TO BROADWAY, TO LIFE!

Geoffrey Block, Series Editor

Series Board

Stephen Banfield   Jeffrey Magee

Tim Carter   Carol Oja

Kim Kowalke   Larry Starr

"South Pacific": Paradise Rewritten
Jim Lovensheimer

Pick Yourself Up: Dorothy Fields and the American Musical
Charlotte Greenspan

To Broadway, To Life! The Musical Theater of Bock and Harnick
Philip Lambert

TO BROADWAY, TO LIFE!

The Musical Theater of Bock and Harnick

Philip Lambert

OXFORD

UNIVERSITY PRESS

OXFORD

UNIVERSITY PRESS

Oxford University Press is a department of the University of Oxford.
It furthers the University's objective of excellence in research, scholarship,
and education by publishing worldwide.

Oxford   New York
Auckland   Cape Town   Dar es Salaam   Hong Kong   Karachi
Kuala Lumpur   Madrid   Melbourne   Mexico City   Nairobi
New Delhi   Shanghai   Taipei   Toronto

With offices in
Argentina   Austria   Brazil   Chile   Czech Republic   France   Greece
Guatemala   Hungary   Italy   Japan   Poland   Portugal   Singapore
South Korea   Switzerland   Thailand   Turkey   Ukraine   Vietnam

Oxford is a registered trade mark of Oxford University Press
in the UK and certain other countries.

Published in the United States of America by
Oxford University Press
198 Madison Avenue, New York, NY 10016

First issued as an Oxford University Press paperback, 2013.

Library of Congress Cataloging-in-Publication Data
Lambert, Philip, 1958-
To Broadway, to life! : the musical theater of Bock and Harnick / Philip Lambert.
p.   cm.—(Broadway legacies)
Includes bibliographical references and index.
ISBN 978-0-19-539007-0 (hardcover); 978-0-19-932806-2 (paperback)
1. Bock, Jerry—Criticism and interpretation. 2. Harnick, Sheldon—Criticism and interpretation.
3. Musicals—New York (State)—New York—History and criticism. I. Title.
ML410.B661L36   2010
782.1′40922—dc22
[B]
2010001966

Publication of this book was supported by the Lloyd Hibberd Publication Endowment Fund
of the American Musicological Society.

1 3 5 7 9 8 6 4 2

Printed in the United States of America on acid-free paper

CONTENTS

* * *

FOREWORD

...

On only their second try Jerry Bock and Sheldon Harnick in 1959 created the music and words, respectively, of a captivating musical based on the early political career of Fiorello La Guardia, the beloved Mayor of New York City from 1934-1945 from his days as a congressman during World World I to the eve of his election as Mayor (and decades prior to the renaming of a New York airport in his honor). *Fiorello!*, directed by George Abbott, ensured its historic stature as the recipient of the third Pulitzer Prize for Drama (following *Of Thee I Sing* and *South Pacific*) and the first of only three winners of Broadway's Triple Crown (the Pulitzer, Tony, and New York Drama Critics Circle awards), a feat later duplicated only by *How to Succeed in Business without Really Trying* and *Rent*. After the death of Hammerstein and end of the Lerner and Loewe partnership, both in 1960, Bock and Harnick, the last major new musical team to enter the Rodgers and Hammerstein era, were the rising creative stars of Broadway's firmament.

Thirty-five years after it took home the crown jewels, *Fiorello!* gained renewed historical distinction in 1994 when it inaugurated an exciting new series devoted to the presentation of worthy but neglected shows, "Encores! Great American Musicals in Concert." In addition to launching the career of Tom Bosley, much later the avuncular co-star of the television sitcom *Happy Days,* the well-crafted and imaginative *Fiorello!* contributed two timelessly biting and funny satiric political songs, "The Little Tin Box" and "Politics and Poker." For most of the latter song, which my cousin can still recite reliably from memory after more than fifty years, Harnick's lyric and Bock's Bowery waltz treat these two high-stakes games as running "neck and neck," before declaring the former vice as the more predictable "because usually you can stack the deck." In 2000 and 2005, respectively, two other worthwhile if uneven Bock and Harnick shows *Tenderloin* (1960) and *The Apple Tree* (1966), the latter starring Kristin Chenoweth, were similarly honored by "Encores!," the latter performance leading to a brief Broadway revival again featuring Chenoweth.

And then came *Fiddler on the Roof* in 1964, almost exactly midway between *Fiorello!* and Bock and Harnick's final show as a team, *The Rothschilds* in 1970. As many reading this foreword doubtless already know, *Fiddler* was and remains an iconic collaboration with choreographer and director Jerome Robbins, whose unwavering insistence on asking "what is the show about?"

led to an unforgettable opening number, "Tradition," and a collaboration of story, movement, words, and music that has long since become a Broadway classic for the ages. When it closed eight years later *Fiddler* had knocked *My Fair Lady* off her pedestal as Broadway's longest run, and over the next four decades the new Broadway sensation would be followed by an elaborately faithful (and musically nearly complete) film in 1971, three Broadway revivals (1976, 1990, and 2004), and a short run at the New York State Theater in 1981. The 2004 revival even introduced a new song, "Topsy-Turvy," the first and perhaps only new Bock and Harnick Broadway song composed since the dissolution of their partnership.

Fiddler, based on stories by Sholom Aleichem, tells the poignant tales of Tevye (originally played by Zero Mostel) and his daughters in a remote place and time, the Russian village of rural Anatevka in 1905. The show vividly conveys how powerful historical and social forces and generational change would challenge and threaten long-cherished traditions. While the words and music for such songs as "Tradition" and "If I Were a Rich Man" exhibit strong traces of Jewish ethnicity and culture, the less overt ethnicity of "Sunrise, Sunset" (a waltz in the minor mode), has since its inception caused copious bittersweet tears to be shed at weddings of nearly every religious persuasion. In fact, ironically, Tevye and his fellow Jews in Anatevka have inspired a musical so universal that at a run-though prior to its opening in Japan a Japanese producer conversing with Harnick and *Fiddler* librettist Joseph Stein felt compelled to inquire how Americans could understand a show that was "so Japanese!"

In addition to *Fiddler, Fiorello!,* and several enjoyable but largely forgotten shows, Bock and Harnick created an intimate show so packed with music that its original LP cast album required two discs to present its nearly two dozen musical numbers. *She Loves Me* (based on Miklós László's play *The Shop Around the Corner*), the first show directed and produced by Hal Prince, debuted one year before *Fiddler* and would be overshadowed, if not totally buried, by its successor. None of its original Broadway or West End productions or revivals inspired long runs, although the latter revival was a critical success and captured the major Laurence Olivier Awards in 1994, including best musical, best director, actor, actress, and supporting performer. Although in its day it played second fiddle to *Fiddler* and other larger-than-life shows like *Hello, Dolly!* and *Man of La Mancha*, Bock and Harnick's jewel has proven remarkably resilient in regional theaters and is widely treasured by directors, audiences, and theater historians. As examples of the latter, Ethan Mordden, in his survey of the 1960s musical *Open a New Window* wrote that this relatively small show presents "a superb story superbly told, an acknowledged glory of the day" and a "classic, because it will always surprise a willing public," and Steven

Suskin in *Show Tunes* asserted unequivocally, not only that "it's time for another revival [of *She Loves Me*]" but that "it's *always* time for another *She Loves Me*."

It is also time to welcome the first comprehensive exploration of the remarkable career of Bock and Harnick into the Broadway Legacies series: *To Broadway, To Life! The Musical Theater of Bock and Harnick*. In this volume, Philip Lambert, the versatile author of *The Music of Charles Ives* (1997) and *Inside the Music of Brian Wilson: The Songs, Sounds and Influences of the Beach Boys' Founding Genius* (2007), treats readers to a generous survey of all seven Broadway shows that first appeared between 1958 and 1970: *The Body Beautiful, Fiorello!, Tenderloin, She Loves Me, Fiddler on the Roof, The Apple Tree*, and *The Rothschilds*. After rigorously but accessibly exploring the formative years of the team before they were introduced in 1956 by the future award-winning co-star of *She Loves Me*, Jack Cassidy, Lambert discusses these seven collaborations from a rich variety of historical, analytical, and critical perspectives.

In the final chapter of *To Broadway, To Life!* Lambert brings readers up to date on the forty-year aftermath that followed the team's creative separation. Here you will learn about the productive albeit largely unheralded musical theater work of Bock (acting as his own lyricist) and Harnick, who, in addition to producing numerous acclaimed translations of classic operas, teamed with talented new composers, including Michel Legrand and Richard Rodgers, the latter on his penultimate musical, *Rex* (1976), a show based on the reign of Henry VIII. *To Broadway, To Life,* to Bock and Harnick, to Philip Lambert, *l'chaim!*

GEOFFREY BLOCK
Series Editor, Broadway Legacies

PREFACE

* * *

Between 1957 and 1970, Sheldon Harnick (b. 1924) and Jerry Bock (b. 1928) wrote lyrics and music for seven Broadway musicals: *The Body Beautiful* (opened in 1958), *Fiorello!* (1959), *Tenderloin* (1960), *She Loves Me* (1963), *Fiddler on the Roof* (1964), *The Apple Tree* (1966), and *The Rothschilds* (1970). They collaborated with major figures of the American theater, including writers Joseph Stein and Joe Masteroff; directors George Abbott, Harold Prince, Jerome Robbins, Mike Nichols, and Michael Kidd; designers Boris Aronson, Patricia Zipprodt, Cecil Beaton, and Tony Walton; and actors Zero Mostel, Barbara Harris, Maurice Evans, Barbara Cook, Tom Bosley, Jack Cassidy, Alan Alda, and Hal Linden. They won Tony Awards and a Pulitzer Prize for Drama. They made an impact on the American stage at a time when the theater was changing along with, and in response to, the world around it. Their most successful opus, *Fiddler on the Roof*, ran on Broadway for almost eight years, while raising issues of cultural identity and Jewish oppression that had never before been addressed in a Broadway musical. In the decades since its premiere, *Fiddler* has been revived on Broadway three times (in 1976, 1990, and 2004), made into an award-winning film, and performed in all sorts of settings around the world.

Now, in the early years of the twenty-first century, as their shows begin to celebrate their fiftieth birthdays, the time is right for a comprehensive look at Bock and Harnick's accomplishments and a full assessment of their contributions to the American theater. The themes and subjects of their shows are broad and diverse: historical or fictional, realistic or fantastic, sentimental or cynical, light or serious. Harnick, the lyricist, is a master of witty wordplay but is equally at home with a love song. He is also a formally trained musician, who has written many songs of his own, and so is deeply sensitive to the musicality of his poetry. Bock, the composer, similarly casts a wide net over styles and forms and moods. He too is keenly aware of the task of his counterpart, having written his own song lyrics from time to time throughout his career. If there is a thread of consistency in their mature work it is their acute sensitivity to drama: they wrote for specific dramatic circumstances and characters, in the best tradition of the integrated musical. They also created little musical dramas within the substance of their scores—dramas of themes, motives, chord types, harmonic progressions, and the like, that interact artfully with the unfolding developments of story and character. They were, in short, a team of expert craftsmen who were more than just great songwriters, whose reputation in the musical theater should rest on a broad range of achievements and contributions, featuring but not limited to their one groundbreaking success.

The names Bock and Harnick are forever intertwined in Broadway history, but by some standards their partnership was relatively short-lived. Their seven shows in fourteen years are eclipsed on the Broadway scorecard by George and Ira Gershwin's fourteen shows in twelve years; Richard Rodgers's nine shows in sixteen years with Oscar Hammerstein II; Rodgers's twenty-six shows in twenty-four years with Lorenz Hart; and the almost forty-two years, and twelve Broadway shows, of John Kander and Fred Ebb. But for Bock and Harnick it was an intense and fertile fourteen years, and it happened at a time when the Broadway musical was in a state of upheaval. After the giant successes of *My Fair Lady* in 1956, *West-Side Story* in 1957, and *The Sound of Music* in 1959, just before Hammerstein's death in 1960, Broadway creators began to reconsider basic elements of the book musical that had evolved since *Oklahoma!* (1943) and to react to the transformations of popular culture happening just outside the stage doors. Artists ultimately responded, in part, with the rock musical, such as *Hair* (1968), and with "concept musicals" inspired by *avant-garde* theater, de-emphasizing linearity and narrative, such as *Cabaret* (1966), *Company* (1970), *Follies* (1971), and *A Chorus Line* (1975). Bock and Harnick stand right on the bridge between the old and the new: their second show and first big success, *Fiorello!*, shared a Best Musical Tony Award with *The Sound of Music*, and their last major effort, *The Rothschilds*, opened on Broadway the same year as Stephen Sondheim's innovative *Company*. Their crowning achievement falls at the midpoint of the period: *Fiddler on the Roof* premiered on Broadway in September 1964.

How *Fiddler* related to the world around it, and how Bock and Harnick have responded to the world around them throughout their careers, as poets, musicians, and creative artists, form the substance of this book. The story begins with interestingly similar early biographies, including approximately seven years of living and working in New York before they became personally acquainted. The central chapters of the book survey all the work they did together in the late 1950s and throughout the 1960s, not only their seven major productions but also additional shows to which they made smaller contributions, other projects that never made it to Broadway, and a variety of other activities in and out of the musical theater. The portrait that emerges blends history and biography with criticism and musical analysis to capture the dynamics of a creative partnership in all its affluence. A final chapter then considers their work in the decades since they stopped writing shows together, including new projects in the musical theater, individually or with new collaborators, and excursions into the new arenas of opera and film. At the end of the book, Appendix A gives historical and statistical details of their Broadway productions, both as a team and in collaborations with others, and Appendix B lists selected media resources for their work, including recordings (audio and video) that were commercially released and some that are available only in public archives.

Both men have lived in New York City and the surrounding area for all of their professional lives. Jerry Bock and his wife Patricia (Patti) raised two children, George and Portia. Sheldon Harnick and his wife Margery also raised two, Beth and Matthew. Their close geographical proximity allowed them to practice their craft in different ways during their fourteen-year partnership, via mailed tapes and lyric sheets, working separately, or in communal songwriting sessions at one or another residence or studio. Usually they would mostly work apart at the beginning of a show's development and then spend more and more time together as the score progressed. After their partnership dissolved in the early 1970s and they began forging other professional affiliations, they also began to take active roles in the promotion and development of songwriting and musical theater, Bock through his involvement with the BMI Foundation and the Jerry Bock Award for Excellence in Musical Theater, Harnick through his association with the Kleban Foundation and the Kleban Award for musical theater lyricists and librettists, the Fred Ebb Award for Musical Theater Songwriting, and the Richard Rodgers Foundation awards. Their joint contributions to American culture and the musical theater have been ceremoniously recognized on several occasions: they were inducted into the Theater Hall of Fame (1990) and jointly honored with the Johnny Mercer Award from the Songwriters Hall of Fame (1990), the Jewish Cultural Achievement Award from the Foundation for Jewish Culture (1990), the Spirit of American Creativity Award from the Foundation for a Creative America (1991), the William Inge Theater Festival Distinguished Achievement in the American Theater Award (2007), and the Oscar Hammerstein Award for Lifetime Achievement in Musical Theater from the York Theater Company (2009). Both have also received honorary doctorates, Bock from the University of Wisconsin (his alma mater), Harnick from Illinois Wesleyan University and Muskingum College.

Bock and Harnick ultimately mastered the art of songwriting, but just as importantly became expert collaborators, productive members of complex creative teams. It helps that they were temperamentally compatible—not alike, just compatible, and in fact on opposite ends of a dispositional spectrum, by their own estimation. Harnick, the self-described pessimist, pinpointed their secret in an interview with Max Wilk in 1971: "Between us, we help bring the other either down to earth, or *up* to earth." On some charmed combination of harmonious temperaments with comparable talent and shared ambitions, the team thrived for more than a decade. The story of their successes and their challenges, the highs and lows of a fourteen-year alliance, opens a revealing window into one of Broadway's most important collaborations, and into the world of the musical theater of a certain time and place.

NOTE ON SOURCES

The research for this book drew from a vast variety of sources, public and private, published and new. The most valuable materials were the sketches, manuscripts, lyric sheets, and drafts donated to the New York Public Library of the Performing Arts by both Bock and Harnick in 2004. Details of these and other important archives are given in section 1 of the bibliography. Other primary source material included published scores and libretti, cast recordings, and videotaped performances that are available for viewing at the Theater on Film and Tape Archive of the New York Public Library of the Performing Arts. Information on these sources is included in the bibliography sections 2 (scores) and 3 (libretti) and in Appendix B (audio- and videorecordings).

The primary sources also included new interviews and written communications with both Bock and Harnick, conducted exclusively for this book in 2008 and 2009. Various members of their creative orbits likewise contributed valuable insights and perspectives in new personal interviews or written communications. Section 4 of the bibliography gives complete information for these new interviews and communications alongside citations for all other previous interviews, published and archival, that provided primary source material. Throughout the main text, any quotations from published or archival interviews are properly noted, while quotations from, or references to, the new interviews and communications are given without bibliographic citation. Readers may assume that any quotations or references that are not cited in the endnotes came from the new personal interviews or communications conducted exclusively for this book.

The most valuable existing monographs on Bock and Harnick are Richard Altman's insider's account of the development of *Fiddler on the Roof* (1971) and Frank Kelly's examination of all of the team's major shows in his doctoral dissertation (1978). Christopher Davis's book *The Producer* (1972) also provides a helpful behind-the-scenes perspective on the team's seventh and last Broadway show. Information on these sources, along with citations for all other secondary sources and newspaper and magazine articles, are given in the general section (5) of the bibliography. Individual reviews of shows are cited by date and source within the main text but are generally not endnoted and not included in the bibliography, unless they hold particular significance and more resemble a "review-essay."

ACKNOWLEDGMENTS

When I began work on this book I hoped to have the cooperation of my two subjects but had no idea what to expect. I knew of their reputation for generosity but would have been satisfied if they had simply agreed not to file restraining orders. As it turned out, the support and cooperation of Sheldon Harnick and Jerry Bock exceeded even my most idealistic expectations. Sheldon sat for a long, detailed interview and then responded to follow-up questions with thoughtfulness and care. Jerry replied to a long list of questions with a twenty-page single-spaced mini-autobiography (last line: "With that, I promise to take two Tylenol, and call my doctor in the morning") and then was equally generous answering numerous emailed follow-ups. A short while later he then outdid himself by sending me four compact discs of unpublished, unreleased musical gems from his post-partnership years. I now find it inconceivable that I would have ever contemplated this project without an assurance of their cooperation. I am deeply grateful to both of them.

Other collaborators of theirs, past and present, were also generous with their time and memories. Larry Holofcener was enormously helpful filling in details about his early work with Jerry. Joe Masteroff and Joseph Stein shared memories of both Jerry and Sheldon when the partnership was in its prime, and Sherman Yellen helped with the years just before and after the team dissolved. Jerry's recent collaborators Sidney Berger and Stuart Ostrow, and Sheldon's recent collaborator Henry Mollicone, likewise provided valuable background information and personal insights.

For assistance tracking down people and resources I thank Richard M. Ticktin, Esq., Mark Saxon of the Songwriters Guild of America Foundation, Mark Spier of Memory Lane Music Group, Mike De Pope of Music Theater International, Anne Reingold and Connie Hamm of the Marton Agency, and Ron Mandelbaum of Photofest. Two online correspondents, Anthony E. Anderson and B. Dietz, were also enormously generous with information and materials. For responses to research queries I thank two authors of valuable scholarly studies, Frank Kelly and Susan Hawkshaw.

The very earliest inspirations for this book came from correspondence with Geoffrey Block, and I am profoundly grateful for his advice and encouragement at every step along the way. I also thank the anonymous reviewer of the first draft of the manuscript, who made many useful, constructive suggestions. At Oxford University Press, I thank Norman Hirschy for his support and guidance throughout the publication process, Madelyn Sutton and Jaimee Biggins for their help with numerous production details, and Susan Meigs for her conscientious copyediting.

The accommodating staff members of the New York Public Library of the Performing Arts, including the Music Division, the Theater Division, and the Theater on Film and Tape Archive, are too numerous to acknowledge individually, but I must give special thanks to Robert Kosovsky, Curator of Rare Books and Manuscripts, for expert advice and assistance, and for helping me obtain extraordinarily valuable rare materials. I also thank staff members at the Dorot Jewish Division of the New York Public Library, the Paley Center for Media, the Library of Congress, the Museum of the City of New York, and the Tamiment Library of the Robert F. Wagner Labor Archives at New York University. And I am indebted, as ever, to the librarians and inter-library loan staff of the William and Anita Newman Library at Baruch College.

My work on this book was supported and facilitated by a fellowship leave from Baruch College, City University of New York, for the 2008–09 academic year. For their support I am grateful to President Kathleen M. Waldron, Dean Jeffrey Peck of the Weissman School of Arts and Sciences, and Professor Terry Berkowitz, chair of the department of Fine and Performing Arts.

For the priceless gifts of time and space, along with her love and support, I thank my wife Diane. I also thank my mother, Joanne Todd, for fostering my early introduction to the Broadway musical, and for all those intangible things that mothers supply.

When I think about the musical theater and the experiences that gave me the impetus to undertake a project such as this, I inevitably look back on some of the teachers who helped form my basic understanding of music and theater, not to forget little things like self-awareness and humanity. Lessons learned from now-departed mentors such as Betty Woods, in whose choruses and theatrical productions I happily performed in my formative years, and Thomas Carey, noted opera impresario and my voice teacher in college (and an acclaimed Porgy), continue to grow with meaning, in and out of the academy. This book is dedicated to their memory, and to my teachers of more recent times, my daughters Charlotte and Alice.

TO BROADWAY, TO LIFE!

1

SUAVE YOUNG MEN
· · ·
CREATIVE STIRRINGS FROM CHILDHOOD THROUGH COLLEGE

The journeys of Sheldon Harnick and Jerry Bock from precocious youth to the Broadway stage were hardly different from those of so many other legends of the American musical theater: urban childhoods in nurturing Jewish families, burgeoning creative gifts seeking expressive outlets in diverse musical entertainments, artistic sensibilities molded by exposure to classic music of the concert hall, radio, and theater. But the stories of these two artists in particular display striking similarities. Bock and Harnick were born about four-and-a-half years apart, showed an early interest in both music and poetry, studied music at Midwestern colleges in close geographical proximity, made the move to New York to pursue Broadway dreams around the same time, gained valuable early experience writing theater music for shows at different summer resorts in the mountains not far from the city, and wrote their first book shows for Broadway around the same time. Their paths finally converged in 1956, and they began writing songs together within a year of their first meeting. The history that predates their partnership almost makes the result seem predestined, a story not of unlikely coincidences but of parallel teleologies.

SHELDON HARNICK: MUSICAL POET

From the moment of his birth, in Chicago on April 30, 1924, Sheldon Harnick was surrounded by performance and creative expression. His father, who maintained a dental practice in the Portage Park section of the city, had a reputation among friends and family as a parlor comic, and his mother wrote light verse to celebrate or commemorate special occasions.[1] His uncle, Milton Kanter, was involved with The Mummers, a group hoping to accomplish in Chicago what the Group Theater had achieved in New York—staging innovative, challenging works with political and social themes. Sheldon and his sister Gloria soon began to write poetry, while brother Jay took an interest in acting. Sheldon's first published poem appeared when he was in fifth grade, in the school newspaper just before Thanksgiving 1934:

> The turkey has my sympathy.
> Why must we be so mean?
> What has the turkey done
> That he deserves the guillotine?[2]

At the same time, musical talents were blossoming. Gloria was becoming an accomplished pianist, Jay eventually gained some proficiency on the marimba, and Sheldon studied the violin. Although the student had little fondness for the instruction he received—he once described his teacher as a "wonderful man, but terrible teacher"—he was impassioned about playing and became a dedicated student, sometimes practicing for hours a day.[3] By the time he reached high school he was performing regularly, for his mother's arts club, in the orchestra for local productions of Gilbert and Sullivan, and at local religious services.[4] On June 23, 1940, at age sixteen, he presented a solo recital in Chicago, accompanied by his sister at the piano.[5]

As his musical studies became more and more serious, his interest in poetry and language developed as well. Following the inspiration of his mother, he contributed comic poems and what he has called doggerel to the high school newspaper. In his junior year he formed a partnership with a slightly older student, Stanley Orzey, Jr., to write comic material for themselves and others, including parodies, sketches, and original songs. At first, Harnick recalled in 2008, he deferred to his partner's superior wit and experience:

> [Stanley] really amused me. We wrote, we wrote a great deal. Mostly he wrote, and I was the secretary, and cleaned it up and typed it up. I contributed what I could, but I was—I wouldn't say intimidated by Stanley—but I was very impressed by what he knew about theater, because I knew almost nothing.

Eventually they became more equal partners and developed a solid reputation among friends for slapstick comedy. They wrote a sketch about their high school teachers that included Gilbert and Sullivan-style parodies. For Harnick's mother's bridge club they wrote a sketch incorporating characters and personalities from the audience; "the ladies screamed with laughter," he recalled decades later.[6] They even sold some comic material to a local comedian. At the suggestion of their drama teacher they also wrote a serious play, *Shades of Business*, that was performed at the school. According to an article in the *Chicago Tribune*, the team hoped to move forward from there to "write, produce, direct, and take part in a play of their own creation" co-starring Stanley's sister Eleanor (who was at that time "playing in a New York show") and Groucho Marx.[7]

One of their songs from this time, "Gus the Gopher," was recorded some years later by Charlotte Rae.[8] Harnick remembers, "I wrote the music, and [Stanley and I] both wrote the lyrics." The A sections of the AABA form, written in a light novelty-song style, employ goofy puns and rhymes such as "gopher/gofer" and "squirrel/Pearl/Earl" to tell the story of a gopher's frustrated love life. A bridge section arrives with immediate musical surprises—a flashier style and hints of the keys of E♭ and G major, far-removed from the original key of B—but these suitably complement the surprising bridge lyric, which moves from a description of Gus's sartorial splendor ("His suits and ties were fabulous / His pants were neatly pressed") to the disarming question, "Whoever heard of gophers wearing clothes?" Finally in the return of the A melody Gus finds true love in Molly the mole, whose visual impairment makes her, alas, Gus's perfect mate.

After graduating from high school in February 1942 Harnick worked as a shipping clerk in a chemical supply house while continuing his artistic pursuits. All the while, he expected to be drafted into the service at any moment. His father persuaded him to attend a technical school, Lewis Institute, in the fall of 1942, where he took classes in geometry, algebra, and mechanical drawing, but toward the end of that semester the call came, and in early 1943 he entered the U. S. Army Signal Corps. He was initially stationed at Robins Field, Georgia, where he received training in radio repair and became part of a five-man team installing blind landing systems. He remembers one "wonderful summer" when another crew was mistakenly sent overseas on orders intended for his team, leaving the officer in charge with no assignment at all for Harnick. Simply told at the beginning of each day to "get lost," he was drawn to a volunteer special service unit run by another serviceman named Sol Lerner, who had worked as a theatrical agent in New York. Harnick recalls,

> He put on a show every Monday night: volunteers, accordion players, guitar players—anybody who volunteered would be in the show. Those of who wanted to do sketches, he would tell us some sketch he remembered seeing in a Broadway revue. He would tell us the premise, he would tell us the punch line, [and] we would go out and improvise it.

Harnick remembers playing violin on some of the shows and performing original satirical songs that "expressed what was happening in my particular outfit."[9] He was one of five second-prize winners in a parody contest in *Yank* magazine. Later during his military service he was in San Francisco and remembers seizing a free evening to attend a production of Hammerstein's *Carmen Jones*, which had opened on Broadway in 1943.[10] Harnick was in the Philippines preparing for an invasion of Japan when the war ended.[11]

A Songwriter's College Education

Back in Chicago after being honorably discharged from the service in early 1946, Harnick worked as a violinist in dance bands, and played in a community orchestra sponsored by a large Methodist church, while making plans to attend college under the GI Bill. He considered joining an Army buddy at DePaul, but two factors persuaded him to attend Northwestern University:

> I was primarily going to school to be a violinist, and the violinist I wanted to study with was the associate concertmaster of the Chicago Symphony [and Northwestern faculty member], Robert Quick. That was one reason, and the other was the Waa-Mu Show, because in the Army I had begun to write songs, and also in high school I had written with Stanley, so I was curious to see if I could contribute anything to the Waa-Mu Show.

Northwestern's renowned Waa-Mu Show—the acronym recognizes the show's co-sponsorship by the Women's Athletic Association and Men's Union—was, and still is, a musical revue written, produced, and performed by students. Productions over the years have featured the likes of Warren Beatty, Karen Black, Cloris Leachman, Ann-Margaret, and Tony Randall.[12] Harnick remembers contributing one song to the Waa-Mu Show during his first year at Northwestern, a "blues song, about a woman, a munitions worker during the war, and it was sung by Charlotte Rae, whose name was Charlotte Lubotsky at the time." Rae remembers the tag line: "I've got those gotta-go-home-alone-tonight blues!"[13] Encouraged by the show's producer-director, Joe W. Miller, to get more involved in subsequent years, Harnick recalls contributing four songs in his second year, six songs in his third year, and then writing "half the show" in his last year of college. Because he was able to apply some academic credits from the Lewis Institute, he actually graduated Northwestern early, so this fourth show would have occurred a few months after he completed his studies. An article in the *Chicago Tribune* dubbed that show "Look Who's Talking" and promised "sly jabs at Grant park concerts, motion picture extravaganzas, Shakespeare, and vaudeville." Sheldon Harnick, announced the article, wrote "most of the music."[14]

Two songs survive from these shows, thanks to Harnick's renditions of them in 1971, in his appearance during the inaugural season of the "Lyrics and Lyricists" series of the 92nd Street Y (then officially known as the Young

Men's and Women's Hebrew Association) in New York.[15] He introduced "The Suave Young Man" by pointing out a "very noticeable Gilbert and Sullivan influence, both in my lyrics and in my music." He is referring to turns of phrase such as "It's the garment indispensable, from varmint reprehensible," and the repetition of the line "He's now the imperturbable, undisturbable man of action" by an echoing chorus. Clearly, he had been listening carefully while playing violin in Gilbert and Sullivan pit orchestras. As he said in 2004,

> Even though I was playing the violin, I could still hear the lyrics. At that time I was turned on by the patter songs, so I began to familiarize myself with Gilbert and Sullivan. I was more fascinated by the virtuosity than anything else. Little by little, I also realized what a fine poet Gilbert was and how imaginative he was, even in the slower songs. So he became an enormous influence.[16]

The last part of "The Suave Young Man," inspired, says Harnick, by Humphrey Bogart, paints a colorful portrait of the "suave young man in the trench coat," who "can laugh with disdain as he's dropped from a plane," who is "at home with a bomb but he's good to his mom," and who "admits no defeat 'til he's wrapped in a sheet." The music is simple and direct, careful not to draw attention away from the words.

The other Waa-Mu relic performed by Harnick in 1971 was "How Could I?," a song written, he says, under the inspiration of E. Y. "Yip" Harburg. Harnick has recalled that Charlotte Rae played him the original cast album of *Finian's Rainbow* soon after its release, leaving him "dazzled" by Harburg's lyrics for the show, with their "marvelous combination" of a "Gilbertian kind of fun with words and at the same time saying something of importance."[17] Indeed Harnick's song "How Could I?" would not be out of place in the *Finian's Rainbow* score, alongside one of Burton Lane's lilting tunes such as "If This Isn't Love" or "When I'm Not Near the Girl I Love." Harburg's influence echoes throughout "How Could I?" in rhymes such as . . .

> I apologize—to you
> And acknowledge eyes—of a heavenly blue

. . . and . . .

> So visible—your charms
> I'm mis'able—when you're not in my arms

. . . adopting the same playful spirit, taking similar liberties with spelling and grammar, as lines in "When I'm Not Near the Girl I Love":

Always I can't refuse 'em
Always my feet pursues 'em
Long as they've got a bosom
I woos 'em.

But Harnick might just as easily have cited Ira Gershwin or Lorenz Hart as models for his wordplay. What especially attracted him about Harburg was the social commentary in *Finian's Rainbow*, for which Harburg also co-wrote the book.

As Harnick's interest in the theater grew during college, he remained committed to the violin; in his baccalaureate recital he played, among other works, the first movement of Saint-Saëns's Third Violin Concerto.[18] In 1950, with a Bachelor of Music degree in hand, he obtained a prestigious position with the Henry Brandon Orchestra, playing dance music five nights a week at Chicago's posh Edgewater Hotel. This was a plum job, but it soon became a source of anxiety. Harnick recalls,

> Five nights a week we broadcast dance music, I believe at midnight. . . . So at midnight these microphones would be lowered over our heads to pick up the orchestral sounds. . . . When they lowered those microphones, I would tense up. And for the couple of weeks that I played that engagement, every night I was so tense that by the end of the engagement I began to have trouble playing. With my left hand I began to have trouble vibrating; with my right hand, my bowing arm, my muscles in my arms were like steel bands. I don't mean that in terms of strength, but just in terms of mobility.

He eventually consulted the family doctor, an Austrian refugee who recognized the symptoms of *Geigerkrampf*, a condition of muscular and nervous exhaustion that he had previously diagnosed in members of the Vienna Philharmonic. The doctor's only recommendation was to "stop playing for a year." Shortly thereafter Harnick was let go from the orchestra anyway for budgetary reasons.

Finding himself at an early crossroads, Harnick began to imagine a future on the creative side of the music business. It began with a decisive encounter after the last Waa-Mu performance in early May 1950:

> The cast, the writers, the orchestra—everybody connected with the show—were invited to meet a Chicago disc jockey. I was a big fan of his; his name was Dave Garroway. He had a program that I used to love. So we met him and some of his staff. He told me how much he liked my work. I said, "Would there be any place for me on your staff?" He said, "Well, I'm leaving

Chicago, I'm going to New York. We're going to have a show originating in New York. That's where the money's coming from. And if I were you, and you want to write for the entertainment world, I would consider going to New York."

Harnick's brother Jay was already there, having appeared in the short-lived revue *Alive and Kicking* in early 1950, then joining the chorus of the more successful *Gentlemen Prefer Blondes*. Charlotte Rae was there as well, writing her friend back in Chicago that New York was in desperate need of good young writing talent. Now, without a violin to help pay the rent, the impetus to make the big move was irresistible.

JERRY BOCK: POETIC MUSICIAN

Music and performance were subtler yet persistent presences in the childhood homes of Jerry Bock, first in New Haven, Connecticut, where he was born on November 23, 1928, then memorably in Flushing (Queens), New York, where the family moved around his second birthday.[19] Bock remembers being entranced by music emanating from the radio, and sometimes playing along with a toy drum. He recalls listening to his mother pick out, on the baby grand piano that he still owns and plays, "popular songs of the day, *sans* sheet music, or ones she approximated after returning from seeing a musical that caught her ear." At some point his grandmother moved into the house, and he fondly remembers her "fragile Yiddish voice" singing "childlike words and music" to him. His father, who was a traveling salesman for automotive supplies businesses, was also a music lover and ardent proponent of musical activities in the home.

Throughout his childhood and teen years, up until the time he finished high school in the spring of 1945, Bock regarded music as a pleasurable pastime, never a source of serious study. During about three years of formal piano lessons, starting at age eight or nine, he displayed formidable talent and yet found himself unable to restrict himself to the notated score. Fortunately, his teacher was "very supportive even to the point of enthusiasm," of her student's free interpretations. About his performance of a Chopin piece she remarked, "lovely, Jerry—not quite the way Chopin wrote it, but very nice." A restless creative spirit led Bock to discontinue formal study as he entered adolescence, clearing the way for unrestricted improvisation and his first attempts at composition. He essentially taught himself the harmonic language of jazz and popular songs, developing a keen ear for melodic gesture

and song structure. He played at parties and for school functions and entertained friends with a clever improvisational game:

> Composing occasionally took the form in high school of challenging myself
> by taking people's phone numbers, translating them to the matching keys
> within a piano scale, and composing on the spot a melody that consisted
> of the phone number, pursuing it to larger improvisations and ending with
> a simple single note reprise of the original phone number.

He also found inspiration in recordings by his "all-time favorite" Glenn Miller,
as well as Benny Goodman, Harry James, and the like, while at the same time
starting to explore music of Tchaikovsky and Rachmaninoff, music that in
2008 he described as a "current passion."

But Bock considered himself just as much an author as a musician. He
wrote both prose and poetry in high school, and in his senior year was editor-
in-chief of the school newspaper and business manager of the school magazine, *Folio*. His poem "Up Close" appeared in the spring 1945 issue of *Folio*.[20]
Another poem, "My World of Music," was included in both the Annual Anthology of High School Poetry for the state of New York and *Songs of Youth*,
the National Poetry Anthology of the Poetry Society of America.[21] Although
Bock had had little formal musical training, and had gravitated toward popular music of the time in his personal musical explorations, his musical frame
of reference in this poem—the "world" in which he resides—is dominated by
orchestral music of the nineteenth and early twentieth centuries. He shows
that he is especially drawn to works with colorful, expressive purposes (Tchaikovsky's or Sibelius's symphonies), music with connections to a specific character or story (Liszt's *Faust Symphony* and *Mephisto Waltzes*, Richard Strauss's
Death and Transfiguration, Rimsky-Korsakov's *Scheherazade*, John Alden Carpenter's *Adventures in a Perambulator*, Prokofiev's *Peter and the Wolf*), and the
more explicit dramatic orientations of music for the opera (Gounod's *Faust*)
and ballet (Ravel's *La Valse* and *Boléro*, Shostakovich's *Age of Gold*).

MY WORLD OF MUSIC
Jerry Bock—Flushing, N. Y.

In a world of music there's all of life.
A contented life spreads o'er this land, which is mine
But may be yours by volition.
Humor here is not found in pantomime or pun,
Heard in voice, or seen in play;

But rather found between the notes of the polka from the Age of the
   Gold Ballet.
Or the whimsical doings of Peter and the Wolf.
And if you've never been in Carpenter's perambulator
You're missing drollery highly sublime,
Which is part of this musical world of mine;—yet may be yours by
   volition.
"What of sadness?" This phrase I hear uttered.—And my answer?
What Tchaikowsky's Fourth, Fifth, and Pathetique,
Whose sadness breeds melancholy, as does Jean Sibelius?
Are death and transfiguration woeful enough for you, O questioner?
Then attend to Richard Strauss's work—Which you easily can,
Here in this, my world of music,—A world which may be yours by
   volition.
"But I want excitement, happiness, and adventure!"
So you cry, eh, persistent one? Well, you'll bathe in a quicksand of
   excitation
When you listen to a tale so cleverly spun by Scheherazade,
Done by a Russian named Korsakoff.—Or perhaps a dance would suit
   your fancy;
Then to The Bolero or La Valse, think Ravel.
Adventure you want? How about hell,
Accompanied by Mephisto and Faust? A treat, I dare say.
Well, Gounod or Liszt will pave the way for you,
Or anyone caring to go, anytime,
Thought only in my universe of musical design, which can be yours by
   volition.
Then satisfied are you? "I am," you say.
You're laughing at the Polka from the Gold Ballet? Do I see tears in your
   eyes
As you listen to the somber cries of Tchaikowsky's music?
You're amazed at Scheherazade's yarn, and so excited you don't give a
   darn about Hell!
Well then this world is not only mine—but yours, by volition.

Bock's dual interests coalesced in the spring of his senior year when he helped write, produce, and perform a two-act musical, *My Dream*, for family and friends at Flushing High School. A cast of ten classmates developed the story collectively, while Bock wrote all the music, including songs and dance numbers, and some of the lyrics (along with classmates Marv Smith and Barbara Kahn). It was a sizable leap forward from his earlier casual improvisations to music with concrete structure and theatrical purpose. It was also an important first exposure to the art of collaboration and the dynamics of multiple creative perspectives.

Although no script of *My Dream* has survived, Bock did save the printed program and some scores and lyric sheets, enough to give a sense of its overall dramatic tone and of the state of his musical development just a few months beyond his sixteenth birthday.[22] The story, as summarized in the program, is a teen-aged soap opera: George dreams of finding the perfect girl but finds himself paired with John's girlfriend Jerry, until he finally realizes that Barbara is his dream girl. Along the way there are ample opportunities for musical excursions, including a dance, a mock wedding, and a fraternity party. The program lists this sequence of musical numbers:

Prologue: "My Dream"
Act I:
   "Sipping a Soda"
   Dance Specialty
   Mock Marriage Numbers
   "This Is Love"
Act II:
   scene 1
      "Flushing High School Blues"
      "Acro-Boogie Dance"
      Comedy Team
      Humorous Dance
      Jam Session
   scene 2
      "Here We Are Alone"
   scene 3
      "I Found You"
Epilogue: "My Dream"

Scores survive for the songs "My Dream," "Here We Are Alone," and "I Found You." Bock also saved a notebook containing melodies written out without text, probably used by the first violinist/conductor to piece together an overture.[23] The music in these scores covers a wide expressive range and demonstrates a thorough familiarity with the idioms and gestures of popular song. But these songs also occasionally manifest a special creative spark, a search for musical ideas that are a little out-of-the-ordinary. "My Dream" (Example 1.1a) uses an unpredictably repeated three-note motive (first heard as "you're my dream," mm. 1–2) to disrupt a strong sense of meter.[24] Metric emphasis most easily falls on the motive's third note (as happens on the downbeat of the second measure), and yet this note does not always occur on strong beats; indeed it happens on weak beats almost as often (e.g., "in the glow," m. 3). "This Is Love" (Example 1.1b), the show's first ballad, consists of a flowing, skillfully shaped C major melody with conspicuous chromatic inflections of

a. "My Dream," mm. 1–10 (Bock Papers, box 6, folders 39, 40)

b. "This Is Love," mm. 1–8 (Bock Papers, box 6, folder 39; box 26, folder 21)

c. "Here We Are Alone," mm. 1–16 (Bock Papers, box 6, folder 40)

Example 1.1: My Dream, *melodic excerpts*

the fourth scale step (F♯) in the first three bars.[25] The chromaticism might lead a thoughtful listener to wonder if indeed the singer's love is true. And "Here We Are Alone" (Example 1.1c), the ballad in the second act in which George declares his love for Jerry, only to discover at song's end that Jerry loves only John, employs an analogous downward inflection of the seventh scale step (B♭), held prominently for the entire second and sixth bars.[26] Such departures from the prevailing scale capture the stirrings of a restless innovator, like a pianist who is unwilling to play a mazurka exactly the way Chopin wrote it.

College Years: Songwriting and Show-Writing

My Dream was a big success, but Bock continued to dismiss music as a career choice. His biographical blurb in the playbill declared, "his ambitions do not lie in music but rather in the field of advertising. To this end he is going to attend college where he hopes to take the course in journalism." And that is exactly what he planned as he arrived for his freshman year at the University of Wisconsin in the fall of 1945. Bock has told the story of his collegiate beginnings and pivotal decisions on several occasions. Here is the version from 2008:

> College was a major magnification of high school's creative energy that started with the most serendipitous of walks up Bascom Hill at the U of W on my way to register for my freshman classes. I was interrupted from my thoughts of becoming a journalism major when I heard, somewhat faintly, music emanating from a small building on my left with a line of students waiting to enter. Curiosity beckoned as I joined the line to inquire what was going on. At the same time I noticed that each member of the line had at least three or four collections of music, including Bach Inventions, Beethoven Sonatas, and a Chopin all-encompassing variety, which I'm sure would be played quite like Chopin wrote it! That no-doubt talented line was waiting to audition for admission to the Music School. And for some unfathomable impulse, I joined that line as it moved toward the designated room wherein three or four professorial types waited to judge the aspirants. And for an even more unfathomable impulse I found myself next to enter that hallowed room, which, having gone this far, I inescapably did, initiating the following scene:
>
> > PROF: Well Mr. Bock, what have you planned to play?
> > JB: Actually I have nothing planned since I've been away from music studies for many years. This was just an impulse and I was unprepared to—
> > PROF: (handing me book of church hymns) Why don't you do a little sight-reading for us.

JB: (in anguish, mutilating the Lord's music beyond recognition) Blasphemy personified! Hymnal Hades!

PROF: (last chance at the classical chorale) Mr. Bock, is there anything you can play for us of your own choosing?

JB: (innocently) Well I do have a series of arrangements of Army bugle calls in the style of various classical composers.

PROF: (holding back disbelief) That would be fine.

And so I did my routine, as I had wowed them at parties, playing "Reveille" in the style of Bach, Chopin, Rachmaninoff, Tchaikovsky, and ending with that foolproof finish—the Boogie Woogie Bugle Call finale.

When I looked up from the keyboard, lo and behold, those stern judicious faces were smiling!

Then came the potential *coup de grâce*:

PROF: Mr. Bock, you do show signs of creativity and inventiveness. However the only possible consideration for entrance would be for you to start from scratch. Literally as a first-time student of music, learning the basic fundamentals as a beginner. It is only under those circumstances we would even consider your entering the Music School. Under those circumstances, would you be interested?[27]

Finally unable to resist an impulse that had been growing year by year, he abruptly changed his major and enrolled in a full program of music study, including courses in theory, counterpoint, and music appreciation, in addition to private lessons in piano and a secondary instrument (violin). He still regarded creative writing as an important interest, but he found himself spending more and more time away from the library, at the piano— "accompanying various performers in school cabaret nights, playing arrangements of well-known songs." He also remembers "meeting and working with two lyricists for different assignments, getting involved in political groups, and even auditioning for roles in the Drama department's productions."

In the summer of 1947, between his second and third years at Wisconsin, Bock began work on his second full-length musical, an entry in a BMI contest that was being held to encourage college students to produce fresh, original material.[28] This time he wrote only music, in collaboration with classmates Jack Royce, who wrote all the lyrics, and Dave Pollard, who wrote the book. For a story they turned to the Paul Bunyan legend, hoping to connect with the celebration of Wisconsin's centennial the following year, as well as the fiftieth anniversary of the organization that would ultimately produce it, the

Haresfoot Club, the university's all-male dramatic society. *Big as Life*, as they called it, was a giant-sized success in the spring of 1948, touring five Wisconsin cities, playing to a full house at the Blackstone Theater in Chicago, and ending with a full week of standing-room-only performances back in Madison.[29] The show was awarded first prize in the BMI competition, and several of its songs were subsequently published.

Bock preserved only excerpts from the *Big as Life* script, but he kept scores and sketches for seventeen songs from the production[30]:

"Almost from the Start"
"Animal"
"The Animal Republic"
"Babe's What They Call Me"
"Bunyan's Are Expectin"
"Ev'rybody Loses"
"Forest in the Sky"
"Great Wisconsin"
"Hear Ye"
"Let's Hit the High Road"
"Logger Beer"
"Skookum"
"Starway Lullaby"
"Timber"
"Today"
"Why Sing a Love Song"
"You Tickle My Fancy"

Again his music demonstrates a wide expressive range and an impressive command of show-music and popular styles. "Ev'rybody Loses" would sparkle in a Glenn-Miller-style arrangement, and "Starway Lullaby" is a lovely ballad that has the melodic elegance of a Jerome Kern song (e.g., "The Song Is You" from *Music in the Air*, 1932). "Babe's What They Call Me" (excerpted in Example 1.2a) calls to mind a self-introductory Gilbert and Sullivan number like "I Am the Captain of the Pinafore" from *H. M. S. Pinafore*, while the syncopated energy of "Great Wisconsin" (Example 1.2b) captures the flavor of a high-kicking show tune in the *Ziegfeld Follies*.[31] "Hear Ye," a sort of vocal fanfare, includes the crossed-out notation "To be sung as a *Round* for 2–3 or 4 parts" (Example 1.2c), suggesting that Bock had picked up some ideas, and skills, from his college counterpoint classes. The show's best song is a Richard Rodgers-style duet, "Why Sing a Love Song," which begins with an arpeggiated F major triad over a D minor 7th chord (Example 1.2d). Still shy of his

a. "Babe's What They Call Me," mm. 0–4 (Bock Papers, box 19, folders 11, 12)

I'm some - what a blue ox, And Babe's what they call me.

b. "Great Wisconsin," mm. 0–4 (Bock Papers, box 19, folder 11)

c. "Hear Ye," mm. 1–6 (Bock Papers, box 19, folder 11)

Hear Ye!_____ Hear Ye!_____ Old Town's young and old

come and hear it told How the Bun - yan Boy is the dev - il's toy

d. "Why Sing a Love Song?" mm. 1–8 (Bock Papers, box 19, folder 11)

Soon we'll both be part - ed, WHY SING A LOVE SONG?

We'd be bro - ken heart - ed twice as much that way.

Example 1.2: Big as Life, *melodic excerpts (music by Jerry Bock, lyrics by Jack Royce)*

twentieth birthday, Bock was writing music that was rich in variety and teeming with wit and character and interesting ideas.

Bock's college education began with a sudden impulse to study music, and, as he started his fourth year in the fall of 1948, a familiar restless energy was nurturing a new impulse that was growing harder and harder to resist. The experience of *Big as Life* helped him envision a future in the musical theater, just as *My Dream* a few years earlier had helped steer him away from advertising and into music school. He also had a new friend, Larry Holofcener, who seemed to share some of his ambitions, or at least seemed open to adventure. By the end of the fall term Bock felt that he had received all the formal education he needed, even though he was still a semester short of graduating. He knew that what he wanted next was an education in the musical theater, and he knew that there was only one place to get it.

2

WONDERS OF MANHATTAN

• • •

PROFESSIONAL BEGINNINGS IN NEW YORK IN THE 1950S

Although Bock and Harnick had both settled in New York by the early 1950s, they had no personal association of any kind until later in the decade. Bock saw Alice Ghostley's showstopping rendition of Harnick's song "Boston Beguine" at a performance of *New Faces of 1952* in New York,[1] and no doubt there were other convergences and near misses as two young aspiring songwriters living in the same city navigated pathways through the same professional networks, but their storylines did not intersect until years later, after each had achieved professional success separately.

SHELDON HARNICK ON BROADWAY

When he arrived in New York in the summer of 1950 Sheldon Harnick was newly married. His wife's small parts on Broadway helped pay the bills, along with money from war bonds and savings. One of his first priorities was to follow up on a conversation he had had with Sol Lerner, the New York theatrical agent, when he was in the Army: "He told me one day, 'You know, you're very good. After you're out of the Army, assuming you live through this, if you decide that you want to come to New York and get into the entertainment world, look me up.'" Through Lerner, Harnick was able to find some work on television, and he remembers writing a thirty-second theme song for the *Cavalcade of Stars* on the DuMont network; this was Jackie Gleason's first variety show, which ultimately evolved into *The Honeymooners*. Harnick also wrote songs with Ed Scott for the *Ray Bolger Variety Show*, and he wrote the opening for the *Larry Storch Show*. At the same time he was writing songs on his own and starting to make inroads in cabarets and off-Broadway revues. Kaye Ballard remembers paying him one hundred and fifty dollars for a song with the lines, "My love gave me a pair of golden earrings but the romance is cold and my ears have turned green."[2] In general he took advantage of "any chance to have a song sung by a good singer, where I could invite people to see it." Occasionally he also sent songs back to Northwestern for Waa-Mu shows.

One of the most important connections Harnick made in his early days in New York was his renewed association with his college friend Charlotte Rae, whose arrival had preceded his by a year or two and who was already making a name for herself as a singing actress specializing in comedy. Through Rae, Harnick was able to meet his idol Yip Harburg, who offered him encouragement and inspiration and important professional contacts. More importantly, Rae asked Harnick to write a song for her, which eventually led to his first big break. The song began to form in the middle of the night:

> I had no ideas for what to write for Charlotte, but one night I woke up about four o'clock in the morning with a song going through my head. I wrote down three stanzas, words and music, and I went back to sleep. The next morning I got up and I said, "I wrote a song last night. It's probably rotten. It's probably one of those four o'clock ideas which turns out to be absolute gibberish the next day." I looked at it and I thought, "My God, this is wonderful!" It needed a fourth stanza, but the fourth stanza was inherent in the way the first three were going. I called it "The Shape of Things."[3]

Rae began to use this song in her cabaret act and planned to perform it in a new revue being put together by Leonard Sillman, to be the fourth in his *New Faces* series. Previous *New Faces* revues had featured debuts of performers such as Henry Fonda and Imogene Coca in 1934, Van Johnson in 1936, and John Lund and Irwin Corey in 1943.[4]

"The Ballad of the Shape of Things" never actually made it into *New Faces* and did not appear in a revue until 1956 (in *The Littlest Revue*, off-Broadway). The timing of its creation, however, makes it a helpful clue to Harnick's creative life very shortly after moving to New York. The song deftly juxtaposes a stiff, madrigal style with a story about lethal revenge taken on the singer's unfaithful lover. A geometric metaphor organizes the narrative: in the first stanza, round shapes symbolize the "lowdown dirty runaround / My true love gave to me"; in stanza two, squares are a ring box, an envelope, a handkerchief, and ultimately "my true love's head"; and in stanza three, rectangles symbolize doors and hotel rooms and, of course, a receptacle with a special solemn function:

> Now, rectangular is the wooden box
> Where lies my love 'neath the golden flocks
> They said he died of the chicken pox

> In part I must agree
> One chick too many had he.

Finally, triangles in stanza four symbolize the "hatchet blade" with which revenge was exacted, and the "relationship / That now has ceased to be," but also a very soft and absorbent piece of cloth strategically situated on a living, breathing memento:

> And, triangular is the garment thin
> That fastens on with a safety pin
> To a prize I had no wish to win
> It's a lasting memory
> That my true love gave to me.

As Henry Hewes noted in *Saturday Review*, "The Shape of Things" is reminiscent of the Rodgers and Hart song "To Keep My Love Alive" from *The Connecticut Yankee* (1927), which has the same stiff, strophic feel and macabre story.[5] But "The Shape of Things" can only succeed if presented deadpan, with somber earnestness, and surely it was a perfect vehicle for a singer with Charlotte Rae's comic gifts.[6]

Production of the *New Faces* revue was delayed for lack of funding in 1950 and 1951, and Charlotte Rae was ultimately lured into joining the cast of a different show, Ralph Blane's book musical *Three Wishes for Jamie* (which opened on March 21, 1952).[7] But Sillman still wanted Harnick to be one of his new faces; soon he signed on another promising new talent, Alice Ghostley, who seemed to share Harnick's comic sensibility, and asked for another song. Harnick's new offering, "Boston Beguine," became one of the highlights of *New Faces of 1952* in its successful run at the Royale Theater from May 1952 through March 1953. He conceived it on a bus trip back from Boston, where his wife was appearing in *Top Banana*. He was angered by some of the shady characters he had encountered in Boston Common, and by a story he had recently read about censorship of books by a Boston church, and so created a musical revenge.[8] The song pulls no punches: Boston has "intrigues and dangers with passionate strangers" and "something in the air; there always is in Boston." At the Casbah, an Irish bar and the "underground hideout of the D. A. R.," you must "watch your heart," but also "watch your purse." In the spell of the city, the song says, "I was drunk with love and cheap muscatel." Ultimately, two lovers find themselves in Boston Common "underneath a voodoo moon," but they can do no better than fall asleep; in being deprived of books they were also deprived of their "dream of adventure," left clueless for any more rapturous sources of sensory stimulation.

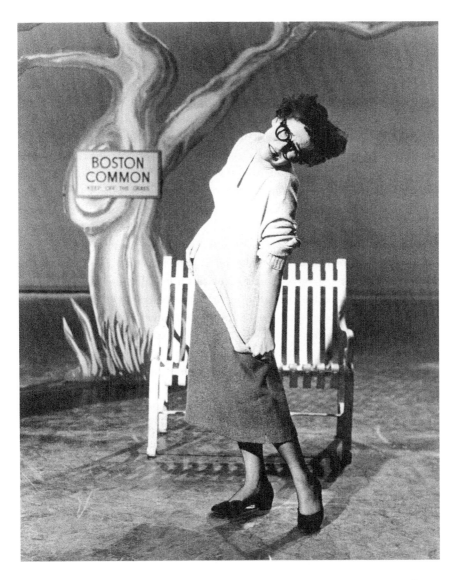

Alice Ghostley performing Harnick's "Boston Beguine" in the revue New Faces of 1952
(Photofest)

Critics praised many facets of *New Faces of 1952*, and several singled out
Alice Ghostley and "Boston Beguine." In the *New York Times* (5/25/52), Brooks
Atkinson described the song as "both intelligent and uproarious." Walter
Kerr called it "probably the evening's happiest inspiration" (*Herald Tribune*,
5/17/52). Ghostley's performance, which can be seen in the 1954 film of the

show, was a skillful blend of subtlety and timing.[9] Atkinson wrote: "Fitted out with some depressing bone glasses, she is dressed like a college student, and her siren bumps and grinds are gauche and inhibited." "What puts it over," said "G. S." in the *Wall Street Journal* (5/17/52), is Ghostley's "painfully accurate and untrammeled rendition of the inept tones and gestures of a raw amateur on a stage." The performance catapulted her to a successful career on stage and screen, as did the work of several others in the cast, including Paul Lynde, Eartha Kitt, and Carol Lawrence. John Stewart describes *New Faces of 1952* as "one of the most influential revues, not only of the 1950s, but of all time."[10] Harnick's song, with its overt echoes of Cole Porter's "Begin the Beguine," has endured as a comic classic, displaying its author's skills with both music and rhyme.[11]

Harnick's success with "Boston Beguine" enhanced his access to producers and revue auditions, as did his inclusion in a showcase for young writers and performers, *Talent '52*, on May 12, 1952, with a musical scene entitled "Rage of the Stage."[12] His next experience on Broadway was *Two's Company*, a new revue featuring Bette Davis in her Broadway musical debut, with music mostly by Vernon Duke, lyrics by Ogden Nash. Harnick recalls some interest in his earlier song "The Suave Young Man" for that show, as a possible scenario for a dance sequence choreographed by Jerome Robbins. After that idea was considered and rejected, the show's producer asked Harnick to write a song that would provide an ending for a sketch about "spacemen, who come from outer space and land in New York, and they are absolutely fascinated and mystified by our obsession with sports." His response, "The Ball Song," was also removed from the show during out-of-town tryouts. Recalling his effort, Harnick observed: "we all should have known: you cannot end a sketch with a song, and especially a song that isn't that funny." This cut, however, left one of the performers, Hiram ("Chubby") Sherman, with too little to do, so Harnick played one of his new creations for him:

> I hired a pianist, or asked a pianist to play for me, and we played for the producer, and the director, and for Chubby Sherman. I did the song. He looked so somber all through the song. And at the end of it there was a long pause, and I thought, "Well, I guess it died." And he said, "That may be the saddest song I've ever heard in my life." And then he said, "I'd like to do it."

And so in December 1952, when *Two's Company*, starring Bette Davis, opened at the Alvin Theater, while *New Faces of 1952* continued its run at the Royale, Harnick had two songs playing on Broadway. The new one, "A Man's Home," was inspired by Frank Lloyd Wright:

When I was thinking of revue songs, and remembering the old imperative adage, "write what you know," it occurred to me that I loved Frank Lloyd Wright, and I thought, "What could I write about him?" I thought it's a funny idea, he uses a lot of natural materials. It would be a funny idea to have somebody who can't actually afford to hire Frank Lloyd Wright, but he would go to one of his disciples, and the man would build him a home out of natural materials, and it would blend so much in with his landscape that one day he leaves home and he can't find it.

"A Man's Home" is more controlled by dramatic narrative, concerned less with distinctive musical gestures, than some of Harnick's other early songs. "The Shape of Things" is purely strophic, and "Boston Beguine" is held together by a consistency of style, but "A Man's Home" is focused on telling a story. And, like "A Suave Young Man," it begins in Gilbert and Sullivan patter style ("If I do say so myself, there is very little romance in me / I'm a practical, tactical, clinical, cynical, hard-bitten business man"), then shifts to a Broadway foxtrot ("I'm in love with my brand new house"). Harnick delivers the ironic ending in rhymed couplets:

> Now, strange as this may sound
> My house cannot be found.
> It's blended with such skill
> Into the surrounding hill.
> I've called the man who designed it
> But even he can't find it.
> He did his job too well
> I hope he roasts in hell!

Reviews were mixed about the song—Brooks Atkinson wrote that he was "grateful" for Harnick's "satirical ballad" (*New York Times*, 12/16/52), while Walter Kerr called it "stubbornly unfunny" (*Herald Tribune*, 12/16/52)—but Hiram Sherman received wide acclaim for his performance throughout the show and won the Tony Award for Supporting or Featured Actor in a Musical in 1953.

Harnick's Broadway experience thus far gave him an inside track to the next project of John Murray Anderson, who had directed *New Faces* and had been brought in for last-minute help with *Two's Company*.[13] After *Two's Company* closed, Anderson put together a revue of mostly young talent, featuring music of a new songwriting duo, Richard Adler and Jerry Ross—who would achieve Broadway acclaim shortly thereafter with *The Pajama Game* (1954) and *Damn Yankees* (1955)—but also including Harnick's song "Merry Little

Minuet," which had at one time been considered for *Two's Company*.[14] *John Murray Anderson's Almanac* opened on December 10, 1953 at the Imperial Theater and ran for 227 performances. New talent Orson Bean performed Harnick's song and the critics raved. The show also featured the Broadway debuts of Hermione Gingold and Harry Belafonte, whose performance earned him the Tony for Best Supporting or Featured Actor in a Musical in 1954.

"Merry Little Minuet" is yet another gem of social commentary in a classic musical framework. As in "The Shape of Things," Harnick's simple music for the minuet is blissfully oblivious to the very somber message of its text. After an introduction in a minor key sets the stage, a lilting triple-meter vocal line, frequently interrupted by a whistled response, presents an apocalyptic lyric, with dire news about armed conflicts, natural disasters, and nationalistic prejudice worldwide. We hear multiple examples of how "the whole world is festering with unhappy souls," and yet that is not the worst of it. None of this matters because we are going to annihilate ourselves anyway: "What nature doesn't do to us / Will be done by our fellow man." The biting satire of "Merry Little Minuet" transports Gilbert and Sullivan, stripped of its subtlety, into the atomic age. It is reminiscent of the best work of Harnick's contemporary Tom Lehrer, with an extra layer of refinement.[15]

Harnick's First Book Show

By the time *John Murray Anderson's Almanac* opened in December 1953, Harnick felt that he had achieved some of his first career goals. He had placed songs in high-profile revues and learned a great deal by studying the audience's reactions. But to move to the next level he decided to heed the advice of Yip Harburg, who had told him, "In my experience, there are more capable theater composers than there are theater lyricists. So you can facilitate your career by writing with other people besides yourself." He began to collaborate with David Baker, the pianist and conductor's assistant in *Two's Company*, following a suggestion by that show's music director, Milton Rosenstock. He also began looking for sketch writers for a new revue and became acquainted with Ira Wallach, the author of *Hopalong-Freud* (1951) and other satirical books, whose work Harnick had seen at a performance at a theater school in New York. As it happened, Wallach was interested in a project more ambitious than a revue, a full-length book musical based on some of the Horatio Alger, Jr. stories. Harnick liked the idea and eagerly signed on as lyricist, bringing in Baker to write the music, in coordination with Wallach's book. It would be the first original musical for each of them.

The project, first known as *The Fair-Haired Boy*, occupied Harnick's creative energies in 1953 and early 1954. With Baker he wrote at least fourteen songs for the show, including ballads, love songs, choruses, waltzes, patter songs, a polka, and a march (see Table 2.1). They were writing the show without performance prospects, but then got a lucky break sometime in early 1954, when Harnick's friend Michael Brown, whose song "Lizzie Borden" was featured in *New Faces of 1952*, contracted mononucleosis and was unable to fulfill a commitment to write a new musical for Margo Jones's theater company in Dallas. Brown put Jones in touch with Harnick, and the Wallach-Baker-Harnick musical, newly named *Horatio*, premiered in Dallas on March 8, 1954. It was an enormous success. Rual Askew, in the *Dallas Morning News* (3/9/54), called it a "real winner" that "keeps an audience in stitches" and lavishly praised every detail of the production and individual performances. The *Variety* reviewer ("Bark") described it as a "laugh-loaded effort" that "should rate further showings on large legit stages." The show first ran until March 27 and was then brought back in May, in repertory with four other new shows from earlier that season.[16]

Understandably encouraged by the reception in Dallas, Harnick, Baker, and Wallach hoped that their musical would next find an audience in New York. It did: in New York *state*, at Green Mansions, a summer resort in the Adirondacks, one of several venues for live theater, music, and dance in the mountains of New York and Pennsylvania. Green Mansions was known for entertainment with higher cultural aspirations than the comedy acts of the

Table 2.1: *Songs written by Sheldon Harnick and David Baker for* The Fair-Haired Boy

"The ABC's of Success"
"Best Loved Girls in Town"
"Class of '88"
"Daydreams"
"Environment—Heredity"
"I've Got a Wonderful Future"
"If I Felt Any Younger Today"
"Let's Evolve"
"Since My Life Began"
"Small Town"
"Temperance Polka"
"That's No Way to Live"
"When I Make Up My Mind"
"The Wonderful Machine"

Borscht Belt in the Catskills. Its programs typically included modern dance, opera excerpts, and chamber music, in addition to theater of all types. In the mid-1950s the resort hired a full staff of actors, musicians, and writers to provide nightly entertainment and produce a new musical revue every week. Among the performers and creators who worked there were Lee Strasberg, Stella Adler, Elia Kazan, Jack Gilford, Imogene Coca, Carol Burnett, Lloyd Bridges, Doris Humphrey, Michael Stewart, Harold Rome, Lee Adams, and Charles Strouse. Harnick was on the staff for the entire summer of 1955 and returned for shorter tours in 1956 and 1957.[17]

Although Harnick speaks of the Green Mansions experience in general as a vital part of his theatrical education—it was when "greasepaint entered my blood," he has said—the first performance there of *Horatio* in the summer of 1955 was memorable for all the wrong reasons.[18] In the first place, the cast that was available was not right for the show: "Non-singers. Dancers who couldn't quite sing. Comics who weren't funny," remembers Harnick. Then on the night of the first performance, everything seemed to be conspiring against them:

> They had a theater, which I think only seated about 250 people. Wooden benches, a very uncomfortable theater. The night we were supposed to perform, it was about ninety-five degrees. There was no air conditioning. There were about four or five hundred people—maybe not that many, but it seemed like it—jammed into that theater that only seated about half that number. It was so hot, and so sweltering, people began to leave during the overture. And I'm standing in the back thinking, "They hate it. They loathe it. They're leaving during the overture. My God, they didn't like the music." Well, during the first act, people left. They just walked out. They were sweltering. By the end of the act there were about fifty people left in the audience. We had the intermission, and about thirty of them came back.

Decades later Harnick regarded that night as a valuable learning experience, because "it couldn't have been worse; it was your nightmare come true." Any future failure could not possibly surpass that one. At least the next night's performance at Green Mansions went better: "It was a nice, cool night. We had a full house, maybe a few standees. No one left. At the end there was a talkback session, and there was a lot of notes on what they didn't like about the show, but no one left."

Perhaps stigmatized by the Green Mansions debut, *Horatio* was not produced in New York City until 1961, when a revised version played off-Broadway under the title *Smiling the Boy Fell Dead*. (This title is the last line of

Robert Browning's poem "Incident of the French Camp.") Critics liked the songs but found flaws in the book. In the *Times* (4/20/61), Howard Taubman wondered if "the ideas . . . were not good enough to begin with. It may also be that this age of innocence is too remote for laughter." Harnick remembers making some revisions in the show, following advice from the New York producers, that ultimately proved problematic.[19] Whatever the case, the production closed after twenty-two performances and lay dormant until 2004, when Harnick turned eighty, looked back on his career, and decided that this was the one project that deserved another chance:

> I found I had four scripts. I read them. Each of them had wonderful material that wasn't in the other scripts. Both the book-writer Ira Wallach and David Baker, they're both gone. So I decided to see what I could do, and I created a new book. I tried to use everything I think I had learned in forty years.

The new version, *Fair-Haired Boy, or the ABC's of Success*, was presented in a rehearsed reading by the Playwrights Theater in Madison, New Jersey, on January 6, 2007. Harnick was pleased and relieved and began looking for opportunities for full stagings of the work, now called *Pluck and Luck, or The ABC's of Success*.[20]

New Phases

Upon returning to New York from Dallas after the *Horatio* performances in the spring of 1954, Harnick went back to work on revue material and constantly searched for performance opportunities. A growing trend had him concerned, however:

> As television got more and more popular, and as television variety shows became more popular, they just obliterated the Broadway revues. There was no need for them. They could do them quicker and faster, they could do them with stars, they could afford stars, they could make them truly topical, which we couldn't. Revues, by and large, disappeared, and with it, my livelihood.

And so over the next few years Harnick's songs were more likely to be heard in off-Broadway theaters before smaller audiences. One of the first opportunities came from a new young producer, Ben Bagley, who was claiming, quite dishonestly, that he had a wealthy father who had promised to fund a new revue.[21] Bagley commissioned contributions from Charles Strouse, Lee Adams, and Michael Stewart in addition to Harnick. In spite of Bagley's unscrupulous practices, the revue, entitled *Shoestring Revue*, was a popular and critical success at the President Theater from February through May 1955. Bagley went on to produce *The Littlest Revue* off-Broadway in May and June of 1956, featuring Charlotte Rae's performance of "The Shape of Things" alongside songs by Vernon Duke and Ogden Nash. The cast included Larry Storch, Tammy Grimes, and Joel Grey. Bagley produced a third revue, *Shoestring '57*, off-Broadway from November 1956 through February 1957, which included a song Baker and Harnick had written for *Horatio*, "Best-Loved Girls." A promising career as a producer was curtailed when Bagley was diagnosed with tuberculosis in 1958, ultimately leading him to enter a less stressful line of work; he went on to produce recordings of lesser-known songs by accomplished Broadway composers that were released on Painted Smiles Records.[22]

Harnick made four contributions to *Shoestring Revue*. "Garbage," for which he wrote both words and music, was performed by Beatrice Arthur, fresh from her recent success as Lucy Brown in the acclaimed off-Broadway production of Marc Blitzstein's translation/adaptation of Brecht/Weill's *The Threepenny Opera*. Harnick has said that his inspiration for "Garbage" was an unnamed popular song of the 1950s in a "tempestuous, passionate, Italianate" style, "the kind which starts with rolling kettle drums and then all the strings sweep up the scale, dramatically preparing for the singer's entrance."[23] This "orchestral buildup would not have been out of place in *Tosca*, but when the soloist began to sing, the banal lyrics sounded like every other limp love song one had ever heard." He says that he found such songs "silly," and that is exactly what "Garbage" is: silliness of the highest order. It begins with an introduction that offers no clues to the subject matter to come:

> I'm carrying a torch
> For the guy who done me wrong
> Why did he done me wrong
> If he done did me right I wouldn't have to sing this stupid song!
>
> Your cruelty to me
> Done hit me like a hammer
> You done destroyed my heart and soul
> And most of all my grammar.[24]

The singer's ironic detachment, commenting on singing and on the song itself, sets the tone. After that Harnick seizes well-chosen opportunities for wordplay on the song's theme, all over a *habañera* rhythmic pattern. The mock seriousness of the music comically clashes with the pedestrian message of the lyric. Harnick shows once again that he is a first-rate parodist, both as a composer and a lyricist. This song also served as a lead-in to what the producer called a "showstopping dream ballet," featuring young newcomer Chita Rivera "leaping head first into a garbage bag trying to retrieve a cigarette butt."[25]

Two of Harnick's songs for *Shoestring Revue* were written with David Baker, perhaps demonstrating some of their initial collaborations, before they began writings songs for *Horatio*. "Someone Is Sending Me Flowers," performed by Dody Goodman, describes in detail a cascade of floral gifts, all as setup to a final punch line (the flowers are being sent "collect"). Baker's harmonic palette may be a bit more diverse than Harnick's, but for the most part the music is not much different from music that Harnick himself had been writing. This song (under the title "Flowers") was also inserted into the program of *John Murray Anderson's Almanac* at some point after the show opened, performed by Hermione Gingold.[26] The other Harnick–Baker effort in *Shoestring Revue* was Arte Johnson's rendering of "The Sea Is All Around Us," a song with a political message like "Merry Little Minuet."[27] As the singer indicates in the song's introduction, Harnick's inspiration was a book by Rachel Carson— presumably *The Sea Around Us* (1951)—with a prophetic message about global warming. The song imagines New York City "at the bottom of a lake," with cross-town submarines, "oysters in the Cloisters," a "shark in Central Park," and so forth. Again Baker's music is similar to what Harnick might have written on his own. They seem to share poetic and musical sensibilities, and the result is another work of razor sharp, all-too-relevant social commentary.

Harnick's other contribution to *Shoestring Revue* was "Medea in Disneyland," a complete comedy sketch he wrote in collaboration with Lloyd Norlin, a fellow contributor to the Waa-Mu Show when they were both at Northwestern. Harnick is credited with the dialogue and lyrics, Norlin with the music, although Harnick believes that he wrote some of the music as well. Their inspiration was Disney's animated version of *Alice in Wonderland*, which he felt had cheapened an "imaginative and stylish masterpiece . . . by turning it into slapstick farce." In response, he "wanted to show the travesty that might result if Disney were to create a sentimental, anything-for-a-laugh version of an acknowledged masterpiece of tragic drama." So "Medea in Disneyland" sets the Medea myth in a Disneyfied world of friendly woodland creatures and fairy godmothers. It played like a condensed, miniaturized version of a full musical and found just the right satirical tone. As Walter Kerr wrote in the *Herald Tribune* (3/1/55),

When narrator Arthur Partington first suggests that, as a first-act finale, the boys and girls are going to do "Medea" in the Disney manner, your hopes aren't too high. Disney is a fairly sharp man himself. But authors Sheldon Harnick and Lloyd Norlin have aimed smack at the chink in the Disney armor—the lush, tinted, harp-twanging sentiment—and the spectacle of a deadpan Dorothy Greener being cheery about bluebirds just before she hacks up her children is, I think, bound to double you up.

Indeed the entire show was very well received and brought early notoriety to cast members Arte Johnson, Dorothy Greener, Dody Goodman, Beatrice Arthur, and Chita Rivera. That it closed when it did, after three months and ninety-six performances, was, said the *Daily News* (4/27/55), "another example of inexperienced management in a tough business."

By 1956 Harnick continued to search for songwriting opportunities even as television increasingly threatened the Broadway revue. Notices occasionally appeared during this time publicizing his involvement in shows that never materialized, such as *Twenty-Nine Rainbows* (*New York Times*, 1/26/56) and *Out of Joint* (*New York Times*, 6/24/57). He became involved with projects that did not really appeal to him, just for the work: *Take All You Can Get*, based on Steve Fisher's novel about the used-car business, brought a paycheck but otherwise only frustration. After a few months' work in collaboration with Jack Brodsky (book) and Robert Fabian (music), the project was abandoned. Harnick did manage to place his Waa-Mu song "The Suave Young Man," now called "Trenchcoat," in a summer tour by Tallulah Bankhead in 1956, along with another original song, "Be Mine." "Trenchcoat" turned up again in 1957, along with a Baker-Harnick song originally written for *Horatio*, "When I Make Up My Mind," in an unsuccessful off-Broadway revue, *Kaleidoscope*. And that same year a Baker–Harnick effort that originated at Green Mansions, "Say, Hello!," was on the program of a nightclub revue, *Take Five*. Harnick also found work on industrial shows, adding new lyrics to existing songs as parts of sales campaigns.[28]

After Green Mansions, David Baker had moved on to other things. One was a performance of *Horatio* back home in Portland, Maine in the spring of 1956, with Linda Lavin, then a high-school senior, playing the female lead.[29] Harnick's reputation as a collaborator and problem-solver brought him work as a "show doctor"—a consultant and contributor to shows that were in development but in need of new creative energy. The producers of *The Amazing Adele*, a musical adaptation of a French comedy, sought Harnick's help as the show floundered in pre-Broadway tryouts, but it closed in January 1956 in Boston. Harnick remembers telling Tammy Grimes, who would have made her Broadway debut in that show, "I wished I had as much faith in my career as I had in hers."[30] Another full-length musical for which Harnick provided last-minute help did make it to Broadway—briefly. *Shangri-La*, a musical adaptation of James Hilton's novel *Lost Horizon*, played for twenty-one performances at the Winter Garden in June 1956. Harry Warren wrote the music, but during the pre-Broadway tour he needed someone new to write lyrics after his original lyricists, Jerome Lawrence and Robert E. Lee, had to shift their attentions to another project (the play *Auntie Mame*, which opened in October). Harnick did some repair work and wrote one new song with Warren, a soft-shoe number that played well but was eventually cut. The one truly beneficial consequence of the *Shangri-La* experience for Harnick, aside from the paycheck, was a social encounter the evening of the premiere, June 13, 1956: at the opening-night party, cast member Jack Cassidy introduced him to Jerry Bock.

JERRY BOCK ON BROADWAY

Jerry Bock and Larry Holofcener left Wisconsin for New York during the winter break of 1948–49. They had met a short time earlier when Holofcener had been asked to sing at a dance and had used Bock as his accompanist, on the recommendation of a mutual friend. After that, Holofcener recalls,

> A dancer friend of mine needed a suggestion for a ballet she was to do for Hillel, the Jewish Community on campus (at Chanukah). I wrote a long tone poem, "Latke"—the Story of the First Potato Pancake. My dancer friend liked it, so I asked Jerry if he'd write some background music for it. Within a day or two, he sat me down and played a beautiful, original ballet score! Needless to say, I was gobsmacked.

Though they had been acquainted for only a month or two and had never written a song together—indeed Holofcener had no experience writing song lyrics at all—they formed a team and got to work immediately after arriving at Bock's parents' house in Flushing. Through a connection with a friend of Bock's parents (Andrew Geoly of Eaves Costumes), they were able to arrange an audition with Max Liebman, producer of the *Admiral Broadway Revue*, a television variety show starring Sid Caesar and Imogene Coca that had just begun broadcasting on January 28, 1949. (It was the forerunner of *Your Show of Shows*.) Bock and Holofcener wrote their first song together with Coca in mind, and then played and sang it, along with three other songs that Bock had written previously with other lyricists, for Liebman and James Starbuck, the show's choreographer. Holofcener recalls,

> Max still said nothing, but he ordered us to come to his apartment at 11 o'clock on Friday night. Biff [Liff, another member of the production team]

explained there was to be a cast party after the broadcast and gave us the address. We hung around the city Friday evening and finally went to Max's huge apartment off Central Park. Noise, music, laughter, food, drink. We were delighted and lost. Max, on seeing us, took us over to a grand piano and told us to play the Coca song. For Coca! And Carl [Reiner] and Sid and Mel Tolkin and Lucille Kallen (sketch writers). As we did the song, I remember (because of the background noise) [seeing] Tolkin's head right [next to] the piano strings to hear the tune. He was a composer, actually, and a wonderful pianist. Max told us to stay and have a good time (or someone did) and offhandedly said to report to work on Monday. We started off with fifty dollars a week each.[31]

Bock and Holofcener were on the writing staff of the *Admiral Broadway Revue* from that moment until the show's final broadcast on June 3 of that year, then again the following year when Sid Caesar and company returned to the air with essentially the same show, now called *Your Show of Shows*.[32] They remained with the newly named show throughout its first season, January 25 until May 20, 1950, and, when it resumed the following fall, through December 1950 and possibly beyond. It is difficult to determine exactly what Bock and Holofcener contributed to each show. Their names do not appear in the opening or closing credits until September 1950, and when they do it is a general credit ("Additional material by Mel Brooks, Larry Holofcener, and Jerry Bock"), not a specific attribution. Many of these shows' scripts are extant, but they give credits only for songs and production numbers—if they give authorship credits at all—and do not indicate smaller contributions such as continuity or dance music or assistance with work done primarily by others. Bock remembers supplying mostly "in-between stuff" and "overall musical production" as opposed to "specific sketch moments" at first, gaining responsibility as time passed.[33] Essentially Bock and Holofcener were considered part of the hired help, and thrilled to be so.

In the scripts saved by Max Liebman and writer Lucille Kallen, credits for Bock and Holofcener appear nine times (see Table 2.2).[34] Restored videos of all of these shows except the earliest one (3/25/49) are in the collection of the Paley Center for Media (formerly the Museum of Television and Radio) in New York.[35] Bock himself saved his score for only one of them, "Heartburn" (4/8/49).[36] "Ingrid the Great" (4/8/49) is a solo turn for Imogene Coca and could well be the first song Bock and Holofcener wrote together, just before their audition for Liebman.[37] Some of the others are large production numbers, with multiple characters and songs and usually some sort of multi-sectional dramatic structure. "Heartburn" (4/8/49) is a movie spoof, and "Clarence the Fireman" (4/22/50) is a melodrama about a fireman who saves his true love

Table 2.2: Scripts for Admiral Broadway Revue *and* Your Show of Shows *with credits for Bock and Holofcener*

Admiral Broadway Revue		
Show No.	Date	Title of Bock–Holofcener number(s)
9	3/25/49	Jim Green
11	4/8/49	Ingrid the Great
		Heartburn
12	4/15/49	Today
13	4/22/49	County Fair
15	5/6/49	The Hero . . . The Heroine . . . and the Man Who's Got the Mortgage
19	6/3/49	Encore
Your Show of Shows		
9	4/22/50	Clarence the Fireman
14	9/9/50	The Hero . . . The Heroine . . . and the Man Who's Got the Mortgage

from a house ablaze. In all these scores it is clear that Bock and his new partner found personal chemistry immediately and were thriving and growing in their show-music crash course. Bock re-used one earlier melody, recycling "Hear Ye" from *Big as Life* (Example 1.2c) with new text as an opening attention-grabber in "Heartburn" ("Listen . . . Listen"), but all the other music is fresh, and it is all filled with character and optimally responsive to dramatic requirements. "Today" (4/15/49) comes across like an opening number for Fred Astaire in a movie musical, and "Ingrid the Great" (4/8/49) is a simple comic song reminiscent of the type of Gilbert and Sullivan number that provides a star performer with multiple verses and silly rhymes, plus an echoing chorus.

Bock and Holofcener were able to build on their experience with Max Liebman and work on other television shows at different times in the early 1950s. Some of these were nonmusical writing assignments: Bock remembers contributing only continuity ("And my next song will be . . .") to the *Mel Tormé Show* and the *Kate Smith Show*.[38] "We hoped we might sneak a song in for them to sing," he recalls, "but we didn't succeed."[39] They did manage to place their song "Milly the Filly" on a broadcast of the *Colgate Comedy Hour* on November 12, 1950, performed by the Skylarks and chorus and dancers. This was a full production number, similar in conception to "Clarence the Fireman," about a filly named Milly and her true love Willie, who helps her win the Triple Crown.[40] They also provided material for nightclub acts by Pat Carroll (who later built a successful career on stage and screen, including playing the stepsister Prunella in the 1965 television version of *Cinderella*) and Dick Shawn (perhaps best known for his portrayal of a hippie actor with the initials "L. S. D." who plays Hitler in the 1968 Mel Brooks film *The Producers*).

Camp Tamiment and Its Impact

By far the most enriching and educational experiences of those years for Bock and Holofcener were the three summers they spent at Camp Tamiment in the Pocono Mountains of Pennsylvania, a "summer camp for adults" similar to Green Mansions in upstate New York, where Sheldon Harnick would do very similar work a few years later. Tamiment had become an important theatrical destination and training arena for young actors, dancers, writers, and songwriters.[41] Each week throughout the summer, from early July through early September, the company wrote, produced, and performed a new revue. Some of the material would ultimately make it to Broadway, and the concept itself became the model for *Admiral Broadway Revue, Your Show of Shows*, and other television variety shows. Imogene Coca had worked there in the 1940s, as had Jerome Robbins, Betty Garrett, and many other well known Broadway performers and creators.

Bock and Holofcener joined the Tamiment staff in 1950, returning in 1951 and 1953. (Bock does not remember why they remained in New York in 1952 but speculates that they were involved with a television project.[42]) They probably got the job through connections with Max Liebman, and by virtue of their inclusion in *Talent '50*, a showcase for aspiring theatrical talent, in April 1950. The program for *Talent '50* included three Bock songs: "Big Top Parade," with lyrics by Holofcener, and "Dear Old College Days" and "Visions on Your Television Screen," with lyrics by Fred Tobias.[43] One of the sponsoring producers, Monroe B. "Moe" Hack, was soon to become Max Liebman's replacement as the producer at Tamiment. Hack also hired performers Pat Carroll and Jack Cassidy from the same showcase for Tamiment. Other young talent at Tamiment during Bock and Holofcener's tenure included Danny and Neil Simon, Dick Shawn, and Barbara Cook.

A typical program for a Tamiment revue included sketches, songs, dances, and production numbers, all written that week for performances on Saturday and Sunday. (Shows toward the end of the summer would often repeat material from previous weeks.) Bock and Holofcener always contributed at least one song to the production, usually many, up to about half of the show.[44] Over their three summers there, they wrote at least seventy-nine songs/sketches together (see Table 2.3). Bock regards the Tamiment experience as the very foundation of his education in the art of musical theater.[45] Each week offered a kind of laboratory in which creators were free to try new ideas and hone developing skills, to workshop a concept in collaboration with a talented performer who could help find what works and suggest refinements. The tight

Table 2.3: Songs or sketches credited to Bock and Holofcener on Tamiment programs in 1950, 1951, and 1953

Title of song or sketch	Performance date(s)	Box. folder in Bock Papers
A Day in the Mountains	8/4/51,8/5/51,9/1/51	
All Abroad	7/25/53,7/26/53	13.11
All the News That's Fit to Sing	9/1/51	
Almost April	7/4/53,7/5/53,8/15/53,8/16/53,9/12/53	13.12
At the Beach	8/11/51,8/12/51	
Bachelor's Hoedown	7/11/53,7/12/53,8/22/53,8/23/53, 9/12/53	13.13
Back to the Indians	8/11/51,8/12/51,9/1/51	
The Ballad of Arthur Central	7/1/50,7/29/50,7/30/50	13.14
[a.k.a. Which Is the Witch]		14.8
Ballad of Smilin' Dave	8/18/51,8/19/51	
Battle of Battle Creek	8/4/51,8/5/51	
Before the Show	8/8/53,8/9/53	13.15
Big Business	8/18/51,8/19/51	
Blues on Sunday	7/7/51,7/8/51	16.22
Breakfast for Two	8/4/51,8/5/51	
The Caddy	8/11/51,8/12/51,9/1/51	
Celestial Hoedown	7/14/51,7/15/51	16.24
Cocoa	8/29/53,8/30/53	13.16
Come to Paris	7/25/53,7/26/53,8/29/53,8/30/53	13.17
Crazy in Love	8/11/51,8/12/51	
Dancing After Five	7/18/53,7/19/53,8/29/53,8/30/53	13.19
Deadwood Gulch on Earth	7/14/51,7/15/51	
Derby Day	9/9/50	
Fallen for the Guy	7/22/50,7/23/50,8/19/50,8/20/50, 9/9/50,7/28/51,7/29/51	
Fiesta in Chile	7/7/51,7/8/51,7/28/51,7/29/51	15.25
Fifth Avenue	7/8/50,8/5/50,8/6/50	
Fly, Little Heart	8/1/53,8/2/53,9/5/53	13.20
Friends	9/1/51	16.30
Gold Rush [a.k.a. Dawson City]	7/8/50,8/19/50,8/20/50	16.25
Goodbye Love	8/11/51,8/12/51	
The Greatest Dance Team	7/25/53,7/26/53,8/22/53,8/23/53,9/12/53	13.18
The Gypsy	7/18/53,7/19/53,8/22/53,8/23/53, 9/12/53	13.22

(Continued)

Table 2.3: (Continued)

Title of song or sketch	Performance date(s)	Box. folder in Bock Papers
High Time	7/28/51,7/29/51	
Home Coming Day	8/8/53,8/9/53	
[a.k.a. Oskiwowity University]		14.1
[a.k.a. Rah, Rah, Rah (Alma Mater)]		14.2
Hungrier'n a B'ar	7/22/50,7/23/50,8/19/50,8/20/50,9/9/50	16.33
I Married a Monster	7/25/53,7/26/53	
It's Nice Out	7/18/53,7/19/53,8/29/53,8/30/53	13.23
It's Simple to be Famous	8/1/53,8/2/53,8/29/53,8/30/53	
Jamaica Lady	7/11/53,7/12/53,8/22/53,8/23/53,9/12/53	13.24
Jim Green	7/11/53,7/12/53,8/22/53,8/23/53,9/12/53	13.25
July	7/21/51,7/22/51,8/25/51,8/26/51	16.38
Just for Love	7/21/51,7/22/51,8/25/51,8/26/51	
Kokomo to Broadway	7/28/51,7/29/51	
Les Enfants de Maman Goose	9/1/51	
Let's Get Away	7/15/50,8/12/50,8/13/50	
The Lindsey Report	7/21/51,7/22/51	
Love on the Phone	7/7/51,7/8/51	16.34
Miami July	7/4/53,7/5/53,8/15/53,8/16/53	13.26
Minsky's Matinee	7/25/53,7/26/53	13.21
Mo'nin'	8/11/51,8/12/51	
Night [a.k.a. Nightime]	7/21/51,7/22/51	16.43
North Pole	9/9/50	
Number Please	8/11/51,8/12/51,8/25/51,8/26/51	
The Old Vaudeville Team	8/18/51,8/19/51	
On the Mall	7/1/50,7/29/50,7/30/50	
On the Road	8/19/50,8/20/50	
One Big Night	7/7/51,7/8/51	
Pals of the Pentagon	7/28/51,7/29/51	
Pennsylvania Sundae	7/28/51,7/29/51	
Phil	7/14/51,7/15/51	
Queen of P. S. 3	7/7/51,7/8/51	
Right on the Wrong, Wrong, Trail	7/14/51,7/15/51	
Rubbin' Noses	7/15/50,8/12/50,8/13/50	
Satin	7/4/53,7/5/53,8/15/53,8/16/53	14.3

(Continued)

Title of song or sketch	Performance date(s)	Box, folder in Bock Papers
Show Me a Town	7/22/50,7/23/50,8/26/50,8/27/50,7/21/51, 8/18/51,8/19/51	
Show Train	7/4/53,7/5/53,8/15/53,8/16/53	14.4
So	8/15/53,8/16/53,9/5/53	14.5
Street Scene	7/14/51,7/15/51	
Summer Shower	8/4/51,8/5/51,9/1/51	
Summer Stock	8/25/51,8/26/51	
TV Caper	7/28/51,7/29/51	
This is Paradise?	8/11/51,8/12/51	
Torch Song	8/18/51,8/19/51	
Wait for Me	7/14/51,7/15/51	
The Want of You	8/8/53,8/9/53,9/5/53	14.7
Who Needs Spring	7/14/51,7/15/51	
Why Travel	8/4/51,8/5/51	
The Wrong, Wrong Trail	8/18/51,8/19/51	
You Can't Fool Me	7/11/53,7/12/53,8/29/53,8/30/53	14.9
You Only Die Once	7/14/51,7/15/51,8/18/51,8/19/51	

time schedule, Bock has said, helped prepare him for the experience of reworking a musical in pre-Broadway tryouts. And it could all happen with a minimized fear of failure: the audience would always be there on the weekend.

The extraordinary value of the Tamiment experience for Bock's development as a Broadway composer is apparent from the range and variety of the music he wrote there.[46] His Tamiment scores include every type of song idiom and theatrical genre, from slapstick comedy ("The Old Vaudeville Team," premiered 8/18/51) to cowboy music ("Gold Rush," 7/8/50). He demonstrates a particular flair for tailoring musical style to dramatic setting, writing in a Latin style for "Fiesta in Chile" (7/7/51) or a Caribbean style for "Jamaica Lady" (7/11/53) or an Eastern European style for "The Gypsy" (7/18/53). He also displays increasing comfort in the language and style of popular music ("Almost April," 8/15/53) and operetta ("Hungrier 'n a B'ar," 7/22/50). The spirit of adventure extends to compositional technique as well. The chorus of "All Abroad" (7/25/53), for example, is first presented as an individual melody, but when it returns it is combined with a new melody in counterpoint. The main tune (stems up in the treble staff of Example 2.1a)

a. *"All Abroad," mm. 1–16 (Bock Papers, box 13, folder 11)*

b. *"Dancing After Five," mm. 1–8 (Bock Papers, box 13, folder 19)*

Example 2.1: Excerpts from Tamiment songs

and the countermelody (stems down) complement each other in rhythm and phrasing, and they are generally consonant with the prevailing harmonic progression.[47] Bock shows no concern for moments when the voices mildly trip over each other: the integrity of the individual melodic lines supersedes dissonances between the G and A in measure 9, or between the As and Bs in measure 13. "Dancing After Five" (7/18/53) supports a sequential melody with a progression of mostly seventh chords on fifth-related roots (Example 2.1b).[48] The sequence progresses consistently in perfect fifths, eventually moving outside of the main key and through all twelve steps of a complete cycle of descending fifths (F–B♭–E♭–A♭–D♭–G♭–B–E–A–D–G–C). And in July of 1951 Bock and Holofcener wrote music and lyrics for "Goin' West," the first of several "mini-musicals" in which writers, composers, and choreographers explored the integration of story, music, and movement within a fuller narrative. From there it was a logical progression to the actual Broadway musical, and in fact full-length musicals were developed (by others) at Tamiment in subsequent years.[49]

Bock's productive partnership with Holofcener endured throughout the early 1950s. In 1954 they signed with a prominent music publisher, Tommy Valando, who paid them a modest stipend to publish their songs, and from that time they wrote many songs together with no apparent connection to a specific project. Bock kept lead sheets for many of these, bearing publication notices and Valando's address in the Brill Building (1619 Broadway). Bock also wrote a number of songs to his own lyrics.[50] Once again, what is most striking about all these songs is not just the composer's familiarity and comfort with popular and Broadway song styles, but his evident desire to test ideas that fall outside normal expectations of style or tone. Clearly he could write a charming pop song in standard style if he wanted to—and "The Day We Fell in Love" is one of his best[51]—but at times he is more interested in being an innovator. The Bock–Holofcener song "Show Me a Better Man," for example, begins with a chromatic ascent from the leading tone that reverses course but eventually peaks on the fifth scale step (F♯) at "on his shelf" (Example 2.2). The second phrase starts similarly but ultimately comes to rest on step 5 by approaching from above, via a lowered and regular step 7 ("Show me a bet-ter man"). In this effort Bock seems to be exploring the possibilities of the chromatic scale within the melodic structure of a pop song, perhaps inspired by the chromatic elements of Richard Rodgers's "Lover" (1932) or Peter DeRose's "Deep Purple" (1934) or Cole Porter's "All Through the Night" (1934).

The affiliation with Valando began to pay dividends. Bock and Holofcener placed two songs in the revue *Ziegfeld Follies of 1956*, "When Papa Would Waltz" and "The Whip."[52] Unfortunately, the show was plagued with financial

Example 2.2: "Show Me a Better Man," mm. 1–8 (Bock Papers, box 17, folder 1)

problems and forced to close before it made it to Broadway; a revised version that played for three-and-a-half months the following year did not include the Bock-Holofcener songs. More encouraging was an engagement to write music for a short documentary film, *Wonders of Manhattan*. Again a spirit of innovation is on full display: "New York Prologue" works as a kind of fantasy on the "lament" chromatic bass line, stepping from 1 down to 5, joining a long list of compositions exploring the harmonic possibilities of that bass pattern.[53] The film, part of the Columbia Musical Travelark Series, was one of two short films submitted by the Motion Picture Association to the Cannes Film Festival in 1956.[54]

In September of 1955 Bock and Holofcener made their Broadway songwriting debuts with *Catch a Star!*, a revue with Tamiment roots. The show's producer, Ray Golden, had been at Tamiment and assembled a revue by combining Tamiment veterans with new talent and material. Neil and Danny Simon wrote most of the sketches, Sammy Fain and Phil Charig wrote most of the music, and Bock and Holofcener contributed three songs: two that had been done at Tamiment in 1953, "Bachelor Hoedown" (7/11/53) and "Fly, Little Heart" (8/1/53), and one new one, "The Story of Alice." Although the overall show was not well received and played for only twenty-three performances at the Plymouth Theater, several reviewers singled out Bock–Holofcener songs for praise, especially "The Story of Alice," an amusing ensemble piece in the style of a dance-hall madrigal. As the singers describe Alice, then her lover Algernon, each verse adds a new contrapuntal layer.[55] By coincidence very much like another faux-madrigal, Harnick's "The Shape of Things," the song ends with the lovers going their separate ways, leaving Alice with a lasting memorial: she is with child. One of Bock's happiest memories about *Catch a Star!* was an article that appeared in the *Daily News* two days after the opening (on 8 September 1955) in which Douglas Watt quoted Richard Rodgers, as he left the theater after the premiere, expressing particular affection for "Fly, Little Heart." This "praise from the master," wrote Bock in 2008, was a "most treasured moment" in his early career.

What is also noteworthy about the history of *Catch a Star!* is one obscure fact that attracted the attention of no one. A touring version of the show, entitled *Joy Ride*, opened in Los Angeles in January 1956. Its program included not only "The Story of Alice" but also Sheldon Harnick's "Merry Little Minuet."[56] For the first time in recorded history, an evening's entertainment featured music of Jerry Bock and Sheldon Harnick.

Bock's First Book Show

The next project for Bock and Holofcener would be the fulfillment of their Broadway dreams; it would also bring about the end of their partnership. Sometime in the middle months of 1955 they had heard through the grapevine that Jule Styne was looking for songwriters for a new musical starring Sammy Davis, Jr. The book was being written by Joseph Stein and Will Glickman, who had written the current hit *Plain and Fancy*, and Styne wanted a fresh sound for the score. Bock and Holofcener were the fifteenth team to audition; they got the job because Styne "liked their energy and moxie."[57] Their first efforts, however, left Styne wondering if he had made a mistake: when Bock and Holofcener played some of the songs they had written for the show at a backers' audition, Styne felt that they had completely missed the mark. He thought that the harmony was too complex and Gershwinesque. He recalls telling them, "Fellows, this isn't an opera."[58] Styne called their agent Tommy Valando and threatened to fire them.

Valando's solution was to bring a more experienced songwriter into the team. Holofcener remembers that Valando first asked for help from Kay Thompson, who had experience as a vocal arranger in Hollywood (and who may have been working on her classic children's book *Eloise* at that time), but after Bock and Holofcener wrote "three or four" songs over a weekend, presumably trying to find a more commercial sound, Thompson heard the results and simply declined to be involved, saying that they "didn't need anyone else." Bock and Holofcener kept working, but at some point Valando enlisted the help of yet another new collaborator, George David Weiss. Weiss had formal musical training and had worked as an arranger and songwriter for over a decade. He had teamed with Bennie Benjamin to write hits for Perry Como ("Surrender," 1946), Patti Page ("Confess," 1948), and Sarah Vaughan ("I Ran All the Way Home," 1951).[59] He had never written for Broadway before, but he certainly understood the marketplace. This placated Styne.

What happened next is remembered differently by those involved. Styne has said that he brought in Weiss because the team needed a stronger lyricist.[60] Weiss remembers tense working sessions with Bock and Holofcener filled with creative disagreements and a strong sense that too many cooks were spoiling the broth, until Valando finally urged them to get the work finished for the sake of their incipient careers.[61] In Bock's memory "a rather difficult and somewhat tense environment" resulted from "two lyricists of varying views," and yet "somehow we managed to survive those emotions." Holofcener believes that Valando brought in Weiss to split up Bock and Holofcener, just as he had earlier turned Weiss against his former partner Bennie Benjamin. Holofcener contends that he and Bock had already written most of the songs for the show by that time, and that after Weiss came along Bock worked exclusively with Weiss to complete the score.

What is not in dispute is that the experience dissolved a songwriting team that had thrived for the previous six years. In Bock's words, "A growing separation in creative ideologies, working techniques, and ultimate ambitions between Larry and myself which had been accumulating finally split us apart, irrevocably."[62] Holofcener went on to search for other songwriting partners and projects for new musicals. He wrote a play, *Before You Go*, that ran briefly on Broadway in 1968, and a musical, *I Don't Live There Anymore*, with composer Gerard Kenny that was performed at the 1993 Spoleto Festival. He also found work as an actor, including a role in *Fiddler on the Roof* in Princeton, New Jersey. Ultimately he became a successful sculptor and painter. In 2008, as he reflected on his work with Bock, he wrote, "Jerry was truly the inspiration for all of my creative life. How he thought I could write masterful (rhyming) lyrics to his beautiful music was some kind of belief that still boggles my mind."[63]

When *Mr. Wonderful* opened at the Broadway Theater on March 22, 1956, the songs were credited to "Jerry Bock, Larry Holofcener, and George Weiss." In the biographical blurbs in a souvenir program, both Holofcener and Weiss are credited with lyrics exclusively, presuming that Bock alone wrote the music.[64] Whatever the division of labor, the new songs were used mostly in the first act, leaving room in the second act for an abbreviated version of Sammy Davis, Jr.'s nightclub act, which included a variety of existing songs by various writers. As Bock has said, the assignment to write a "half score" was a good steppingstone to full-length musicals down the road. But the original songs in the first act make a strong showing alongside the standards in the second act, and two of them, "Mr. Wonderful" and "Too Close For Comfort," emerged outside the context of the show in multiple separate recordings. Indeed, recordings of these songs were released before the show opened in New York, "Too Close For Comfort" by Davis and his group, the Will Mastin Trio, and the title song by Sarah Vaughan (which reached the thirteenth spot on the pop charts). Other versions of "Mr. Wonderful" appeared that same year by Peggy Lee (13 on the pop charts) and Teddi King (18).

Stein and Glickman's story is tailored to feature the star performer and encapsulate his rise to fame. The Davis character, Charlie Welch, is a talented entertainer but seemingly content to play small clubs for modest paydays, accompanied by his father and uncle (played by Davis's father, Sammy Davis, Sr., and uncle, Will Mastin). Another performer, Fred Campbell (played by

Sammy Davis, Jr. in Mr. Wonderful *(1956) (Photofest)*

Jack Carter), wants to make Charlie a star. He convinces his wife, Lil (Pat Marshall), to let him invest their savings in Charlie's future. Charlie deliberately fails in his first big chance and is similarly reluctant to make a commitment to his girlfriend, Ethel Pearson (Olga James). Eventually Fred gets Charlie a booking at the prestigious Palm Club in New York and convinces him to give it his best shot. The show ends with Charlie's performance at the club. He is a big hit.

It may not be one of Stein and Glickman's most inspired creations, but it gave the audience what it wanted. (An earlier version of the script began in Paris and featured a theme of racial equality, but this aspect did not play well in pre-Broadway performances in Philadelphia and was removed.[65]) In the final scene Davis was free to entertain directly to the audience just as he would in an actual nightclub. This act could vary from show to show and might include whatever singing, dancing, and mimicry seemed right for that moment. When critics in New York liked the star and his final nightclub act but objected to just about everything else—Brooks Atkinson in the *Times* (3/23/56) called it a "spectacular, noisy endorsement of mediocrity"—Davis vowed to work even harder for his fans in the audience who were clearly enjoying themselves. He wrote in his autobiography,

> I'd just finished doing the impressions in the Palm Club scene when a woman in the audience stood up and shouted, "The critics are crazy. We love you, Sammy." I threw her a kiss. "So tell your friends!" The audience cheered. It was eleven-fifteen and I was ready to go into the last number but I cued Morty and I did an extra thirty minutes.[66]

The show played for eleven months and 388 performances, closing not because of waning ticket sales but because Davis had obligations elsewhere.[67] All in all, *Mr. Wonderful* had to be considered a success—but a success of showmanship, not of theater.

Bock's songs for *Mr. Wonderful* embrace the same diversity of style and structure as his work at Tamiment (see Table 2.4). The show opens with a syncopated attention-getter, "1617 Broadway," echoing the spirit of Cole Porter's "Another Op'nin', Another Show" (from *Kiss Me, Kate*, 1948) and essentially paying tribute to the concentration of publishers and songwriters in the Brill Building in New York (in reality located at 1619 Broadway). The other classic show tunes include the duet between Fred and Lil "Without You, I'm Nothing," Charlie's love song "There," and the song Fred sings about his discovery, "Charlie Welch." "Too Close for Comfort" deserves its place in the canon, but it is extraneous to the story and was almost cut during previews; it stayed because the audience apparently knew the tune from the radio and

Table 2.4: Overview of Mr. Wonderful

ACT 1

1. 1617 Broadway, New York City.
      "Without You, I'm Nothing"
2. The Bandbox in Union City, New Jersey.
      "Jacques D'Iraq"
      "Ethel, Baby"
      "Mr. Wonderful"
      "Charlie Welch"
3. 1617 Broadway, two weeks later.
      "Charlie Welch" (reprise)
      "Talk to Him"
      "Too Close for Comfort"
4. Fred and Lil's apartment, several days later.
      "Without You, I'm Nothing" (reprise)
5. An audition hall.
      "Rita's Audition"
      Dance Improvisation
      "The Audition"

ACT 2

1. The Bandbox after hours, several months later.
      "There"
2. An arcade in Miami, Florida, next day.
      "Miami"
      "I've Been Too Busy"
3. Backstage at the Palm Club, Miami Beach.
4. Charlie's dressing room.
      "Mr. Wonderful" (reprise)
5. The Palm Club.
      The Act
      Finale: "Mr. Wonderful" (reprise)

"applauded warmly" when the orchestra played it during the overture.[68] Also extraneous but preserved was "I'm Available," a song inserted to feature relative newcomer Chita Rivera. The ballads Charlie and Ethel sing about each other, "Ethel, Baby" and "Mr. Wonderful," apparently represent some of Bock and Holofcener's first efforts for the show and somehow survived despite Jule Styne's initial objections. "Ethel" is harmonically lush and could easily be the song with "Gershwin harmony" that Styne wanted them to simplify.

"Mr. Wonderful" retains its elegance despite being cut down from its original "operatic" length, in Styne's characterization.[69] Actually, "I've Been Too Busy," a quartet for the four principals, is the show's most opera-like, or operetta-like, number, with voices contributing different melodies to a layered, often contrapuntal texture. Both this song and "Ethel, Baby" were added during the pre-Broadway tour in Philadelphia: apparently, at some point Styne realized that Gershwin and opera were not such bad things after all.

What is missing in *Mr. Wonderful* is an integration of music with drama. The songs all respond to characters and moments in the story, but they fulfill no real dramatic function.[70] When Lil sings "Miami" in Act 2, for example, she has a lot to say about a great American city, but none of it has any bearing on Charlie Welch's life in show business. The song comes across as a perfectly fine show tune that would be just as much at home in a revue. That may explain why "Miami" could be so easily removed from the show at some point during the New York run, perhaps to make more room for the final nightclub scene.[71] (The producers may have encouraged such cuts as Davis's nightclub act began to extend the show's length and thus involve overtime wages for cast and crew.) But many other songs in the score are also dramatically expendable. Bock himself said as much in 1985: "*Mr. Wonderful* was, in a sense, my first book show, but I treated it, I think, like a revue—songs, scene, songs, scene, not working close together."[72] It was an ideal assignment for a Broadway songwriter's debut, and Bock seized the opportunity to produce a solid score that sparkles with musical invention, but he also recognized that he still had much to learn.

The personal conflicts within the *Mr. Wonderful* team left Bock without a clear vision of his professional future. Jule Styne announced plans for the entire collective—Stein, Glickman, Bock, Holofcener, and Weiss—to adapt Garson Kanin's story *Do Re Mi* for the musical stage, but this never happened; Styne wrote the music for this show himself a few years later.[73] Meanwhile, Bock's commercial potential seemed to be growing, not only in the various individual recordings of "Mr. Wonderful" and "Too Close For Comfort" but also in the releases of two songs he wrote with George Weiss: "Never," which was recorded by Sarah Vaughan in 1955, and "Never Mind," recorded by Steve Lawrence in 1956.[74] These songs may be evidence that Bock and Weiss had worked together with the thought of establishing a partnership, or the songs may simply be rejects from *Mr. Wonderful*. Bock also continued to write both music and lyrics on occasion and may have considered going forward without a partner.[75] Four songs with words and music by Bock were recorded around this time as instrumentals (ironically) by the Nick Acquaviva Orchestra: "Always the Sea," "Joni," "One Moment More," and "This Might Be Love."[76]

Jerry Bock may have been a composer in transition, but his music was most certainly in the air the evening of June 13, 1956, from radios and phonographs and in the performance of *Mr. Wonderful* at the Broadway Theater, when he attended the premiere of *Shangri-La* two blocks down the street, and Jack Cassidy introduced him to Sheldon Harnick.

STYLISTIC FINGERPRINTS

Although still at embryonic stages of their careers when they first met in 1956, Harnick and Bock had already displayed traits and trends that would become their calling cards—the stylistic fingerprints of essentially all their subsequent work. Harnick emerged as a master lyric craftsman with an eye for detail, an ear for musical speech, a taste for unusual rhymes, and a nose for offbeat humor, often delivered with a touch of social consciousness. Bock had proven to be a prolific inventor with a seemingly endless supply of original, fertile musical ideas, a mastery of the complexities of style, and a focus on challenging conventional creative boundaries. As their sensitivity to drama grew in the fourteen years of their partnership, and as they became expert practitioners in the art of collaboration, they would ultimately reach a rarefied place in the pantheon of Broadway songwriting teams.

Sheldon Harnick the lyricist follows in the footsteps of Oscar Hammerstein II and Yip Harburg. Like Hammerstein, writes Thomas Hischak in his book about Broadway lyricists, Harnick is "steeped in tradition and yet subtly breaking rules to achieve self-expression."[77] From Harburg, Harnick inherited not only linguistic dexterity but also social awareness.[78] All this is evident in the clever humor of songs such as "Boston Beguine" or "Garbage," and in the satiric social messages in songs such as "Merry Little Minuet" and "The Sea Is All Around Us." In his book about Broadway lyricists, Lehman Engel emphasizes the novelty of some of Harnick's subject matter (the organizing role of geometric shapes in "The Shape of Things") and the humor arising from his use of irony (between the apparently innocent verse and the catastrophic refrain in "Merry Little Minuet") or creative rhymes (as seen in chapter 1 in "How Could I?").[79]

And yet these examples are all stand-alone songs: Harnick's most important strengths as a lyricist lie in his ability to work within a dramatic context, to use a song to develop themes and enrich characterization. This is something that began to emerge with his experience on his first book show, *Horatio*, and that would reach maturity in his most artistically successful collaborations with Bock. As Engel points out, Harnick became a master at finding humor in characters and situations, without using "ephemeral jokes that would limit their life-span," and without laughing at the expense of others.[80] Hischak agrees: "We may laugh at the character's foolishness or indecision or self-deception but our laughter is one of recognition, not derision."[81] Above all, observes Hischak, Harnick writes for characters with compassion and tolerance, stopping short of excessive sentimentality. His songs may not be "brassy" and "expansive," but they are also not "dull or lifeless." Harnick finds "excitement in the ordinary," writes Hischak. "In a theater too often impressed with glorious noise, Harnick speaks in a whisper."[82]

Harnick also gleaned from Harburg a perspective on the lyricist's role, and secrets of the art of collaboration, that he would carry with him throughout his career. Harnick remembers Harburg telling him,

> Always listen to the composer, and try to serve his needs, because the stronger the melody is, the stronger the lyric will be. . . . What's going to happen, especially with a comedy song—the first time the audience hears it, they will laugh. The second time they hear it, they know the jokes, and the thing that keeps [the song] alive is the charm of the music.[83]

Harnick's generosity of spirit and adaptability, not to forget his strong musical background, gave him the temperament and knowledge that have been keys to his success. Lyric-writing, he said in 1971, "is a combination of . . . creating a sculpture and doing a crossword puzzle. . . . A lot of it is really carpentry."[84]

Quite naturally for a theatrical songwriter of his generation, Jerry Bock at first worked in the shadow of Richard Rodgers. He has also named Irving Berlin and George Gershwin among his musical role models.[85] There is no apparent limit to the variety of Bock's melodies: they can be classically phrased, as in "Why Sing a Love Song?" (Example 1.2d), or filled with unexpected twists and turns, as in "My Dream" (Example 1.1a). The rhythmic playfulness of "My Dream" is also a trademark. Bock's harmonic palette is robust, ranging from basic diatonic and applied chords ("Why Sing a Love Song?," Example 1.2d), to progressions enriched by chromatic motions ("Show Me a Better Man," Example, 2.2; also "New York Prologue" from *Wonders of Manhattan* and "Ethel, Baby" from *Mr. Wonderful*), to reliance on extended root movement by fifth ("Dancing After Five," Example 2.1b; also "Without You" from *Mr. Wonderful*). In 2008 Bock confessed that as a composer he is "drawn to the circle of fifths."

He is also drawn to notes outside the diatonic scale, especially ♯4 and ♭7. Lowered seventh steps can follow the "Oh What a Beautiful Mornin'" model and resolve down to step 6, as do the B♭'s in "Here We Are Alone"

(Example 1.1c), or they can pull upward to the regular diatonic seventh step, as do the E♭ in "Great Wisconsin" (Example 1.2b) and the A♮ in "Show Me a Better Man" (Example 2.2), or they can simply hold on to the Mixolydian sound without resolution, as the G♭'s do in "Hear Ye" (Example, 1.2c). Raised fourth steps occur with conspicuous frequency in Bock's melodies, sometimes simply as lower chromatic neighbors to step 5, elsewhere as part of a major triad on step 2 (this is a likely harmonization of the G♯ in "Babe's What They Call Me," Example 1.2a) or part of a diminished seventh chord rooted on step 1 (the notated harmonization of the B♮ in m. 3 of "All Abroad," Ex. 2.1a). The F♯ in "Why Sing a Love Song" (Example 1.2d) and the E♯ in "Show Me a Better Man" (Example 2.2) are raised fourths harmonized with major triads on step 7 (the latter with an added seventh). The F♯ in "This Is Love" (Example 1.1b) could work in any of these harmonizations. The Lydian sound of the raised fourth step became such a favorite element for Bock that it eventually evolved to be an expected feature of at least one song, usually more, in any large-scale project throughout his career. This reaches back to his high-school musical *My Dream* (in the songs "This Is Love" and "Mock Marriage"), and goes forward to his college musical, *Big as Life* ("Babe's What They Call Me"), television ("The Hero" from the *Admiral Broadway Revue*), Tamiment revues ("All Abroad," "Goldilocks," "The Gypsy," "Jim Green," "Miami," "Satin from Lower Manhattan"), stand-alone songs written under contract to Tommy Valando ("Show Me a Better Man," "Have a Heart," "The New You," "Can You Forgive Me?," "Never"), the *Ziegfeld Follies of 1956* ("When Papa Would Waltz"), *Mr. Wonderful* ("Ethel, Baby," "Mr. Wonderful"), and beyond. His raised fourth steps are often not just subtle chromatic departures, as at the end of the bridge in an Irving Berlin song, when the harmony prepares the dominant with a secondary dominant,[86] but vibrant, distinctive musical moments, making a dramatic impact on the language of the song, as in the first note of Richard Rodgers's melody for "Spring Is Here" or the third note of his "Bali Ha'i." But Bock's usage far surpasses that of his role models. It has a spiritual kinship with Leonard Bernstein's treatment of the raised fourth step, and especially the tritone between steps 1 and ♯4, in *West Side Story* (1957).[87]

Less prominent, but no less distinctive, is Bock's affection for counterpoint. Although he recalls having difficulty with formal contrapuntal studies in college, he says that he is "constantly sensitive" to contrapuntal possibilities when "examining the song assignment" and has an "impulse to surprise with an unexpected coupling of separate melodic moments." Perhaps, he has joked, this is an "effort to make up for my impaired fugal facility" in college. Indeed it was not until after college that layerings of "separate melodic moments" begin to appear in his scores, first in the 1953 Tamiment song "All Abroad" (Example 2.1a), later in "The Story of Alice" from *Catch a Star!* (1955) and "I've Been Too Busy" from *Mr. Wonderful* (1956). Perhaps by this time he had also become more aware of the musical and dramatic potential of contrapuntal practices, after hearing Irving Berlin's "You're Just in Love" from *Call Me Madam* (1950), or Frank Loesser's "Fugue for Tinhorns" from *Guys and Dolls* (1950).[88] The early effort "All Abroad" (Example 2.1a) is typical, not only in its rhythmic interplay but in its tolerance for occasional dissonant clashes between the voices. It would be a mistake to dismiss such moments as the work of an inexperienced contrapuntist; he allows these kinds of momentary, inconsequential conflicts to arise in contrapuntal passages throughout his career.

The range of Bock's compositional technique encompasses an array of styles and idioms. He demonstrated this range in one of his earliest creative acts, the improvised variations on "Reveille" in various styles that he played at parties in high school and for his college audition. As he began to write for the theater, he began to tailor style to setting and character, to create what Lehman Engel calls a "musical costume."[89] John Bush Jones describes this aspect of Bock's work as a "major contribution to completing the integrated musical."[90] As Engel points out, opera composers had begun to invoke stylistic imitations since *Aida* (1871) and *Carmen* (1875), and composers of operettas followed suit shortly thereafter. Early musical theater was overly clichéd, but by the time Bock arrived on Broadway he was surely familiar with recent evocations of style such as Frederick Loewe's flavors of Scotland in *Brigadoon* (1947) and Frank Loesser's hints of Victorian England in *Where's Charley?* (1951).[91] Of course Bock's experience at Tamiment provided golden opportunities for exploring musical style and ethnic identities, in songs with titles such as "Fiesta in Chile," "Jamaica Lady," and "The Gypsy." Musical costumes would become for Bock second nature, a natural implement in his composer's toolkit. He would use them with particular dexterity when the ethnicities they depicted were part of his own identity.

3
POLITICS AND POKER
• • •
THE BODY BEAUTIFUL AND *FIORELLO!*
AND THE LATE 1950S

Bock had "no thought of working together" when he and Harnick first met in
June 1956. Harnick, however, had hoped to be considered for the job as lyricist for *Mr. Wonderful* a year or so earlier and had recently seen and admired
Eydie Gormé's performance of Bock's "Too Close for Comfort" on television.[1]
He was well aware of Bock's work and "envious" that Bock had already done a
book show—a substantial part of one, at least—and eager to find a new collaborator for a large project.[2] Harnick had also signed on with Tommy
Valando, the publisher with whom Bock, Holofcener, and Weiss had had con-
tracts for several years.[3] The personal and professional orbits of Jerry Bock
and Sheldon Harnick were finally overlapping. They were each in search of
work and partnership, and the time was right for them to enter a new phase
in their professional lives.

THE BODY BEAUTIFUL

The idea for a musical about boxing began with Joseph Stein and Will
Glickman sometime in 1955 or 1956, when they were still involved with
Mr. Wonderful. They had immediately secured the support of producer Richard
Kollmar, who had also co-produced their successful musical *Plain and Fancy* in
1955. At some point Albert Selden became a co-producer. After Stein and
Glickman completed a first draft of a libretto, they began looking for song-
writers to complete the creative team. They may have considered Albert
Hague and Arnold B. Horwitt, who wrote music and lyrics for *Plain and Fancy*.
They apparently did offer the job to the *Mr. Wonderful* trio, but Holofcener did
not want to revive the tension of that experience, and Bock and Weiss also
decided to go their separate ways. The impetus to team Jerry Bock with Sheldon Harnick came from a convergence of several forces. Stein knew and

admired Harnick's work and had recently attended a backers' audition for *Horatio*, the musical Harnick wrote with David Baker and Ira Wallach.[4] Harnick also recalls sending the *Horatio* score to Richard Kollmar, seeking his endorsement for the new project with Bock.[5] Tommy Valando surely played a role as well, as the publisher of two partnerless songwriters in search of work; indeed Harnick remembers Valando telling him, "I've managed to persuade [Kollmar] to let you two guys do the score."[6] Lewis Funke made the announcement in his "News and Gossip of the Rialto" column in the *New York Times* on January 27, 1957: "Jerry Bock and Sheldon Harnick will compose the score for *The Body Beautiful*."

For Bock, this would be a more substantial assignment than his previous Broadway score, now requiring a full two acts of music. For Harnick, it would be a first chance to write a full-length musical specifically for a Broadway stage. But for both of them, the transition was smooth and energizing. As Bock recalled in 1968, "Sheldon and I had great *simpatico*, mutual respect, and the first blush of collaboration was marvelously exciting." And: "It was love at first write."[7] Harnick agrees: "In terms of personalities fitting together, visions fitting together, tastes fitting together, Jerry and I hit it off."[8] They soon developed the working method they used throughout their partnership. It starts with study and discussion, followed by a period of separation in which Bock composes a series of what he calls textless "musical guesses" that seem right for the story while Harnick continues to think about song placement and do background research. Harnick explains,

> When [Jerry] reaches the point of having composed anywhere from ten to twenty pieces, he will put them on tape and give me the tape to take home to listen to. Usually there are a number of things on the tape that I find so exciting musically I can't wait to put words to them so I can sing them. If anything on the tape strikes me as being very right for a particular idea I have, then I will plunge in and start that way.[9]

At the same time, if Harnick has an idea for a lyric that does not fit with anything on the tape, he writes it out completely and gives it to Bock for musical setting. "It goes back and forth," says Harnick; "we work both ways." Especially the comic songs often originated with Harnick's lyric. In the end, they both estimate that half of the songs for any of their shows originated with one partner, half with the other.[10]

Their collaborators on *The Body Beautiful* included Broadway veterans and some old friends. Although directing a musical for the first time, George Schaefer had extensive experience with non-musicals on Broadway and had co-produced John Patrick's Tony Award-winning play *The Teahouse of the*

August Moon in 1953. Milton Greene, whom Bock remembered well from Tamiment and *Catch a Star!*, directed the orchestra and did the vocal arrangements. Another Tamiment alumnus, choreographer Herbert Ross, had worked on Broadway as a performer and dance designer since 1943. The production designers, William and Jean Eckart, were working on their fourteenth show—they had also designed scenery and costumes for the very successful *Damn Yankees* a few years earlier—and Noel Taylor, veteran of twenty-four previous Broadway productions, designed the costumes.

Of the seven major musicals Bock and Harnick would write together between 1957 and 1970, *The Body Beautiful* is the only one set in the present, and the only one completely based on an original (non-adapted) story with entirely fictitious characters. The first act begins in a training gym for boxers, where Dave, a fight manager, is training a group of decidedly untalented and undermotivated fighters. Bob, a recent college graduate with some boxing experience, arrives to try to arrange a boxing exhibition for some teenagers at a local community center, but instead spars with Harry, one of the boxers in Dave's stable. We soon learn about the love lives of each of the three main male characters: Dave has two ex-wives, Florence and Jane, hounding him for alimony checks; Bob becomes smitten with Ann, the gym receptionist; and Harry struggles to justify his volatile and financially unstable chosen profession to his wife Marge. Eventually Bob and Harry fight each other in a professional arena, but Harry loses the fight intentionally to help jump-start Bob's career. This creates relationship problems—for Harry, because his wife now sees no future for him in boxing, and for Bob, because he now wants to continue fighting even though he had promised Ann that he would stop.

At the beginning of Act 2, Dave's love life gets even more complicated when he arrives with new flame Gloria at an outdoor training camp in the mountains. The remainder of the act takes us through the resolution of each of the three romantic conflicts. Although Gloria is warned about Dave by both of his ex-wives, she accepts his marriage proposal and submits to his sweet-talking. (This is the most dubious resolution of the three, but somehow sparring with women verbally, like watching men spar in the ring, seems to be Dave's modus operandi.) Harry and Marge reconcile when he confesses that he threw his earlier match with Bob, and she supports his plans for a rematch, with the winner getting the opportunity to take on the champion. Finally Ann welcomes Bob back into her good graces when he intentionally loses the rematch, so that Harry will have a chance at the championship, and so that Bob can then retire from the ring. The teenagers from the community center attend the fight and welcome Bob back into their lives as well.

The Body Beautiful *Score*

In 1985 Bock described *The Body Beautiful* as a "human story," not so much a "boxing story" but "a story of a guy who wanted to do something better than boxing."[11] It is also a love story in triplicate. When Bock and Harnick set out to write their first songs together for the show, they focused mostly on these aspects of the show and very little on boxing. A script dated May 20, 1957 indicates that in the first four months of their partnership, they appear to have written at least twenty songs together (see Table 3.1).[12] These include "Hidden in My Heart," a ballad that Bob and Ann sing to each other, acknowledging their blossoming love; "Somebody Beautiful," another love song for Bob and Ann with a soaring melody reminiscent of Richard Rodgers ("Something Wonderful" from *The King and I*, perhaps); and "Ooh, Merci Beaucoup," a jazzy love duet for Harry and Marge. Five other early songs were also about relationships: in "Leave Well Enough Alone" Ann tries to convince herself not to get involved with Bob, but then agrees to see him later anyway; in "Just My Luck" she worries about the progress of their relationship, while acknowledging that her strong feelings will not be going away; "Responsibility" was a rough sketch for a song for Harry and Marge about the pressures of growing older together; Dave sings "Blonde Blues" about his affection for women with a certain hair color; and "The Honeymoon Is Over" is a trio in which Dave's two ex-wives counsel Gloria about the perils of matrimony. Bock and Harnick also wrote one song, "Every Man for Himself," for the teenagers at the community center to express their feelings about growing older, and two songs just for flavor and humor: "Summer Is" (calling to mind the Medieval song "Sumer is icumen in") celebrates warm weather, and "Nobility" is a brief quartet sung by the boxers when Harry decides to let Bob win their first fight. The only songs from this early batch that specifically involve boxing are "Where Are They?," the opening number in which Dave and his trainers wonder why success in the ring has been so elusive, and "Mother, Come and Fight With Me," in which Bob explains the sport to his mother. Two other titles in the script, "Fighters" and "He's a Killer, He's a Murderer, So We Love Him," appear to point to songs about boxing, but no scores or lyric sheets for these songs are extant, and the titles did not reappear in subsequent script revisions. "You Got to Be Cultured" and "My Miserable Life" suffered similar fates.

The excitement of the "first blush of collaboration" is evident in the variety and character of all these initial efforts.[13] Bock's gifts as a melodist are widely evident, in the flowing lines of "Hidden in My Heart" or the syncopations of "Ooh, Merci Beaucoup." Harnick had already proven himself as a witty parodist, and his work here is no exception ("Blonde Blues": "For my type of

Table 3.1: Overview of an early version of The Body Beautiful *(from script dated May 20, 1957), with titles that remained in the show for the New York opening in* **bold**

ACT 1

1. Dave's office.
   "Where Are They?" (Dave, trainers)
2. Section of Gym.
   "Where Are They?" continues
3A. Mrs. Stockton's living room—in One—That afternoon.
3B. Mrs. Stockton's Living Room.
   "Mother, Come and Fight With Me" (Bob, mother)
   "Song - To Finish" [no other information]
4. Corridor—Jersey City Arena—In One—The following night.
   "Leave Well Enough Alone" (Ann)
5. Section of Gym—The next afternoon.
   "Responsibility" (Harry, Marge)
6. Dave's office—That afternoon.
   "Blonde Blues" (Dave)
7A. Outside of Community Center—In One—That afternoon.
   song for Boys [no other information]
7B. Community Center Playground and Exterior—That afternoon.
   song for Boys (reprise)
   "Hidden in My Heart" (Bob, Ann)
8. Section of Arena Dressing Room—In One—Several weeks later.
9. Summer Resort—Exterior—Several weeks later.
   "Summer Is" (Ensemble)
   "You Got to Be Cultured" (Mrs. Stockton, Boxers)
   "Nobility" (Boxers)
   "Summer Is" (reprise)
10. Dave's Office—A week later.
   "My Miserable Life" (Dave)
11. Hartford Arena—A week later.
   a. Harry's Dressing Room
   b. Bob's Dressing Room
   "Somebody Beautiful" (Bob, Ann)
   "Somebody Beautiful" (reprise) (Ann)
12. Section of a Bar.
13. Section of corridor beneath Arena.
14. Section of Bar as in Scene 12.

(Continued)

ACT 2

1. Summer Resort—Exterior—Several months later.
    "He's a Killer, He's a Murderer, So We Love Him" (Ensemble)
    "The Honeymoon Is Over" (Gloria, Florence, Jane)
    "Just My Luck" (Ann)
2. Boathouse—In One—The same.
    "Summer Is" (reprise) (Dave, Gloria)
3. a. Community Center Exterior—Several Days later.
    b. In one, as in Act One Scene 7A
    "Every Man for Himself" (teenagers at the community center)
4. Steam Room in Turkish Bath—The next day.
5. New York Street—In One—The following day.
    "Ooh, Merci Beaucoup" (Harry, Marge)
6. Stockton Living Room—That evening.
    "Fighters"
    "Somebody Beautiful" (reprise) (Bob, Ann)
6A. Section of living room as in Act One Scene 3A.
    "Just My Luck" (reprise) (Ann)
7. Arena—Split Dressing Rooms (as in Act One Scene 11)—Ten days later.
    duet: Ann, Marge [no other information]
    "Ooh, Merci Beaucoup" (reprise) (Bob, Ann, Harry, Marge)

fellow / The girls that I follow / The hair must be yellow / The head may well be hollow"), but he also shows an ability to write a touching love song ("Somebody Beautiful": "Your tender smile / Reveals a heart / That seems to me / A work of art"). These early songs especially sparkle when they respond very specifically to a dramatic moment in the story. "Where Are They?" begins with Dave asking why he fails to attract good fighters to his gym ("Where are they / The fighters with style / The fighters with flair / I get the lads with the delicate air"), then moves to a contrasting melody sung by the boxers, asking why they cannot seem to find beatable opponents ("There's one thing alone, makes the picture incomplete / We can't seem to find any fellas we can beat"). The boxers' melody was originally a separate song, "The Manly Art of Self-Defense," but the harmony aligns with Dave's melody, so the song ends with both melodies combined. This is what Bock was thinking of in 2008 when he described his affection for counterpoint as an "impulse to surprise with an unexpected coupling of separate melodic moments." The trio "The Honeymoon Is Over" similarly charms with style and flavor, as Dave's ex-wives tell Gloria what to expect from marriage ("The man you married was good and kind / A tender lover was he / But sweet Sir Galahad overnight / Turns into Simon Legree"). Throughout their work in this early collection of songs for *The Body Beautiful*, the overall sense is that finally, for the first time, both partners are flourishing in the company of an equally talented counterpart.

Only a handful of these early songs remained in the show for the Broadway opening, a typical circumstance (see the **bold** titles in Table 3.1). Bock and Harnick have estimated that they wrote at least two or three times as many songs for any show as they eventually used. In Harnick's words,

> I never mastered the knack of getting the right idea the first time around. In fact, what I found about myself was that each draft acquainted me with another level of a character's personality, so successive drafts made the character more real to me, more three-dimensional, which in turn affected the show as a whole. I always took to heart the truism "Shows are not written; they are rewritten."[14]

"Somebody Beautiful," for example, appears in no scripts subsequent to the one dated May 20, 1957; the beginning phrases of its verse were recycled as the verse for "Leave Well Enough Alone."[15] "Responsibility" was also dropped after the May version. "Mother, Come and Fight With Me" survived into the next version, a script dated October 15, 1957 (with revisions dated November 26), but not beyond.[16] And two of the early songs, "Ooh, Merci Beaucoup" and "Every Man for Himself," were listed on the program for the pre-Broadway tryout in Philadelphia (which opened on December 26) but eliminated before the show moved to Broadway a few weeks later. Some of the eliminations are understandable—"Mother, Come and Fight With Me" became irrelevant when the character of the mother was written out of the script—but others must have hurt. "Every Man for Himself," probably cut because it was deemed extraneous to the dramatic flow, is an affecting song about adolescent angst. "Ooh, Merci Beaucoup," which Harry and Marge were to sing to celebrate their reconciliation in Act 2, is one of Bock and Harnick's finest songs, from any stage in their careers. An opening dialogue between the two voices dissolves symbolically into a phrase sung together in thirds, and later the bridge is sung entirely in thirds. The style of the song is reminiscent of an up-tempo arrangement by Glenn Miller or Benny Goodman, particularly at the approach to the repetition of the title as a hook ("Used to think how simple it would be / To take you on my knee and spank you / But my heart kept gettin' in the way / Now all that I can say is thank you / Thank you / Ooh, merci beaucoup").

Six songs appeared for the first time in the October version of the script.[17] "He's Our Boy," an Act 2 opener celebrating Bob's victory over Harry, was cut during the Philadelphia run, but the other five made it to Broadway (Table 3.2).

Marge and Harry sing "Fair Warning" in Act 1, as an exploration of their marital difficulties, even while their mutual affections are barely suppressible. Bock uses the interplay of major and minor to help capture the gloomy ultimatums of the lyric, displaying once again his mastery of classic jazz style. Soon after that the style shifts to 1950s rock-and-roll in "Uh-Huh, Oh Yeah," sung by the teenagers at the community center. This song has all the clichés and exaggerations of an effective caricature, with a lyric about the finer things of adolescence, delivered in inexact rhymes (sublime/divine, wealth/myself, wine/time) to portray a lack of refinement or sophistication in the genre. Also added was a second Act-1 love song (in addition to "Hidden in My Heart") for Bob and Ann, "All of These and More," expressing the elation of newfound love. Bock's four-note main motive for this song, a rising fourth falling down a step and then down a third, perfectly captures the imagery of Harnick's lyric, "A shooting star / A rising tide / A sea-gull sailing on the breeze / You make me feel as though / I'm all these and more." The remaining two new songs in October are both classic Bock–Harnick creations, illustrating how far they had come after only a few months of work. The boxers and some rather cultured young women sing "The Art of Conversation" at a party in Act 2. Bock's music provides a simple foundation for Harnick's patter between the girls, who only want intellectual conversation, and the boxers, whose desires are rather more elemental:

> GIRL 2:   I'll convert you—to existentialism
> Albert Camus—Colin Wilson
> I have the key to what Jean-Paul Sartre meant.
> BOXER 3: And while you're at it here's the key to my apartment.[18]

As a break from the patter, Bock inserts a chorus in a completely different style ("The art of conversation / Fills all the social gaps . . ."), showing that he and Harnick both have a strong affinity for Gilbert and Sullivan. Lastly, "A Relatively Simple Affair," which breathes new life into a melody that was originally known as "A Word of Wisdom," brings together Ann and Marge at the end of Act 2 to sing about the complications of being in love.[19] After each has sung a complete chorus, Ann reprises hers while Marge sings a chromatic line previously heard only in the accompaniment. In the bridge Marge sings an imitative countermelody with a few fleeting dissonances toward the end (especially in the sixth bar), showing Bock's characteristic focus on line over contrapuntal conventions (Example 3.1). The interplay of the two voices captures the differences between the two characters' perspectives.

After watching the show play before live audiences in Philadelphia, where it opened on December 26, 1957, the creative team made fairly substantial changes in the sound and structure of *The Body Beautiful*. The largest one

Table 3.2: Overview of The Body Beautiful *as first presented in New York, with titles that appeared in the earlier script version in* **bold**

ACT 1

1. Dave's office.
   "Where Are They?" (Dave, Boxers)
2. A gym.
   "Where Are They?" continues
   "The Body Beautiful" (Ann, Boxers)
3. A section of the gym.
   "Fair Warning" (Marge, Harry, Company)
4. Dave's office.
   "Leave Well Enough Alone" (Ann)
   "Blonde Blues" (Dave)
5. A street in the vicinity of the community center.
6. Playground at the center.
   "Uh-Huh, Oh Yeah" (teenagers at the community center)
7. The street.
   "Hidden in My Heart" (Bob, Ann)
8. Montage and section of a fight arena.
9. The gym.
   "Nobility" (Boxers)
10. Dave's office.
11. Two dressing rooms.
    "All of These and More" (Ann, Bob, Company)
12. Inside the arena.
    "The Body Beautiful" (reprise) (Ann)

ACT 2

1. Training camp traveler.
   "Summer Is" (Boxers, Campers)
2. The training camp.
   "The Honeymoon Is Over" (Gloria, Florence, Jane)
3. Montage and Dave's office.
4. A steam bath.
5. The street.
   "Just My Luck" (Ann, teenagers)
6. Terrace of the Stockton home.
   "All of These and More" (reprise) (Marge, Harry)
7. Stockton living room.
   "Art of Conversation" (Boxers, College Girls)
   "Gloria" (Dave, Gloria, Boxers)

(Continued)

8. Dressing rooms.
   "Relatively Simple Affair" (Ann, Marge)
   "Uh-Huh, Oh Yeah" (reprise) (Company)

Example 3.1: "A Relatively Simple Affair," bridge, vocal parts (Bock Papers, box 19, folder 31)

involved moving the scene at the outdoor training camp from late in Act 1 to the beginning of Act 2, thus giving new prominence to the song "Summer Is" as the second-act opener. Smaller changes included adding a reprise of "All of These and More," now sung by Harry and Marge and so drawing parallels between their love story and that of Bob and Ann, who first sang the song in Act 1. Bock and Harnick also wrote two new songs between the Philadelphia and New York openings. They added a title song for Ann to sing early in Act 1, just after she has met Bob for the first time, explaining her preference for intellect over physical strength or appearance ("When I go for a guy / I want more than meets the eye / Just plain brawn / Makes me yawn!"), while also revealing that Bob's physique has hardly escaped her notice. And they beefed up Dave's romance with Gloria by giving him a new song, "Gloria," to sing to her in Act 2. His sleaziness is charmingly captured both by Bock's soft-shoe music and by Harnick's rhymes, such as "Gloria, darlin' Gloria / You're the only girl I love—named Gloria!" and "Gloria, you're so feminine / You're a cup of tea with cream—and lemon in."[20]

Audiences and Critics

Bock and Harnick's first Broadway show opened at the Broadway Theater in New York on January 23, 1958, about nineteen months after they first met and about a year after they started writing songs together. The cast included no major stars to compete with Judy Holliday, who was still playing Ella Peterson in the long run of *Bells Are Ringing* at the Shubert, or Robert Preston, who had just opened as Harold Hill in *The Music Man* at the Majestic, but it did include Jack Warden as Dave, fresh from his role in Sidney Lumet's classic film *Twelve Angry Men*, and Mindy Carson, a pop singer of moderate success, as Ann. Mostly the cast consisted of young actors with little or no Broadway experience, such as Steve Forrest (Bob), who would subsequently find success working in film and television, and Barbara McNair (Marge), who would go on to a successful career as an actor and recording artist.

Reviews were mixed. John McClain in the *Journal-American* (1/24/58) found the show "funny, swift-moving and tuneful" and predicted that it "should be with us for many a moon." Thomas R. Dash in *Women's Wear Daily* (1/24/58) described it as "altogether diverting and beguiling," granting Bock and Harnick "ringside seats hereafter in the theater's arena." Falling

Mindy Carson (Ann), Lonnie Sattin (Harry), and Steve Forrest (Bob) in
The Body Beautiful *(1958) (Photofest)*

somewhere in the middle were Frank Aston in the *World-Telegram* (1/24/58), who found parts of the show "extraordinarily beguiling" but other parts "commonplace," and Rowland Field in the *Newark Evening News* (1/24/58), who called it "spirited and likeable," even though the book was "something less than inspired." The most influential critics, however, were not so kind. In the *Times* (1/24/58), Brooks Atkinson found the show "heavy-footed, hackneyed, and mediocre." Walter Kerr (*Herald Tribune*, 1/24/58) called it "on the one hand inoffensive and on the other indifferent." Wolcott Gibbs (*New Yorker*, 2/1/58) wrote that the show was "vulgar and feeble-minded in about equal degrees." The show failed to attract an audience and closed on March 15 after sixty performances. (Joseph Stein: "It closed during a week where we had a terrible snowstorm that crippled the city. We've always said, 'The show ran six weeks, but if it weren't for that snowstorm, it could have run seven.'"[21]) Plans to record a cast album were scrapped.

Many have blamed the book for the show's failure. Frank Kelly observes that the three parallel love stories are too similar and lack "sufficient dramatic time or space to develop distinctively." Without a "clearly discernible principal dramatic line," writes Kelly, "*all* the lines seem secondary."[22] Stein and Glickman had been successful in their adaptation of an existing play for *Plain and Fancy*, but seemed to struggle more with original stories in *Mr. Wonderful* and *The Body Beautiful*; Stein's subsequent projects (alone or with different partners) were mostly adaptations.[23] The music is full of personality but also cannot escape blame for the show's lack of success. As in *Mr. Wonderful*, Bock had not fully considered the dramatic aspects of song content and had approached the score as if writing for a revue or Tamiment sketch:

> [*The Body Beautiful*] was closer to a revue than an integrated book show in that the scenes were basically funny sketches and the songs were kind of revue songs. I think we simply were not informed or knowledgeable enough at that point to consider integration, to explore the book more carefully, to deal with our own words and music more carefully or differently.[24]

Harnick was probably thinking of both book and music when he told Harold Flender in 1971 that the show "had a lot of good things in it but it was hollow at the core."[25] While some of the songs do fulfill legitimate dramatic purposes—most of the relationship songs develop the romances adequately, and "Where Are They?" is an effective scene-setter, for example—others play just for laughs and work against continuity and plot development. The characters have no dramatically productive reason to sing about the joys of summer at the beginning of Act 2, and "The Art of Conversation" places the story on hold for bantering between the boxers and college girls. These and other issues could have received more attention early on, but the show's director, George Schaefer, was not able to join the creative team until just one week before rehearsals began. Without a director to oversee revisions, explains Harnick, "all the time we spent on the road was spent in making improvements that should have been made before we went into rehearsal, and consequently, the show we opened with in New York was the show we should have gone into rehearsal with."[26]

The Body Beautiful lay dormant until 2007, when the York Theater Company in New York presented a concert version in its Musicals in Mufti series, part of a Joseph Stein retrospective. Even with spare resources and minimal rehearsal, the performances allowed the charm and wit of Bock and Harnick's songs to shine through. As for the overall show, Stein was circumspect: "We weren't trying to make any important philosophic points, but just be entertaining. We all knew it wasn't a masterpiece."[27] The following year the same troupe then recorded the musical's first cast album, which was released along with bonus tracks of previously released individual songs (including "Hidden in My Heart" and "Just My Luck," recorded by Mindy Carson with Sherman Edwards and His Orchestra) and composer demos. The score began to receive long-overdue exposure and respect, if mostly among hard-core aficionados.

For the new songwriting team in 1958, it was a "major heartbreak" to devote a year of exhilarating work to a show that found so few admirers.[28] The lessons learned about dramatic integration would serve them well in projects to come. At the same time, they could take enormous satisfaction from the music they produced together, considered alone, as independent songs. If these songs are not great show tunes, at least they are catchy numbers, and some of them continued to pay dividends, in recordings by Frankie Laine ("All of These and More"), Steve Lawrence ("Uh-Huh, Oh Yeah"), and Eydie Gormé ("Just My Luck"), among others. It was not the ideal Broadway debut, not the one songwriters dream about, but it inaugurated a partnership that showed great promise.

SONGWRITERS AT WORK

The team of Bock and Harnick was not yet an established partnership, however, nor was it a financially lucrative one in 1958; the immediate aftermath of *The Body Beautiful* brought more small jobs to help make ends meet. Harnick worked as a musical amanuensis for Ogden Nash, who was writing lyrics for Prokofiev's melodies from *Peter and the Wolf* for a television special,

Art Carney Meets Peter and the Wolf.[29] Harnick also had another experience as a last-minute show doctor, this one for a legendary Broadway disaster, *Portofino.* Richard Ney had written the book and lyrics, to music by Louis Bellson and Will Irwin, but called in Harnick to help rescue the show when it was having problems on the road in Philadelphia, just after *The Body Beautiful* opened in New York. Harnick recalls,

> I wrote as much as I could, and I saw [Ney] getting increasingly frustrated. And then the night before they opened he had a meeting on the stage, and he said to everybody, "I don't like what Mr. Harnick has done. My work was better and more in keeping with what this musical is about, so I want you to go back to my lyrics." This was the night before [the opening]. They had been doing my lyrics for a week and a half. And I went to him and I said, "Mr. Ney, you can do what you want, it's your show, but you cannot do this to our lead, because he's French, and he has a language problem." And he said, "Okay, he can do your lyrics, but nobody else can." Oh, it was awful. People would start his lyric, go to my lyric in the middle, or forget altogether, or improvise: it was terrible.

Portofino opened on February 21, 1958 and closed the next day. Harnick: "The opening night party lasted long enough to be the closing night party."[30]

Bock and Harnick remained under contract to Tommy Valando and continued writing songs together, hoping to arouse interest from the popular market. Their creations from 1958 and 1959 include the modest swing number "Penny For Your Thoughts," a witty love song, "Fireworks," and a bluesy cabaret number, "Gently."[31] In some of these stand-alone songs Bock's tendency to push the envelope of style or custom is strongly evident. "I Can't Remember Who I Am," for example, depicts the uncertainty of the title sentiment with frequent returns to a raised fourth scale step as the arrival tone of a phrase, held for one-and-a-half measures without melodic or harmonic resolution.[32] Even at the end of the song, when the lyric seems to profess an epiphany of self-awareness ("I just remembered who I am!"), the music undermines this by coming to a final stop on the dissonant raised fourth step, held for the last five bars.

Evidence abounds of two gifted artists drawing inspiration and creative energy from each other. When given the assignment to write four songs to help the Ford Motor Company introduce a new line of tractors and implements to dealers, Bock and Harnick produced not just cookie-cutter show tunes but music of real charm and invention, in a show called *Ford-i-fy Your Future.*[33] Their song "More Power to You" includes a most poetic summary of farm work ("There's always mowing, towing, baling, nailing, / Seeding, breeding, spreading, shredding, / Clipping, stripping, shaking, raking") and a chromatic bridge that contrasts nicely with the largely triadic chorus. In "Any Speed for Any Need" a female soloist and then a male chorus present different melodies to express wonder and delight over multi-gear tractor transmissions, then sing their parts together, another of Bock's signature "unexpected coupling[s] of separate melodic moments." Each of the four songs for this project serves its purpose of providing information and inspiration, and yet holds additional appeal for the tractor dealer with discerning musical taste.

FIORELLO!

The second full-scale musical by Bock and Harnick, *Fiorello!*, began its journey to Broadway in the spring of 1958. Arthur Penn, the Tony-nominated director of William Gibson's *Two for the Seesaw*, which began its successful Broadway run one week before *The Body Beautiful* opened in January 1958, had earlier done research for a television documentary about Fiorello H. La Guardia, the congressman, soldier, and beloved New York City mayor, and had been struck by his essential theatricality.[34] Penn then proposed a musical about La Guardia to Harold S. Prince and Robert E. Griffith, whose ground-breaking production of *West Side Story* had opened in September 1957, and they agreed to produce. Penn planned to direct the show, and may also have begun drafting a libretto, but he eventually yielded writing duties to Jerome Weidman, a novelist (*I Can Get It for You Wholesale*, 1937) with little theatrical experience but a keen interest in moving in that direction.[35] To write the music, Prince and Griffith hired Jerry Bock. Prince and Griffith had been in the audience opening night of *The Body Beautiful* and had heard great potential in the score, even while finding less to like overall. They did not initially hire Sheldon Harnick to be the lyricist, however, because Weidman was planning to write lyrics of his own. Anyway, Prince and Griffith were not convinced that Harnick could adopt an appropriate tone for their show; they admired his satiric gifts but wanted lyrics that were "earthy and warm."[36]

Weidman's first efforts produced some effective scenes, but he also wrote song lyrics that Bock found unworkable. "Weidman was turning in not song lyrics but . . . epic poems," Bock told Harnick.[37] Prince and Griffith convinced Weidman to devote himself exclusively to the book, and the search began for a new lyricist. Bock wanted Harnick, and Harnick wanted the job, but the decision was out of their hands. Yip Harburg was considered at one point.[38]

The producers offered the job to Stephen Sondheim, who had already made a splash as Leonard Bernstein's lyricist for *West Side Story*, and who at that time was writing lyrics with Jule Styne for *Gypsy*, but Sondheim was looking for a project for which he could write both words and music.[39] Finally, remembers Harnick,

> it narrowed down to Marshall Barer, lyricist for *Once Upon a Mattress*, and me. Hal [Prince] called and said, "I'll be honest. I don't think you're the right person for this, but if you're willing to write four songs on speculation—without pay—and prove us wrong, you have the opportunity." I said, "I'd love to." I worked with Jerry, and he was so cooperative. They wanted a song that sounded like an Irving Berlin tune from [1917], a waltz for a big going-away party. Jerry went off and wrote four waltzes. He came back and played them and asked me, "Which one do you like best?" I picked one, and he said, "Oh, good, I like that one too."[40]

They performed this waltz and three other new songs for Prince and Griffith, and Harnick was hired. An announcement of the renewed partnership appeared in the *Times* on March 20, 1959, about four months after Bock had signed on to write the music.[41]

Development of the Libretto

Disagreements began to arise about the tone of the show. Penn favored internal conflict and psychological undertones, as in *Two for the Seesaw*. Weidman, Prince, and Griffith wanted to move in a more nostalgic direction, to create a "lament for a bygone manageable New York, for the loss of heroes, of the innocence of speakeasies and payoffs and gang wars."[42] Penn was eventually overruled and replaced as director by George Abbott, a Broadway legend with a stellar track record as both book author and director, working with the likes of Rodgers and Hart (*The Boys from Syracuse*, 1938; *Pal Joey*, 1940), Leonard Bernstein (*On the Town*, 1944; *Wonderful Town*, 1953), Frank Loesser (*Where's Charley?*, 1948), Irving Berlin (*Call Me Madam*, 1950), and the recent rising stars Adler and Ross (*The Pajama Game*, 1954; *Damn Yankees*, 1955). Abbott was busy directing *Once Upon a Mattress* up until its premiere on May 11, 1959 and joined the *Fiorello!* team after that. Abbott also became coauthor with Weidman, and the "1st Weidman–Abbott draft" of the libretto is dated May 25, 1959.[43]

Weidman's starting point for the story was an assortment of published material on La Guardia, including his autobiography, *The Making of an Insurgent*, and a memoir of one of his law clerks, Ernest Cuneo's *Life with Fiorello*.[44] Yet at some point, wrote Weidman,

The creative team for Fiorello! *(1959) and* Tenderloin *(1960): standing from left, George Abbott, Jerome Weidman, Sheldon Harnick; at the piano, Jerry Bock (Photofest)*

my thoughts turned more and more to my own relationship with La Guardia, what I had known of him and what he meant to me. Out of that came the notion of telling not the story that one might expect—the account of the well-publicized last years of his career—but the story that very few know.[45]

Weidman focused the narrative on the years leading up to La Guardia's first nomination for mayor in 1933, and on his two wives: Thea, who died of tuberculosis in 1921, and Marie, who had been his secretary and to whom he was married from 1929 until his death in 1947. Weidman and Abbott decided to introduce the character of Marie early in the show and tell both love stories simultaneously, rather than focusing exclusively on one wife in the first act and another in the second. Marie's affections are brought out in bits and pieces throughout the first act, even as Fiorello's relationship with Thea is progressing toward matrimony. The actual Marie La Guardia, who survived her husband by thirty-seven years, gave her blessing to the project at several points along the way.[46]

The basic storyline remained the same throughout rehearsals and the pre-Broadway tryouts in New Haven and Philadelphia. It begins with a Prologue presenting a familiar image of La Guardia as mayor, reading the comics into a radio microphone. We then flash back to the 1910s, and in the first act follow La Guardia's progression from legal advocate to congressman to soldier. Marie is a member of La Guardia's staff, along with Neil, a law clerk, and Morris, the office manager. We first meet Thea when La Guardia helps her get out of jail, after she and other striking workers at the Nifty Shirt Waist Company have been framed by police. A secondary love story emerges between Dora, one of the striking workers, and Floyd, one of the cops. We also meet Ben Marino and the party politicians, who feebly attempt to control La Guardia's political destiny. A film montage at the end of Act 1 depicts La Guardia's heroic exploits during the First World War, which include fulfilling a promise to Thea to help liberate Trieste, her homeland, from imperialistic invaders. Just before the curtain falls, La Guardia returns home and Thea accepts his marriage proposal.

The second act begins about ten years later, with La Guardia and Thea happily married and La Guardia campaigning for mayor against the incumbent Jimmy Walker. Their personal and political fortunes spiral downward, however, as Thea is ailing and the Tammany political machine is plotting to ensure La Guardia's defeat. Dora and Floyd, who has gone from police work to garbage contracting, abet the conspiracy, but then Dora tells Marie about plans to disrupt a La Guardia campaign event. The disruption succeeds anyway, after news arrives that Thea has died. Then La Guardia loses the election. The final two scenes move ahead four years, with Ben Marino and his political hacks contemplating the next mayoral election, and Marie supporting her boss but worried about her personal life. The future is looking brighter as the show comes to a close: La Guardia commits himself to another mayoral campaign, and to another marriage. "I think you can learn to love me," he tells Marie. She replies, "Yes, I think I can. I've been practicing for fifteen years."

The story compresses and adapts historical facts, often with obvious debts to La Guardia's autobiography and Cuneo's memoir.[47] The secondary love story between Dora and Floyd, however, is entirely invented. Cuneo himself is the model for the character of Neil, although Cuneo actually joined La Guardia's staff later than Neil does. Thea's death, and La Guardia's second marriage, actually happened earlier than they do in the retelling. The details of La Guardia's successful campaign for Congress in 1916, his military service, and his loss to Jimmy Walker in 1929 are essentially correct in the musical, although the time compression between acts omits his congressional service in the 1920s, and the time compression of the last two scenes skips over his unsuccessful campaign for re-election to Congress in 1932. Many details travel from pages in the La Guardia and Cuneo books to Weidman and Abbott's libretto. When Fiorello tells Dora that "They sold rotten food to the Army in the Spanish-American War—and my father died" (Act 1, scene 1), he echoes a passage from the end of the first chapter of La Guardia's autobiography:

> One of the worst scandals of our entire military history occurred during this short Spanish-American War and made a lasting impression upon me, for my father was one of its victims. Corrupt contractors supplied the Army with diseased beef. . . . My father died in 1901, a victim of condemned Army meat.[48]

A comment from Fiorello about the image of Italians—"When people think of Italians, I want them to think of Michelangelo, Caruso, Garibaldi; not of Ponzi and the Mafia" (Act 1, scene 3)—draws inspiration from a passage in Cuneo:

> When the Lindbergh baby was kidnapped, Fiorello did say to me, "I hope that bastard kidnapper doesn't turn out to be Italian." So did I. The Italian immigration had taken place only three decades before, and its publicized effects on the country were mostly lamentable, centering around tabloid headlines about the Capones, Fiaschettis, Costellos, and similar scum of gangland.[49]

Also in the first act (scene 8), the portrayal of La Guardia's support for American involvement in the First World War, and for the Draft Act, despite widespread opposition among his constituency, draws from the sixth chapter of his autobiography ("Congress in Wartime"). Later, the ploy to disrupt La Guardia's campaign in Act 2, scene 3, involving a tripped fire alarm and a baby carriage filled with paving blocks, comes from Cuneo's account of La Guardia's 1932 campaign for re-election to Congress.[50] Fiorello's comical instruction to Neil, to strike a policeman if necessary to thwart the disruption, carries the weight of historical accuracy. Cuneo's recollection of his boss's directive ("If the Law can't protect us, we can protect ourselves.") matches Fiorello's orders for Neil almost word for word ("Tell him if the law won't protect us, we'll have to protect ourselves.").[51]

The Songs of Fiorello!

The libretto given to Bock and Harnick for Harnick's audition as lyricist included markings to indicate four presumptive song locations, all in the first act.[52] (Probably only the first act had been drafted by that time, early 1959.) The Irving Berlin-style waltz, "'Til Tomorrow," was written for Thea to sing at a farewell party for La Guardia near the end of Act 1, as he prepares to go overseas. It is, then, a "diegetic" number, or "set piece," experienced as music by the characters in the drama.[53] Harnick remembers drawing inspiration for the lyric from an old song:

> I had done all my period research, and I had an idea of the kind of "lace valentine" sound the lyric should have, but an old song kept coming to the surface of my mind: [singing] "Just a song at twi-light . . ." I have no idea when that song was actually written, but it had exactly the quality that I wanted to achieve. The word "twilight" seemed a perfect period word to begin the song with, and eventually we arrived at this.[54]

He was thinking of the chorus of "Love's Old Sweet Song," the Irish ballad written by James L. Molloy and J. Clifton Bingham in 1884. Indeed "'Til Tomorrow" borrows not just the first word but the tone and character of "Love's Old Sweet Song," which it shares with any number of waltzes of the late nineteenth or early twentieth centuries, by Irving Berlin or by others. Another audition song, "Unfair," also known as "The Strike Song," was written for Fiorello and the garment workers to sing in protest of working conditions at the shirtwaist factory. As Fiorello motivates and energizes the women to stand up for their rights, the music grows in intensity towards heavier accents and pulsating rhythms. Bock simplifies the melody to bring more attention to the heavier accompaniment, and to Harnick's percussive poetry in passages such as "Proudly we picket / The men who pick the pockets / Of the poor hard-working poor."

Harnick remembers that Prince and Griffith were duly pleased at the audition with "Unfair"—and with "'Til Tomorrow," after choreographer Peter Gennaro helped convince them that its sentiments were sincere—but that the other two audition songs were greeted with less enthusiasm.[55] One of them was "Take a Flyer," a song for the end of Act 1 about rivalries between branches of the military. Griffith told Harnick that this song suffered from "research poisoning": its military metaphors overwhelmed any sense of poetic elegance.[56] The other rejected song may have been "The Bum Won," a song for the political hacks to sing after Fiorello defies their predictions and wins a seat in Congress. If this song met with early disfavor, however, the producers later changed their minds, after a few vital revisions that George Abbott had advised, and it became part of the show during the pre-Broadway tour in Philadelphia. With good reason: "The Bum Won" is one of Bock and Harnick's contrapuntal showpieces, with separate parts for Ben Marino and three groups of political hacks. First each part is presented alone, each in a different key, and then all four parts combine in the same key. Each melody is distinctive and easily distinguished from the others, and yet their combination minimizes dissonant conflicts or rhythmic awkwardness. If Bock had at one time felt insecure about his contrapuntal technique, by this time he was clearly comfortable and adept.

Bock and Harnick wrote songs for *Fiorello!* throughout the spring and summer of 1958, anticipating rehearsals in the fall, openings in New Haven on October 19 and Philadelphia on October 28, and opening night in New York on November 23 (Bock's thirty-first birthday). As usual, the experience of seeing songs play before an audience motivated strategic shifts or cuts. "Business Is Fundamentally Sound," which was cut in New Haven, "was given an expressionistic staging with actors wearing masks, and it seemed stylistically at odds with the rest of the show," reports Frank Kelly.[57] In Philadelphia, "Marie's Law," in which Marie makes it clear to Morris that she has more than a professional affection for her boss, was moved from a late scene in Act 1, where it had been falling flat, to an earlier one, where it instantly succeeded.[58] Songs cut in Philadelphia were "When the Bootlegger Comes," "Impatient," and "Where Do I Go From Here?," a lush ballad for Marie to sing when she first hears about Fiorello's engagement to Thea. This latter excision, according to Prince, was necessary to prevent Fiorello's relationships with Thea and Marie from becoming "lugubrious and sentimental."[59] Harnick remembers agreeing with Bock and Abbott, and with the audience response, that the song made Marie seem too "mopey."[60] Musically, it is a loss, however: the soaring melody of "Where Do I Go From Here?" is one of Bock's finest, and Harnick shows again that he is more than just a satirist. The song was included in the published vocal selections from the show, and was recorded by Robert Goulet, Peggy Lee, the Four Freshmen, and, more recently, Liz Callaway.[61]

The final score of *Fiorello!* is aptly balanced between romance, politics, and comic diversions (Table 3.3). The opening number, "On the Side of the Angels," helps establish the character of Fiorello through the words of his staff, by describing his efforts on behalf of clients. Harnick probably got the idea for the lyric from a sentence in Cuneo's book: "This episode marked the first of many occasions that prompted me to speculate on what might happen to Fiorello if he weren't on the side of the angels."[62] First Neil, and then Morris, sing about Fiorello's work and concern for poverty and injustice: "Penniless and helpless / Ignorant and scared / He collects 'em all!" Then, after some dialogue, three of the downtrodden who are seeking assistance sing new melodies, and these are eventually combined with the trio of Neil, Morris, and Marie singing the earlier melodies. In this case the contrapuntal writing allows fleeting dissonances and momentary rhythmic entanglements, as in the early "All Abroad" (see chapter 2, Example 2.1a) and as in "A Relatively Simple Affair" from *The Body Beautiful* (Example 3.1). The differences between the contrapuntal lines help bring out contrast between the two parts, the clients and the staff—unlike the contrapuntal layers in "The Bum Won," in which four political hacks express essentially the same points of view and do so with very few musical conflicts.

Also expressively structured in "On the Side of the Angels" is the chorus melody itself (Example 3.2). In the first two phrases, for example, prominent chromatic tones occur on the downbeats of the first and third full measures ("**proud**-ly" and "**hard**-ships"), then return with heightened frequency and drama in bars 5–7 ("**Work**-ing **with** this **man** on the **side** of the **an**-gels"), each resolving upward by half step to a chord tone. As these figures continue to appear throughout the song's choruses, they repeatedly offer little moments of tension and release, little anxieties that are quickly whisked away, like a legal advocate protecting the rights of a client. The metaphor is particularly resonant as it appears in concentrated form in the refrain, "Working with this man on the side of the angels." This refrain happens twice in each chorus, and the chorus is sung three times in each section—first by Neil, then by Morris, then by both of them and Marie—and so by the end of the song our ears are saturated with the chromatic notes and their immediate resolutions. (The dissonances are a mixture of appoggiaturas, passing tones, and neighboring tones.) Further, in the third section, when the texture is thickened by the additional parts sung by the clients, the chromatic notes often clash directly with notes in the new contrapuntal lines before moving to their resolutions. It is a drama of characters, circumstances, and tones.

The colorful comic sensibility of the show is further established in the next scene, when Ben Marino and the political hacks compare "Politics and Poker." Harnick wrote this lyric by adapting some of Weidman's dialogue:

Table 3.3: Overview of Fiorello!

ACT 1

Prologue
1. Law offices of Fiorello La Guardia in Greenwich Village, shortly before the First World War.
    "On the Side of the Angels" (Neil, Morris, Marie, Clients)
2. Main room of the Ben Marino Association on West 3rd Street, the same day.
    "Politics and Poker" (Ben, Politicians)
3. Street outside strike headquarters, the same day.
    "Unfair" (Fiorello, Girls)
4. Fiorello's office, immediately following.
    "Marie's Law" (Marie, Morris)
5. Three street corners, 1916.
    "The Name's La Guardia" (Fiorello, Company)
6. Street near the Ben Marino Association, right after election day.
    "The Bum Won" (Ben, Politicians)
7. Roof of a Greenwich Village tenement house, 1917.
    "I Love a Cop" (Dora)
8. Fiorello's office in the Congressional Office Building in Washington, D. C., shortly after preceding scene.
9. Street near the Ben Marino Association, a few weeks later.
    "I Love a Cop" (reprise) (Dora, Floyd, Company)
10. Main room and yard of the Ben Marino Association, immediately after preceding scene.
    "'Til Tomorrow" (Thea, Company)
11. Gangplank of a troopship for soldiers returning from overseas, sometime after the Armistice.
    "Home Again" (Company)

ACT 2

1. The La Guardia home, 1929.
    "When Did I Fall In Love" (Thea)
2. The terrace of Floyd and Dora McDuff's penthouse apartment shortly after preceding scene.
    "Gentleman Jimmy" (Mitzi [a Broadway star], Dancing Girls)
3. Fiorello's law office, the following week.
4. Madison Avenue and 105th Street, that night.
5. Fiorello's law office, later that night.
6. Street near Fiorello's law office, election night, 1929.
    "Gentleman Jimmy" (reprise) (Company)

(Continued)

7. Main room of the Ben Marino Association, 1933.
    "Little Tin Box" (Ben, Politicians)
    "(I'll Marry) The Very Next Man" (Marie)
    "Politics and Poker" (reprise) (Ben, Politicians)
8. Fiorello's office, the next morning.
    "The Very Next Man" (reprise) (Marie)
    Finale ("The Name's La Guardia" reprise) (Politicians)

Example 3.2: "On the Side of the Angels," chorus melody, mm. 0–7

One of Jerome Weidman's early drafts of *Fiorello!* contained a scene in which a number of ward-heelers were playing poker when they should have been attending to the business of choosing a candidate to run for Congress from their district. As written, it was an amusing scene which seemed certain to play well. Now, I had long had a desire to write a lyric involving poker terms which had struck me as especially colorful and tangy ever since I had played a lot of it in the Army. When I read Mr. Weidman's scene, I had an instant vision of an effective song which could incorporate much of the scene and to which I felt I could contribute a great deal. I asked him if he would mind if Jerry and I tried to "musicalize" his scene. Generously, he told us to go ahead and to feel free to use anything in the scene which we felt would be valuable. . . . When we played the song for Mr. Weidman, he was genuinely delighted, which must have taken great generosity of spirit indeed, for he must have seen that he would get no credit for a number of funny notions in the song, including the notion of the punch line ("You idiot, that's me!").[63]

The result—a first-act showstopper—is one of the show's signature songs. "Politics and Poker" has three main sections, each beginning with expressions from a poker game ("King bets / Cost you five. / Tony, up to you. / I'm in." and so forth), followed by a verse about politics ("Gentlemen, here we are, and one thing is clear / We gotta pick a candidate for Congress this year"), and eventually a chorus about both ("Politics and poker . . ."). In a bit of dialogue between the second and third sections, Marie and Fiorello convince Ben to support Fiorello for Congress, and so the final verse and chorus are more specifically about Fiorello's brazen gamble.

After Harnick had created the lyric from Weidman's dialogue, Bock at first set it as "a kind of foxtrot," recalls Harnick, and they had a heated dispute over the style of the song.[64] When Bock reset it, in a "mock-Verdian way," as a "big, Italian hurdy-gurdy waltz," however, the improvement was obvious to both. Poker and politics are first addressed separately with the introductory poker expressions followed by the politically themed verse, but Bock's music helps make the connection between them by using similar chromatic ascents. In the first section, for example, the poker expressions gradually work their way upward from D on "King bets" to E, F, and F♯ on "Cost you five / Tony, up to you," to G on "So am I" and G♯ and A on "Me, too," all over a prolonged dominant D chord in the key of G. Then in the lead-in to the first chorus (Example 3.3a), when singing about politics, embellished chromatic ascents return, from G♯ up by half steps to B in the phrase "I say neither one / I never even met 'em," and from A♯ up by half steps to D (skipping over C♮) on "I say when you got a pair of jacks, bet 'em." After that the chorus begins (Example 3.3b), and the last two notes of the ascent just completed (C♯ – D on "bet 'em") become the first two notes of the chorus, initiating a double-neighbor figure around scale step five (C♯–D–E–D) that begins the melody and returns frequently throughout. The C♯'s—raised fourth scale steps again—also look back to the ubiquitous chromatic inflections of "On the Side of the Angels," as do the cadential notes of the first phrase of the chorus (on the word "joker") and virtually all of the figures in the phrases immediately preceding (Example 3.3a). Indeed the G♯–A on "I say" and "I never," and the A♯–B on "neither one" and "met 'em" (Example 3.3a) work exactly like the chromatic resolutions on "proudly" or "hardships" or "working with this" (for example) in the preceding song (Example 3.2). The similarities provide subtle musical continuity in the show despite considerable stylistic differences between the songs.

We hear these chromatic resolution figures again in scene 4 of Act 1, when "Marie's Law" begins with the same kinds of resolutions from chromatic notes upward to scale tones, on each pair of notes in "My law" and "shall state" and "to whom." The figures are not pervasive in the song, but they help plant the seeds of a connection between Marie and Fiorello. Otherwise, "Marie's Law" is enlivened by Harnick's clever wordplay relating legalisms with romance ("In re, my law / Ad hoc, to wit, to woo" and so forth). It gives the song a Gilbert and Sullivan flavoring, as do Morris's echoes of many of

a. Transitional phrase into chorus

I say nei - ther one I ne - ver ev - en met 'em

I say when you got a pair of jacks bet 'em

b. Beginning of chorus

Pol - i - tics and po - - ker pol - i - tics and po - - ker

shuf - fle up the cards and find the jo - - ker

Example 3.3: "Politics and Poker," excerpts

Marie's phrases, taking down her "laws" in dictation. Indeed many aspects of the song, the general sound and style of its melodies and patter, owe a debt to the masters of English operetta.

The first act reaches fever pitch in a song following Fiorello along the campaign trail, "The Name's La Guardia." Harnick recalls that the idea for the song came from Arthur Penn.[65] Important details may have been inspired by sections of La Guardia's autobiography, where he describes campaigning techniques and his constituencies. In describing his first (unsuccessful) run for Congress in 1914, for example, La Guardia explains that his district "included some of the tenement sections of the lower East Side, teeming with Italian and Jewish immigrants. My knowledge of Italian and Yiddish came in handy."[66] So in "The Name's La Guardia" he sings first in English, then in Italian, and finally in Yiddish, leading to an exuberant Hora by the local residents. Bock and his collaborators on the sound of the show, orchestrator Irwin Kostal and dance music arranger Jack Elliott, recast the original music with ethnic flavorings, first like an Italian folk song, then like a Yiddish folk song and dance, sounding very much like a forerunner of the wedding scene in *Fiddler on the Roof*. Otherwise, what also makes the song effective are frequent statements of a six-note motive, first heard at the very beginning on the phrase "Now here's another name," then for "But you can change it all" and "Go use the ballot box," until finally these same notes intone "The name's La Guardia."

Chromaticism and dissonance treatment make conspicuous returns at the beginning of Act 2, in Thea's ballad about her relationship with her husband, "When Did I Fall In Love?" The sound of this song made a striking impression on Ethan Mordden, who noted a "bizarre harmonic dissonance on the second beat that resolves on the fourth beat yet keeps returning, as if questioning this beauty-and-beast mating."[67] Kenneth Tynan, reviewing the show in the *New Yorker*, may have been thinking of these clashes when he blamed orchestrator Irwin Kostal for a "sour contrapuntal accompaniment" in the song.[68] The clashes occur in dissonant clusters on second beats in many bars of the song, consisting of either E♭ or E plus F♮ and G♯, followed by a more consonant sound, often a D major tonic triad, on the third beat. The continuous back-and-forth between clusters and consonance therefore revives an idea heard earlier in the melodic chromaticism of "On the Side of the Angels," with its parallels to conflicts and resolutions in the lyric. In "When Did I Fall In Love?" the resolutions capture the progression of Thea's feelings, from someone who "never once pretended that I love him," to someone who misses her husband "more with each good-bye." She is "astonished" at her transformation and does not know when or how it happened. Meaningful chromatic resolutions happen in the melody as well, not only in cooperation with the clusters in the accompaniment ("what night, which day" and so forth) but also in phrases not accompanied by clusters ("unfelt, ignored"). Bock and Kostal punctuate the ending of the song with one final dissonant blast and resolution in the orchestra, after Thea sings her final phrase, "Until the end of my life."[69]

Chromaticism plays a different, yet equally meaningful, role in Marie's song later in Act 2, "(I'll Marry) The Very Next Man." Here she expresses the frustrations of her love life by promising to leave Fiorello behind and settle for just anyone who comes along. Her pledges ring hollow, of course, and only generate greater sympathy and anticipation, preparing Fiorello's marriage proposal in the next and final scene, when Marie reprises the song as she accepts and the words take on a whole new meaning. Bock creates undercurrents of doubt and anxiety in the chromatic accompaniment, beneath a melody that is simple and direct, often staying on the same note repeatedly. At the beginning of the chorus, for example, major triads on A♭, G♭, and F♭ circulate below a melody that stays mostly on notes of the tonic A♭ major triad. In the third and fourth phrases, as the melody stays on those notes but adds chromatic lower neighbors (at "mar-**ry** the **ve**-ry **next** man"), the harmony enacts a mostly chromatic ascent from the first up to the fifth scale steps, especially intensified in the last four bars, on C, D♭, D, and E♭ major triads. The harmonic language is unusual for a show tune, but it is an artful response to the dramatic circumstances.

Two comic songs in *Fiorello!* offer productive diversions from the main dramatic and musical storylines. Dora sings "I Love a Cop" in Act 1 to develop her relationship with Floyd. It is an effective song, even if the characters are essentially superfluous to the drama; Prince described this secondary love story as a "major flaw" in the libretto.[70] The other comic song in Act 2, however, in which the political hacks sing about a "Little Tin Box," is anything but superfluous. It was the last to be written, added during the pre-Broadway run in Philadelphia after George Abbott decided that the second act needed a showstopper. Weidman recalls using the title phrase in a hastily written draft of a scene for Ben Marino and his political cronies, bemoaning corruption in the mayoral administration of Jimmy Walker; the phrase also appears in Cuneo's memoir.[71] It refers to the response of a corrupt sheriff (Thomas M. Farley) to the questioning of reformer Judge Samuel Seabury, who wondered how the sheriff was able to save so much money: he replied that he kept it in a "little tin box." After reading Weidman's scene, Harnick's imagination was sparked, but he could not work on a song right away with Bock, who had gone to the movies. Instead, he wrote a lyric to go with the music of one of their rejects, "Take a Flyer," the song about service rivalries that they had used in their audition. Harnick recalls,

> I wrote three choruses, —[but] there was nothing in the existing music that would give me the actual chorus, "little tin box, little tin box." So, I went to meet Jerry when the movie broke and he said, "Hi." I said, "We wrote a song tonight." And he said, "How was my music?" And I said, "I believe you'll like it." So we went back to his hotel room, where he had a piano, and I showed him what he had done. And he loved it. He said, "Okay, let me work on the rest."[72]

The result is a perfect 11 o'clock number and another of the show's signature songs. The music of the "Little Tin Box" verse fits with the melody of "Take a Flyer," note for note.[73] One of the political hacks asks a question as if he is Judge Seabury conducting an inquiry, wondering how the corrupt official can afford an extravagant lifestyle on his government salary; then Ben Marino answers as if he is a Tammany official, offering ridiculous explanations such as "For one whole week I went without my lunches / And it mounted up Your Honor, bit by bit." In the music of Marino's responses Bock transposes phrases as if stepping up a tonal ladder, moving through the keys of G♭, G, A♭, and B♭. This is a favored harmonic technique in this show, also heard in "Politics and Poker" (in the transitions between verse and chorus, most extensive before the second chorus, "How about Dave Zimmerman . . ."), "Marie's Law" (in the bridge, "Here's another law . . ."), and "The Name's La Guardia" (stepping *down* a tonal ladder starting with "Now there's a double 'M' in Tammany . . ."). Then for the newly (and hastily) written chorus, Bock returns to an old standby, the sleazy soft-shoe number, as he did for "Gloria" in *The Body Beautiful*. The hacks sing the chorus together, seizing multiple opportunities to ham it up, especially in the Gilbert-and-Sullivan-like phrase echoes (e.g., "That he got was put aside").

Musical Language and Period Flavor

"Little Tin Box" is not only a showstopper and comic masterpiece. It is also part of a web of musical connections involving other important songs from earlier in the score. The main melodic idea of the chorus, for example, is a double-neighbor figure (Example 3.4a) also heard in different rhythmic settings in the opening of the "Politics and Poker" chorus (Example 3.4b) and throughout "'Til Tomorrow" (Example 3.4c). The motivic recurrence has no obvious dramatic significance in the show—it connects the two songs of the political hacks, but any association of these songs with Fiorello's goodbye song seems a bit of a stretch—and yet it provides an element of consistency in the musical language, even among songs in diverse styles. We find intrashow musical cross-references of this sort with increasing frequency in Bock's scores over the course of his career. It is one of his contributions to the development of the integrated musical, a fuller exploration of practices that Mark N. Grant traces back to Jerome Kern and that had evolved through the work of Frank Loesser, Leonard Bernstein, Meredith Willson, and others.[74]

The harmony of the "Little Tin Box" chorus, featuring repeated use of root movement by fifth, provides another element of consistency. At the

a. "Little Tin Box," chorus opening

b. "Politics and Poker," chorus opening

c. "'Til Tomorrow," first phrase

Example 3.4: Some double-neighbor motives in Fiorello!

beginning of the chorus, for example, the harmony circulates through fifths progressions twice, first VI–II–V–I and then III–VI–II–V–I. (The Roman numerals indicate root movement but do not specify chord qualities or triadic alterations or added sevenths and the like.) This happens initially in the first two lines ("Into a little tin box / A little tin box") as the harmony moves away from I to VI and then proceeds by fifths to II and V before returning to I at the beginning of the next phrase. After that the harmony moves away from I to III, before continuing by fifths to VI, II, and V (" . . . a little tin key unlocks / There is nothing unorthodox") and finally returning to I.

These are very routine progressions, but their presence and recurrence here deserve special attention nonetheless. Bock is attempting to capture the flavor of an era, and his harmonic practice plays an important role in doing so. He would face essentially the same challenge for his next show, *Tenderloin*, which is set a few years earlier, in the 1890s, but which shares important musical affinities with *Fiorello!*'s music of the World War I era and 1920s. One good source for examining music that he might have used as models, for example, is an album of music from the 1890s that Bock specifically recalled in 1993, in an interview for the liner notes of the CD reissue of *Tenderloin*:

> I remember I had an album that a lady named Beatrice Kay did, a Gay Nineties album, and I had it for such a long time that I'm sure that rang in my head as I started to think about the score—just style-wise.[75]

He is apparently remembering *Beatrice Kay Sings Gay 90s*, an album released in the 1950s that included sixteen songs of the 1890s.[76] Many of the songs on that album employ progressions by fifths in similar ways; it is a stylistic hallmark, not just an outgrowth of the tonal system they all share.

The classic "You Tell Me Your Dream and I'll Tell You Mine" is typical of the songs on the album (Example 3.5).[77] Before the fifths progression begins we hear a double-neighbor figure employing a raised fourth step ("You had a dream"), perhaps a model for Bock's double neighbors in "Politics and Poker" and "'Til Tomorrow" and "Little Tin Box." The raised fourth harmonized by a diminished triad (in the second measure) is likewise a likely model for this stylistic fingerprint in Bock's compositional language in general. Then in the fourth measure, as arranged in standard fashion on the album by Gerald Dolin, the fifths progression begins on VI ("dear") followed by four bars of II ("I had one too") and four bars of V ("I know mine's best 'cause it") before returning to I ("was"). After a half cadence the progression starts to unfold again in the third phrase ("Come sweetheart . . .") but is aborted by the IV at the beginning of the fourth phrase (where the lyric begins to feature the song title). In this last phrase we hear a stock technique in many songs of this era:

Example 3.5: "You Tell Me Your Dream and I'll Tell You Mine," chorus (as harmonized by Gerald Dolin in Beatrice Kay Sings Gay 90s)

a climactic, specially dramatized arrival on VI ("your___dream") near the end, and then one last completion of the fifths progression to II ("I will"), V ("tell you"), and I ("mine"). Something similar happens in the last phrase in more than half of the songs on the Beatrice Kay album; in some cases (e.g., "She's More to be Pitied than Censured") the climactic chord is III and so the culminating fifths progression is one chord longer, III–VI–II–V–I.

One reason that "'Til Tomorrow" is a highlight of the *Fiorello!* score is that it adapts this model so artfully. Initially Bock spreads out the progression over two long phrases, starting on III ("everything"), moving to VI ("ends, 'Til"), II ("tomorrow, tomorrow"), V ("Since we must part / Here is my heart, 'Til"), and I ("tomorrow, tomorrow"). Next there is a moment of melodic contrast ("Clouds drifting by . . .") that uses the progression again (VI on "such sweet," II on "sor-," V on "-row," returning to I on "I'm drifting too"). Then the final phrase recalls the beginning but collapses the progression into a single phrase: III ("dreaming of"), VI ("you, 'Til to-"), II ("-mor-"), V ("-row"), I ("comes"). The final climactic moment is not especially emphasized when it is first presented, nor when the entire melody is repeated instrumentally as dance music, but the third time through, when the gathered crowd sings the song in a choral setting, the final phrase is dramatized by its *a cappella* performance, by a little extra dissonance and resolution within the climactic chord ("dreaming of **you**"), and by an expressive *ritardando*.

In the show's other diegetic number, "Gentleman Jimmy," we hear how this harmonic signature of 1890s parlor songs persisted in 1920s dance music.

The song appears in Act 2, first in scene 2, as Floyd hosts a group of political operatives plotting La Guardia's defeat in the 1929 mayoral election, and later reprised in scene 6, as New Yorkers celebrate Jimmy Walker's victory. Using period clichés and syncopated rhythms, the first phrase of the chorus arrives on III at "silk hat," moving from there to VI ("gray spats"), II ("striped pants"), V ("Why that's"), and I ("gotta be"). The progression happens again in the bridge ("Say Jim we promise . . ."). The sound of "Gentleman Jimmy" is modeled on songs like "Charleston" (Cecil Mack and Jimmy Johnson, 1923) and "Five Foot Two, Eyes of Blue" (Art Landry, 1925), which utilize identical fifths progressions and set them in much the same way. Bock returns to the same two notes (G♯–A) on "silk hat" and "striped pants," for example, and to another pair of notes (C♯–D) on "gray spats" and "Why that's," similar to the repeated note pairs over changing harmonies on "some dance" and "some prance" in "Charleston." Bock also connects "Gentleman Jimmy" to the trend of dissonance treatment in the *Fiorello!* score, with chromatic inflections resolving to chord tones on "silk hat," "gray spats," "Gentleman Jimmy," and elsewhere, brought out especially in the flashy ending, "Jimmy / Jimmy / Jim Jim Gentleman Jimmy."

In the context of such stylistic hallmarks, we can make reasonable connections between harmonic practices in these two diegetic numbers and songs in the *Fiorello!* score that are not written to evoke period flavor. In addition to "Little Tin Box," instances of progressions by fifths leap out of obscurity in "On the Side of the Angels" ("share / working on the side of the angels" [Example 3.2]), "Politics and Poker" ("We gotta pick a candidate for Congress this year") and "Marie's Law" ("He must love her in return"). The contrasting material in "Unfair" presents the fifths progression with special force and flair ("Let's put a stop to the sweatshop" and so forth). We hear these progressions as well in the main verse of "I Love a Cop," in the contrasting phrase of "When Did I Fall In Love?" ("How could the moment pass . . ."), and with colorful embellishments in the bridge of "(I'll Marry) The Very Next Man." "Home Again," sung by the chorus when Fiorello returns from the war, simply repeats the fifths progression over and over, bookending his war years by recalling the harmonic basis of the song heard just before he left for battle, "'Til Tomorrow." Considered separately, apart from their context within the show, these progressions are mostly routine and unremarkable. Heard alongside the stylized harmonies throughout the *Fiorello!* score, however, they help establish thematic significance and meaningful inter-song connections.

Bock confesses to no grand plan for creating musical continuity through harmonic patterns, in this or any other show, but he has said that he is "drawn to the circle of fifths" and that he engaged in "spontaneous noodling" as "a way of supporting or even discovering a melody revealed by those progressions." Whether or not the acts were conscious, it is evident that he approached the writing of *Fiorello!* with a new awareness of musical consistency and intra-show cohesion. Indeed it is clear that both he and Harnick understood so much more about the integrated musical in *Fiorello!*—that they had learned some valuable lessons from their experience on Broadway up to this time. They had been weaned on the musical revue, and Bock, in his work on *Mr. Wonderful* and his work with Harnick on *The Body Beautiful*, adopted a revue mentality. Now they were giving more thought to the story: not helping to write it, but using their songs to advance plot and develop character, without fluff or dramatic diversions. Harnick has said that he did not become truly attentive to the book until his fourth show with Bock, *She Loves Me*, but *Fiorello!* is a step in that direction.[78] As Bock said in 1985, "*Fiorello!* was actually the beginning of my curiosity as to what the other guy—the author—was doing."[79]

Audiences and Accolades

The songwriting team's second Broadway opening, on November 23, 1959 at the Broadhurst Theater, was as different as it could be from their first one, for *The Body Beautiful* twenty-two months earlier. Critics not only adored *Fiorello!*, praising everything from the direction to the scene design to many individual performances, they also took special notice of the songwriting. Brooks Atkinson wrote in the *Times* (11/24/59) that Bock's score has "a good deal of the ingenuity of Frank Loesser's music," and that Harnick was "in an unfailingly humorous frame of mind." Richard P. Cooke of the *Wall Street Journal* (11/25/59), felt that "the greatest excitements of the evening come when the composer, lyricist, and director predominate." Robert Coleman in the *Daily Mirror* (11/24/59) found the music "bouncy and nostalgic," with lyrics that "captured the flavor of a hectic period." Reviewers expressed admiration for several individual songs but reserved special praise for "Politics and Poker," "'Til Tomorrow," and "Little Tin Box." Whitney Bolton wrote in the *Morning Telegram* (11/25/59) that "'Til Tomorrow" "not only will be a hit wherever people dance this winter but, undoubtedly, will lead to 8000 marriages between couples dancing to it. It is that kind of song." All doubt was now dispelled: the Bock–Harnick style reached beyond satire and wit to embrace romance and nostalgia as well.

Critics were also taken with Tom Bosley, making his Broadway debut in the title role. The casting director had noticed Bosley in an off-Broadway show (presumably George Farquhar's Restoration comedy *The Beaux' Strategem*, which opened at the Phoenix Theater in February 1959), and the production team had chosen him over some two hundred other candidates. Prince at first wanted Eli Wallach for the role but discovered that Wallach's singing skills were limited.[80] Mickey Rooney had also been seriously considered.[81] Bosley could not only act and sing, but also looked like the former mayor: "the physical resemblance is uncanny, even to the high-pitched excitement-packed voice," wrote Robert Coleman in the *Daily Mirror* (11/24/59). According to John McClain in the *Journal-American* (11/24/59), Bosley's "similarity to the original Fiorello is such that when an actual newsreel of La Guardia is flashed on the screen, it brings an involuntary gasp from the audience." The physical resemblance aside, Bosley gave a "commanding and brilliant performance" (John McClain, *Journal-American*, 11/24/59). "He is no mere impersonator," wrote John Chapman in the *Daily News* (11/24/59); "he is a good actor who remains top man of a show which has been built around him." Bosley was recognized with a Tony Award the following spring, emerging from a pool of distinguished nominees that included Theodore Bikel (*The Sound of Music*),

*Howard Da Silva (Ben Marino), Tom Bosley (Fiorello La Guardia),
and company in* Fiorello! *(1959) (Photofest)*

Jack Klugman (*Gypsy*), and Bosley's castmate Howard Da Silva (playing Ben Marino).[82]

The category for Bosley's Tony was for "featured actor in a musical," not for the starring role, and yet most reviewers were not troubled by a musical with a title character who rarely sings and is not a pervasive presence on stage. As Ethan Mordden points out, even when Fiorello does sing, in "Unfair" and "The Name's La Guardia," the songs help develop personality, not emotional core. "This show is constructed more *around* its protagonist than *through* him," writes Mordden. "Much of the book, the score, and the overall feeling of the show is not who he is but how his associates and constituents regard him."[83] Frank Kelly observes that "Fiorello is portrayed as a dynamic man of action who, in a sense, lights musical fires among those around him and then moves on to another scene. . . . The drive of Fiorello's rise to power is not interrupted by his musical introspection."[84] The second act has considerably less music than the first and might be a logical place for an additional song by the title character. Indeed, the creators have often discussed a musical enhancement of the moment in the second act just after La Guardia's electoral defeat. Although Bock was initially inclined to leave it as it stood, with just a very brief reprise of "The Name's La Guardia," Harnick began to feel that it "*needed* a musical statement from La Guardia, something that expressed both his anger and his grief." They have tried extensions of the reprise, new monologue material, and even a new short song within the reprise. In 2009 they were still tinkering with it.[85]

Bosley's debut had plenty of support from Broadway veterans in the other starring roles. Howard Da Silva (Ben Marino) had worked on Broadway since the 1930s, and in film since the 1940s; he originated the roles of Larry Foreman in *The Cradle Will Rock* (1938) and Jud Fry in *Oklahoma!* (1943). Nathaniel Frey (Morris) had appeared almost exclusively in musicals directed by George Abbott, including *A Tree Grows in Brooklyn* (1951), playing the husband opposite Shirley Booth, and *Damn Yankees* (1955), initially as the catcher and later replacing Ray Walston as the Devil. A relative newcomer, Patricia Wilson, played Marie, but Ellen Hanley, playing Thea, had worked on Broadway since 1946—Harnick may have first seen her singing Vernon Duke songs on the same program with his "A Man's Home" in the Bette Davis revue *Two's Company* (1952). Pat Stanley, playing Dora, had recently won a Supporting Actress Tony for *Goldilocks* (1958).

Even with a dialogue-heavy second act, the first run of *Fiorello!* was a great success. It played for 796 performances, until October 28, 1961. (Prince believes it would have run longer but was weakened by an eleven-day hiatus resulting from a labor dispute, and by an ill-advised move to a larger theater.[86])

In addition to Bosley receiving a Tony Award, Abbott was recognized as Best Director, and, for the only time in Tony history, the award for Best Musical went to co-winners, *Fiorello!* and *The Sound of Music*. Music director/conductor Hal Hastings was also nominated, as were choreographer Peter Gennaro and scene designers William and Jean Eckart. The show was also named Best Musical by the New York Drama Critics' Circle.

If this was already more success than the creators might have anticipated, they certainly could not have been prepared for the next honor, the Pulitzer Prize for Drama. Only two other musicals had been so recognized up to that time, George and Ira Gershwin's *Of Thee I Sing* (awarded in 1932) and Rodgers and Hammerstein's *South Pacific* (1950). (A third, Rodgers and Hammerstein's *Oklahoma!*, was given a "special citation" in 1944, arguably an equivalent honor because the committee awarded no regular drama prize that year.[87]) Even the nominating jury was caught by surprise: its members had enthusiastically nominated Lillian Hellman's *Toys in the Attic* for the drama prize, after also considering Saul Levitt's *The Andersonville Trial*, William Gibson's *The Miracle Worker* (which won the Tony for Best Play), and Paddy Chayefsky's *The Tenth Man*. They had never discussed *Fiorello!* at all.[88] But the Pulitzer advisory board, which held final authority, felt that *Toys in the Attic* did not represent Hellman's best work, and had little enthusiasm for the other plays considered by the jury, and made its own decision.[89]

For Weidman, Abbott, Prince, Griffith, Bock, and Harnick, it was a "joyful shock" that "stimulated their work for some time thereafter."[90] For many others, the prestigious honor raised questions about the dramatic and artistic merit of *Fiorello!* and the sources of the show's success. Harold Prince himself called it a "good musical rather than good drama," noting that *Gypsy* failed to receive well-deserved recognition the same year, as did *West Side Story* two years earlier.[91] *Fiorello!* is vulnerable to criticisms of its relentlessly upbeat attitude toward its title character, whose idealism is never tested or questioned. The creative decision to emphasize nostalgia and sentiment, rather than follow Arthur Penn's impulses to explore psychological conflict, gave the story a sense of inevitability that is soothing and comfortable, not challenging or complex. Politics too is sanitized, played strictly for laughs. "The mayor's crooked political enemies," writes Gerald Bordman, "came out of the show as likable grafters. It was, the authors seem to be saying, all good fun."[92]

Further, in the telling of the story the authors depended on biographical awareness brought by the audience to the theater. The dénouement, for example, might be satisfying to anyone with independent knowledge of La Guardia's subsequent terms as mayor of New York, but Kenneth Tynan, the

British critic who in 1959 "knew little more about Fiorello La Guardia than that he was one of New York's smallest and least corruptible mayors," found the ending inexplicable and anti-climactic: "the curtain comes down on La Guardia's decision to marry his former secretary; the election itself is omitted, and all sense of triumph is lost."[93] This issue of course has repercussions for other productions of *Fiorello!* aimed at audiences who are likely to be less familiar with the background story and New York City's political history. The producers of the London production that opened in October 1962 addressed the problem by interjecting explanatory narration, by a man standing at a lectern, throughout the evening. Unfortunately, as Harnick has pointed out, each moment of narration stripped the ensuing scene of its drama, making it "unnecessary."[94] Some of the London reviewers seemed unable to understand why the show had been such a success in New York. (W. A. Darlington in the *Daily Telegraph and Morning Post* [10/9/62]: "Do American political campaigns thrill you? If so, *Fiorello!* at the Piccadilly is just your musical.") In 1985, for a revival at the Goodspeed Opera House in Connecticut, Bock and Harnick felt compelled to go back to the script and find places to "clarify who some of these people were and what some of the issues were."[95] The solution of the Chicago's TimeLine Theater Company in 2008, which may be fairly typical, was to provide a detailed lobby display including a biographical timeline, background information on major figures, and explanations of important story elements such as Tammany Hall.[96]

The show has fared well in revivals in all sorts of venues, if not on the strength of ageless appeal then certainly on an abundance of warmth and charm, and on the dynamic theatricality of the title character. The first New York revival came soon after the show closed, in fifteen performances at City Center in June of 1962, starring Sorrell Booke, who had been Tom Bosley's standby in the original production but had never gotten the call. Marie's song "Where Do I Go From Here?" was reinstated, adding welcome musical substance to Act 2.[97] Bosley himself revived the title role at the Paper Mill Playhouse in New Jersey in 1962, and at the Westbury Music Fair in 1985 (after achieving television immortality as the father in the nostalgic situation comedy *Happy Days*), in a production directed by Sheldon Harnick's brother Jay. Efforts to bring the show back to Broadway have fallen short several times. A revival was announced in 1984 but fizzled, and Harnick has said that he hoped the Goodspeed production the following year would be transferred to Broadway, but this too failed to happen, perhaps because of a sour review from Stephen Holden in the *Times*.[98] The show's most noteworthy production in New York since the premiere occurred in 1994, when it became the inaugural offering in City Center's vaunted "Encores!" series of concert or semi-staged performances of neglected or obscure musicals. A parade of stars supplied the talent, including Jerry Zaks (Fiorello), Faith Prince (Marie), Philip Bosco (Ben), Adam Arkin (Morris), Gregg Edelman (Neil), Liz Callaway (Dora), and Donna McKechnie (Mitzi).

What the City Center concert performance showed above all, and what critics and commentators on diverse productions over the years have consistently emphasized, is that the music of *Fiorello!* is one of its greatest strengths. Even reviewers who find fault with the book, or who long for a Fiorello with Tom Bosley's air of authenticity, usually concede that the show is still worth seeing, for the period flavor of "'Til Tomorrow," or for the colorful musical characterizations of "The Bum Won," or for the inspired coalescence of music, lyrics, and circumstance in "Little Tin Box." In *Fiorello!* Bock and Harnick established themselves as a formidable songwriting team, with comparable talent, complementary personalities, and a shared ambition to embrace the musical-comedy traditions set forth by the legends with whom they now shared a Tony Award, Richard Rodgers and Oscar Hammerstein II. At this early stage in their careers Bock and Harnick were still exploring those traditions, and still developing their own distinctive voice, but after a wild swing from an inauspicious first show to an astonishingly successful second, their future could not have been brighter.

4

LITTLE OLD NEW YORK
• • •
TENDERLOIN AND THE EARLY 1960S

Bock and Harnick first began writing songs together in early 1957, but their work on *The Body Beautiful* did not gain them automatic acceptance as an established partnership. They were hired separately for their second collaboration, *Fiorello!* By the time that score was complete, however, an exclusive partnership had been formed. Their compatibilities, artistic and personal, were abundantly apparent and were receiving recognition and respect from the Broadway community. For the foreseeable future, major projects would be conceived as a team.

TENDERLOIN

The team's third project began while its second was still in production. Harold Prince had obtained galley proofs for a new novel by Samuel Hopkins Adams, *Tenderloin*, sometime in 1958, and had acquired stage rights with Bobby Griffith by October of that year. By the following September, when *Fiorello!* was just going into rehearsals, Prince had recruited the same creative partners—Abbott, Weidman, Bock, and Harnick—to start adapting Adams's novel for the musical stage.[1] In Prince's words, the group "could not bear splitting up" after they had "had such a good time doing *Fiorello!*"[2] Bock recalled a spirit of "Kids, let's do another musical."[3] For Weidman the new project was his "diploma for the theatrical education I received from George Abbott" while working on *Fiorello!*, his first libretto.[4] Eventually three other *Fiorello!* veterans were brought on board as well: music director Hal Hastings, orchestrator Irwin Kostal, and dance music arranger Jack Elliott. Abbott and Weidman completed the book by January 1960, and Bock and Harnick worked on the score throughout the spring and early summer, in preparation for pre-Broadway runs in New Haven and Boston in September and early October, and the New York opening at the 46th Street Theater in mid-October.

The new show was not only an extension of a successful collaboration. It was also a further exploration of colorful episodes from New York City history. Adams's novel took the team back decades before the La Guardia era, to a culture of corruption and debauchery in the 1890s. *Tenderloin* also represented a pendulum swing from the political idealism of *Fiorello!* to a grittier, earthier snapshot, tempered by the religious idealism of aspiring reformers. In the world of Broadway, its portrait of the city recalled a musical from the beginning of the 1950s, *Guys and Dolls* (1950), and a subsequent series of shows with New York themes, including two Brooklyn musicals with music by Arthur Schwartz and Dorothy Fields—*A Tree Grows in Brooklyn* (1951) and *By the Beautiful Sea* (1953)—and two of Leonard Bernstein's greatest works—*Wonderful Town* (1953) and *West Side Story* (1957).[5] *Tenderloin* shares only themes and settings with such an esteemed array, however; the heady optimism at the show's inception ultimately gave way to questionings and disappointments.

Adams's novel is centered around Tommy Howatt, a young, ambitious newspaper reporter who is simultaneously pursuing insider information about police activities and the affections of Laurie Crosby, a beautiful socialite. To appear worthy of Laurie's attention Tommy joins a church choir and becomes a confidant of its pastor, Reverend Brockholst Farr. Reverend Farr gains fame as an outspoken advocate against sin and vice, and for a while Tommy plays the double agent, feeding information back and forth between the forces of morality, represented by Reverend Farr, and the soiled underbelly, embodied in the corrupt policemen and the houses of prostitution. Ultimately, however, some of Tommy's underworld associates force him to assist in a frame-up of the Reverend, who resigns in disgrace. This at first turns Laurie away, but she eventually comes to understand Tommy's true intentions and, at the end of the novel, prepares to accept his marriage proposal. Reverend Farr too attains some sort of redemption in the final pages when he helps engineer a political victory for reformers over corrupt Tammany officials. The story is based on actual events from the 1890s involving Dr. Charles H. Parkhurst, pastor of the Madison Square Presbyterian Church, and his moral crusades.[6] Corruption and prostitution were common throughout the city, but the most notorious area, catering to upscale clientele, was the part of midtown controlled by the 19th Police Precinct on West 30th Street (24th to 42nd Streets between Fifth and Seventh Avenues), known as the Tenderloin district. The name came from a corrupt police captain who was moving from a precinct with modest payoffs into the 19th and told a reporter for the *Sun*, "I've had nothing but chuck steak for a long time, and now I'm going to get a little of the tenderloin."[7]

Abbott and Weidman's libretto features the novel's young lovers, now named Tommy and Laura, and moral crusades by a prominent clergyman, renamed Reverend Brock, but shifts the central focus away from the love story and onto the Reverend. The writers apparently made the decision to change the emphasis fairly early in the writing process and by December 1959, before the script was complete, had obtained a commitment from the acclaimed Shakespearean actor Maurice Evans to play the role of Reverend Brock.[8] Although Evans had a solid reputation in the classical repertoire, he had only played in one previous musical, *Ball at the Savoy*, in London in 1933.[9] The first act is dominated by Reverend Brock's initial efforts to shut down the brothels, first by notifying the police, who feign ignorance, and then, when he realizes that his protests are ineffective, by visiting one himself (in disguise) to gather evidence firsthand. In the second act he testifies about the sin and corruption at an official inquiry, until a police lieutenant brandishes a doctored photograph of the Reverend in a compromising position. Tommy tells the judge that the photograph is a forgery, but the scandal Brock has created, and the unwanted attention he has drawn to his church and his parishioners, cost him his job. Tommy's prospects with Laura are likewise jeopardized, because he must flee the city to evade police retribution, and in the final scene he and Laura part ways, presumably forever. In an epilogue, Dr. Brock is seen starting a new crusade against pleasures of the flesh, from a pulpit in Detroit.

The Music of Tenderloin

Bock and Harnick apparently consulted with Abbott and Weidman early in the development of the libretto—including during a December 1959 retreat in Puerto Rico[10]—but most of the actual songwriting appears to have commenced after the book writers were substantially finished. An early typescript, dated January 1960, includes a few music cues and song ideas but no lyrics and appears to be Bock and Harnick's initial reference script.[11] The list of musical numbers from the program for the New Haven opening in Table 4.1 summarizes the results of their initial efforts.

A reverential choir, reminiscent of the band of believers in *Guys and Dolls*, started this version of the show with "Bless This Land," a hymn to the homeland, extolled as a place of "freedom and friendship" and "hope and promise," offering "faith in the future" and "help to the fallen." Tommy soon meets Laura for the first time and sings "Finally" about his search for love. Next we are introduced to the denizens of the Tenderloin district, led by two of the

Maurice Evans (Reverend Brock), Pat Turner (Maggie, center), Nancy Emes
(Prostitute, seated), and Dargan Montgomery (Waiter in background)
in Tenderloin *(1960) (Photofest)*

working girls, Nita and Gertie, singing "Little Old New York" to express their
outrage over attempts to clean up their lifestyles: "Don't want no bible spou-
tin' / Gospel shoutin' / Preacher nosin' aroun' / Dryin' everythin' up / Closin'
everythin' down." In the style of an up-tempo vaudeville dance number, they
explain that New York is "good enough for me" just the way it is, "wide open"
and filled with opportunities for chasing a "golden goose." Tommy soon
realizes that the way to Laura's heart is through her pastor and sings a stylish
parlor song, "Artificial Flowers," as a kind of audition for the choir at her
church. He then meets Reverend Brock and offers to help with the crusade; in
"What's In It for You?" they ponder suspiciously how each might be able to
help the other. Next Brock confronts the police, and in "First Things First"
they express their differing perspectives, Brock feeling self-satisfied and the au-
thorities wishing he would just go away. Subsequently the focus shifts to Laura,
whose growing awareness of love and intimacy, fueled by her acquaintance with
Tommy and by the spotlight Reverend Brock is shining on recreational sex,

Table 4.1: Musical numbers in Tenderloin *as listed in the New Haven program*

ACT 1

"Bless This Land"

"Finally"

"Little Old New York"

"Artificial Flowers"

"What's In It for You?"

"First Things First"

"I Wonder What It's Like"

"The Picture of Happiness"

"Lovely Laurie"

"The Army of the Just"

ACT 2

"Good Clean Fun"

"Gentle Young Johnny"

"The Picture of Happiness" (reprise)

"The Trial"

"The Tenderloin Celebration: Old Doc Brock"

"The Army of the Just" (reprise)

"Bless This Land" (reprise)

inspires her to speculate about such things in her duet "I Wonder What It's Like" with her friend Jessica. But Tommy is still playing both sides of the fence, and he is soon back in the Tenderloin, singing "The Picture of Happiness," a tale of a lecherous man corrupting an innocent girl, to entertain patrons at a notorious haunt, Clark's. He is nevertheless aware of the complexities of his romantic aspirations and sings "Lovely Laurie" as he hopes for Laura's patience while he climbs the "mountain [that] separates Laurie and I." Act 1 of this early version ends with another reverential hymn, "The Army of the Just," in which the parishioners reaffirm their faith and moral convictions as Reverend Brock, who has realized that the police are part of the problem, decides to intensify his crusade and visit the brothels himself.

Act 2 opens with a church retreat and a celebration by the faithful of the many wholesome ways to have "Good Clean Fun," from poetry to parlor games. They are celebrating victory: the Reverend's efforts have succeeded, and the Tenderloin has been shut down. This leads one of the working girls, Nita, to wonder about her future and hope for a "Gentle Young Johnny" to rescue her. She gets her wish when Joe, a wealthy member of Reverend

Brock's flock, offers to take her away to China, with marriage as a necessary condition. Her girlfriends sing a chorus of "The Picture of Happiness," retexted as a tribute to her surprising good fortune. The centerpiece of Act 2 is "The Trial," in which various characters provide a musical narration of the climactic appearance of Reverend Brock at the official inquiry. After the Reverend is shamed by the adulterated photograph, the girls in Clark's celebrate victory in "The Tenderloin Celebration: Old Doc Brock." But Tommy helps clear the Reverend's name the next day, and the show concludes with the forces of virtue celebrating their triumph in reprises of "The Army of the Just" and "Bless This Land."

This version of the show somehow made it through the development period in the spring and summer of 1960, and through rehearsals starting on August 10, but when it fell flat in its New Haven opening on September 12, the creative team shifted into crisis mode. Harnick remembers a meeting after opening night in which Abbott posed the problem succinctly: "Well, gentlemen, I had a concept for this show, and it doesn't work. Any suggestions?"[12] Two new writers, William and James Goldman, were on hand as observers and offered advice for book revisions.[13] Another outside observer, Richard Altman, who had received a Ford Foundation grant to chronicle the show's creation, and who would later serve as Jerome Robbins's assistant on *Fiddler on the Roof*—and write a book about the experience—remembers observing a heightened reliance on Bock and Harnick to become the saviors of *Tenderloin*. "The pressure was never off the composers to keep coming up with new and better material," writes Altman. "They worked around the clock."[14] Frank Kelly identifies three main problem areas that the songwriters found themselves toiling to repair: the role of Reverend Brock, the Tommy–Laura romance, and the finales of both acts.[15]

As a result, by the end of the pre-Broadway tour—one week in New Haven, three in Boston—Bock and Harnick had written six new songs, plus additional reprises, and helped with some radical restructuring (Table 4.2, with the new titles in **bold**). They took out Tommy's "Finally" but moved "Little Old New York" to the opening scene, as an effective, attention-grabbing counterpart to "Bless This Land." They also removed the superfluous "First Things First" but added a new song, "Reform," to give the Tenderloin girls a chance to express their cynicism about the system in which they find themselves ("Reform, reform / It's only a passing storm"). The Brock character was bolstered by two new songs in the first act: "Dr. Brock," a reflection by the Reverend about the complications of meeting everyone's needs; and "Dear Friend," in which he encourages his parishioners to enjoy themselves during a beach outing, essentially an expression of naive optimism about the status of his moral crusade. The romance of the young lovers was reworked by adding the new song "Tommy, Tommy" in Act 1, which has Laura telling Tommy to relax and be himself as she is obviously growing attracted to him, and by removing Tommy's song to her, "Lovely Laurie." Laura's duet with Jessica, "I Wonder What It's Like?," was also eliminated, in part as a response to questions about the "propriety of having two young girls speculating about making love."[16] In addition, Tommy and Laura develop their romance in Act 2 with a new number, "My Miss Mary," ostensibly a love song to a girl named Mary but ultimately an oblique expression of mutual affection.

The finales underwent significant revisions. The collaborators kept the hymn to self-righteousness, "The Army of the Just," near the end of Act 1, but Bock and Harnick wrote a new song, "How the Money Changes Hands," as the big Act 1 finale, with Brock visiting the brothel and figuring out how everything works: "So the men pay the girls / And the girls pay Liz / And Liz pays the cops," and so forth, all the way up to "The Alderman pays the Mayor." The idea for this song, Harnick has recalled, came from George Abbott.[17] The second act finale likewise shifted focus from the reformers to the riff-raff, as the reprises of "Bless This Land" and "The Army of the Just" were abandoned altogether, and instead Reverend Brock's sermon to his new followers is gradually overtaken by a new version of the prostitutes' earlier anthem: "Little old Detroit is plenty good enough for me. . . ."

The score by this time was larger and richer, and filled with Bock–Harnick calling cards. The diegetic numbers repeat the success of *Fiorello!*'s "'Til Tomorrow" and "Gentleman Jimmy" in capturing period flavor and style. "Artificial Flowers" and "My Miss Mary" sound like authentic 1890s parlor songs, and "Bless This Land" and "The Army of the Just" are convincingly solemn. "The Picture of Happiness," which is diegetic when first presented, then a reflective book song when reprised in Act 2, adopts the spirit and rhythms of a vaudeville dance-hall extravaganza, not unlike "Gentleman Jimmy" from *Fiorello!* The ballads, "Tommy, Tommy" and "My Gentle Young Johnny," meet the songwriters' customary standards for Broadway-style melodic grace and lyric eloquence, although two of the cut ballads, "Lovely Laurie" and "I Wonder What It's Like," are just as musically engaging, if not more so. (Both were included in the collection of published vocal scores from the show.[18]) The prominence of the raised fourth scale step in the "Lovely Laurie" melody calls to mind Bock's tune for "Ethel, Baby" from *Mr. Wonderful*, among other earlier songs, just as the lowered seventh steps in "My Gentle Young Johnny" move forward his interest in things Mixolydian. The score includes simple character-building numbers in contemporary styles ("Dr. Brock," "Dear Friend") but also complex musical scenes ("How the Money Changes

Table 4.2: Overview of the final version of Tenderloin, *with titles that were added after the New Haven opening in* **bold**

ACT 1

1. A darkened stage.
   "Bless This Land" (Choir)
   "Little Old New York" (Nita, Gertie, Chorus)
2. Street outside the church.
3. Parish house.
   "Dr. Brock" (Brock)
   "Artificial Flowers" (Tommy, Chorus)
   "What's In It For You?" (Brock, Tommy)
4. Street in front of the 19th Precinct.
5. The 19th Precinct Police Station.
6. Street in front of the 19th Precinct.
   "Reform" (Bar Girls)
7. Laura's living room.
   "Tommy, Tommy" (Laura, Tommy)
8. Street in front of Clark's.
9. Inside Clark's.
   "The Picture of Happiness" (Tommy, Margie, Chorus)
10. Street in front of Clark's.
11. A beach.
    "Dear Friend" (Brock, Parishioners)
    "The Army of the Just" (Brock, Parishioners)
12. Street in front of Clark's.
13. Clark's, 11:00 p.m.
    "How the Money Changes Hands" (Nita, Brock, Tenderloin Denizens)

ACT 2

1. Central Park.
   "Good Clean Fun" (Brock, Parishioners)
   "My Miss Mary" (Tommy, Laura, Company)
2. A street.
3. Clark's.
   "My Gentle Young Johnny" (Nita)
   "The Picture of Happiness" (reprise) (Tenderloin Girls)
4. The trial.
   "The Trial" (Company)
5. Clark's.
   "The Tenderloin Celebration" (Tenderloin Denizens)

(Continued)

Table 4.2: (Continued)

6. Parish house, Night.
7. Precinct street.
8. The courtroom.
9. A street.
    "Reform" (reprise) (Tenderloin Girls)
10. Parish house.
    "Tommy, Tommy" (reprise) (Laura, Tommy)
Epilogue (Detroit).
    "Little Old New York" (reprise) (Company)

Hands," "The Trial"), in a line of development with songs with similar dramatic objectives in *Fiorello!* such as "Unfair" and "The Bum Won." The songwriters again display their affection for dramatically motivated contrapuntal textures in "What's In It For You?," when both Tommy and Reverend Brock express their skepticism simultaneously, and in "Good Clean Fun," when eight separate groups of believers gradually enter with different suggestions for sin-free entertainment—doubling the number of layers of political hacks in *Fiorello!*'s "The Bum Won."

Parody and Continuity in the Tenderloin *Score*

Looking deeper into the *Tenderloin* score, it is easy to appreciate the sensitivity and intelligence with which the songwriters approached their tasks, whether in the comfort of their home studios early in the development process, or against last-minute time pressures in a hotel room in New Haven or Boston. "Artificial Flowers," probably one of the first songs to be written for the show, gains specific inspiration from Tommy's first performance in Adams's novel, in which he brings an audience in the Tenderloin to tears with his rendition of "The Picture That Was Turned Towards the Wall."[19] This turn-of-the-century "pathetic ballad" by Charles Graham laments the tragic destiny of a "tender loving lassie" who lived a "happy life" in a loving family until she "left them all one evening" and her father "turned her picture toward the wall." Adams has Tommy singing a variation on a few lines of the chorus:

> There's a name that's never spo-kun.
> There's a heart that's almost bro-kun.
> There's a pick-shure that is turned towards the wall.[20]

Harnick's lyric for "Artificial Flowers" similarly tugs at the heart-strings with a story of "poor little Ann," an orphan who labors for hours a day making artificial flowers, but perishes from exposure to the cold weather drifting into her tenement room. Harnick adroitly straddles a fine line between genuine pathos and clever parody:

> With paper and shears, with wire and wax
> She labored and never complained
> 'Til cutting and folding her health slipped away
> And wiring and waxing, she waned.

In the end Ann is imagined in "heavenly gardens and bowers," wearing not a halo but a "garland of genuine flowers."

Bock's music for "Artificial Flowers" likewise adopts and personalizes stylistic signatures of the era, as he did in *Fiorello!*'s "'Til Tomorrow" a few months earlier. Inspired in part by the Beatrice Kay album (see chapter 3), he continues to follow standard harmonic practices as found in "You Tell Me Your Dream and I'll Tell You Mine" (Example 3.5) and many other songs of the 1890s. In "Artificial Flowers" he contrasts a largely triadic verse, reminiscent of "After the Ball Is Over" and "Bicycle Built for Two" and other songs on the album, with another use of the double-neighbor figure in the chorus (Example 4.1a), just as he had done in "'Til Tomorrow" (Example 3.4c), mimicking, for example, the opening notes of the "You Tell Me Your Dream" chorus (Example 3.5). Indeed the other parlor song in *Tenderloin*, "My Miss Mary," uses the double-neighbor figure as well (Example 4.1b). The *Tenderloin* parlor songs also adopt the model's climactic arrival on VI in the last phrase, followed by a return to tonic via a fifths progression (VI–II–V–I), quite like "'Til Tomorrow" (and like more than half of the songs on the Beatrice Kay album). In "Artificial Flowers" the melody dramatizes the moment by jumping out of the neighbor figure and up a fourth (on "Ar-ti-fi-cial **flow**-ers"), followed by a completion of the progression ("Fashioned from Annie's despair"). In "My Miss Mary" it is the harmony and bass line that give the final climax extra emphasis: the arrival on the climactic VI ("Mary don't be shy, **Miss**") is approached by a chromatic bass descent harmonized by a dominant seventh

Example 4.1: Double-neighbor figures in (a) "Artificial Flowers" and (b) "My Miss Mary"

chord (on "don't be") and a minor triad (on "shy"). After the VI ("Miss") the progression unfolds as usual ("Mary won't you marry me").

As with *Fiorello!*, the pervasive presence of fifths progressions in *Tenderloin* is a style element, not just a reflection of the structure of the tonal system. Of course such progressions are especially prominent in stylistic evocations such as "Picture of Happiness" (most conspicuously in the chorus) and "How the Money Changes Hands" (verse), but they also undergird important parts of ballads (e.g., the bridge of "My Gentle Young Johnny") and basic show tunes (e.g., the end of the chorus in "Good Clean Fun"). Simple diatonic fifths progressions in "Dr. Brock" and "I Wonder What It's Like" would not normally attract special attention, but in this context they do relate suggestively to similar harmonic patterns in the other songs. "Little Old New York" essentially endows a fifths progression with thematic status right at the beginning of the show, each time the chorus repeats "Little Old New York is plenty good enough for me" over and over while the harmony in the orchestra cycles through I–VI–II–V–I several times. When the bar girls sing "Reform" in Act 1, they begin by recalling strains from "Little Old New York," but it is just the lyric and fifths progression that recur, not the melody. Then the main melody of "Reform" features the same progression once again. The fifths progression becomes the spirit of the city that infiltrates and inhibits the efforts of the reformers, just as it permeates the people and music of the Tenderloin district, and of *Tenderloin*.

The thematic symbolism of "Little Old New York" is not limited to the fifths progression. Right at the beginning of the song we hear a motto ("Why can't this damn do-gooder . . .") that continually reappears at the ends of verses, giving exaggerated prominence to a ♭VI chord (first heard on the phrase "Keep his hands off" in the introduction). When ♭VI chords are similarly featured in later songs, our ears start to make connections back to "Little Old New York," and with the pervasive New York spirit. This happens especially prominently in "How the Money Changes Hands" (in the refrain, "Just as long as the **money** changes hands"), "Good Clean Fun" (on "I'm in the mood for fun, my friends," leading to a key change), and "My Gentle Young Johnny" (at the end of the verse, leading to the cadential dominant). "Little Old New York" also establishes a tonal relationship used elsewhere in the score when the key shifts to the subdominant for the bridge ("Right now she's wide open" and so forth), forecasting subdominant key relations in "Dr. Brock," "Reform," "The Picture of Happiness," "My Miss Mary," "The Trial," and "How the Money Changes Hands."[21] And whole-step relationships become thematic when "Little Old New York" shifts up by that distance within the bridge and before the last chorus, starting a trend that is followed by "Artificial Flowers," "What's In It For You?," "Tommy, Tommy," "Dear Friend," "My Miss Mary," and "The Trial."[22] Tonal relationships of this sort, by fourth and by whole step, are common enough in show and commercial music, but not so common that they might typically be heard with this frequency, and not an element of such prominence in Bock's work in general—just in the *Tenderloin* score.

Whatever problems the show might have faced with its libretto or first production, Bock and Harnick wrote vital, interesting music that advanced the progress of their evolving partnership. The squareness of the opening hymn is established not only by the dry rhythms and churchy organ accompaniment but also by a predictably conservative voice-leading structure, simply moving stepwise down a scale from an opening phrase starting on the upper tonic ("Bless this land of freedom and friendship") to phrases starting on steps 7 ("Bless this land of hope and of promise"), 6 ("Land that offers faith in the future"), 5 ("Help to the fallen"), and 4 ("Home to the homeless"). The octave achieves completion at the end of the number, when the women sing "Bless this holy land" on steps 5–4–3–2–1 while the men hold the tonic note. Later, the other song of the faithful, "The Army of the Just," has slightly more musical variety but uses analogous basic voice-leading patterns, mostly involving scalewise ascents. A song like "Tommy, Tommy," by contrast, amasses all its rhetorical resources to avoid any such simple resolutions. The lyric is filled with uncertainty and insecurity, as Laura first asks Tommy to be himself, then confesses that she too is resisting a full display of genuine feelings. So Bock's melody, tinged with chromatic flavorings, struggles and wavers on its way to resolution. It seems headed toward some sort of repose after the first two phrases (after "Byron second-hand" in the first verse, "not a bit like me" in the second), but then veers into a progression by fifths away from tonic (starting with "If you like me" in the first verse, "You confuse me" in the second). When the main melody returns it makes several attempts to rise chromatically to tonic before finally attaining its goal as Laura finishes her point in the first verse ("Let the nice young man come through"), and confesses her attraction in the second ("Something slowly draws me to you, closer every day").

In "What's In It For You?" we hear the state of Bock's contrapuntal technique after a decade of professional songwriting. The dramatic moment provides a perfect opportunity, as two very different characters, Brock and Tommy, display contrasting points of view while trying to gain a competitive advantage. First Tommy sings two verses, the second a whole step higher than the first, expressing doubt about Brock's purity and intentions, followed by a summarizing chorus: "What's in it for you?" Then Brock does the same, casting a skeptical eye on Tommy but also hoping that he can be trusted to help with the crusade. When Brock gets to his chorus, Tommy echoes him, line for line. This sets up a subsequent section in which the characters continue to sing in dialogue but now on slightly different melodies (Brock: "Shall I accept him as an ally?"; Tommy: "I need him and he needs me"). Finally they become completely contrapuntally entangled on repetitions of the phrase "we shall see." The characters accept the challenge and hold their ground; the result is a standoff. They then sing one final echoing chorus and some concluding interplay, ending with a unison spoken punctuation: "Your move."

Mixed Receptions on Broadway and Beyond

The new songs and pre-Broadway restructuring improved *Tenderloin* significantly, although not enough to satisfy most of the New York critics after the October 17 opening. The ones who liked it—John Chapman in the *Daily News* (10/18/60), Frank Aston in the *World Telegram* (10/18/60), and Rowland Field in the *Newark Evening News* (10/18/60)—were so bedazzled by the singing and dancing, they were willing to overlook unspecified "flaws" in the libretto (Chapman) and "low spots" in the first act (Aston). Many of the harshest critics were also enamored with the score: Howard Taubman in the *New York Times* (10/18/60) had basic reservations about the adaptation but wrote that "Sheldon Harnick's lyrics and Jerry Bock's music are the best excuse for *Tenderloin*." The defect most often cited was central to the show's basic conception: "When it concerns itself with dedicated, happy baggages and trulls it is a walloping and vivid and excitingly funny show, but when it turns to admire the sleek impregnables of virtue, it is duller than dishwater" (Whitney Bolton, *Morning Telegraph*, 10/19/60). We are expected to sympathize with the moral forces, the Reverend and his flock, but these characters are upstaged by the singing and dancing hedonists. As Walter Kerr wrote in the *Herald Tribune* (10/18/60), "Maurice Evans has an extremely unsympathetic part. . . . He plays a crusading minister who wants to eliminate the production numbers."

The show's creators, in subsequent reflections on the *Tenderloin* experience, have reached similar conclusions. Harnick's words echo many of the New York critics:

> Most of the fun was when people were doing naughty things, when they were going to the Tenderloin; that was where it was colorful. There was nothing really evil about it; it was a musical comedy version of bawdiness. But every time the church came onstage, every time the minister came on,

the fun was over. As much as we tried to make the minister human and a fun-loving man, it never quite worked—and we were stuck.[23]

The problems stemmed from a basic creative decision, made in the beginning, to focus the story on the minister. The Reverend, writes Hal Prince, "turned out to be not such an ideal character for a musical."[24] In Adams's novel, the character of the Reverend is secondary, essentially a role player in the drama of the culture of the Tenderloin. The focal point of the novel is Tommy and his movements back and forth between two divergent sides of New York society in pursuit of a socialite's affections. Prince imagines a reconceptualization of the musical centered on Tommy as a "parable of contemporary morality, the young leading man utterly amoral, triumphing, a forerunner of J. Pierpont Finch in *How To Succeed in Business Without Really Trying*."[25]

We are less aware of these shortcomings in the first act, because the moral forces have not yet triumphed. "Little Old New York" highlights a strong opening scene, and "How the Money Changes Hands" is a very effective send-off to intermission. But the Reverend's successful push for reform in Act 2 comes across as a defeat for the most appealing characters in the show, the life-blood of the Tenderloin district. The audience's moral sense wants to savor Brock's victory, but its dramatic sense leaves its sympathies with the vanquished. We come to agree with Nita, who starts off the opening song-and-dance number by asking "Why can't this damn do-gooder / Keep his hands off / Little . . . Old New . . . [York]." The libretto's ambivalence is perfectly captured, with unfortunate irony, in the show's Epilogue, as Reverend Killjoy begins yet another sermon about the wages of sin, only to be superseded by one last glimpse of those lovable dancing prostitutes.

Likewise, the libretto does not promote a strong interest in Nita's search for marital bliss. We prefer Nita as she was, a bar girl hustling customers in Clark's, not as Joe's traveling companion on a slow boat to China. The relationship we want to see consummated, between Tommy and Laura, fizzles into heartbreak. It is a rare musical comedy indeed that follows the blossoming love of two young, appealing characters and then, in the end, sends them their separate ways.

The strong cast mostly escaped blame. Reviewers seemed surprised to learn that Maurice Evans, an experienced interpreter of Shakespeare and Shaw, could sing and dance. Ron Husmann, fresh out of Northwestern when he played one of the politicians in *Fiorello!* the previous year, received high praise for his portrayal of Tommy. Also earning critical acclaim were Wynne Miller (bandleader Glenn Miller's niece) playing Laura, and Eileen Rodgers, another *Fiorello!* veteran, playing Nita. Among the actors who brought extensive Broadway experience to their roles as bar girls was Lee Becker (Gertie), who originated the role of Anybodys, the tomboy member of the Jets gang in *West Side Story* (1957). The role of another bar girl, Margie, was played by Margery Gray, who had played Dora during the run of *Fiorello!* and who would become Sheldon Harnick's wife a few years later. *Tenderloin* received three Tony nominations, for Actor in a Musical (Maurice Evans, who lost to Richard Burton for *Camelot*), Supporting or Featured Actor in a Musical (Ron Husmann, who lost to Dick Van Dyke for *Bye Bye, Birdie*), and Costume Design in a Musical (Cecil Beaton, who lost to Adrian and Tony Duquette for *Camelot*). The show closed after its 217th performance on April 23, 1961. Investors did suffer a financial loss, although the damage was less severe than it might have been because of a large advance sale.[26] Two blocks away, the first run of *Fiorello!* was still going strong well into its second year.

Since that time *Tenderloin* has moved in and out of public consciousness. Just after closing, an abridged eighty-minute version of the show played for six weeks at the Dunes Hotel in Las Vegas, with the same cast except for a few of the lead roles.[27] The musical premiered in Europe in 1971 by the Rickmansworth Players of Watford, England. The next New York performances came in a three-week run by the Equity Library Theater in 1975, appraised by Clive Barnes in the *Times* (11/11/75) as "tasteful but modest." For this production Bock and Harnick restored three songs that had been cut in 1960, including Laura's duet with her friend Jessica, "I Wonder What It's Like." Barnes wrote that the song "should not have gone astray on the way to the 46th Street Theater"; Kelly calls it a "striking fleshing-out of their characters."[28] The rethinking continued for the concert version presented by the City Center "Encores!" series in 2000, with the director Walter Bobbie and Jerome Weidman's son John trimming the script down by some thirty pages, according to Harnick's estimate. Because the cuts "get to the musical numbers faster" and "allowed the audience to spend more time with the Tenderloin girls," they were "all to the good," believes Harnick.[29] Meanwhile, the heart of the show's appeal may still be experienced in a new recording of the music by the 2000 cast, and in the original cast album (reissued on CD), which stayed on the *Billboard* charts for thirty-four weeks in 1961, peaking at fifteenth. Ken Mandelbaum considers *Tenderloin*, like Sondheim's *Merrily We Roll Along*, Loesser's *Greenwillow*, and Harold Arlen's *House of Flowers*, to be "a classic example of a flop whose cast album leads people to believe that the show must have been sensational."[30]

Both composer and lyricist regard the *Tenderloin* experience as an inspiration for an important change in their working methods. Bock had been growing more and more aware of dramatic issues in all the shows he had written, starting back even as far as *My Dream* and *Big as Life*, but with *Tenderloin* he realized with new clarity "that it was important for us to get involved, much more intrinsically involved, in the making up of the whole musical," that the songwriting team should be "on top of the book," that is, "more sensitive to what was happening in terms of how the book was being written."[31] Harnick believes that his conversion arrived with an epiphany he had during the meeting of collaborators after the New Haven opening. Up until that time he had considered his job to be to "read the script, to be told where the song should go, or discover places on my own where the songs should go, and write the lyrics with the composer." But when faced with George Abbott's request for help, he realized that he should do more:

> I resolved right then and there that in my next show, whatever it was, I would really study the book, try to anticipate where the weaknesses were, try to be able to know the book so well that I could make contributions in one way or another. It really changed my professional life.[32]

Their heightened sensitivity would result not only in stronger libretti but also closer integrations of music with drama.

THEMES AND VARIATIONS

Just as Bock and Harnick's third Broadway musical, *Tenderloin*, had begun gestating before their second, *Fiorello!*, opened, so did the drive to produce a fourth show begin while *Tenderloin* was still in development, sometime in 1960. But the concept that the team began to discuss at that time would ultimately be realized as their fifth show, *Fiddler on the Roof*, in 1964. Their fourth major collaboration, *She Loves Me*, intervened in 1962 and 1963. And they were in no hurry to get something on stage. With the success of *Fiorello!* giving them some sort of financial stability, and the disappointment of *Tenderloin* helping them keep things in perspective, they were able and willing to take their time and do things right. Never again would the interval between their major shows be as brief as the 329 days between the New York premieres of *Fiorello!* and *Tenderloin*.

They also pursued smaller projects and did work outside the partnership during this time. The same night that *Tenderloin* opened in New Haven (September 12, 1960), the revue *Vintage '60* opened on Broadway, featuring two songs that Harnick wrote some years earlier with David Baker, "Ism" and "Forget Me."[33] The show closed after eight performances; Howard Taubman in the *Times* called it "bubbly and flat."[34] And while *Tenderloin* played on Broadway Harnick certainly devoted considerable energies to the New York premiere of his Horatio Alger musical, now titled *Smiling the Boy Fell Dead*, at the Cherry Lane Theater on April 19, 1961, four days before *Tenderloin* closed (see chapter 2). Also during this period Bock's theme music for a television program, *The Joke and the Valley*, appeared on NBC's Hallmark Hall of Fame (May 5, 1961). Jerry McNeely, a speech professor and theatrical director at the University of Wisconsin-Madison, wrote the teleplay, which was selected for airing from among 1500 other submissions in a writing competition.[35] And as a team, Bock and Harnick were in discussions with Arthur Penn about writing music for a show about horse racing, based on an original story by Penn and written by Walter Bernstein. Although the project was announced in the *Times* on January 24, 1962, with Bock and Harnick's participation described as "likely," it never came to fruition.[36]

In the early 1960s Jerry Bock became devoted to music for children, no doubt drawing inspiration from his own parenthood. He began writing a series of songs—words and music—for an educational radio program in New York, which culminated in an entire album of fifteen songs, *New Songs We Sing in School*.[37] He sings the songs himself on the record, accompanied by a small chamber group, to a receptive and energetic group of children. The music demonstrates the composer's customary stylistic array, from simple songs in the style of standard children's fare ("I Bet I Can Make You Smile"), to basic show tunes ("Sing Something Special"), to a catalogue song ("Since I'm Eight (Or Nine)"), a two-part canon ("Round Ground Round"), and a Latin shuffle ("Peter Minuit"). Bock clearly has an affinity for the project, and for children's sensibilities, especially in clever conceptions such as "Swiss Cheese Yodel" (in which one may produce a yodel by singing into a hole in Swiss cheese), "Aw, Mom" (an argument against overbundling on cold days: "I wish you were like Mother Nature / Now she has a right to boast / 'Cause she never puts the animals in three pairs of snow pants / And yet they're warm as toast"), and "Music That They Play in Outer Space" (a speculation about music of other planets, including this lyric: "Are their instruments familiar / Like the tuba, flute, and harp? / Or is everything electronic string and pitch? / Are their pianos shaped like arrows / So the music comes out sharp / Do they have a song they can beep along with Mitch?"). Even when writing for children Bock does not suppress his urge to use blue notes, half-step inflections, and chromatic lines in inner voices; as children's music goes, it is far from routine.

During this time both Bock and Harnick also continued to write independent, stand-alone songs with an eye toward commercial opportunities. Bock's archive includes songs he wrote alone such as "Better is Love" (1961) and "Said My Heart" (1961), and songs he wrote with Harnick such as "The Lonely Stage" (1962) and "The Right Word" (1963).[38] Their most marketable independent song of this period was "Since My Canary Died" (1962), which was recorded by the vocal group the Brothers Four on their *Cross-Country Concert* album (1963) and by the Smothers Brothers on their album *Tour de Farce: American History and Other Unrelated Subjects* (1964).[39] Harnick recalls this song title and lyric popping into his head sometime earlier, as he was writing lyrics with another composer (identified only as "one of Frank Loesser's protégés"). He gave the lyric to his new partner, and Bock's setting was performed in cabarets around New York, by Portia Nelson and possibly others. It is a classic Harnick lyric recalling the old revue days of "Boston Beguine" and "Merry Little Minuet," about the loss of a canary (beloved, even though "he was molting / and looked revolting") and the consequences for the cat. Bock's music provides enough variety to keep the song interesting and still leaves plenty of room for text projection and, especially in the case of the Smothers Brothers, clowning around.

Separate projects from these years included Harnick's song "Metamorphosis," a humorous oddity rhapsodizing the transformation of a pitiable caterpillar into the "king of insects," which appeared on a live album by the Journeymen in 1962.[40] The song originated as a nonsense poem in high school, which Harnick set to music "in the style of a Schubert art song" after he moved to New York. Also, Bock's "Since I've Been to You," an up-tempo jazz number in the spirit of "Too Close for Comfort," was recorded by Ethel Ennis and released in 1964 on her album *Once Again*.[41]

During this time Bock and Harnick made a small contribution to a show that became their most successful Broadway venture prior to *Fiddler on the Roof*. Indeed Sumner Arthur Long's play *Never Too Late*, for which Bock and Harnick wrote the one and only one song, opened on November 27, 1962 and was still playing when *Fiddler* opened in September 1964; it ran for 1007 performances, until April 24, 1965. George Abbott directed the play, about a married couple of advancing years who unexpectedly discover that they are going to be parents again. John Kander wrote incidental music, but Bock and Harnick wrote the "Never Too Late Cha-Cha" for the place in the script that calls for the father to perform a song and clumsy dance. Harnick's lyric sets the tone ("Never, never too late / For that buried desire / Stir those ashes and you'll find ashes of fire"), and Bock's stylish cha-cha includes his signature raised fourth step in the second bar (harmonized with a tonic diminished seventh chord) and several trips through fifths progressions starting on VI.[42]

The most extensive project Bock and Harnick completed between *Tenderloin* and *She Loves Me* was a rarity, at least until *Avenue Q* came along: a musical puppet show on Broadway. The guiding spirits were Bil and Cora Baird, whose marionettes had made featured appearances two decades earlier in a Broadway revue, *Ziegfeld Follies of 1943*, and in *Flahooley* (1951), a quickly forgotten musical by the author-lyricists for *Finian's Rainbow*, Yip Harburg and Fred Saidy, in collaboration with composer Sammy Fain. The Baird marionettes had also played an important role in the development of early television in the 1950s, appearing on programs such as *Your Show of Shows* and *The Steve Allen Show*, and producing original programs of their own, including *Life with Snarky Parker* and *The Whistling Wizard*. Some of their adaptations of classic tales had played in smaller theaters in New York and around the world, and in December 1955 they presented their first show in a larger house (the Phoenix), including a musical version of *Ali Baba and the Forty Thieves*, at show times that would not interfere with the main attraction. This was a success for both audiences and critics, and the following September they presented a similar show for a nine-day run in a theater not being shared (the Playhouse). Their next venture was a new musical based on an original story and playing solo at a legitimate Broadway house: *Davy Jones' Locker* played at the Morosco Theater in March and April 1959. Mary Rodgers wrote original songs for this show; it was technically her composing debut on Broadway, preceding *Once Upon a Mattress* by a couple of months.

Harnick had worked on a project involving the Bairds when he assisted Ogden Nash on the television special *Art Carney Meets Peter and the Wolf* in 1958. Sometime in 1961 or 1962 he and Bock were brought in to write songs for another new puppet musical, *The Man in the Moon*, based on an original story by Bil Baird and written by Arthur Burns, who had co-written *Davy Jones' Locker* (with M. L. Davenport). *The Man in the Moon* premiered at the Biltmore Theater on April 11, 1963 and played twice daily until April 21, two days before *She Loves Me* opened at the Eugene O'Neill. Critics had mostly kind words for the 70-minute musical, although they were perhaps more charmed by a general puppet variety show presented after intermission, which included interaction with the audience, a pageant of puppets from around the world, and a finale featuring the Ponyettes from Rodeo City Music Hall.[43]

Baird and Burns's story for *The Man in the Moon* concerns Jerry, a boy who uses a short-wave radio to contact the citizens of the moon. The moonfolk choose him to be the first Earth ambassador and beam him skyward, but a jewel thief and his henchmen, escaping the police, somehow get transported on the same beam. On the moon they find a girl, Chandra, who is threatened by the bad guys, and they also find the Man in the Moon, who is enraged by the behavior of his unwelcome guests. Jerry eventually finds a friend in a dim-witted Giant (played by an actual person, not a puppet), who helps him rescue Chandra by sending the gangsters into orbit. Jerry returns to Earth a hero.

Bock and Harnick wrote five songs for the show, in styles and idioms that stretch across their creative range.[44] "Look Where I Am," which Jerry sings after his lunar landing, sounds at times like some of the music they were imagining for their still-nascent show about a poor Russian milkman and his daughters, especially when raised fourth and flatted second scale steps predominate. "You Treacherous Men," sung by the Man in the Moon to the evil interlopers, also occasionally sounds like a distant cousin to the *Fiddler* score, especially one of the Tevye monologues. For the jewel thief's moment in the spotlight, Bock turns to his favorite genre for sleazy characters, the soft-shoe number: "Itch to be Rich" follows a trend reaching back to "Gloria" in *The Body Beautiful* and "Little Tin Box" from *Fiorello!* Equally sinister is a *waltz macabre* sung to Chandra by the bad guys, "Ain't You Never Been Afraid."

The standout is Chandra's song of friendship to Jerry, "Worlds Apart." Harnick chose to showcase this number in his appearance in the "Lyrics and Lyricists" series at the 92nd Street Y in 1971, as an example of the kind of song he had not been able to write in his younger days. In introducing it he told his audience that many of his earlier attempts at writing love songs lacked "emotional content—and that can be a serious flaw in a love song." An earlier predilection in his lyrics for images of "breaking down walls," he surmised, "must have originated in my need to break through my own emotional defenses."[45] In 1997 he credited psychotherapy for helping him find his tender side: "Prior to analysis, my love songs were satiric. I had a certain amount of difficulty just writing lyrics that dealt with love, but I began to open up in therapy."[46] Well, there are tender moments in his earlier work—"Somebody Beautiful," a song written for, but never used in, *The Body Beautiful* is one[47]—but it is generally true that many of Harnick's early love songs somehow stand at an emotional distance or approach their subject obliquely. "Hidden in My Heart" (*The Body Beautiful*), for example, is affecting, but the sentiments are, after all, "hidden." "When Did I Fall In Love?" (*Fiorello!*) raises the subject in the form of a question, as if afraid to make an emotional commitment. And the expressions of love in *Tenderloin* come in Laura's "Tommy, Tommy," a song filled with insecurities, and in "My Miss Mary," where the two young lovers express their love to each other only by transferring affections expressed for Mary onto themselves. "Worlds Apart," on the other hand, embraces its subject with directness and candor:

Yesterday, we were worlds apart
Your world was far away, a world unknown
I was sure, we'd stay worlds apart,
But since I've talked to you, how close we've grown.

Before we met, I would have bet,
I wouldn't like you
Now I like you—
Strange how suddenly . . .

A change takes place, when we're face to face,
It's just like tearing down a wall
Our universe is growing very small
And we're not worlds apart after all.[48]

Bock's music is similarly open and direct, with lush but straightforward harmonies and a skillfully shaped melody. By this time they had nothing left to prove as songwriters. They did, however, have plenty of directions to go as dramatists.

5

TO BROADWAY WITH LOVE

• • •

SHE LOVES ME AND THE 1964 WORLD'S FAIR

By the time their third show, *Tenderloin*, closed in 1961, Jerry Bock and Sheldon Harnick had experienced the theater in all its glory and infamy. They had enjoyed stunning successes and endured major disappointments. They had been toasted and roasted. They had written a show based on a completely original and fictitious libretto, a show retelling historical events in a libretto adapted from nonfiction sources, and a show with a libretto adapted from a historically inspired novel. Their musicals all included important love elements, following in the best of Broadway traditions, but the general themes and dramatic contexts of their shows had ranged from boxing to politics to public morality. The decision to make their creative experience broad and diverse, to grow in every direction, was a conscious one. "Whenever we finish something," Bock told Max Wilk in 1971, "we've always wanted to do an about-face and go somewhere else. To do something hopefully that will give us the opportunity to break new ground, to write fresh, or to explore territory we haven't been in before."[1] In the early 1960s, as Bock and Harnick approached what would become the midpoint of their fourteen years of collaboration, and the fourth of the seven major musicals they would ultimately write together during that time, their search for unexplored territory took them to a genre that has been explored more than any other in the musical theater: the pure love story.

SHE LOVES ME

In 1961 and early 1962 Bock and Harnick were developing at least two show ideas simultaneously. Their main focus since *Tenderloin* had been a musical adaptation of some of Sholem Aleichem's Tevye stories. They wrote some songs with this in mind, and Joseph Stein had begun drafting a libretto. But in the fall of 1961, when they were approached with a proposal for a musical adaptation of the Ernst Lubitsch film *The Shop Around the Corner*, they were so charmed by the idea that they could not say no.[2] They began conceptualizing this project even as they were looking for a producer and director for the Aleichem dramatization. Bock made a tape of song ideas that was a mixture of musical possibilities for both shows.[3] Then in early 1962 they met with Harold Prince to discuss the Tevye project and he advised them not to go forward with it unless and until they could get Jerome Robbins to direct.[4] They agreed, but Robbins was unavailable, so they gradually began to devote more attention to the film adaptation, and by the end of the summer they had set the Tevye material aside.[5] It was easier in any case to move a project of their own devising to the back burner than to delay a project that had been initiated by someone else.

Lubitsch's 1940 film was itself an adaptation, by Samson Raphaelson, of the play *Illatszertár*, written in 1936 by the Hungarian playwright Miklós László. This play, usually known by its French title *Parfumerie*, had been performed extensively in Europe but never in the United States.[6] A musical adaptation of the material had already appeared on film in 1949, as *In the Good Old Summertime*, starring Judy Garland and Van Johnson, but the music for this version consisted entirely of existing songs presented as set pieces. As early as 1955 Cy Feuer and Ernest Martin had tried to attract interest in an adaptation with newly composed, integrated songs, and in 1956 they had received a commitment from Cole Porter. Porter told an interviewer in 1956 that *The Shop Around the Corner* was his next project, after he completed work on a movie musical for MGM based on *The Philadelphia Story*.[7] Neither project materialized, and Porter's attentions turned to a new movie-musical, *Les Girls*, starring Gene Kelly and Mitzi Gaynor (1957). In the meantime the *Shop Around the Corner* property passed through other producers' hands, including Emil and Gabriel Katzka, then Max Liebman, before being taken over by Lawrence Kasha (who had worked for Feuer and Martin) and Philip C. McKenna (an oil and real-estate tycoon in Arizona), and they eventually offered it to Bock and Harnick.[8] A few months later Harold Prince became a co-producer as well.[9] At first known by the same title as the film, the name for the new show was eventually changed, so as to make a clear distinction between the two, to *She Loves Me*.[10]

To write the libretto, the creative team recruited Joe Masteroff, whose play *The Warm Peninsula* (1959) had played on Broadway a few years earlier. Masteroff had no previous experience writing a book for a musical, but his work had struck a chord with Harnick. Masteroff remembers working primarily from Raphaelson's screenplay, not from the László script, despite the show's official credit line ("based on a play by Miklós László," with no mention of Raphaelson or Lubitsch). Masteroff's adaptation therefore became one of the first Broadway musicals based primarily on a Hollywood film, after *Silk Stockings* (adaptation by George S. Kaufman, Leueen MacGrath, and Abe Burrows, music and lyrics by Cole Porter, 1955), *Destry Rides Again* (adaptation by Leonard Gershe, music and lyrics by Harold Rome, 1959), and *Carnival!* (adaptation by Michael Stewart, music and lyrics by Bob Merrill, 1961).[11] The creators apparently did not consider *In the Good Old Summertime* as a potential source. Bock said in 1994, "I think had we seen *In the Good Old Summertime*, it would have been far less appealing to us as a project."[12]

George Abbott, who had recently had yet another huge success directing *A Funny Thing Happened on the Way to the Forum* (opened 5/8/62), was invited to direct, and reportedly gave the matter serious consideration in the late summer and fall of 1962.[13] When he withdrew, the job was offered to Gower Champion, whom Bock remembered well from his work on the Sid Caesar television shows in the early 1950s, and who had since made his name on Broadway directing *Bye Bye Birdie* (opened 4/14/60) and *Carnival!* (4/13/61). Champion was interested but involved in something else and asked the team to delay production until he was free.[14] Rather than wait, Bock and Harnick turned their attentions to a friend with a stellar track record as a producer but little directing experience, Harold Prince. At that point Prince had directed only twice: early in 1962 he had stepped in to rescue the early John Kander musical, *A Family Affair*, during its pre-Broadway tour, and more recently he had staged a production of Thornton Wilder's *The Matchmaker* (the source for *Hello, Dolly!*) for a tour of New York state on behalf of the Phoenix Theater.[15] Prince was announced as the director of *She Loves Me* in Sam Zolotow's column in the *New York Times* on November 5, 1962; he continued to serve as co-producer. Bock and Harnick remained loyal to Prince even after Champion's other project fell through and Prince offered to step aside. (Coincidentally, Prince had just declined an offer to direct the show that would soon become a huge success for Champion, then known as *Dolly! A Damned Exasperating Woman*, later renamed *Hello, Dolly!*[16]) Harnick has embraced the ultimate decision, praising Prince's directorial gifts and compatible artistic vision, even though at that time he was an "unknown quantity." Harnick speculates that Champion might have "changed direction so totally that I probably would have been fired."[17]

For the remainder of the production team Bock and Harnick welcomed several previous collaborators. Musical director Hal Hastings and incidental music arranger Jack Elliott had both worked on *Fiorello!* and *Tenderloin*, and scenery and lighting designers William and Jean Eckart had designed scenery, lighting, and costumes for *Fiorello!* Orchestrator Don Walker had scored Harnick's song "A Man's Home" for *Two's Company* in 1952 (see chapter 2) and was a familiar presence on Broadway, scoring shows such as *Carousel* (1945), *Call Me Madam* (1950), *The Pajama Game* (1954), *Damn Yankees* (1955), and *The Music Man* (1957). Otherwise the *She Loves Me* production team included new collaborators for Bock and Harnick. Costume designer Patricia Zipprodt was well into a distinguished career that would include Tony awards for *Fiddler on the Roof* (1964), *Cabaret* (1966), and *Sweet Charity* (1966), plus seven other nominations. The modest dance sequences in *She Loves Me* would be staged by Carol Haney, who had first lit up the stage in *The Pajama Game* in 1954.

The Story and Its Sources

The plot of *She Loves Me*, in Masteroff's adaptation, concerns the owner and staff at a parfumerie in a "city in Europe," presumably Budapest. The store's proprietor, Maraczek, oversees three clerks: Georg, a young single man who also helps manage the store; Sipos, an older man with a wife and family; and Kodaly, a rakish man in his middle years with expensive tastes and a boastful air. Also on the staff are the cashier Ilona, who is approaching middle age and growing tired of the single life, and a young delivery boy, Arpad. Act 1 opens on a morning in mid-summer, the store busy with customers buying perfumes, soaps, and creams. It soon develops that Georg has become infatuated with a woman he knows only through a series of letters but has never met. He does not even know her name, so he is oblivious when this very same woman arrives in the shop seeking employment. The woman, Amalia, is also unaware that she has stumbled upon her beloved but anonymous pen pal. She succeeds in gaining Maraczek's respect, and a job in the shop, when she convinces a customer that a leather musical cigarette box is actually a candy box, its music serving as a reminder not to overindulge, and making a sale. We also learn that Ilona and Kodaly are romantically entangled, although it is clear that for Kodaly, Ilona is one of many, and for Ilona, Kodaly is hardly her knight in shining armor.

A transition then takes us some months forward to a day in early December, when Georg and Amalia, still in passionate, anonymous correspondence—although clashing daily in person—have agreed to meet. Unfortunately, Maraczek asks the staff to stay and hang Christmas decorations that very same evening, and Georg releases the tension of the moment in a heated exchange with Maraczek that ends with Georg's resignation. We soon learn that Maraczek is happy to see Georg go because he believes that Georg is having an affair with his wife. When he is told by a detective that it is Kodaly who is the adulterer, Maraczek is so distraught that he tries to shoot himself.

Meanwhile, Georg is so upset by the circumstances of his resignation that he finds himself unable to meet his secret lover as planned. Instead he goes to the meeting place, the Cafe Imperiale, expecting to send Sipos in to give the woman, known only as Dear Friend, a note. When Georg realizes that Amalia and Dear Friend are one and the same, he stays and torments Amalia, who still, when the curtain falls on Act 1, has no idea what is going on.

Act 2 begins the next day, with a reconciliation between Maraczek, who has only injured his arm in his suicide attempt, and Georg. Georg is placed in charge of the shop, with instructions to fire Kodaly at once. Georg also tries to reconcile with Amalia and visits her at home, where she is feeling the effects of too many glasses of wine while waiting for Dear Friend the night before. Georg tells Amalia that he spoke to her soulmate outside the restaurant and was told that he had to leave town suddenly on urgent business, and Amalia feels better. But she also realizes that she is touched by Georg, because he cared enough to visit, and because he brought her a carton of ice cream to cheer her up. Back at the shop, Ilona announces that she has found a new love, an optometrist she met at the library, and then Kodaly says his flamboyant goodbyes. As Christmas approaches, Georg and Amalia are growing increasingly affectionate towards each other, but she is still smitten with— and in the dark about—Dear Friend. She has arranged a new first meeting with him at her house for Christmas Eve dinner, and she also invites Georg. Finally at closing time on the night before Christmas, with everyone going their separate ways, Georg and Amalia reminisce about their first meeting and find themselves unable to suppress their mutual affection any longer. Georg reveals the truth by quoting a passage from one of Amalia's letters. Their warm embrace as the curtain falls tells us that Amalia bears no hard feelings for Georg's deception. We assume that she will even forgive him when she realizes how long it went on.

Because he worked primarily from Raphaelson's screenplay, Masteroff adopted several substantive changes in László's original story.[18] Both Raphaelson and Masteroff place the love story at the center of the drama, whereas László devotes roughly equal attention both to the young lovers and to the shop-owner's marital crisis. This means, in part, that some of Raphaelson's and Masteroff's best scenes are not in the original at all. In László, for example, the *ingénue* already works at the store at the beginning of the play and has no scene like the film and musical where she arrives looking for work and auditions by selling the cigarette/candy box. The confrontation at the cafe and the scene in her home are also entirely new with Raphaelson, retained by Masteroff. At the end of the story, László has the two young lovers expressing their mutual affection and planning Christmas Eve together, but the consummation never happens onstage. The man never reveals himself as the woman's correspondent, and does not intend to do so, preferring to cultivate the relationship as it stands.[19]

But in other respects Masteroff does not follow Raphaelson and instead either incorporates ideas from László or develops new elements of his own. Masteroff does not recall ever reading the László script and so apparently got ideas from a team member who had—probably Harnick, making good on his *Tenderloin*-inspired promise to take an active role in the development of the book. Masteroff moves the setting, for example, back to a parfumerie; in Raphaelson the shop sells leather goods. (Masteroff: "How do you sing leather?") Some character names—Amalia, Sipos, and Arpad—likewise connect László directly with Masteroff.[20] Masteroff and László, but not Raphaelson, also include the secondary love story (between the characters named Ilona and Kodaly in Masteroff's version), which is broken off in the end when the woman finds true love outside the shop. More generally, Masteroff gave the story a warmer, more affectionate ambience than Raphaelson, making the group of co-workers seem more like a family, even if richly dysfunctional. Masteroff's dialogue is less argumentative, his characters more comic and endearing. As he puts it, he converted the roué (Kodaly), for example, from a "contemptuous toad" to a "charming egomaniac."

Music in She Loves Me

Previously Bock and Harnick had worked with librettists who would "write a scene and put, in parentheses, that there could be a song at such a point about such and such a subject." For this project, however, they decided to try something different. Harnick recalls,

> Joe Masteroff, the playwright, had never written a musical before and what we asked him to do was kind of an experiment all the way around. He was to write a play and let us search through the scenes and find the emotional moments or comic moments which we thought could be well expressed in song, and that is the way we did it. I don't think Joe ever wrote in a scene that there should be a song there.[21]

Bock and Harnick found Masteroff's initial effort to be "drenched with music" and took advantage of many opportunities to convert dialogue into song lyrics.[22] It was, said Harnick, "like looking at a raisin cake and plucking out pieces of fruit."[23] Masteroff's opening scene, for example, in which the characters arrive for work (just as they do at the beginning of Raphaelson's screenplay, and in the first scene of László's second act), was completely reworked in song as "Good Morning, Good Day." This segues into a scene inside the shop in which clerks and customers interact musically in the song "Sounds While Selling," also inspired by Masteroff's dialogue. Whenever a customer leaves the shop, the clerks assemble for a recurring choral refrain, "Thank You, Madam," which originates in a line found in four different spots in Masteroff's first draft: "Good day—thank you—please call again."[24] The notion of a recurring chorus actually comes not from Raphaelson but from László; some variation of "Goodnight, Madam, thank you very much, call again," spoken together by the clerks, appears nine times in *Parfumerie*.[25]

Masteroff may not have specifically indicated song locations or possibilities, but he did include "a number of lengthy monologues" in his original draft, where he was "trying to say to Sheldon, 'You know, this oughta be a song.'"[26] When Amalia sells the cigarette/music box as an audition for Maraczek in the second scene of Act 1, for example, Masteroff initially gave her this to say:

> Let me tell you. It's been a life-saver to many, many women. They have a slight tendency to over-weight. And don't we all? We sit reading a good book—or listening to a symphony—and, without realizing it, our hand slips into the candy box. But now—with this revolutionary new box—that can never again happen. The minute we lift the lid—Music!! "No bon-bons for *you*—no bon-bons for *you*!" In a way, it's like the voice of God.[27]

Harnick kept the first few lines, up through "our hand slips into the candy box," as spoken dialogue, but used the rest as inspiration for—or as actual lines of lyric in—Amalia's song "No More Candy":

> We become indiscreet
> Eating sweet after sweet—
> Tho' we know all too well
> Where that may lead.
>
> So this box was designed
> With the two of us in mind
> As the kind of reminder we need.
>
> When you raise the lid
> The music plays
> Like a disapproving nod.
>
> And it sings in your ear:
> No more candy, my dear.
> In a way, it's a little like the voice of God.[28]

For a scene later in Act 1, Masteroff originally wrote a monologue in which the older clerk, Sipos, explains his worldview to Georg:

> Just look at it the way I do. Here I am: Ladislav Sipos—merely one of many employees in this Parfumerie—which is merely one of many Parfumeries in this city—which is merely one of many cities in this country—which is merely one of many countries on this continent—which is merely one of many continents on this planet—which is merely one of many planets in this solar system—which is merely one of many solar systems in this universe . . . So who am *I* to get excited if the boss yells at me?[29]

From this Bock and Harnick wrote the song "Perspective," which includes a recitative-like section with these lines:

> I am only one of several in a rather small Parfumerie
> Which is only one of several in this city
> Which is one of many cities in this country which is only one of many
>   countries
> Which are on this continent
> Which is only one of seven on this not so special planet
> Which is one of many in our solar system
> Which is only one of many solar systems
> In this vast and inconceivable affair that is the universe.
> So—in this infinite, incomprehensible scheme
> If a dot called Maraczek should scream
> At a speck called Sipos—
> What—on earth—does it matter?[30]

Elsewhere in Masteroff's draft are the origins of Amalia's song "I Don't Know His Name," in which she tells Ilona that she is deeply in love with someone she knows only through anonymous letters, and two songs from the Cafe Imperiale scene at the end of Act 1: "A Romantic Atmosphere," sung by the *maître d'*, and "Tango Tragique," sung by Georg in an attempt to make Amalia feel even worse. Masteroff has said that he was complimented, not offended, by the adaptations of his original text, because "the function of the book is to serve the music."[31] Masteroff "had no ego about salvaging scenes, lines, jokes," remembered Bock. "His attitude, which became our unified attitude, was to absorb most of that play into music."[32]

And absorb they did, perhaps too much at first, according to Harnick: "everything wanted to be sung." At first they wrote not only "songs and developed pieces" but also "musical bits" or "musical fragments." They eventually had to prune this back, fearing that the audience would be oversaturated and would just "stop hearing."[33] At the same time, they wanted the music for this show to be more closely connected to the drama than any of their previous scores had been. They would not only work more closely with the librettist to fashion and shape the story—applying the lessons of the *Tenderloin* experience—they would also try to give music a more integral organic presence. As Bock said in 1979, "We had always instinctively felt like writing the so-called integrated musical, and this was an opportunity for us to really explore that in depth."[34]

As a result, *She Loves Me*, like Masteroff's original draft of its libretto, is drenched with music (Table 5.1). The opening sequence of "Good Morning, Good Day" and "Sounds While Selling," concluding with the refrain "Thank You, Madam," develops plot and character without spoken dialogue, setting an operatic tone that lingers throughout the show. Songs with operatic conceptions, motivated primarily by dramatic circumstances and eschewing traditional song forms, appear frequently: "Three Letters" moves the action in Act 1 forward from summer to winter; the clerks sing "Goodbye, Georg" after Georg resigns, in counterpoint with "Sounds While Selling" sung by customers, and end with a variant of "Thank You, Madam"; the scene in the restaurant features the songs "A Romantic Atmosphere" and "Tango Tragique" (which ends with Amalia's dramatic tantrum, originally listed as a separate number, "Mr. Nowack, Will You Please?"); and in the last scene in Act 2, the song "Twelve Days to Christmas" provides a musical narrative of the holiday shopping season, alternating with a version of "Thank You, Madam" sung by customers ("Thank you, thank you / We'll call again"). Operatic elements also emerge in the recitative section in Sipos's "Perspective"; in the hints of Gilbert and Sullivan in the middle section of "Try Me," Arpad's attempt (ultimately successful) to persuade Maraczek to hire him as a clerk; and in vocal lines and figures in the series of songs in Act 2, beginning with "Ice Cream," Amalia's reflection on Georg's visit to her home, and continuing with a direct segue to Georg's joyous outpouring of his heart, "She Loves Me." Shortly thereafter we hear Ilona's aria "A Trip to the Library," a richly detailed account of her discovery of love in the stacks.

Songs more consistent with musical-comedy traditions are equally abundant. In his only solo number, "Days Gone By," Maraczek reflects fondly on the innocence and idealized happiness of his younger days. This lilting waltz brings to mind some of Bock and Harnick's earlier nostalgic waltzes, especially "'Til Tomorrow" (*Fiorello!*) and "Artificial Flowers" (*Tenderloin*). Also in Act 1, Georg releases nervous tension over his impending meeting with Dear Friend in a patter song, "Tonight at Eight." When that song is followed fairly closely by Amalia's attempt to convince Ilona that she is in love with a virtual

Table 5.1: Overview of She Loves Me

<hr>

ACT 1

1. Exterior of Maraczek's Parfumerie, midsummer.
    "Good Morning, Good Day" (Clerks)
2. Interior of the Parfumerie.
    "Sounds While Selling" (Clerks, Customers)
    "Thank You, Madam" (Clerks)
    "Days Gone By" (Maraczek)
    "Thank You, Madam" (reprise) (Clerks)
    "No More Candy" (Amalia)
    "Thank You, Madam" (reprise) (Maraczek, Clerks)
3. Georg at his writing desk.
    "Three Letters" (Georg)
4. Exterior of the Parfumerie.
    "Three Letters" continues (Georg, Amalia)
5. Interior of the Parfumerie, early December.
    "Tonight at Eight" (Georg)
6. Workroom of the Parfumerie.
    "I Don't Know His Name" (Amalia, Ilona)
7. Interior of the Parfumerie.
    "Perspective" (Sipos)
    "Thank You, Madam" (reprise) (Clerks)
8. Workroom of the Parfumerie.
9. Interior of the Parfumerie.
    "Goodbye, Georg" (Clerks, Customers)
10. Exterior of the Parfumerie.
    "Will He Like Me?" (Amalia)
11. Interior of the Parfumerie.
    "Ilona" (Kodaly, Sipos, Arpad)
    "I Resolve" (Ilona)
12. Exterior of the Parfumerie.
13. Interior of the Parfumerie.
14. Cafe Imperiale.
    "A Romantic Atmosphere" (*Maître d'*)
    "Tango Tragique" (Georg, Amalia, *Maître d'*)
    "Dear Friend" (Amalia)

ACT 2

1. A private room in a hospital, the next day.
    "Try Me" (Arpad)
    "Days Gone By" (reprise) (Maraczek)

(Continued)

Table 5.1: (Continued)

---

2. Amalia's bedroom.
    "Where's My Shoe?" (Amalia, Georg)
    "Ice Cream" (Amalia)
3. A park.
    "She Loves Me" (Georg)
4. Maraczek's office.
    "A Trip to the Library" (Ilona)
5. Interior of the Parfumerie.
    "Thank You, Madam" (reprise) (Clerks)
    "Grand Knowing You" (Kodaly)
6. Exterior of the Parfumerie.
    "Twelve Days to Christmas" (Carolers)
    "Thank You, Madam" (reprise) (Customers)
7. Interior of the Parfumerie, Christmas Eve.
    "Thank You, Madam" (reprise) (Clerks, Customers, Carolers)
8. Exterior of the Parfumerie.
    "Ice Cream" (reprise) (Georg, Amalia)

---

stranger, "I Don't Know His Name," this helps make a connection between Georg and Amalia, even though neither character is yet aware that they are amorous pen pals. Ilona adds skeptical contrapuntal interjections in the last section of the song ("Supposing he snores like a locomotive? / Supposing he grinds his teeth? / Supposing he's a knuckle-cracker?"), but by the end is starting to think it might work out anyway ("How I could have used / One long revealing letter"). Amalia's insecurities are laid bare later in Act 1, in a touching ballad, "Will He Like Me?" Similarly, the secondary love story is developed in Act 1 by Kodaly's sleazy come-on to his sometime lover, "Ilona," followed shortly thereafter by her promise to have higher aspirations, "I Resolve." Act 1 ends with Amalia's brutal speech to Georg, to which he can only respond by exiting the restaurant, and Amalia's expression of heartbreak in her poignant slow waltz, "Dear Friend." Here Bock follows waltz models he has used frequently, arriving at the climactic VI chord in the last phrase ("Don't break my **heart**") just as he had done in "'Til Tomorrow" and "Artificial Flowers" and "My Miss Mary." In fact the melodies of both "Dear Friend" and "'Til Tomorrow" are saturated with exactly the same four-note rhythmic motive.

In Act 2 we hear the show's first duet between Georg and Amalia, "Where's My Shoe?," a frenetic number when she is threatening to return to work while Georg is encouraging her to stay home. This song, as Ethan Mordden observes, "isn't about what it thinks it's about. . . . It's actually Georg's first chance to get his hands on Amalia."[35] Their emerging affection is vividly portrayed by rapid exchanges of disparate phrases (Amalia: "Where's my shoe?"; Georg: "You shouldn't be on your feet," and so forth) that eventually come together in harmony at the ends of the choruses (Amalia's "My right shoe" in parallel sixths with Georg's "Back to bed!"). And later in the second act, just before the Christmas sequence, Kodaly says goodbye in a song dripping with sarcasm, "Grand Knowing You." This comes shortly after Ilona's "A Trip to the Library" and so makes a pairing of songs within the secondary love story that balances the pairing of "Ilona" and "I Resolve" in Act 1.

The series of songs and scenes has an especially compelling structure and shape, a sense of puzzle pieces coming together with maximal dramatic impact and emotional resonance. Because of such sequences, *She Loves Me* has earned a reputation as a "perfect musical," a label first affixed by John Simon in 1993: "The creators of *She Loves Me* have fashioned the perfect intimate musical. (Perfect? Yes, damn it, perfect.)"[36] The sense of "perfection" is especially strong in the second act, with its succession of Georg and Amalia's duet "Where's My Shoe?," Amalia's "Ice Cream," Georg's "She Loves Me," Ilona's "A Trip to the Library," and Kodaly's "Grand Knowing You," followed by the crescendo built into "Twelve Days to Christmas" and, finally, Amalia's climactic epiphany, woven into a reprise of "Ice Cream." Masteroff explains: "It's just a progression of songs, all of which move the plot forward, all of which involve a main character, and all of them terrific songs." Each number is indispensable to the development of the character singing it, whose personality it perfectly captures with every melodic phrase and lyrical nuance. Each song strikes just the right emotional chord and uses up just the right amount of space in the development of the story. It is a musical and a dramatic progression of uncommon artistry.

Motivic Threads and Ethnic Markers

The integration of music with drama has other dimensions as well. In the opening of Act 1, for example, the first notes of "Good Morning, Good Day" announce primary motivic ideas for this song and others (Example 5.1a). It begins with the three notes of the B major tonic triad in order, with the fifth in the lower octave ("Good morn-ing. Good"), followed by a step up to the sixth scale degree G♯ ("day"). Then we hear a series of stepwise scale segments moving up and then down ("How are you this beautiful day?"). As the song unfolds we hear these motives again and again, the triadic figure announcing a new beginning, the scalar figure playfully winding around as if searching for a convenient place to rest. When a scale segment finally does reach completion on a tonic note, it is on Georg's phrase "Let's all run away."

a. "Good Morning, Good Day," mm. 1–2 (over a B-F♯ ostinato)

b. "Sounds While Selling," mm. 1–4

c. "Thank You, Madam"

Example 5.1: Shared musical ideas in the first three songs of She Loves Me

The immediate segue from "Good Morning, Good Day" into the second song helps highlight a connection: "Sounds While Selling" also begins with a triadic figure (Example 5.1b). This time the tonic note E is decorated with a double-neighbor turning figure ("I would like to see"), followed by the lower fifth and upper third ("a face"). The ensuing stepwise figure ("But we carry—") is another double-neighbor figure, the first of many variants of this song's opening gesture. Complementing, in a way complicating, the motivic interconnections is the strategy of constantly moving melodic fragments among different singing voices (akin to the "hocket" technique in Medieval music), with humorous results. (In Example 5.1b, typically, three characters contribute elements to the composite sentence "I would like to see a face like yours cracked.") The shopping spree reaches a fever pitch in an unaccompanied madrigal-like section where the customers contrapuntally exchange motives, mostly the triad with double-neighbor decoration from the opening bar ("What have I forgotten," and so forth).

"Sounds While Selling" ends with an immediate segue to the first instance of "Thank You, Madam" (Example 5.1c). This refrain starts with four notes on a vibraphone—resembling a door-opening signal—and then the clerks sing in four-part parallel harmony. The effect is striking because it is the first time we have heard the characters sing together in harmony; until now they have sung together only in unison or in dialogue. As the show progresses we hear this refrain several more times, at first sung by clerks, later by customers (with slightly different text), and its impact is always striking, often artfully disruptive to the dramatic flow. The rhythm of the refrain emulates speech and places an agogic accent on "do," in the way an ingratiating clerk might give extra emphasis to this word when speaking that phrase. The parallel movement of voices, at first by distances that are mostly within an E major scale (with chromatic inflections, notably the Mixolydian lowered seventh), then at the end by half-step distances, also projects an ingratiating air, as if the clerks are being excessively friendly. Each chord in the refrain is the same: a major triad with added sixth. It is, in other words, another variation on the opening of "Good Morning, Good Day," the first five notes of which (B-B-D♯-F♯-G♯) also present a triad with added sixth (Example 5.1a).

The added-sixth chord can be formed in different ways: the introduction to "Thank You, Madam" shows a nontriadic conception (Example 5.1c). These four vibraphone notes serve one important purpose, to give the singers their pitches, but they also demonstrate how the added-sixth chord can be broken down into two perfect fifths, between steps 1 and 5 of the scale (E and B in the lower staff) and between steps 6 and 3 (C♯ and G♯ in the upper). As we hear these four notes whenever "Thank You, Madam" returns throughout the show, they grow to function as a musical mooring, elevating the added-sixth chord to a kind of "tonic" status for the score. (At one point Bock and Harnick considered having the four notes sung by the clerks, on the words "good day thank you."[37]) This sense is then strengthened by the other prominent instances of this chord type in the score, and by the related instances of interaction between the sixth scale step and the fifth step as the upper tone of a tonic major triad. In some songs the sixth step is simply a stopping point for melodic gestures, as it is at the beginning of "Good Morning, Good Day" (the G♯'s in Example 5.1a). A phrase in the middle section of "Days Gone By," for example, comes to rest on step 6 on the words "Around, around, around."

But in several very prominent places the sixth step carries more dramatic heft. The main melody of "Will He Like Me?" moves back and forth between steps 5 and 6 in the key of G, as if unable to decide whether or not to stay in the main triad of the key, reflecting Amalia's insecurity (Example 5.2a). Amalia's "Dear Friend" ends with an instrumental melody that comes to rest on step 6 (B♭ within a D♭ major triad), making the major triad plus added sixth the last sound heard before the curtain falls on Act 1 (Example 5.2b). By the time we get to "Ice Cream," the turning point of Amalia's feelings in Act 2, her melody is no longer unsure about the role of step 6: now it is decisively a decoration to step 5 (Example 5.2c). Indeed the interplay of steps 6 and 5 (C♯ and B in E major) dominates the first few phrases of this melody, first encircling 5 with upper and lower neighbors ("Ice cream, he brought me ice cream, vanilla ice cream, imagine"), then coming to rest on 6 (on "Imagine **that**"), which is also decorated by upper and lower neighbors ("Ice cream, and for the first time, we were together without a spat!"), followed by a return to 5 and its upper and lower neighbors ("Friendly, he was so friendly, that isn't like him, I'm simply"), and a final arrival on 6 ("stunned!"). When this song segues into "She Loves Me," Georg gets into the act, first with 5–6–5 (E♭–F–E♭) gestures in the key of A♭ in the opening phrases (Example 5.2d: "and to my amazement," "knowing that she loves me"). These whole steps, and the whole steps between scale steps 2 and 1 ("she **loves me**"), take over Amalia's focus on that interval from the preceding number. Then in the big finish of "She Loves Me" Georg belts out a sixth step (F) for four full measures (one with a fermata) within an added-sixth chord (Example 5.2e). Later, in the show's final scene, after Georg finally reveals the true identity of Dear Friend, we hear the recurrent scale-step interplay one last time, with the words "Dear Friend" now replacing "Ice Cream" on steps 6 and 5.

The double-neighbor, or turning motions in "Ice Cream" ("Ice cream, he brought me ice cream," and so forth) call attention to another prominent element in the *She Loves Me* score. We first hear this kind of neighboring figure in the main melody of "Sounds While Selling," surrounding step 1 in E major ("I would like to see" in Example 5.1b). Later, in the scene in the Cafe Imperiale, turning figures surround step 5 in E minor with half-step neighbors on steps 6 and ♯4. This happens both in the melody of "A Romantic Atmosphere" (Example 5.3a) and in the dances for the waiters (Example 5.3b). In the latter instance the turning figure carries "Hungarian" connotations, in keeping with the setting of the original play. As Jack Gottlieb has observed, this turning figure, in his words a "seductive swivel," is a "cliché in Slavic and Russian-Gypsy music."[38] More generally, it is a signature gesture of what has been named *style hongrois*, the method of cultural reference practiced by

Example 5.2: Scale-step 6 in She Loves Me

a. "A Romantic Atmosphere," first phrase

b. "A Romantic Atmosphere," three bars from a dance tune

Example 5.3: Scale-step 6 in chromatic double neighbors in She Loves Me

many Western European composers, including Haydn, Beethoven, and Schubert, probably best-known via Brahms's Hungarian Dances and Liszt's Hungarian Rhapsodies.[39] The main features of the *style hongrois* also include imitations of native instruments and distinctive rhythmic patterns. Bock has said that he knows this music well and certainly drew inspiration from it. He surely also got ideas from Werner R. Heyman's soundtrack for the Lubitsch film, which features the chromatic turning figures of the Russian-Gypsy ballad "Otchi Chorniya" (Example 5.4a). We hear this melody coming from the cigarette/candy box in the film, and it is also played by the orchestra in the cafe scene. The film in fact opens with the orchestra playing two turning motives derived from this tune, before proceeding to a lilting melody in F major that includes a diatonic version of the turning figure (bracketed in Example 5.4b).

Bock's employment of the *style hongrois* opens a window into a broader consideration of the nature and roots of his compositional palette. He has Hungarian heritage: an early biographer, who interviewed him, wrote that his father was a "salesman of Hungarian background."[40] He told another interviewer that he is a "Russian-Hungarian-German Jew, mostly Russian."[41] Some of his stylistic fingerprints reflect these roots. A Hungarian musical pedigree may help explain, for example, his general affection for the raised fourth scale degree, described by Jonathan Bellman as a common feature of melodies in the *style hongrois*.[42] This would help tie together the Hungarian setting of *She Loves Me* with melodies (in various styles) featuring ♯4 at several spots in the score, including many chromatic neighboring figures (Examples 5.2c, 5.3a, 5.3b), but also including melodies with a prominent raised fourth that is not part of a turning gesture. (There are many examples of this in the score; the G♮ in the main melody of "Dear Friend," excerpted in Example 5.2b, is a very prominent one.) From these connections follows a broader association between Bock's Hungarian heritage and the raised fourth degree throughout his work (e.g., Examples 1.1b, 1.2a, 2.1a, 2.2, 3.2, 3.3a, 3.3b). The tonal basis of such melodies may be either a harmonic minor scale with

a. "Otchi Chorniya"

b. Overture melody

Example 5.4: Chromatic double neighbors in The Shop Around the Corner

raised fourth degree, also known as a "Gypsy Scale," or the major scale with the Lydian raised fourth. Both can be considered resources for *style hongrois* melodies, although the minor version is more common.[43]

In *She Loves Me*, the music is the main contextualizing factor. The characters' names are intended to suggest Hungarian heritage, but otherwise no dialogue or stage direction situates the action in a specific city or culture. The published libretto only places the action in "a city in Europe" in the 1930s.[44] Bock's overture sets the tone, with newly composed Hungarian-scented cadenzas in the accordion and violin; later, the most concentrated and sustained moments of *style hongrois* occur in the Cafe Imperiale scene. In the company of these vivid cultural references, similar musical figures throughout the score, in songs of diverse styles, may connect with the Hungarian elements, or at least serve as musical reminders of the show's cultural milieu. These can include the chromatic double neighboring heard in the introduction to, and then throughout, "Where's My Shoe?" (Example 5.5a), as well as diatonic turning figures in "Sounds While Selling" ("I would like to see" in Example 5.1b), "Perspective" (Example 5.5b), "A Trip to the Library" (Example 5.5c), and other songs. Surely this was one thing Bock had in mind when he told an interviewer in 1979 that the key to, or guiding principle of, the *She Loves Me* score is "Hungarian":

> The word "Hungarian." And that is, you know, very general, mind you, but it gave me a sound, a shape, a period, and a feeling, that I began to string melodic notions and guesses around that kind of instinct. Europeans, particularly Hungarians. Not that all the songs are Hungarian, but that gave me a platform from which to take off.[45]

a. "Where's My Shoe?," first vocal phrase

b. "Perspective," contrasting melody within main verse

c. "A Trip to the Library," first phrase

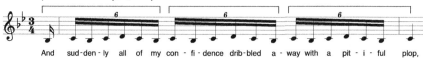

Example 5.5: Other double-neighbor figures in She Loves Me

When *She Loves Me* opened its pre-Broadway tour in New Haven on March 16, 1963, many of the score's most appealing moments were already in place, with just a few remaining to be written. Songs that had been in the libretto since its earliest versions include "Good Morning, Good Day," "No More Candy," and "Will He Like Me?"[46] Bock and Harnick had written "Days Gone By" for their first choice in the role of Maraczek, Broadway veteran Luther Adler, although Adler decided not to take the part.[47] (They would, however, work with him a few years later, as he went on to play Tevye in *Fiddler on the Roof*, on Broadway and on tour.) The New Haven program also included "Sounds While Selling," "Thank You, Madam," "Tonight at Eight," "I Don't Know His Name," "She Loves Me," "A Trip to the Library," and most of the other stalwarts of the score. By the time the tour arrived in Philadelphia, opening on March 26, they had added "Ilona" and "Ice Cream." Harnick remembers having had the idea for "Ice Cream" much earlier but not knowing exactly how to execute it until he watched the scene play before an audience.[48] It replaced the song "The Touch of Magic," which was another musical conceptualization of a Maseroff monologue; when that song came out, the monologue went back in.[49]

They made several cuts because the show was just too long. Songs were working, but members of the creative team felt that they were asking the audience to "absorb so much music." Harnick observed in 1994: "With the current kind of wall-to-wall music show, they don't use that many songs. They use a lot of motifs. So you're not constantly introduced to new stuff. But we kept throwing new themes at them."[50] While the show was in Philadelphia they cut "Hello Love," which Maraczek sang while on the phone with his wife, and "Christmas Eve," sung by Maraczek and his employees near the end of Act 2; they re-used the "Hello, Love" material as transitional music for scene changes.[51] One of the more painful deletions may have been Amalia's "Tell Me I Look Nice," a sophisticated 5/4 number that was said to be a favorite of Stephen Sondheim's.[52] (This is no surprise: it has the freshness and wit of a Sondheim song.) Also in Philadelphia they tried a number, "Seasonal Changes," to show the passage of time from summer to winter in Act 1 but eventually simplified the matter with the song "Three Letters."[53] And it was during this time that they added the reprise of "Ice Cream," retexted as "Dear Friend," to the end of the show, replacing a reprise of "No More Candy." One of their boldest, ultimately wisest, changes was to replace the song "My Drug Store" (sometimes called "My North American Drug Store") that Kodaly had been singing to say goodbye near the end of Act 2.[54] Jack Cassidy, who had first introduced Bock and Harnick to each other in 1956, was stopping the show with the song nightly, but the songwriters felt that "it was diversionary. It wasn't really a character song, the kind of character song that everybody else had."[55] It was also mean-spirited, with a basic message of spite and vengeance against the store and co-workers Kodaly was now leaving. The new song, "Grand Knowing You," has Kodaly saying goodbye in a sarcastic, grandiose tone that is more consistent with his character. Cassidy at first resisted the change but agreed to give it a try and was soon charming the audience just as much with the new song.[56]

The Show and Its Legacy

The reaction of the New York critics, after *She Loves Me* opened at the Eugene O'Neill Theater on April 23, 1963, was effusive. Reviewers dusted off some of their most fulsome superlatives for the occasion. (Walter Kerr's dissenting voice in the *Herald Tribune* [4/24/63] was essentially outshouted.[57]) John Chapman in the *Daily News* (4/24/63) found the show "so charming, so deft, so light, and so right, that it makes all the other music-shows in the big Broadway shops look like clodhoppers." Howard Taubman wrote in the *Times* (4/24/63) that "a bonbon of a musical is on display, and it should delight who knows how many a sweet tooth. . . . You keep thinking that you cannot digest an array of desserts, no matter how attractive and tasty they are, but you find yourself relishing nearly all of them in *She Loves Me*." Richard P. Cooke in the *Wall Street Journal* (4/25/63) found "substance and flavor not often discovered in such entertainments. . . . It is as nice a dish of its kind as a theatergoer is likely to get for a long time." "With a full and happy heart, may I tell the good, good word," wrote Norman Nadel in the *World Telegram* (4/24/63): "this theater season finally has a musical play with which everyone can fall in love." Whitney Bolton in the *Morning Telegraph* (4/25/63) wanted to put it "under a glass bell and look at [it] with pleasure for a long time." The score, wrote Martin Gottfried in *Women's Wear Daily* (4/24/63), consists of "a whole batch of lovely, lovely songs that are original, singable, and completely integrated into the action." *She Loves Me*, in the estimation of John McClain of the *Journal American* (4/24/63), was "here to stay."

And yet it closed relatively soon, on January 11, 1964, after 302 performances, recouping only a small portion of its $300,000 investment. What happened? Many believe that *She Loves Me* was a victim of its times, that it was, in Harold Prince's words, a "soft-sell" show in an era of the "noisy, heavy-sell musical."[58] Joe Masteroff remembers hearing comments from *She Loves Me* audience members like "Oh, wasn't that cute! That was darling!" But, he laments, "cute and darling doesn't really work"; the show "doesn't have balls enough." In Clive Barnes's view, "Broadway embraced the wiseguy strutting of Damon Runyon and Walter Winchell, and in the naive yet brash New World, the original *She Loves Me* seemed like a nostalgic Old World refugee."[59] Edward Sothern Hipp asked: "What is there about the economics of Broadway that seems to make it impossible for a tuneful, wholesome, and unpretentious offering to compete with the blockbusters?"[60] In the spring of 1963 audiences were flocking to shows like *Oliver!*, which had opened in January; *A Funny Thing Happened on the Way to the Forum*, then finishing its first year; *How to Succeed in Business Without Really Trying*, well into its second year; and *The Sound of Music*, which was nearing the end of its three-and-a-half-year first run. An intimate show with a small cast, no chorus, and only a smattering of dancing could not compete.

Harold Prince has voiced additional theories. He wrote in his 1974 memoir that the theater where it played, the Eugene O'Neill, was too small to generate sufficient box-office receipts. He acknowledged that the O'Neill was aesthetically ideal for this show, and that "there is a kind of play that needs an intimate theater," but *She Loves Me* "would have played equally well in a theater half again as large."[61] This has often been a point of contention between Bock, Harnick, and producers. They feel that the show is "comfortable in a smaller house" and gets "lost" in larger ones, as Harnick witnessed in a large theater in Los Angeles in 1987. They have declined to license productions of the show in large theaters, most notably an offer by the New York City Opera for a production in the cavernous New York State Theater.[62] For Prince, the kind of intimacy that Bock and Harnick seem to require "exists only Off-Broadway or in the Booth Theater," although it is "common to England and the Continent." Prince wrote: "I know of nothing that could not be trans-ferred painlessly from a six hundred seat house to a twelve hundred seat house."[63]

Prince also blames casting decisions for the financially disastrous first run. The production team had originally offered the role of Amalia to Julie Andrews, who was a proven Broadway commodity from her Tony-nominated performances as Eliza Doolittle in *My Fair Lady* (1956) and Guenevere in *Cam-elot* (1960). Andrews wanted to play Amalia but was busy filming *The Ameri-canization of Emily* at the time and asked if the opening could be delayed until the fall. Prince believes that the show "might have run three years" if they had waited the six months.[64] Even so, the actor ultimately chosen for the part, Barbara Cook, could not have been any less brilliant, as Bock and Har-nick have been quick to point out.[65] Cook had already proven herself on Broadway, in leading roles in *Flahooley* (1951), *Plain and Fancy* (1955), and *Can-dide* (1956), and had a won a Supporting Actress Tony for her portrayal of Marian Paroo in *The Music Man* (1957). Nor were Cook's castmates any less capable or distinguished. Daniel Massey, playing Georg, was the son of actors Raymond Massey and Adrianne Allen who would go on to be a prominent figure in the Royal Shakespeare Company and Royal National Theater. Lud-wig Donath, playing Maraczek, had acted extensively on European stages before the Second World War and in American films since fleeing the Nazis in 1940. The cast also included Barbara Baxley (Ilona), who had trained at the Actors Studio under Elia Kazan and received a Tony nomination for Tennes-see Williams's *Period of Adjustment* in 1961; Nathaniel Frey (Sipos), a familiar face from the cast of *Fiorello!*; and, of course, Jack Cassidy, playing the kind of part that he would go on to play often and well for the rest of his career on stage, television, and film.

Whether or not a marquee name would have helped at the box office, *She Loves Me* may simply have been a victim of its own fluffy reviews. Critics expressed their affections using confectionary metaphors: they called the show a "bonbon" (Taubman, *New York Times* 4/24/63), a "rich plum cake" (George Oppenheimer, *Newsday* 5/1/63), and a "delicious pastry decorated with won-derful, intricate dabs and curls of musical frosting" (John Chapman, *Daily News* 4/24/63), telling a "warm, appealing story dripping of sentimentality like

Barbara Cook (Amalia), Gino Conforti (Violinist), and Daniel Massey (Georg) in SheLoves Me *(1963) (Photofest)*

a chocolate drop" (Leonard Hoffman, *Hollywood Reporter* 4/24/63), "filled with all the rich Mittel-European pastry-stuffing of a bygone day" (Henry Hewes, *Saturday Review* 5/11/63). They gave the impression that the show was light and frothy, lacking dramatic or artistic substance. In fact the show's genuine appeal comes from its sophistication, from the richness of musical invention, the vividness of characterization, and the close integration of music and drama. Potential ticket-buyers for this type of show may have been turned away by the nature of the critical reception. Such an audience pool is limited anyway, as Harnick has observed: "[*She Loves Me*] has immense appeal for very sophisticated theater-goers, and for very sensitive people. Once we begin to run out of those, the show goes downhill."[66]

The critical outpouring also helped obscure another key facet of *She Loves Me*: it has a dark side. What Avery Corman wrote of the Lubitsch film also holds true for the musical adaptation:

> For all the romance, harsh reality is never far away. People are desperate for work, desperate for love, manipulative. There is a betrayal, an attempted

suicide. When the movie was released, the refined Mitteleuropa of the 1930s was being destroyed by World War II. Lubitsch, a director who had come to America from Europe, suggests darkness in all the corners of the piece.[67]

Joe Masteroff was closely attuned to these shadows:

> I was always fascinated with the thought that the show took place about 1938, and I said in two years a lot of the people are going to be dead, or their lives totally ruined, and it fascinated me. It gave the material such another twist that there was always that underlying darkness. And maybe some of the cynicism in the script came from that.[68]

The film takes a gloomier tone than the musical, but they both have darker layers running deeper than their main love stories. Reviewers and audiences—and producers and directors—too easily overlook these elements in a show whose most famous song celebrates a frozen dessert.

It probably did not matter that *She Loves Me* premiered too late for the 1963 Tony Awards and was considered instead the following year, well after it had closed. The competition was formidable both years, from big productions that were drawing all the crowds: *A Funny Thing Happened on the Way to the Forum* (eight nominations, six wins, including one for producer Harold Prince) and *Oliver!* (ten nominations, three wins) in 1963, and *Hello, Dolly!* (eleven nominations, ten wins) and *Funny Girl* (eight nominations) in 1964. Still *She Loves Me* received nominations in 1964 for its book, director, producer, and for Best Musical, and Jack Cassidy won the Tony for Supporting or Featured Actor in a Musical, giving *Hello, Dolly!* (Charles Nelson Reilly) its only defeat out of eleven nominations.

The disappointments continued when the first London production of *She Loves Me*, premiering in April 1964, was even less successful than the original. This version of the show featured a new song, "Heads I Win," in place of "I Resolve," for the Ilona character, played by Rita Moreno. Harnick believes that it was Prince's idea to make the substitution, which made sense at the time but did not become permanent. The production was directed by Julie Andrews's husband, Tony Walton, but again did not star Andrews, who was busy making movies. Walton has suggested, only half in jest, that the show suffered at that time from confusion with the Beatles song "She Loves You," which was then dominating the airwaves on both sides of the Atlantic.[69] The production closed after 189 performances.

Efforts to produce a film version of *She Loves Me* began in 1967, when MGM pledged support for an adaptation directed by Harold Prince and starring Julie Andrews, who remained eager to play Amalia.[70] Initial plans imagined something quite different from the stage musical, possibly with a different title and some new songs. This is evident in notes Bock made, dated November 17, 1967, summarizing three new song possibilities: "Every Girl's Dream," to be sung by Amalia after she convinces Maraczek to employ her in his shop; "Today's the Day," perhaps a duet sung by Georg and Amalia in cut-away shots from one home to another; and "My Wonderful World," for Maraczek on his way to work.[71] (In his notes Bock indicates that the role of Maraczek would be played by Maurice Chevalier.) An extant screenplay for this version from 1968, of unknown authorship, is actually much closer to Raphaelson's screenplay for the Lubitsch film than Masteroff's original libretto is. It essentially uses the Raphaelson script as a starting point and then inserts songs from the musical at appropriate places.[72] Masteroff has no recollection of producing this draft—nor does he recall who did—although he did write another version (undated) that also reads like a very close adaptation of Raphaelson, but without new songs.[73]

After a period of Hollywood indifference and neglect, Blake Edwards, who had recently married Julie Andrews after her split with Tony Walton, stepped in and wrote a third version of the screenplay, again using the Raphaelson version as a starting point, and without new songs.[74] MGM committed itself to the project in August 1969, with Edwards directing.[75] Harnick remembers a meeting from that time that offered encouraging signs:

> I had gone out to California to meet with Michael Kidd, who was supposed to do choreography, and Blake Edwards. They showed me the mock-up of the part of Hungary they were going to film in. I met with Julie. And on the way back to the airport, before I left, I asked Blake, "Is there any chance of this falling through?" He said, "With Julie Andrews, not a chance."[76]

Not long after he returned to New York, however, he learned that MGM was under new management and revisiting some of its commitments. The *She Loves Me* film, which had been budgeted for ten million dollars, was canceled.[77]

The musical was never able to benefit from the publicity it might have received from a Hollywood feature film. And yet John McClain was right: *She Loves Me* was here to stay. Fans and critics who are resistant to the lure of the show-biz extravaganza have always cherished its warmth and humanity, its elegant integration of song and story. An early indication of its potential for longevity came when the original cast album, a two-record set, won the Grammy Award for Best Score From An Original Cast Album in 1963. Then in the years after its premiere the show began to develop a following among regional and academic theater groups who had mounted successful productions, presumably in small, intimate venues. Bock and Harnick gradually began receiving letters of appreciation from some of these groups, with messages like: "We don't understand why the show had such a short run on Broadway. We love it. We think it's wonderful, and our audiences love it."[78] It became a "cult show," appreciated by a small group of passionate cognoscenti. It came back to New York in modest productions by the Equity Library Theater in 1969 and by the York Players in 1976, and began to emerge into the mainstream with high-profile limited runs at Town Hall in 1977 (a concert version, starring Madeline Kahn and Barry Bostwick) and at the Goodspeed Opera House in Connecticut in 1978. Also in 1978 the BBC aired an abbreviated version (with the creators' blessings) that was well received and critically acclaimed. This is not a cinematic adaptation but essentially a film of the stage musical, with bits of dialogue converted to British idioms, "Will He Like Me?" relocated later in Act 1 and set in Amalia's home, and some strategic cuts to trim the show's length (notably the songs "Days Gone By," "Goodbye, Georg," and the opening [tango] section of "Tango Tragique"). The show remained alive in New York in the 1980s in a second production by the Equity Library Theater (1985) and in a production by the Opera Ensemble of New York (1989).

Finally in 1993 *She Loves Me* celebrated its thirtieth birthday with a Broadway revival by the Roundabout Theater Company, starring Boyd Gaines and Judy Kuhn and directed by Scott Ellis. Gaines won the Tony for Best Actor in a Musical, and the production received eight other nominations. Again the critics gushed forth ready-made advertising copy. Frank Rich called it a "continuously melodic evening of sheer enchantment and complete escape" (*New York Times*, 6/11/93). Clive Barnes found it "magical and faultless (faultlessly magical, magically faultless—Polonius himself would be at a loss for words if not enthusiasm)" (*New York Post*, 6/11/93). For William A. Henry III it was "a 2 1/2-hour nonstop smile punctuated by laughter and a lacing of sentimental tears" (*Time*, 6/21/93). Of the changes made for this production, the most important was the removal of "Tango Tragique" from the scene at the Cafe Imperiale: Harnick came to feel that it "took too long to say what it had to say."[79] Bock agreed to the change, on the condition that they restore a verse to "Dear Friend" that had been eliminated in 1963.[80] When this production moved to London in 1994, "Tango Tragique" was back in, but the "Dear Friend" verse stayed as well. The London cast virtually swept the Laurence Olivier Awards in 1995, winning for Best Musical Revival, Best Direction of a Musical (Scott Ellis), Best Actor in a Musical (John Gordon Sinclair), Best Actress in a Musical (Ruthie Henshall), and Best Supporting Performance in a Musical (Tracie Bennett, playing Ilona).

No longer a cult show, *She Loves Me* has finally established itself as one of the most artful and imaginative American musicals, as tuneful and colorful as Rodgers and Hammerstein, as musically rich and sophisticated as the best of Bernstein or Loesser. For its creators, *She Loves Me* has finally provided the kind of satisfaction that unaccountably eluded them during its initial Broadway run. They have even dared to speak of it in the same breath as some of their subsequent work that was more commercially successful. Harold Prince, one of the most acclaimed producer-directors in Broadway history, wrote in 1974 that *She Loves Me* was "one of the best things this office has done, and as far as I'm concerned, it's as well directed as anything I've ever done."[81] Joe Masteroff, whose subsequent show, *Cabaret*, would win the Tony for Best Musical in 1967 (with Prince co-producing), remarked in 1994: "All of us went on right from *She Loves Me* to do enormously successful gold mines of musicals, and yet, speaking for myself and I think for Jerry and Sheldon, *She Loves Me* is the one that really is closest to our hearts." Listening to Masteroff make this comment during a three-way interview, Bock and Harnick agreed, although Harnick quickly added, "Along with *Fiddler*, I have to say."[82] *She Loves Me* and *Fiddler on the Roof* have emerged as strikingly different but comparably compelling masterworks in the center of Bock and Harnick's seven-show corpus. *Fiddler* is the commanding presence whose scope and impact are bigger than itself. *She Loves Me* is the dear friend whose warm company never grows old.

BROADWAY LOVEFEST

After the opening of *She Loves Me* in April 1963, while returning to work on the Tevye materials leading up to the premiere of *Fiddler* in September 1964, Bock and Harnick also found time for one smaller project. It began with a commission to provide musical continuity and new material for a Las-Vegas-style Broadway spectacular at the 1964 World's Fair, hosted by the Texas Pavilion. The show was produced by George Schaefer, who had directed *The Body Beautiful*, with financial backing from Angus G. Wynne, Jr., a Texas real-estate magnate who had recently opened the Six Flags Over Texas amusement park near Dallas. Morton Da Costa, known for staging *Plain and Fancy* (1955) and *The Music Man* (1957), among other Broadway musicals, directed. The show was a ninety-minute whirlwind tour through the history of the American musical called *To Broadway with Love*.

Bock and Harnick surely appreciated the irony of turning their attentions from a show that was defined by its intimacy to one that was boldly, ostentatiously extravagant. Not only was *To Broadway with Love* a much larger theatrical event than *She Loves Me*, it easily out-glitzed even the most lavish Broadway musical. Two rotating casts of seventy-five actor-singer-dancers played three shows a day, seven days a week, on a 186-foot stage—86 feet wider than that of Radio City Music Hall—in a newly built, specially designed 2500-seat auditorium on the grounds of the World's Fair. Flashy costumes and parades of dancers and chorus lines presented production number after production number, taken from shows throughout Broadway history, starting with Stephen Foster and minstrelsy, progressing through vaudeville and operetta, and touching on major book musicals of the 1940s and '50s. Each era was introduced by a movie montage projected on a large screen. Bock and Harnick wrote the show's opening and closing numbers, some transitional music, and six other original songs.[83] They only contributed the requested original material and did not participate in conceptualizing or planning the rest of the show, which consisted of excerpts from the *Ziegfeld Follies* ("Would You Rather Be a Colonel"), *Kiss Me, Kate* ("Another Op'nin', Another Show"), *Annie Get Your Gun* ("There's No Business Like Show Business"), *South Pacific* ("Bali Ha'i"), and other Broadway signposts.

This commission allowed Bock and Harnick to write the kind of material that they had made their trademark: stylized parodies and witty evocations. Their opening number "To Broadway with Love," also used as the Finale, is a syncopated, up-tempo attention-grabber, in the mold of Cole Porter's "Another Op'nin', Another Show" and reminiscent of Bock's song "1617 Broadway" from *Mr. Wonderful*. When the historical survey moves through the Ziegfeld era, their song "Beautiful Lady" calls to mind Irving Berlin's "A Pretty Girl Is Like a Melody," originally from the *Ziegfeld Follies* of 1919.[84] Harnick's ideal of beauty is not a melody but a bird: "Beautiful lady, it just occurred to me / Beautiful lady, you're like a bird to me." Bock's music breathes life into all the clichés of the era, a familiar exercise from his work on the scores for *Fiorello!* and *Tenderloin*, but the harmony here is even more saturated with fifths progressions, and he milks every last drop of schmaltz from the climactic VI chord in the last phrase, on the last word of the line "I would love to build a beautiful nest with you." Thomas Thompson, reviewing the production in *Life* magazine, colorfully captured the poetry of the spectacle:

> Waves of beauties, awash in turquoise ostrich plumes, pour over a staircase in a Niagara of loveliness. Other girls, gilded and gorgeous, come sailing on in flying birdcages. One stunning creature, wearing very little at all, commands her attendants to affix a richly sequined cape which

Company members in To Broadway With Love *(1964): from left, Jane Zachary, Barbara Swisher, Shirley de Burgh, Bradford Craig (Billy Rose Theater Division, The New York Public Library for the Performing Arts, Astor, Lennox, and Tilden Foundations)*

then grows and grows, as it unrolls behind her, until it seems to billow over a full half acre of stage. Wow! Flo himself could not have staged it better.[85]

The largest concentration of Bock and Harnick songs came near the end of the show, when the panorama turned toward the Broadway of the future. In "Mata Hari Mine" they wonder what a song from a musical about Mata Hari might sound like, citing other recent biographical musicals such as *Fiorello!*, *Gypsy*, *The Sound of Music*, and *Funny Girl*. In "Remember Radio" they reminisce about the golden era of radio, taking a cue from recent nostalgic shows such as *Hello, Dolly!*, *The Music Man*, *Take Me Along*, and *Wish You Were Here*. Their last song before the Finale is "Popsicles in Paris," a commentary on societal changes in the Jet Age. Because innovations in transportation and communication have made cultures so much more accessible to each other, the song says, we can now have

Popsicles in Paris
Shish kebab in Shanghai
Sweet potato pie in Rome;

Crackerjack in Cairo
Curry in Caracas
Alka-Seltzer back at home.[86]

Bock's music of the future is a stylish jazz waltz traveling around the circle of fifths (circling the globe?) counter-clockwise, as he had done in the bridges of "Where Do I Go From Here?" (*Fiorello!*) and "Tommy, Tommy" (*Tenderloin*). Here the movements around the circle are even more extensive than in those earlier songs, involving more chords and occurring in both the verse and bridge sections. In fact, the progression in "Popsicles in Paris" is almost exactly like that of a more recent effort, "No More Candy" from *She Loves Me*: both songs move from I to IV, ♭VII, ♭III, and ♭VI before returning to the dominant to set up the next phrase, and do so repeatedly.

To Broadway with Love was an enormous critical success after its formal opening on April 29, 1964.[87] Reviewers seemed almost surprised to be entertained by such a spectacle, but recognized that it accomplished what it set out to do. Howard Taubman in the *Times* (4/30/64) liked the combination of "nostalgia, corn, and fun." The *Newsweek* critic (5/11/64) found the show "surprisingly enjoyable, considering that it jams forty-one songs and twenty-eight lavish production numbers into ninety minutes." Lee Silver in the *Daily News* (4/30/64) called it a "whopping, affectionate valentine to the song and dance men and women who delighted the country and the composers and lyricists who created the words and music." For Bock and Harnick it was a loud, aggressively affectionate valentine, to complement the modest, gentle one they had given to Broadway a year earlier.

But they may have barely noticed when *To Broadway with Love* closed prematurely in late July, a victim of high costs, poor attendance, and mismanagement of resources.[88] In the year between the openings of *She Loves Me* and *To Broadway with Love*, and in the three months while the extravaganza was playing at the World's Fair, Bock and Harnick had focused most of their creative energies on the development of their next major musical, set for a Broadway premiere in September 1964. It was a project with great promise, but significant obstacles. They regarded it with both passion and apprehension. They had no inkling of how successful it might be, or what kind of impact it might have, on the world of Broadway or on the world at large.

6
TRADITION
• • •
FIDDLER ON THE ROOF

On July 21, 1971, when the curtain fell on the evening performance at the Broadway Theater, *Fiddler on the Roof* became the longest-running musical in Broadway history up to that time, its 2845 showings eclipsing a recent milestone by its former neighborhood rival, *Hello, Dolly!* Less than a year later, on June 17, 1972, *Fiddler* set the mark for Broadway shows of any kind, with 3225 performances surpassing a record held by *Life With Father* for some twenty-five years. By the time *Fiddler* finally closed in early July of that year, following its 3242nd consecutive performance, it had established a standard that would remain for another seven years, five months (until the performance of *Grease* on December 8, 1979) and had ignited an explosion of worldwide popularity that continues to this day. *Fiddler on the Roof* has been performed across the globe in many languages and at every level of theatrical endeavor, from school and amateur productions to major runs in London, Paris, Austria, South Africa, Australia, Tokyo, and Israel, copious national tours, and Broadway revivals in 1976, 1990, and 2004. The original Broadway production virtually swept the 1965 Tony Awards, while Norman Jewison's 1971 film was nominated for eight Oscars, winning three. Cast recordings have been released around the world, as have interpretations of songs from *Fiddler* by the likes of Cannonball Adderley (1964) and Gwen Stefani (2004). Critical accolades have flowed forth from every direction, and in 1999 *Fiddler on the Roof* placed ninth on the American Theater Critics Association's list of "twenty-five significant American musicals of the twentieth century."[1]

What is it about this show? How has a story with such specific ethnic themes, exploring issues of utmost seriousness and concluding in decidedly un-Broadway-musical fashion, on an empty stage with a sobering commentary on a dark chapter in human history, earned such enormous popularity? It is a success that no one in the original production team could have predicted, not the potential backers who had felt that the show was "too special, too ethnic and parochial for any kind of open audience," certainly not the *Variety* reviewer of a preview performance in Detroit, who wrote that the show "may have a chance for a moderate success on Broadway."[2] Harnick himself remembers modestly hoping that "maybe we would last a year" beyond the show's Broadway opening on September 22, 1964.[3] What happened instead was a landmark event in the American musical theater, and the defining work of the Bock–Harnick partnership.

TEVYE AND *FIDDLER*

In 1960, the year of *Tenderloin*, Jerry Bock recorded the origins of *Fiddler on the Roof* with an entry in a diary: "Sheldon gave me a novel called *Wandering Star*."[4] He was referring to Sholem Aleichem's 1910 novel about Jewish life and a Yiddish theatrical troupe touring Russia around the turn of the twentieth century, whose main characters ultimately seek their fortunes in America. Bock and Harnick, along with Joseph Stein, who had gone on from *The Body Beautiful* to write musicals with Marc Blitzstein (the unsuccessful *Juno*, 1959) and Robert Merrill (the successful *Take Me Along*, 1959), began to imagine a musical based on Aleichem's novel. Eventually, however, they found *Wandering Star* "too sprawling" for a theatrical treatment.[5] Instead they began to consider some of Aleichem's Tevye stories and met and brainstormed several times through mid-August 1961, according to Bock's diary, at which time Stein began a first draft of the libretto. The team developed script and music over the next few months before approaching Harold Prince in early 1962 and receiving his advice to delay the project until Jerome Robbins was available to direct.[6] While Bock and Harnick refocused their efforts on their adaptation of Lubitsch's *The Shop Around the Corner* with Joe Masteroff, Stein turned his attentions to his dramatization of Carl Reiner's semi-autobiographical novel *Enter Laughing*, which played on Broadway concurrently with *She Loves Me* in 1963 and early 1964. Not long after those shows opened, all three collaborators were back at work on the Tevye project.

By this time they had sharpened their focus to Aleichem's short stories about Tevye and his three eldest daughters, Tzeitel, Hodel, and Chava, and about the expulsion of Russian Jews by Tsarist decree. It would not be the first dramatization of these tales. Aleichem himself had made a theatrical adaptation of some of the same material, entitled *Tevye Der Milkhiger: A Family Portrait in Five Scenes*, that premiered at the Yiddish Art Theater in New York in 1919, three years after his death. The play was very well received and eventually entered the repertory of the Yiddish theater; it was also successfully produced in Warsaw, Moscow, and Tel Aviv.[7] Maurice Schwartz, the director and lead actor of the New York production, then adapted Aleichem's play into his film *Tevye Der Milkhiker* in 1939. The first theatrical adaptation of this material with music appears to have been Irving Elman's *Tevye's Daughters* in 1949, described as a drama "embroidered with folklore tunes."[8] This property was optioned by Rodgers and Hammerstein, who hoped to fashion a musical using unpublished songs by Jerome Kern, but was never produced.[9] Then in the next decade three more nonmusical adaptations of Aleichem's stories emerged. Arnold Perl's *The World of Sholem Aleichem* (adopting the title of Maurice Samuel's book) played off-Broadway in 1953 but did not incorporate specific Tevye stories, while his *Tevya and His Daughters*, which premiered off-Broadway in 1957, adapted some of the same material, as did the previous versions. Also in 1957, Chewel Buzgan's *Tevie der Milchiger* premiered in London.[10]

Fiddler's primary source material comes from four of Aleichem's stories: "Modern Children," which concerns the eldest daughter Tzeitel; the eponymous stories "Hodel" and "Chava"; and "Get Thee Out," about the pogrom leading to the Diaspora, which includes an ending to the Chava saga.[11] Both Perl, in *Tevya and His Daughters*, and Stein, in his libretto, follow the original Tzeitel story fairly closely: Tevye thinks he has a husband for his daughter in the butcher Lazar Wolf but learns that Tzeitel has defied tradition by pledging her own hand in marriage to the poor tailor Motel Kamzoil. Tevye reluctantly agrees to the arrangement and invents an outrageous dream in order to convince his wife Golde to go along. Perl's version of the Hodel story is closer to the original than Stein's. Both depict her infatuation with the revolutionary Perchik and ultimate decision to leave home and join him where he has been imprisoned, but in Perl, as in Aleichem, the two are actually married, whereas in Stein, Hodel leaves home to join her betrothed with only a promise to marry "under a canopy." Stein has said that he never saw Arnold Perl's play *Tevya and His Daughters*, but did "read it after we had finished the draft of *Fiddler*."[12] Harnick recalls seeing both of Perl's plays but dismisses the possibility of direct influence. For one thing, as he and Stein have both observed, Perl presents the stories as discrete dramas—as a collection of short plays, analogous to Aleichem's grouping of short stories—whereas in *Fiddler* the stories are interwoven. Even so, Perl owned a license on the material at that time and so is allotted a share of the *Fiddler* royalties and acknowledged in the show's official credit listing with the phrase "by special permission of Arnold Perl."

The Chava story does not appear at all in Perl's adaptation but provides the primary storyline for Schwartz's film (and thus Aleichem's play). The *Fiddler* creators were familiar with this film but found it too "lachrymose" to use as any kind of model; indeed Harnick believes that they stopped watching it before the screening was finished. In this story, Chava has decided to marry the Gentile Fyedka, and Tevye, who reluctantly agreed to break with traditions and give his blessing to the marriages of his two older daughters, cannot support marriage outside the Jewish faith. He not only withholds his blessing but he disowns Chava, refusing even to acknowledge her existence. The story reaches its apogee as the family is preparing to evacuate in response to the Tsar's orders. Aleichem, in "Get Thee Out," provides no real resolution to the conflict, as Chava returns to say goodbye but Tevye cannot decide whether to shun or embrace her, and the story ultimately leaves the question dangling: "What should Tevye have done?"[13] The conclusion of Schwartz's film answers the question by showing that Chava has left her husband to join Tevye in the exodus. Stein's solution is to have Tevye simply and touchingly acknowledge his daughter with the phrase "God be with you," spoken into the air but intended for Chava's ears, before they go their separate ways.

As an adaptation, Stein's libretto is more like what Jerome Weidman and George Abbott did for *Fiorello!* than like the other adaptations Bock and Harnick had worked with, from a novel (*Tenderloin*) and from a film and play (*She Loves Me*). As in *Fiorello!*, the *Fiddler* narrative weaves original story elements together, occasionally altering or adding details. Although the character of the matchmaker originally appears in Aleichem's Hodel story, in *Fiddler* it is Tzeitel whose ill-fated betrothal to Lazar Wolf is arranged by the matchmaker Yente. Also, Aleichem's matchmaker is a man, following custom, and so by switching the character's gender Stein also uniquely, if anachronistically, tips the balance of power within the *shtetl* in the female direction.[14] When Tzeitel does marry Motel, the ceremony and celebration are the high point of *Fiddler*'s first act, a much more elaborate event than anything described in the original stories, for Tzeitel or Hodel. The renowned opening scene of *Fiddler*, in which the audience is introduced to the characters and setting, has no specific counterpart in Aleichem's work but drew inspiration from the book *Life Is With People*, an anthropological study of the *shtetl* that Harnick has often cited.[15] And the character of the "fiddler" himself, and thus the show's title, were inspired by Marc Chagall's paintings such as "Green Violinist."[16] Tevye says in his opening monologue, "You might say that every one of us is a fiddler on the roof, trying to scratch out a pleasant, simple tune without breaking his neck."[17]

This title came late in the process, just before rehearsals began in June of 1964. Before that the show had been provisionally known as *The Old Country* or *Tevye*. Stein's early scripts with these titles show him working with the tone and characterization and attempting to capture the spirit of the original stories, which are framed as conversations between Tevye and Sholem Aleichem.[18] Stein remembers: "Although we stayed with the essence and the feeling of the original material, very little of the scenes and the dialogue came directly from the original material." Harnick adds:

> We all thought that there was a lot of dialogue from the stories which would work onstage. What we all discovered was that, when spoken aloud, it lost its quality. It was literary. Joe had to invent material—particularly the malaprops and the whole style of speech for Tevye—out of his own imagination.[19]

In some of Tevye's dialogue early in Act 1, for example, Stein has Tevye talking to God about his poverty:

> I'm not really complaining—after all, with Your help, I'm starving to death. I realize, of course, that it's no shame to be poor, but it's no great honor either.[20]

These lines have no specific precedents in Aleichem's texts but generally echo sentiments from several stories in the Aleichem collections, including "Tevye Wins a Fortune," which explains how Tevye became a dairyman, and "The Bubble Bursts," in which Tevye loses money in a bad investment.[21]

Another bit of dialogue, and one of Tevye's best-known quips, follows a more specific sequence of derivation. It has origins in a passage about wealth from Aleichem's Hodel story:

> [Perchik] tries to tell me that money is the root of all evil. Money, he says, is the source of all falsehood, and as long as money amounts to something, nothing will ever be done in this world in the spirit of justice.[22]

In his earliest script, dated October 17, 1961, Stein adapted this text into an exchange between Perchik and Tevye early in the first act:

> PERCHIK: And why, Tevye, must everything be put in terms of making a living, of money? Money is the source of all falsehood, of all evil.
> TEVYE: Ah, then, that explains it.
> PERCHIK: What?
> TEVYE: Why I have such a perfect character. Because I have no money.
> PERCHIK: You may joke, Tevye, but where people seek to make money from the work of others, when one man exploits another, there is no justice.[23]

Sometime after producing this draft, Stein held story conferences with Bock and Harnick and began to map out a new draft that he would complete the following January. At this time, by his own recollection, he also became acquainted with Perl's script for *Tevya and His Daughters*, which included a similar dramatization of the same source material:

FEFERAL: Don't talk to me about the rich. They're no friends of mine. It's the poor who count.

TEVYA: I know. In your opinion poverty is a gift of God. Listen, sonny, work is noble, but money is comfortable.

FEFERAL: Money is a curse.

TEVYA: May Tevya be so cursed and never recover.[24]

Stein's next draft, dated January 18, 1962, moves the Perchik–Tevye exchange later in the first act and incorporates two additional lines (shown in **bold** below) that reflect the influence of Perl:

PERCHIK: And why, Tevye, must everything be put in terms of making a living, of money? Money is the source of all falsehood, of all evil.

TEVYE: Ah, then, that explains it.

PERCHIK: What?

TEVYE: Why I have such a perfect character. Because I have no money.

PERCHIK: I repeat, Reb Tevye . . . money is the world's curse!

TEVYE: May the lord smite me with it! And may I never recover! . . .

PERCHIK: You may joke, Tevye, but where people seek to make money from the work of others, when one man exploits another, there is no justice.[25]

By the time *Fiddler* reached Broadway Stein had moved the exchange back to an earlier scene, trimmed it down, and folded it into a discussion of Tzeitel's marriage arrangement:

PERCHIK: (*sarcastic*) Congratulations, Tzeitel, for getting a rich man.

TEVYE: Again with the rich! What's wrong with being rich?

PERCHIK: It is no reason to marry. Money is the world's curse.

TEVYE: May the Lord smite me with it! And may I never recover![26]

In other cases the similarities between Perl and Stein are not so specific but simply reflect similar responses to the task of adapting the same source material. Generally, when original text is not converted to dialogue between characters, it is adapted, in Perl, as a dialogue between Tevye and his horse or a monologue to the audience, and, in Stein, as a dialogue with God, who seems to be sitting in the audience, off to the side in the front of the balcony.

Seth L. Wolitz has written insightfully about the changing characterization of Tevye from Aleichem's text and Schwartz's film to Perl's play and Stein's libretto.[27] In Perl, Tevye has become a "jolly Jewish peasant," lacking the "restraint and dignity of the earlier characterizations," writes Wolitz. Perl's Tevye "indulges the American taste for romantic love" and presents an "idealized and sentimentalized" figure "who conformed to the liberal ideology of the 1950s theater world." In *Fiddler* the process of "Americanization" is complete: "American ideals of individual rights, progress, and freedom of association are assimilated into the Judaic tradition." Tevye has become the "universal grandfather of Jewish America." Yet the story of *Fiddler* is not just a universal tale of folkloric characters and their responses to a changing world. It is also a very personal exploration of the cultural legacies of its creators and the histories of their families and ethnic sensibilities.

FIDDLER'S MUSIC

By the end of the summer of 1963, Jerome Robbins was available and had agreed to direct.[28] He told his collaborators that he was touched by the material because of his Polish-Jewish ancestry and because he wanted to "give another twenty-five years of life to that *shtetl* culture which had been devastated during World War II."[29] (Robbins's surname at birth was the same as Sholem Aleichem's actual surname, Rabinowitz.[30]) As a condition of Robbins's participation, Harold Prince became co-producer, and eventually sole producer when Fred Coe dropped out to work on a film.[31] The completion of the production team came with the inclusion of *She Loves Me* veterans Don Walker (orchestrations) and Patricia Zipprodt (costume design), and *Body Beautiful* survivor Milton Greene (music direction and vocal arrangements). Boris Aronson took the job of scene designer after Marc Chagall declined.[32] Aronson had designed for the theater since 1932, for shows such as *Awake and Sing!* (for the Group Theater, 1935) and *The Crucible* (1953), and won the Tony in the first year he was nominated, 1951, for *The Rose Tattoo*, *The Country Girl*, and *Season in the Sun*. He would win Tony Awards for his designs five more times in a long and distinguished career.

What Is This Show About?
Jerome Robbins's impact on the development of the material was enormous, as he proposed countless rewrites and conceptual changes. "We went through

the show song by song, scene by scene, character by character," remembers Stein. "Jerry [Robbins] is very painstaking, and sometimes I would take the same scene and write it three or four different ways—just fool around with it, really, to see which way had more spark. . . . He examined everything micro-scopically."[33] At the same time, Robbins was also asking broader questions, and these eventually led to the show's powerful opening number, "Prologue–Tradition." Harnick remembers:

> [Robbins] asked what I thought was a surprising question. And he kept asking and hammering at us for months: "What is this show about?" If we gave him an answer like, "Well, it's about this dairy man, and he has three daughters," he would reply, "No. If that's what the show is about, then it's the previous adventures of the Goldberg family, and it's not enough." He said, "We have to find out what it is that gives these stories their power." And he kept asking that same question: "What's it about? What's it about?" I don't know which one of us finally said it. . . . But *somebody* said, "Do you know what this play is about? It's about the dissolution of a way of life." Robbins got very excited. "If that's what it's about," he said, "then we have to show our audience more of the way of life that is about to dissolve. We have to have an opening number about the traditions that are going to change. This number has to be like a tapestry against which the entire show will play."[34]

And so a show that had begun, in the earliest drafts of the script, with a chance encounter between Tevye and Perchik, or with the daughters pre-paring their house for the Sabbath, evolved to begin with a series of introduc-tions set to music.[35]

The opening finally crystallized very late in the process, after rehearsals had already begun in June 1964.[36] With verbal narration from Tevye and mu-sical narrations from the chorus, the Prologue introduces the society and values of the community of Anatevka. Each of these descriptions can be traced to passages from *Life Is With People*. When the men of the community describe their roles by singing these lines, for example . . .

> Who, day and night must scramble for a living,
> Feed a wife and children,
> Say his daily prayers?
> And who has the right
> As master of the house
> To have the final word at home?
> [ALL: The papa . . .]

. . . they echo text such as this from *Life Is With People*:

The creative team for Fiddler on the Roof *(1964): standing from left, Sheldon Harnick, Joseph Stein, Jerome Robbins; at the piano, Jerry Bock (Photofest)*

The realm of the father is the spiritual and the intellectual. He has the official authority, the final word on matters of moment.[37]

For the women, these lines from the *Fiddler* Prologue . . .

> Who must know the way to make a proper home,
> A quiet home, a kosher home?
> Who must raise a family and run the home
> So papa's free to read the holy book?
> [ALL: The mama . . .]

. . . express these sentiments from *Life Is With People*:

The good wife and mother helps her husband to fulfill his obligations. She is responsible for the observance of the dietary laws and for maintaining or implementing all the domestic ritual.

The woman of the house is mother of the whole family, including the father. She is the one who tends, cares for and above all feeds the family.[38]

Life Is With People includes this same sort of source material for the roles described in the *Fiddler* Prologue for the sons, the daughters, the match-maker, the beggar, and the rabbi.[39] After we have heard about each group, Tevye concludes the song with a summarizing exclamation: "Without our tra-ditions, our lives would be as shaky as—as a fiddler on the roof!"

Bock's music for the Prologue weaves a sonic tapestry to symbolize the social one. First we hear the "Fiddler" theme (Example 6.1) and then, under-neath Tevye's opening narration, the Fiddler theme in counterpoint with the Papa theme (Example 6.2). After that we hear the Papa theme again, this time with the descriptive, introductory text sung by Tevye and the Papas, followed by a new melody sung by the Mamas (Example 6.3). The subsequent melodies sung by the Sons and Daughters recall the Fiddler theme. With small varia-tions, these themes are all based on the same chord progression, a repeating tonic harmony for two measures followed by one measure of a triad on the flatted second degree of the scale and then another measure of tonic. In the Mama theme, for example, the progression consists of two measures of A major, one of B♭, and one back on A major during the first phrase (first four measures), and then the same chord succession again underlying the second

Example 6.1: "Fiddler" theme

Example 6.2: Fiddler and Papa themes in counterpoint

Example 6.3: Mama theme

Example 6.4: Groups in counterpoint

phrase. The identical harmonic foundations for the various themes help make it possible to present them in the same key and in combination, and in fact that is what happens after all four groups have been introduced (Example 6.4). What is surprising, however, is that this dramatic choral presentation realigns the melodies—the Papas enter one measure before the other three groups—and so the identical harmonic progressions do not actually line up. It is a twist that adds an element of surprise, and some conspicuous dissonance, to a series of introductions that had previously been unfolding in a quite orderly manner. Raymond Knapp calls it a passage of "near chaos" filled with irony when phrases such as the Papas' "Say his daily prayers" conflict with the Mamas' "A quiet home."[40] Even so, the parts come together at the end of this section, as they do throughout the song, when they repeat the song's title, indeed the entire show's central essence, "Tradition."

The scenes, songs, and dances that follow this rather unusual opening conform to a more typical Broadway musical structure (Table 6.1). In the first scene after the Prologue the women in Tevye's family prepare for a Sabbath meal. Yente arrives to speak with Golde about a match for Tzeitel, and the daughters vocalize their anxieties about leaving their fates in the hands of a matchmaker and their father ("Matchmaker, Matchmaker"). Next we find Tevye outside the house musing about his modest circumstances and his standing in the community ("If I Were a Rich Man"). He meets Perchik and invites him to join his family for the Sabbath. In the next scene the whole family, including two younger daughters (Shprintze and Bielke) and Perchik and Motel, sit for their Sabbath meal as Tevye and Golde sing a prayer for the health and safety of their family, eventually joined by a chorus of other families in other homes upstage ("Sabbath Prayer").[41] Tevye has been told that the butcher Lazar Wolf wants to speak with him, so in the next scene the two men meet in the tavern to discuss the arranged marriage of Lazar and Tzeitel ("To Life"). They celebrate their agreement in a boisterous dance with neighbor men, including a group of Russians. On the way home Tevye is warned by the Russian constable of an impending "demonstration" against the Jewish members of the community.

The next morning, Perchik displays his progressivism by showing Hodel that a man and a woman can dance together; she is startled but interested. Then Tevye speaks to Tzeitel about the marriage arrangement but learns that Tzeitel wants to marry Motel instead; he delivers his first musical rumination about his changing world ("Tevye's Monologue") but nevertheless gives Tzeitel and Motel his blessing, and they rush off to express their joy ("Miracle of Miracles"). Tevye is left with the formidable task of telling Golde what he has done, and does so by convincing her that her grandmother came to him in a dream and told him that Tzeitel should marry Motel, not Lazar Wolf ("The Dream"). Meanwhile, Chava starts to notice the Gentile Fyedka when he protects her from harassment by some of his Russian comrades. Act 1 ends with Tzeitel's wedding, featuring a musical meditation by Tevye and Golde on the marriage of their eldest child ("Sunrise, Sunset") and a series of celebratory dances, including some between men and women, instigated by the radical

Table 6.1: Overview of Fiddler on the Roof

ACT 1

Prologue: Exterior of Tevye's house.
    "Tradition" (Tevye, Company)
1. Kitchen of Tevye's house.
    "Matchmaker, Matchmaker" (Tzeitel, Hodel, Chava)
2. Exterior of Tevye's house.
    "If I Were a Rich Man" (Tevye)
3. Interior of Tevye's house.
    "Sabbath Prayer" (Tevye, Golde, Villagers)
4. The inn, the following evening.
    "To Life" (Tevye, Lazar Wolf, Men)
5. The street outside the inn.
6. Exterior of Tevye's house.
    "Tevye's Monologue" (Tevye)
    "Miracle of Miracles" (Motel)
7. Tevye's bedroom.
    "The Dream" ["The Tailor, Motel Kamzoil"] (Tevye, Golde, Grandma Tzeitel,
    Fruma-Sarah, Company)
8. A village street and the interior of Motel's tailor shop.
9. Part of Tevye's yard.
    "Sunrise, Sunset" (Tevye, Golde, Perchik, Hodel, Villagers)
10. Entire yard of Tevye's house.

ACT 2

Prologue: Exterior of Tevye's house.
1. Exterior of Tevye's house.
    "Now I Have Everything" (Perchik, Hodel)
    "Tevye's Rebuttal" (Tevye)
    "Do You Love Me?" (Tevye, Golde)
2. The village street.
    "The Rumor" ["I Just Heard"] (Yente, Villagers)
3. Exterior of the railroad station.
    "Far From the Home I Love" (Hodel)
4. The village street, some months later.
5. Motel's tailor shop
6. A road, late afternoon.
    "Chava Sequence" ["Chavaleh"] (Tevye)
7. Tevye's barn.
    "Anatevka" (Company)
8. Outside Tevye's house.

Perchik. The revelry comes to an abrupt end when the Tsar's soldiers arrive to cause mayhem, leaving a community in tatters and fear.

In the second act we turn our attention to the other two daughters. First Hodel and Perchik profess their love for each other ("Now I Have Everything") on the eve of Perchik's departure for Kiev to act on his political convictions. Tevye once again yields to his daughter's wishes and offers his blessing to their betrothal, while exclaiming further about the world that is changing around him ("Tevye's Rebuttal"). This leads him to wonder if love plays any role in his own marriage, and so he asks Golde this very question in an affecting duet ("Do You Love Me?"). During the ensuing scene change, Yente and some villagers spread the news that Perchik has been imprisoned ("The Rumor"). Hodel must catch a train to join him in Siberia, and sings her poignant goodbyes to her father ("Far From the Home I Love"). The next scene skips ahead some months, as Motel and Tzeitel have become parents and Motel has finally acquired his sewing machine. Their joy is counterbalanced, however, by the unwelcome news of Chava's engagement outside of the faith. At last Tevye has reached the limits of his tolerance for change and cannot give his blessing to such a union; he expresses his anguish in a musical monologue ("Chava Sequence"). Now the family, along with their neighbors, must prepare to disperse and they sing a hymn to their beloved home ("Anatevka"). The show ends as the characters make their departures: Tevye, Golde, and their two youngest daughters to America; Tzeitel and Motel and their baby to Warsaw; Chava and Fyedka to Cracow. (Fyedka: "We cannot stay among people who can do such things to others.") In the underscoring of the final scene we hear fragments of the themes first heard in the Prologue but at last hear the Fiddler theme in its entirety: the world may change but the spirit endures.

The *Fiddler* score achieves satisfying balances across dramatic and musical terrains. Comic and serious moments blend together artfully and comfortably, often within the same song. Of course the musical showpiece of the score, "If I Were a Rich Man," belongs to Tevye, but his other solo numbers are essentially recitatives (his three monologues), and his other musical highlights are shared with others. Golde has no song to herself but joins Tevye in a second-act centerpiece, "Do You Love Me?," and in two duets with choral support in the first act, "Sabbath Prayer" and "Sunrise, Sunset." Hodel is the only daughter with a solo number ("Far From the Home I Love"), but her sisters are also featured in one of the relatively few trios in a Broadway musical, "Matchmaker, Matchmaker." The characters of two of their suitors are developed in solo numbers: the simplicity and directness of the humble tailor's love song to the eldest daughter, "Miracle of Miracles," counterbalances the harmonic sophistication and melodic complexity of the political activist's love song to her sister, "Now I Have Everything."

Taken together with expressions of community in the ensemble numbers ("Tradition," "To Life," "The Dream," "Anatevka") and the dance music, the full musical roster holds a formidable presence in the dramatic structure and storytelling. It starts with the Prologue, of course, but the songs that follow this singular beginning consistently live up to the same high standard of musical integration and dramatic impact. If *She Loves Me* achieves some sort of "perfection" on a more intimate scale, *Fiddler on the Roof* reaches the same rarefied plateau with broader gestures. As Clive Barnes wrote in 1976, reviewing the first Broadway revival: "The book, the music, the lyrics, are absolutely perfect. There is not a song—and in this it is like the only other 'perfect' musical, *My Fair Lady*—that you could consider being changed" (*New York Times*, 12/30/76). It was the artistic and commercial success that Bock and Harnick had been imagining since they began writing songs together almost eight years earlier.

Evolution of the Score

Four of Bock's earliest musical inspirations for *Fiddler*'s music, from the tape of song ideas he made for Harnick, were released as bonus tracks on the CD reissue of the original London cast recording. Tracks 14 and 17 are recordings of Bock playing and humming two melodies eventually used in "The Dream," while track 15 has the melody that Harnick used for "Sabbath Prayer," and track 16 the melody that became "Sunrise, Sunset." Harnick has said that he wrote lyrics for "The Dream" first, in September 1961, and so this tape presumably dates from that time, when Bock's diary indicates that he began working on the score.[42] Some of Bock's verbal introductions on the recordings confirm a memory of Harnick's about Bock's typical expectations for his wordless melodies:

> I must say that on the tape Jerry would say, "Well, I see this number for the butcher," or, "I think this number is for somebody else." My reaction was almost always, "Wrong. That's not the butcher." The most exciting numbers were always the ones where I would hear his voice saying, "I don't know what this is." For some reason, those were always the best.[43]

Indeed Bock does not express a clear sense of a possible lyric for the two "Dream" melodies (tracks 14 and 17), but for another tune on the tape (track 15) he provides this preamble:

Shel, this theme may be Tevye's theme, whatever that is, or may not. It's got a certain Yiddish-Russian quality. It's overly sad, which might be a point of humor. On the other hand, it could also be legitimately sad, which might be more poignant than humorous. And here it is.

Bock's expectations are not much different from Harnick's response in this case, as the lyricist used this melody to create a moment of great solemnity, "Sabbath Prayer." For another tune on the tape (track 16), however, Bock provided this introduction:

Shel, I just hit something that I'm very happy about. It has an authentic folk-Russian feel, à la Moiseyev. It gives me the spirit of the girls in *Tevye*, on a flirting idea—"coquette"—and it has the bubble, the slight tease, but it's unashamedly sentimental.[44]

When Harnick gave text to this tune it became something quite different, "Sunrise, Sunset"—sentimental, yes, but far from playful or coquettish. The simple undulation of Bock's chorus melody (up a step on "sun-**rise**," down a step on "sun-**set**") became a metaphor for the all-too-swift passage of time in the lives of parents and their children.

Each of these songs is mentioned at an appropriate place within the second version of the script, the one dated January 18, 1962.[45] This version also references "To Life" but otherwise indicates songs that were incorporated into other numbers ("The Tailor Motel Kamzoil," part of "The Dream"), or songs that did not survive into later revisions ("Poppa, Help Me"). To provide an overview of *Fiddler*'s songwriting history, Tables 6.2 and 6.3 collate all extant song scores, lyrics, fragments, or simple references, specifying in which versions of the script (if any) each song is included. Whereas the first version of the script includes no specific song titles—just suggestions for lyric themes and placement—Table 6.3 shows exactly what music was mentioned in the second and subsequent versions. It also gives a sense of how

Table 6.2: Extant versions of the Fiddler *libretto*

Version	Date	Show title	Box.folder in Bock Papers
1	10/17/61	The Old Country	21.01 (first act only)
2	1/18/62	Tevye	21.04
3	[Summer 1963?]	Tevye	21.06 (first act only)
4	[Fall 1963?]	Tevye	21.05
5	[Spring 1964?]	Tevye	21.07

Table 6.3: *Extant scores, lyrics, or fragments of songs written for* Fiddler on the Roof

Song title	Bock Papers box.folder	Harnick Papers (Wisc.) box.folder	Libretto version				
			2	3	4	5	FINAL
Anatevka	3.12,20.20	4.12					
Any Day Now	3.13,20.21						
As Much as That	3.14,20.22	4.13					
Baby Birds	20.23						
Brand New World	20.24						
Butcher's Song	20.25	4.14	x	x			
Chava Sequence	3.17,20.26	4.15		x			x
The Curses of Fruma-Sarah	3.19						
Dear Sweet Sewing Machine	3.20,20.27	4.16		x	x		
Do You Love Me?	3.21	4.10					x
The Dream	3.22						x
Far From the Home I Love	3.23,20.28	4.11					x
Fiddler on the Roof		4.17					
Get Thee Out	3.27,20.29	4.18					
Here in Anatevka	20.30	4.19					
Horse Song				x			
I Can't Wait		4.20					
I Had a Relative	4.01,20.31	4.21					
I Just Heard		4.22					x
If I Were a Rich Man	20.32	4.03		x	x		x
If I Were a Woman	4.02,20.33	4.23					
Letters from America	3.11,20.34		x		x	x	
Little Bird	4.06						
A Little Bit of This	4.07,20.19	4.24					
Make a Bigger Circle	4.25						
Matchmaker		4.02					x
Miracle of Miracles	20.35	4.06					x
A New World		4.26					
Now I Have Everything	4.09,20.36	4.09					x
Poppa, Help Me	20.37	4.27	x				
Pots - Pans - Etc.	4.10						
Promise Me	20.38	5.01					
The Richest Man in Town	20.39	5.02		x	x		
Sabbath Prayer	20.40	4.04	x	x	x	x	x
Somehow the Time Will Pass	20.41	5.03					
The Story of Jacob	20.42	5.04					

(Continued)

Song title	Bock Papers box.folder	Harnick Papers (Wisc.) box.folder	Libretto version				
			2	3	4	5	FINAL
Sunrise, Sunset	4.11,20.43	4.08	x	x	x	x	x
The Tailor Motel Kamzoil	20.44	4.07	x	x	x	x	x
Tevye's Monologue				x	x	x	x
Tevye's Rebuttal				x			x
That's Life	20.45	5.05					
To Life	4.12,20.46	4.05	x	x	x	x	x
To Marry for Love	4.13,20.47	5.06		x	x	x	
Tradition	4.15,20.49	4.01		x	x	x	x
We'll Work for Tomorrow Today	20.50	5.07					
We're Very Lucky	20.51	5.08					
We've Never Missed a Sabbath Yet	4.18,20.52	5.09	x				
What Should I Do?	20.53	5.10					
When Messiah Comes	4.19,20.54	5.11			x	x	
Where Poppa Came From	20.55	5.12					
Why Gentile, Why Jew	4.20,20.56	5.13					

many songs Bock and Harnick wrote that never found their way into the show. Indeed, these may not be the only ones: Bock and Harnick both estimate that they wrote approximately three songs for every one that was eventually used.[46]

Songs may be interrelated in various ways. In the first scene of version two of the script, for example, the daughters prepare the house for Sabbath dinner and sing "We've Never Missed a Sabbath Yet." This song was eventually replaced by "Prologue–Tradition," but, as Bock points out in the liner notes to the London cast recording CD reissue, one melody from the middle section of "We've Never Missed a Sabbath Yet" was re-used as the Papa theme in "Tradition" (lower staff of Example 6.2).[47] The main melody of "We've Never Missed a Sabbath Yet" survives in certain instrumental transitions and scene changes. Another recycled song that originally appeared in the second version of the script was "Letters from America." Harnick explains:

> We had a scene . . . in which Tevye read a letter from his brother-in-law in
> America. It was an amusing scene, and it led to a song called "Letters from

America" or "Anatevka" in which the people sang of how very happy they were about being in Anatevka. "America may sound fine but we are very, very happy in Anatevka." After that scene and that song were dropped, a piece of that happy song became the basis for the song now known as "Anatevka." It was just slowed down and became almost what might be called a dirge.[48]

Elsewhere within the second version of the script are indications for various song placements but no actual titles, suggesting work still to be done.

Later versions of the script mention a number of songs that were excised before the show went into rehearsals, including "A Butcher's Soul" and "The Richest Man in Town." Harnick has described the latter, for example, as a love song from Motel to Tzeitel that was dropped because "the development of their romance was restructured so extensively that the song was no longer called for."[49] Others survived throughout rehearsals and well into the preview period, until they were finally eliminated or replaced because of audience reactions. Harnick remembers that "When Messiah Comes" was removed during the pre-Broadway tour because it "made the audience very uncomfortable" by "asking them to laugh at the same time the situation onstage said not to."[50] "Dear, Sweet Sewing Machine" had been a cast favorite during auditions and rehearsals but was cut after it repeatedly fell flat in previews for reasons that were never entirely clear. Robbins believed that it disrupted the show's forward momentum.[51] Several of these songs have been recorded: "Messiah" and "Sewing Machine" surfaced on two of the *Lost in Boston* discs (sung by Lee Wilkof and Emily Loesser, respectively), while Harnick himself sang "Messiah" and "The Richest Man in Town" at the 92nd Street Y in 1971, and "Butcher" a few years later in a similar setting.[52]

Still other songs in the archives, including the duet for Hodel and Perchik, "If I Were a Woman," and "Why Gentile, Why Jew," are never mentioned in any extant version of the script and survive only as vocal scores, or just sketches. Harnick recalls that "If I Were a Woman" was tried during rehearsals, until Jerome Robbins demonstrated that he could achieve the same dramatic purpose in a brief dance.[53] Such deletions made space for new songs, inspired by watching the material play in rehearsal or on stage. Some of the score's highlights, including "Matchmaker" and "Do You Love Me?," were created very late in the development process, toward the end of the rehearsal or preview periods.[54] When at the last minute Perchik's song "As Much as That" was deemed unsuccessful and replaced with "Now I Have Everything," which had been sung by Motel, Bock and Harnick immediately needed a new song for Motel to sing about his love for Tzeitel, and "Miracle of Miracles" was born.[55]

Musical Ideas and Continuities

The origins of "Matchmaker" draw attention to another important element of the *Fiddler* music. In a discussion of casting issues, Harnick remembers an early song for the daughters, "To Marry for Love," that was not working:

> It was just too difficult for them. So we had to write a new song for them quickly. The song that we had originally written to open the show was called "We've Never Missed a Sabbath Yet." Jerry took part of the melody of that song and converted it into "Matchmaker, Matchmaker."[56]

Bock demonstrated this musical derivation at the piano in a television program in 1964, shortly after *Fiddler* opened on Broadway.[57] The main melody of "We've Never Missed a Sabbath Yet" (as heard on track 18 of the original London cast CD reissue, also found in transitional music such as "Act I—Opening" and "End of Scene 2") begins on the fifth step of the G major scale, leaping up a fourth to the tonic and then moving stepwise to the second, third, and raised fourth degrees (Example 6.5a). "Matchmaker" opens with exactly the same initial scale-step sequence, excepting the concluding raised fourth, in E major and in a different meter and rhythm (Example 6.5b). The step sequence they have in common—scale-step 5 leaping up a fourth to steps 1–2–3—is a familiar one, in melodies such as "How Dry I Am," "You Are My Sunshine," Lehár's "Merry Widow Waltz," and the third movement of Beethoven's "Pathétique" Piano Sonata (in a minor key).[58] We hear it in *Fiddler* in the key of B♭ in Tevye's first two musical soliloquies (Example 6.5c and 6.5d) and in F major as the opening notes of "Do You Love Me?" (Example 6.5e). When the pattern first occurs it has a character of anticipation, as the girls prepare for the Sabbath (Example 6.5a) or speculate about their futures (6.5b). But when Tevye takes over the motive (6.5c, 6.5d) it carries the expression of his questioning about the changes happening around him, leading, ultimately, to the question he asks about his own life and love (6.5e). The evolution of the idea from song to song follows the evolution in Tevye's worldview, unfolding a series of musical linkages that underscore dramatic ones.

The opening interval of this motive further relates to the rising fourths heard prominently elsewhere in the score: the opening two notes of the Fiddler theme (Example 6.1); the beginning of the Prologue refrain ("Tra-di-tion"); the two notes played by the English horn in the introduction to "Sabbath Prayer," acting as a shofar calling celebrants together[59]; the initial interval of "Sabbath Prayer" itself ("May the Lord protect and defend you");

a. "We've Never Missed a Sabbath Yet," opening gesture (cf. "Act I–Opening" and "End of Scene 2")

b. "Matchmaker," opening gesture

c. "Tevye's Monologue," mm. 45–46

d. "Tevye's Rebuttal," opening gesture

e. "Do You Love Me," opening gesture

Example 6.5: Motivic recurrences

and the first two notes of the "Sunrise, Sunset" verse ("**Is this** the little girl I carried"). If the show is about "tradition," then it only makes sense that the singers sing this interval when they proclaim the show's theme at the beginning, and that the Fiddler himself plays this same interval at the beginning of his ubiquitous melody. As the Fiddler embodies the feelings and spirit of the characters and community, the germinal interval of the Fiddler's theme binds together the musical expressions of their thoughts and dreams.

Such craftsmanship is apparent throughout the score. In Tevye's musical soliloquies Bock takes counter-clockwise fifths progressions even farther around the circle than in the recent "No More Candy" (*She Loves Me*) and "Popsicles in Paris" (*To Broadway with Love*): "Tevye's Monologue" in Act 1 makes a full half-circle from C major to its tritone antipode (C–F–B♭–E♭–A♭–D♭–G♭), and "Tevye's Rebuttal" in Act 2 travels almost as far (B♭–E♭–A♭–D♭–G♭).

These progressions give an impression of searching for a home key, as a depiction of Tevye's rambling questions and exclamations. As they project the 5–1–2–3 motive through each step around the circle, they demonstrate the changes and uncertainty of the "tradition" often sung on the motive's first two notes, until finally reaching a moment of revelation. In both soliloquies this revelatory moment arrives with one last statement of the motive at the end of the number, as Tevye realizes that he cannot possibly dismiss or deny the look of hope and love in his daughters' eyes.[60]

"Do You Love Me?," which Harnick wrote out first as if drafting dialogue, stubbornly avoids a melodic resolution while Tevye repeats his question and Golde struggles to respond. Tevye's melody rises, stating the questioning motive, to the third scale degree in F major (Example 6.5e), but Golde's initial response is almost a shriek that moves the melody far away to step 6 ("Do I **what**?"). Later responses move up still farther, to ♭7 ("go lie **down**," "why **talk about** love right now"), but eventually Golde warms to the question. When she finally gives her answer at the end of the song—"twenty-five years my bed is his. If that's not love, what is?"—she moves up to ♭7 one last time (on the word "is") and then Tevye takes over for her and steps away from ♭7 to steps 6–5–4 in his phrase "Then you love me?" followed by Golde's return to step 3 on the last note of "I suppose I do" (Example 6.6a). Tevye's subsequent phrase "And I suppose I love you too" ends on tonic, but still it is not a melodic resolution that connects with the previous stepwise descents: this phrase jumps down to the leading tone and resolves *up* by half step to tonic. We must wait a few more bars, until the song's final phrase, "It's nice to know," for the downward stepwise resolution that the previous phrases seem to have been struggling to achieve (Example 6.6b). Only when the matter has been fully settled, when the two characters have finally opened their hearts to each other, do we hear a musical conclusion of commensurate finality. It is the final stage in this motive's evolution since the early part of the show: what was once anticipation (Example 6.5a, 6.5b), then questioning (6.5c, 6.5d, 6.5e), finally leads to a gesture of resolution in Tevye's stepwise descent to tonic (6.6b).

FIDDLER'S MUSICAL ROOTS

Although Bock and Harnick had worked with ethnic idioms before, their musical evocation of time and place becomes a more important matter in the *Fiddler* score. The techniques of *style hongrois* in *She Loves Me*, for example, set a certain tone and ambience but are not integral to the drama; the story of love among anonymous pen pals does not require a specific ethnic context.

Example 6.6: "Do You Love Me?," ending

And, clearly, the adoption of a particular musical identity, or "musical costume," was one of their specialties, whether modeling turn-of-the-century parlor songs ("'Til Tomorrow," "Artificial Flowers"), or 1920s dance music ("Gentleman Jimmy"), or the musical sounds of New York City neighborhoods ("The Name's La Guardia"). But in *Fiddler* the music must help carry the dramatic weight of the "Jewish" aspects of the drama; it is as much a part of the storytelling as the scenery or costumes. For this reason, some have objected to those songs in *Fiddler* that do not evoke Russian-Jewish culture. As Walter Kerr wrote in his review of the original production (*New York Herald Tribune*, 9/23/64), "I think it might be an altogether charming musical if only the people of Anatevka did not pause every now and again to give their regards to Broadway, with remembrances to Herald Square."

Indeed, "Matchmaker," "Miracle of Miracles," "Now I Have Everything," and "Do You Love Me?" may serve as melodious reminders of a culture beyond the *shtetl*. But Broadway historian Abe Laufe finds these songs "not completely incongruous, for they did illustrate the desire of the young people to break with tradition."[61] As Raymond Knapp observes, "'Matchmaker' . . . presents the girls' perspective as a dramatic and musical foil to Tevye, which again calls for contrast" with the style of other songs in the show.[62] Further, these songs do not require a musical stereotyping of the characters who are singing them, in the same way, for example, that the music of "Prologue–Tradition" must establish and capture the ethnic flavor of the show's setting and *dramatis personae*. Whatever the case, the mixture of musical styles must find a balance between ethnic portrayal and audience communication. On the one hand, as Joseph Swain observes, musical stereotyping is useful for context and cultural identification; on the other, the strongest medium of communication is the "musical language of the culture viewing the drama." Swain advises: "If intelligibility is compromised in the interest of ethnic authenticity, communication breaks down and so does the drama."[63]

Further, in some respects the *Fiddler* creators aimed specifically to avoid ethnic references, fearing that the show would seem too insular or parochial. Harnick had seen Lenny Bruce's nightclub act and noticed that whenever Bruce used Yiddish expressions, "they would elicit laughter from a few people here and there, but many of the other people in the club turned to each other and said, 'What'd he say? What'd he say?'" The laughs that did occur were shallow and insubstantial. The *Fiddler* team decided it would be "useful to use a couple of Yiddish words in our show, in the dialogue and in the lyrics—just a couple, for flavoring—but if anyone laughs when they're used, they come out. And also, when they're used, they have to be used in a way that the audience will know what they mean."[64] Thus the show's book avoids Yiddishisms almost completely, and in the two song lyrics with Yiddish expressions, Harnick leaves no doubt about their meaning: "To life, to life, *l'chaim*" (in "To Life"), and "A blessing on your head, *mazeltov, mazeltov*" (in "The Dream"). If either expression does elicit laughter, it is in response to humor rooted in the story and characterizations, not Borscht Belt shtick.

Issues of realism and style in the portrayal of Jewish themes and characters arose in several Broadway theaters in the early 1960s, when *Fiddler* was in development. Nonmusical plays on Jewish themes such as Paddy Chayefsky's *Gideon* (premiered 11/9/61) and Elick Moll's *Seidman and Son* (10/15/62) had respectable runs, along with four musicals that, in the words of John Bush Jones, "marked the beginnings of a new Jewish consciousness in the United States."[65] The first of these, *Milk and Honey* (10/10/61), was Jerry Herman's first score, with a story about American Jews in Israel. It includes an "Independence Day Hora" and allusions to Jewish music in "The Wedding" alongside many other songs in traditional show-tune styles. The second, *A Family Affair* (1/27/62), was a star vehicle for comedian Shelley Berman, with music by John Kander (working with lyricist William Goldman, just prior to Kander's first score with Fred Ebb). It contains many references to the lives of American Jews but no elements of Jewish music. Next came *I Can Get It For You Wholesale* (3/22/62), set in New York's Garment District. Harold Rome's music for this show includes a typical mixture of Broadway styles with occasional evocations of Jewish musical traditions, most conspicuously in "The Family Way" and "Momma, Momma." Finally, Jule Styne's music for *Funny*

Girl (3/26/64) is also set in typical Broadway idioms. References to Jewish aspects of Fanny Brice's life and identity during her rise to fame are underplayed, except when employed to elicit the kind of laughter that Harnick witnessed during Lenny Bruce's performance.

When songs from such shows do evoke Jewish musical traditions, they generally mimic ethnic characterizations of an earlier time, trends that first emerged in vaudeville alongside stereotyping of other ethnic identities. About Irving Berlin's early novelty songs, for example, Charles Hamm writes:

> The music is likewise sketched with broad strokes suggesting ethnic-specific stylistic features. German characters sing tunes resembling ländler, with beer-garden oom-pah-pah backing; Italians sing graceful melodies with accompaniments invoking plucked mandolins, tarantellas, or street serenades; Jews sing tunes in minor modes spiced with augmented seconds.[66]

Ten of Berlin's Jewish novelty songs survive, with titles like "Yiddle, On Your Fiddle, Play Some Ragtime" (1909) and "Yiddisha Eyes" (1910).[67] Minor keys, especially E minor, are prominent in all of them, as are shifts to the relative major in the chorus.[68] Jack Gottlieb labels these songs "Yingish" (dropping the "l" in the older word "Yinglish" to give Yiddish and English "equal status" in the coinage) and offers a broad summary of the genre, encompassing songs by Berlin and by others. He notes that in Yingish songs the "verses are usually in minor with choruses in major."[69] For Andrew P. Killick there are "two main types of musical image that we will find in association with Jews: the rustic dance and the synagogue chant." He agrees that the minor mode is an "obvious musical marker of Jewishness."[70] In fact statistical overviews have confirmed that the minor mode is much more common than the major in Jewish folk music.[71]

The minor mode predominates throughout the *Fiddler* score, often arriving as a counterpart to its parallel major.[72] In the bridge of "Anatevka," among other places, it occurs in harmonic form and is therefore "spiced" with the augmented second between steps 6 and 7, to borrow Hamm's characterization of Irving Berlin's Jewish evocations. But the augmented second has an equally strong, and equally evocative, presence in other scales as well.[73] We hear this right away in the Papa theme of "Prologue—Tradition," between the D♭ at the end of the third (or seventh) bar and the ensuing E♮ (lower staffs of Example 6.2). In this case the augmented second occurs between the second step (D♭) and third step (E♮) of the Jewish mode *Ahavah rabbah* on C, widely familiar as the basis of the celebratory dance song "Hava Nagila." In other *Fiddler* songs we find augmented seconds between steps 3 and 4 of the source scale, characteristic of the Jewish mode *Mi shebberakh*. These two modes, along with a scale that does not feature an augmented second, *Adonai malach*, combine with harmonic minor as the scales most often used to evoke Jewish folk music in *Fiddler*. Indeed they are the scales that most strongly characterize Jewish folk music in general.[74]

Although these modes probably have Oriental roots, with histories extending at least as far back as that of their Western counterparts, scholars have often categorized them according to similarities with Western church modes.[75] *Ahavah rabbah* (Example 6.7a) is also known as *Frigish* because it can be understood as Phrygian with a raised third step (Example 6.7a with an E♭ would be C Phrygian). *Mi shebberakh* (Example 6.7b) has been called *Altered Dorian* because it can be understood as Dorian with a raised fourth, or *Ukrainian-Dorian* because of its association with Ukrainian music (Example 6.7b with an F♮ would be C Dorian).[76] (*Mi shebberakh* also shares important features—specifically, the first five steps, highlighted by the augmented second between steps 3 and 4—with the Gypsy scale, or Hungarian minor, a tonal resource for some of the *style hongrois* in *She Loves Me* [see chapter 5].) *Ahavah rabbah* and *Mi shebberakh* are essentially different modal rotations of harmonic minor: Example 6.7a is the fifth rotation of F harmonic minor (F harmonic minor rotated to start on step 5), and 6.7b is the fourth rotation of G harmonic minor (G harmonic minor rotated to start on step 4). *Adonai malach* (Example 6.7c) is a major scale with a ♭7, as in Mixolydian, plus ♭3 in the upper octave.

In *Fiddler* we hear *Ahavah rabbah* and *Mi shebberakh* with special prominence and clarity in Act 1, as the basis of instrumental melodies within two big dance sequences: the evening of drunken revelry celebrating Lazar Wolf's engagement in "To Life" (*Ahavah rabbah*, Example 6.8a), and Tzeitel's wedding (*Mi*

a. Ahavah rabbah

b. Mi shebberakh

c. Adonai malach

Example 6.7: *Modal sources for some* Fiddler *melodies*

shebberakh, Example 6.8b). Bock used *Mi shebberakh* in a similar way in *Fiorello!*, as the basis of dance tunes when La Guardia campaigns in a Jewish neighborhood. *Fiddler* tunes with the Mixolydian ♭7 do not involve the upper ♭3 as in *Adonai malach* but nevertheless relate suggestively to Jewish musical traditions. One of *Fiddler's* Mixolydian tunes, Tevye's heartbroken lament after learning that Chava has married Fyedka (Example 6.8c), can be associated with Jewish idioms when heard in this context, although taken by itself it is equally evocative of other musical traditions. (The ♭7 and triple meter and harmonic repetition may remind some listeners of Ravel's *Boléro*, which Bock explicitly

a. "To Life," mm. 142–149, vocal line (Ahavah rabbah)

b. "Wedding Dance–No. 1," mm. 17–28, main melody (Mi shebberakh)

c. "Chava Sequence," verse 1 (Adonai malach)

Example 6.8: Excerpts from Fiddler *melodies with specific modal origins*

quoted in "A Trip to the Library" from *She Loves Me*.) Much earlier in the show, however, the ♭7 in "If I Were a Rich Man" provides a very strong ethnic marker, expressed in nonsense syllables to evoke a Hasidic tradition.[77] Further, "Rich Man" moves back and forth between parallel major and minor and so employs both versions of the third step of the scale, as if collapsing together notes that appear in *Adonai malach* in two different octaves. And a slow passage in the center of the song resembles a kind of synagogue chant, concluding with a turning figure highlighting augmented seconds ("Boi-boi-boi-boi-boi-boi-boi-boi"). Most significantly, "Rich Man" captures a style of performance Bock and Harnick had witnessed at a Hebrew Actors Union benefit featuring "a mother and a daughter who sang a Hasidic song that was all 'boy-boy-boy-boy-boy-boy-boy-boy-boy' and in thirds and sixths most of the way through." Harnick mixed regular text, inspired in part by Aleichem's story "The Bubble Bursts," with syllables such as "Daidle deedle daidle digguh digguh deedle daidle dum" that he had heard at the benefit and at a Simchas Torah celebration in Brooklyn.[78]

This is a rare instance in which the composers explicitly acknowledge a musical model for their work. Harnick referred to "Rich Man" as "the only piece of music [written for *Fiddler*] that I can think of that was definitely influenced by some Jewish music."[79] With this one exception, Bock too has consistently stated that he "never felt the urge to research the score" of *Fiddler* because he was able to draw from the experience of hearing Yiddish and Russian folk songs sung to him by his grandmother during his childhood.[80] He has claimed no specific knowledge of Jewish modes, just a process of drawing from "whatever I had heard in my Jewish head."[81] In a 2004 interview he described his inspiration this way:

> I knew the ambience was going to be "Russian," and that it took place in a *shtetl*, but I had no compulsion to research either early Klezmer or particularly Russian music at the turn of that century, or just before the turn of the century. What happened was that for some inexplicable reason, the music that I hadn't been able to write, with all our shows, was something that I had silently deposited in my creative mind, and the opportunity to now express myself with that kind of music just opened up a flood of possibilities for me.[82]

In 2008 he was more succinct: "I simply could not stop the brood of melodies and harmonies that waited to be born."

Any specific connections between *Fiddler* songs and existing music, therefore, simply reflect the depth of Bock's connection to his musical heritage and personal familiarity with the styles and idioms of *Fiddler*'s setting. Jack Gottlieb, who wrote a book to make his case for the Jewish roots of American popular music, finds precedents for some of the *Fiddler* material in several Yiddish sources. His most convincing claim finds a resemblance between "To Life" and a Yiddish melody variously known as "Papirosn," "Nemele," and "Drey iber dem redl."[83] The first phrases of the songs have similar profiles: both begin with a move up from the fifth step of the scale to the third and then generally descend back down to steps 1 and 5 (Example 6.9). The second phrases match less well but contain similar moves toward the subdominant. Gottlieb also suggests sources for the Fiddler theme in a pair of Yiddish songs about fiddlers, and for "Anatevka" in a group of Yiddish "*shtetl* songs."[84] Gottlieb's overall agenda does not require precise derivational relationships, but he certainly feels that Jewish music influenced many American popular songs, even those that employ no explicit Jewish idioms. His liberal methods would likely allow him to find some sort of Jewish roots for all of the music of *Fiddler*, including songs crafted in familiar show-tune styles.

Kate Mostel, wife of the original Tevye, Zero Mostel, makes a more specific biographical claim about *Fiddler*'s musical origins. She remembers a meeting with Bock and Harnick in 1964 at which "Zero sang them some old Yiddish songs he remembered from his childhood. . . . Some of [these] later found their way into the play, slightly altered for Broadway."[85] Similarly, in a 2001 article Theodore Bikel, one of the greatest and most practiced Tevyes, was said to believe that Bock "referred to Mr. Bikel's recordings [of Jewish folk music] for stylistic—even melodic—inspiration" when he was composing *Fiddler*.[86] Bock himself told Harold Flender that some *Fiddler* tunes are "parodies or melodies borrowed from traditional Jewish music and . . . set in contemporary fashion."[87] And Bock drops another hint about sources when he says that one of the songs on a demo tape—the melody that Harnick transformed into "Sunrise, Sunset"—"has an authentic folk-Russian feel, à la Moiseyev."[88] He is referring to Igor Moiseyev, the great Russian dancer-choreographer who released albums of instrumental versions of Russian folk music in the late 1950s and early 1960s.

a. "Papirosn," first two phrases

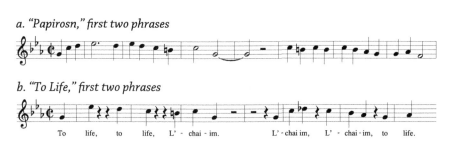

b. "To Life," first two phrases

Example 6.9: Gottlieb's source for "To Life" (Funny, It Doesn't Sound Jewish, 49)

Although no further evidence survives to clarify Kate Mostel's recollection, the albums by Bikel and by the Moiseyev ensemble contain several intriguing parallels with the music of *Fiddler on the Roof*. Bikel released thirteen albums from 1955 to 1962, a time when he was also making a name for himself on Broadway, most famously as the original Captain Von Trapp in *The Sound of Music*.[89] Four of his albums are devoted exclusively to Jewish and Russian folk music: *Theodore Bikel Sings Jewish Folk Songs* (Elektra, 1958), *Songs of a Russian Gypsy* (Elektra, 1958), *Theodore Bikel Sings More Jewish Folk Songs* (Elektra, 1959), and *Songs of Russia Old and New* (Elektra, 1960). The Moiseyev albums from the pre-*Fiddler* days include *Russian Folk Dances of the Moiseyev Dance Company* (Monitor, 1958–1961), *Moiseyev Dances, Vol. 2* (Monitor, 1958–1961[?]), and *Moiseyev Spectacular* (Artia, 1961). It is easy to hear general similarities between many songs on these albums and the *Fiddler* score. Minor keys are common, and instances of *Fiddler*'s three prevalent Jewish modes are not hard to find. In a few cases melodies display very close resemblances. A Yiddish song about a train ("Di ban," *Theodore Bikel Sings Jewish Folk Songs*, side 1, band 4) shares many features with the Fiddler tune itself (Example 6.10, cf. Example 6.1). The Fiddler tune's first phrase (first four measures) matches the Yiddish song's first phrase very closely, and the Fiddler tune's second phrase begins like the first but then ends with the lowered second step approaching the final tonic, just like the end of the Yiddish song. A Yiddish song from another Bikel album ("Drei techterlech," *Theodore Bikel Sings More Jewish Folk Songs*, side 1, band 5) includes a phrase outlining the *Mi shebberakh* mode very much like the melody in that mode from the *Fiddler* wedding scene (Example 6.11, cf. Example 6.8b). Appropriately, in the text of this Yiddish song a father expresses his feelings about the marriages of his three daughters:

> When we marry off our eldest daughter I will dance and sing—a burden will be lifted. Musicians, play with feeling, for my eldest is getting married. Only God and the man who has daughters can understand my joy.

> When I see my second daughter in her wedding dress, I will drink and rejoice—to marry off a child, and a daughter to boot!

> When the music plays for the last wedding of my youngest daughter, I will sadly think: the youngest daughter also gone, then what else is left? How hard it was with three daughters—it will be worse without them—Play, musicians, with tears, for the last bed will be vacant tonight.[90]

Other tunes on the Bikel and Moiseyev albums have less specific resemblances to *Fiddler* melodies but simply offer further evidence of how skillfully and sensitively Bock captured the musical essence of the culture he was portraying. When

Example 6.10: "Di Ban" (Theodore Bikel Sings Jewish Folk Songs, side 1, band 4)

Example 6.11: "Drei techterlech," excerpt (Theodore Bikel Sings More Jewish Folk Songs, side 1, band 5)

Hodel and Perchik dance together, first in private and later at Tzeitel's wedding, the instruments play a dance tune (Example 6.12a) that would not be out of place on a Moiseyev album, alongside a tune like "Ukrainian Dance (Hopak)" (Example 6.12b, *Moiseyev Dances, Vol. 2*, side 2, band 1). The opening rhythm of "If I Were a Rich Man," and occasionally the actual pitches as well, permeate another Russian tune from a Moiseyev album ("Trepak No. 1," *Russian Folk Dances of the Moiseyev Dance Company*, side 1, band 4). The main melody of "To Life" resembles not only the tune cited by Gottlieb (Example 6.9a) but also a melody from one of Bikel's Russian albums ("Yamshchik Gani-Ka K Yaru," *Songs of Russia Old and New*, side 1, band 2). And "Sabbath Prayer" has distinct commonalities with one of Bikel's Yiddish songs, "Kinder Yorn" (*Theodore Bikel Sings More Jewish Folk Songs*, side 1, band 7), especially in the transition between the second and third verses, and later in large parts of the entire fourth verse, when we hear the same Dorian-based chord progression found in Bock's creation, rocking back and forth between G minor and C major harmonies. Such resemblances help amass a rich essence of Russian-Jewish musical sensibility, alongside other frequent motivic affinities, including connections Knapp describes between parts of "Sunrise, Sunset," "Anatevka," and "Hatikvah," the Israeli national anthem.[91]

Perhaps the truest sense of *Fiddler*'s musical roots is that demonstrated by Bock himself, in the early demo recordings made for his songwriting partner.[92] In the inflections of his textless singing, his voice becomes another instrument as if from the Moiseyev ensemble, infused with a sensitivity and feeling on a par with Bikel's. The nuances of his expressive performance communicate the trenchancy of his musical understanding and acuity of his cultural appreciation. That Bock and the other members of the *Fiddler* creative team were able to preserve and maintain this spirit in the long process from demo tape to award-winning, record-setting Broadway run, and beyond, is testament to the depth of their passions, and to the unity of their artistic vision.

a. "Perchik and Hodel Dance" (excerpt)

b. "Ukrainian Dance (Hopak)" (Moiseyev Dances, Vol. 2, side 2, band 1)

Example 6.12: Comparison of dance melodies

FIDDLER PLAYS

When casting began in the fall of 1963, Tevye, of course, was a top priority. The creative team considered, or at least fielded inquiries from, a long list of Hollywood and Broadway notables for the role, including Danny Kaye, Frank Sinatra, Alan King, Julius La Rosa, Red Buttons, Danny Thomas, Jack Gilford, Walter Matthau, and *Fiorello!* veterans Tom Bosley and Howard Da Silva.[93] In the end, however, the casting of Zero Mostel seemed all but inevitable. Mostel provided the star power that *She Loves Me* lacked, having recently won Tony Awards for Ionesco's *Rhinoceros* (1961) and the Sondheim/Prince musical *A Funny Thing Happened on the Way to the Forum* (1962). He had also acted in Arnold Perl's *The World of Sholem Aleichem* on television a few years before, although not in the role of Tevye.[94] Casting of the other parts fell into place gradually over a long audition period through the first half of 1964.[95] For the mature roles the creative team cast Maria Karnilova (Golde), an old friend of Robbins who was a charter member of the American Ballet Theater with solid Broadway credentials, including a memorable performance as the stripper Tessie Tura in *Gypsy* (1959); Beatrice Arthur (Yente), acclaimed for her portrayal of Lucy Brown in revivals of *The Threepenny Opera* (1954, 1955); and Gluck Sandor (Rabbi), renowned for his dancing and teaching in addition to his decades of acting experience. Some of the actors cast in the younger roles were just embarking on distinguished careers in the theater. Austin Pendleton (Motel) had already acted under Robbins's direction, playing the son in Arthur Kopit's *Oh Dad, Poor Dad, Mamma's Hung You in the Closet and I'm Feelin' So Sad* (1962), and would later make a name for himself as a writer, director, actor, and teacher; Joanna Merlin (Tzeitel) would become a well-known casting director in addition to starring in film and television; Bert Convy (Perchik) went on to a successful career as actor, singer, and television game-show host; and Julia Migenes (Hodel) would subsequently make the transition from *Fiddler* to opera houses and concert stages.

The show rehearsed for eight weeks in New York in June and July 1964. Robbins insisted on such an unusually long rehearsal period, as he had for *West Side Story* a few years earlier, and indeed only a director of Robbins's stature would have been granted such a luxury. From there the show moved on to the Fisher Theater in Detroit, where the pre-Broadway tryout tour began on July 27. Local reviewers were muzzled by a newspaper strike, although the mostly positive views of at least one, Jay Carr of the *Detroit News*, were aired on local television and radio.[96] Laudatory notices also appeared by Peter Bellamy in the *Cleveland Plain Dealer* (7/31/64) and by Richard Christiansen in the *Chicago Daily News* (8/9/64). The review that received the most attention from the *Fiddler* cast and production group, however, appeared in *Variety* (7/29/64) under the byline "Tew." This reviewer, who was, according to Kate Mostel, an "automobile executive who doubled as the *Variety* critic in Detroit,"[97] described the show as "mildly amusing," "completely predictable," and musically "ordinary and serviceable, rather than singable or haunting." Joseph Stein called the *Variety* piece "devastating"; Richard Altman, who was on hand as Jerome Robbins's assistant, believed that the review "all but destroyed the morale of the company."[98] Even so, the creative team was well aware of changes that needed to be made, especially in the second act, and worked feverishly during the month of August to trim the length—notably by shortening an elaborate ballet scene expressing Tevye's anguish over Chava's marriage outside the faith—and to generate new material such as "Do You Love Me?" In fact, audiences were responding warmly, despite all the problems.[99] Further, any fears that the show might be "too Jewish" were proving to be unfounded. Stein remembers that opening night in Detroit was a benefit for a Jewish organization, and that some audience members wondered aloud, "Well, we like it, but I don't know if *they* will like it." In subsequent performances, when audiences of no particular ethnic or cultural composition were equally charmed, Stein recalls feeling that "we had something rather special."[100]

By the time a substantially improved version of the show opened at the National Theater in Washington on August 27, audiences were enthusiastic and houses packed. Reviews were mostly positive, describing the music as "exceptionally fine, wedded beautifully to the action" (Harry MacArthur, *Washington Star*, 8/28/64) and "thoroughly in keeping with the people, and in nearly all cases sung outstandingly well" (Leo Sullivan, *Washington Post*, 8/28/64). The show played there for sixteen days, through September 12, undergoing just a few additional refinements, notably the addition of the acclaimed "bottle dance" in the wedding sequence and—as the final decisions about the ending were reached— the removal of the song "Get Thee Out" and the transformation of "Letters from America" into "Anatevka."[101]

The critics in New York, following the opening at the Imperial Theater on September 22, had minor quibbles but found much to admire. Howard Taubman in the *Times* (9/23/64) described the show as "an integrated achievement of uncommon quality," even if the material occasionally veered too far away from the tone of Sholem Aleichem's original stories for his taste. Whitney Bolton (*Morning Telegraph*, 9/24/64) raised similar concerns while recognizing the strength of the show's book, score, and dancing; Norman Nadel (*World Telegram and Sun*, 9/23/64) and George Oppenheimer (*Newsday*, 9/23/64) wished that some of the singing voices had been stronger, even while praising everything else. Some critics could only gush superlatives: Martin Gottfried (*Women's Wear Daily*, 9/23/64) described *Fiddler* as a "rich, sunbursting, magnificent show," and John Chapman (*Daily News*, 9/23/64) called it "one of the great works of the American musical theater" and a "work of art." The critical outpouring overruled Walter Kerr yet again (*Herald Tribune*, 9/23/64); he described the show as a "very near miss" because of a "failure to be entirely honest with itself," among other shortcomings.

The one thing that all the reviewers could agree on was the brilliance of Zero Mostel. For Howard Taubman (*New York Times*, 9/23/64), Mostel's Tevye was "one of the most glowing creations in the history of the musical theater." Richard Watts, Jr. (*New York Post*, 9/23/64) attributed the show's success primarily to Mostel's "brilliantly resourceful and intelligent performance," and John McClain (*Journal American*, 9/23/64) described the whole show as a "great tribute to the comic gifts of the star." The role of Tevye, wrote Norman Nadel (*World Telegram and Sun*, 9/23/64), "must have been waiting all these years for Zero Mostel." "Mr. Mostel's praises have been sung to the skies," rejoiced Martin Gottfried (*Woman's Wear Daily*, 9/23/64), "but it is time to sing them to the heavens. To see him dance is to see an angel in underwear, to listen in on his conversations with God is to be privy to the secret of life." Raves for Mostel continued in the coming days—even in otherwise lukewarm or mixed assessments of the overall production—from *Time* (Mostel has "the gift for reaching the heart of a character and sympathetically synchronizing every heartbeat in the house with his"), *Newsweek* (Mostel is "the show's powerful heart and conquering soul"), and *The Nation* ("unpredictably fantastic—altogether beyond the known or rational"). The *Variety* critic ("Hobe," 9/30/64) summarized the recurring theme: *Fiddler on the Roof* is "Mostel's show."

The star apparently agreed. Mostel had played an active role in the development of the Tevye character since early in the process and helped make

Zero Mostel (Tevye) in Fiddler on the Roof *(1964) (Photofest)*

staging decisions in virtually every scene, most substantively in "If I Were a Rich Man." Bock has described Mostel's creative contributions and character development during rehearsals as "an elating experience, . . . marvelous, dynamic, creative, unpredictable."[102] Many such contributions arose when Mostel would deviate from the script. At first, during rehearsals and on the tryout tour, Bock found this "constructive, very creative," providing "new insights into the character."[103] "He would feed *us*," remembers Bock, "improvising in such a way that we'd want to rush back and capture something he'd show us."[104] In the weeks and months after Mostel received his critical raves, however, he began to improvise more liberally, and more destructively. Cast members have told remarkable stories about Mostel's antics during New York performances that might include substantial additions to dialogue, out-of-character pandering to the audience, and unprofessional interplay with other actors.[105] This went far beyond harmless playfulness but would "change the focus of a scene," remembers Harnick.[106] Mostel was also doing something the creators had tried assiduously to avoid—getting cheap laughs by inserting Yiddish expressions. In the words of John Stewart, the actor "stopped playing Tevye as the creators had made him, and started playing Zero Mostel."[107] Any attempts to restrain him were met with hostility or defiance. Clearly, Mostel believed that *Fiddler* was his show, and that he had the license to fiddle with it as he pleased.

When the producers gave the role of Tevye to Luther Adler after Mostel's initial nine-month contract expired, Mostel predicted that the show would last only "a few weeks, a month or two at most" without him.[108] Harnick recalls approaching the star at a party following his final performance, telling him that he was sorry to see him go; Mostel replied, "No you're not. You're sorry to see the grosses fall."[109] Bock remembers thinking that Mostel may have been right: "That was perhaps the first time we had to assess *Fiddler*'s success—was it the show or was it Zero?"[110] But it was not only Mostel who received a Tony Award in 1965: the show was named Best Musical and won nine overall, for Maria Karnilova (Supporting or Featured Actress in a Musical), Jerome Robbins (for Direction and for Choreography), Harold Prince, Bock and Harnick, Joseph Stein, and Patricia Zipprodt (Costume Design). (It received only one other nomination, for scene designer Boris Aronson, who lost to Oliver Smith's designs for *Baker Street*, *Luv*, and *The Odd Couple*.) The show was also named Best Musical of 1964–65 by the New York Drama Critics' Circle. And then there was the memory of a few performances in Washington, when Paul Lipson played Tevye while Mostel was ill, and two weeks in January 1965 when Luther Adler played Tevye while Mostel took a vacation.[111] The show continued to hold its power and appeal in those performances, and it survived portrayals of Tevye in very different styles over the next seven years of its first Broadway run, by Luther Adler, Herschel Bernardi, Harry Goz, Jerry Jarrett, Paul Lipson, and Jan Peerce. Early audiences may have been lured by the performance of a legendary actor, but as the years wore on, it became evident that it was Tevye himself, not the actor portraying him, who was the star attraction. As the show toured the United States and began to play all over the world, audiences of every conceivable demographic were being easily persuaded that *Fiddler* was not a phenomenon of one actor or one production or even one culture. They were embracing *Fiddler* as if it were their own personal possession, like the Japanese producer who could not understand the show's appeal in America because "It's so Japanese!"[112]

By the time Mostel returned to the role, on a multi-city tour culminating with the first Broadway revival at the Winter Garden in 1976–77, he still misbehaved but generally seemed to have less energy for that sort of thing.[113] (He died at the age of 62 on September 8, 1977, 110 days after the limited run closed.) The Tevyes of the next two decades included Theodore Bikel, on tour and in a shortened version in Las Vegas,[114] and the Israeli actor Chaim Topol, who first played the role in Tel Aviv in 1965, filling in occasionally for Bomba J. Zur, and then earned the part outright for the first London production in February 1967.[115] Topol also starred in the second Broadway revival at the Gershwin in 1990–91, for which he received a Tony nomination. Harnick has said that his favorite Tevye, because of his acting and musicality and the "paternal quality" of his performance, was Herschel Bernardi, a veteran of the first Broadway run and also the star of a production at the New York State Theater in 1981, for which he received a Tony nomination.[116] A list of other memorable Tevyes from the early years should also include Teddy Smith, the teenaged boy who played the role in a production in May 1969 by the students of Junior High School 275 in Brownsville, Brooklyn, in the midst of a teacher's strike and violent community resistance, as chronicled by their teacher-director Richard Piro in his book *Black Fiddler*.[117]

Mostel was seriously considered for the role in the film version, but the part went to Topol because the production team felt that he would be a warmer screen presence. (They fended off inquiries from, among others, Herschel Bernardi, Richard Burton, Danny Kaye, Walter Matthau, Frank Sinatra, Rod Steiger, and Danny Thomas. Yossi Yadin, who had played the part on stage in Germany, was a strong contender but lacked proficiency in English.[118]) Topol's Tevye may be the one that is most widely known, thanks to video rentals, but he has been criticized for minimizing the humor in the role: Harnick found him "not as comfortable with the verbal humor" because English is not his first language; Peter Stone said that he played the role as a "leading man and not a comic."[119] Topol rises in his own defense with an axiom learned from performing Tevye many times on stages around the world: "Don't make them laugh too much in the first act; otherwise they won't cry in the second act."[120] Director Norman Jewison found in Topol's Tevye a powerful "dignity and strength" and a "sense of destiny as, and pride in being, a Jew."[121] By 2009, when Topol brought Tevye to American audiences once again in a multi-city tour, he was hardly hesitant at all to draw the humor out of the character and yet had no trouble generating deep emotional responses in Act 2.

The film in general, not just Topol's performance, is darker than most stage versions of *Fiddler on the Roof*. The visual aspect is literally darkened: cinematographer Oswald Morris shot the entire film through a scrim of brown women's hosiery stretched over camera lenses. In scene after scene, the camera lingers meditatively on stark, dramatic images. The jokes are still there in Joseph Stein's adapted screenplay, but they seem less vital to the storytelling than they typically do onstage. A new song Bock and Harnick wrote for the film, "Any Day Now," would have contributed to the darker ambience by replacing Perchik's upbeat celebration of his engagement to Hodel, "Now I Have Everything," with an anthem to his political beliefs, soaked with minor-key passages and Russian folk idioms.[122] Jewison ultimately decided to use neither the new song—because it "had a quality of waving the red flag"—nor the original one.[123] At that point in the film, Hodel and Perchik make their plans and then run off to inform Tevye, without pausing to celebrate the moment or express their elation in song.

A sober, earnest sensibility lies at the heart of the film's vivid realism. When Tevye first meets with Lazar Wolf, he visits him in his opulent home rather than meeting him in the tavern, thereby highlighting exactly what Tzeitel will be passing up when she chooses to marry a poor tailor instead. (This is also how it happens in Aleichem's original story.) Stein and Jewison also added new scenes, of the Russian constable receiving his fateful orders, of Perchik being arrested at a rally in Kiev, of Golde entering a church in search of Chava and her Gentile boyfriend, all shot on location in and around a small village in Yugoslavia. Cinematic techniques lend extra horror and sur-realism to "The Dream." Flashbacks add depth and texture to "Far From the Home I Love" and "Chava Sequence." Striking images of local villagers and their environs lend special power to the score's most touching moments: the celebration of family and community in "Sabbath Prayer"; the marriage of an eldest daughter in "Sunrise, Sunset"; and the ending, when a subdued, hummed "Anatevka" enfolds the imagery of an entire exiled village standing anxiously on a barge floating across a river.

The film is not universally admired, but *New Yorker* critic Pauline Kael, for one, called it "the most *powerful* movie musical ever made."[124] It features strong performances by Norma Crane (Golde), a veteran of Broadway and television; Molly Picon (Yente), an acclaimed star of the Yiddish theater; and Paul Mann (Lazar Wolf), an influential teacher at the Actors Studio in New York. In the younger roles are familiar faces such as Leonard Frey (Motel), who had been the original Mendel, the rabbi's son, on Broadway and who was developing a solid reputation on stage and screen; and Paul Michael Glaser (Perchik), soon to be popularly known as Detective David Starsky in the tele-vision series *Starsky and Hutch*. The film won Academy Awards in 1972 for Cinematography (Oswald Morris), Adapted Score (John Williams), and Sound (Gordon K. McCallum and David Hildyard), and received nominations for Best Actor, Supporting Actor (Leonard Frey), Art Direction (Robert Boyle, Michael Stringer, Peter Lamont), Directing, and Best Picture. It also won Golden Globes for Best Actor and Best Picture.

What remained constant as *Fiddler on the Roof* aged into its second and third decades—in the film, national tours, and New York stagings on

Bottle dance in the wedding scene from Fiddler on the Roof *(1964) (Photofest)*

Broadway in 1976 and 1990 and at the New York State Theater in 1981—
was the profound impact of Jerome Robbins on the musical's central essence, and on its power and longevity. Robbins's choreography became as
much a part of the show as Tevye's quips or Bock and Harnick's songs. Robbins, who died in 1998, played active roles in many productions of the show
during his lifetime, either as an on-scene director-choreographer or by
entrusting one of his protégés with the responsibility of teaching his
movements and direction, of preserving his legacy. More generally, Robbins's early insistence on a coherent theme and focus for the show helped
ensure its enduring universal appeal. In the story of Tevye's family he
found his own story, and he helped make it ours.

FIDDLER'S SOUL

Audiences around the world have finally affirmed that *Fiddler on the Roof* is
not the exclusive property of a particular actor or character nor of the audience members or cultural communities who share Jewish heritage with Tevye
and his Anatevka neighbors. Some critics will continue to ask, however, at

what expense such universalism has been attained. Robert Brustein raised the question first, in an article in *New Republic* shortly after the show first opened in 1964.[125] If "even Chinamen" could enjoy *Fiddler's* "slick, colorful, and energetic" production, wrote Brustein, then the "serious Yiddishist" is likely to take offense. Brustein lamented that the world of Sholem Aleichem had been falsified and homogenized and that the great Zero Mostel was wasting his talent. Irving Howe concurred the next month in *Commentary*, writing that in *Fiddler* "Sholem Aleichem is deprived of his voice, his pace, his humane cleverness and boxed into the formula of a post-*Oklahoma* musical."[126] Howe went further to condemn Americans of Jewish descent who fail to care about, or at least recognize, the transformation of Old World Jewish culture, and to excoriate the "Yiddish press" who had lost sight of "important issues concerning the dignity of the Jewish tradition and the values of the contemporary Jewish world."

Critiques of this sort have appeared now and again in the decades since *Fiddler's* premiere,[127] and in 2004 the issues resurfaced with special fury surrounding the show's third Broadway revival, opening at the Minskoff on February 26. Eleven days before opening night (but twenty-three days after the first preview), novelist and cultural critic Thane Rosenbaum renewed calls for a *Fiddler* that stayed closer to its Jewish roots.[128] The new production, wrote Rosenbaum, had "in some profound, perhaps even intentional way, an absence of Jewish soul." As other critics and journalists began to react to Rosenbaum's charges, a related issue emerged, focusing on the ethnicity of the actor playing Tevye, the Spanish-Italian (and non-Jewish) Alfred Molina. According to the *New York Post*, people with inside knowledge were saying that the show had been "de-Jewed."[129] Ben Brantley reported in the *Times* that the production had earned a nickname in the Broadway community: "Goyim on the Roof."[130] With Molina as Tevye, many other apparently non-Jewish actors in lead roles, and all under the direction of the British (and non-Jewish) David Leveaux, some critics were wondering just how "Jewish" this *Fiddler* was, and how "Jewish" it should be.

In other words, the debate surrounding the 2004 revival not only revisited centuries-old controversies about character portrayal and ethnicity, voiced by critics throughout the history of opera and other forms of drama, it also essentially revived questions that the creators themselves had been asking from the very beginning. They had made a decision to emphasize universality over specificity, and the result was a spectacularly successful entertainment for the masses, not a history lesson. As Harnick says in Rosenbaum's article: "We didn't want the show to only play to Jews, and, at the same time, we had no ambition to teach the world about Jews." Further, "It's not really an accurate depiction of the *shtetl*. It's more like having false memories of a longing for community." To those critics who long for the authenticity and Yiddish flavor of the original source material, the show's creators might respond, with Stephen J. Whitfield, that "Sholem Aleichem is not so fragile, so badly in need of protection, that *Fiddler on the Roof* posed a threat to his availability to serious readers."[131] As Ami Eden wrote in *Forward*, the problem was not in the show or in the production but in the critics themselves, who have "misguided definitions of Jewish authenticity and lack of imagination."[132] Reflecting in 2009, Joseph Stein questioned whether critics

> understand the concept of adaptation. I mean, Sholem Aleichem wrote in a different language, for a different audience, in a different medium. . . . I adapted it in my own way into a language that's understandable in theater terms. . . . And yet I wanted, consistently, to stay true to the essence of the Sholem Aleichem stories. I think I succeeded. . . . There are some purists who apparently would like the show to be read as monologues. Which is fine with me. I mean, if you want to have somebody get up and read the stories, that's fine.[133]

Jerry Bock responded to the criticisms in a letter addressed to Michael Riedel of the *New York Post* (but never mailed):

> For your colleague Rosenbaum to have put the term "de-Jewing" in David Leveaux's hands is an abomination. That phrase is more likely to be found in the dictionary of The Holocaust. It will never be found in this production of Fiddler on the Roof. In each case this incomparable cast was chosen for their lasting talent, not by their last names. To have even suggested that point is not only pointless and perverse, but exposes his deplorable ignorance of the theater process, and demeans the creators along the way. For you to have mined this mud, sullies your hands as well.[134]

John Heilpern reasonably asked, "Where is it written that only a Jew can play a Jew? If that were the case, Laurence Olivier, the son of a priest, wouldn't have given us his memorable Shylock, and Nathan Lane, a Catholic, wouldn't have been able to play Max Bialystock."[135] Charles Isherwood wondered "whether a production of *The Sound of Music* with a Jewish actress as Maria would be accused of having an absence of 'goyish' soul."[136]

So the critics changed their names but hardly changed their tunes in the forty years between the first *Fiddler* and its third Broadway revival. At the same time, the show itself has aged gracefully over that period, refining and redefining its place in American culture. Alisa Solomon makes this point very eloquently in an article that appeared in the *Village Voice* just before the 2004 premiere.[137] *Fiddler*'s impact on "America's sense of Jewish history can hardly be exaggerated," writes Solomon. The show was born in a time when American Jews needed to "stake a claim to an ethnic past" and to be "assured of being fully American." Forty years later, Jewish families have proven their upward mobility and "no longer dream of becoming rich men (and women) in 'a big tall house with rooms by the dozen.'" *Fiddler*'s pogrom once reminded audiences of "Jewish powerlessness," writes Solomon, but now reminds Jews of their "bygone innocence." She quotes Jeffrey Shandler, a professor of Jewish studies at Rutgers University: "Until the Six-Day War [of 1967] it was *Fiddler* that was the source of public Jewish-American pride." In the "post-*Seinfeld* era," says Shandler, "we've got much more complex and forthright statements about Jewishness in popular art." Further, writes Solomon in a two-part follow-up in *Forward*, in an era of "hybrid cultural invention," *Fiddler* today gives new generations of Jewish artists opportunities to explore their heritage in very different ways.[138] If *Fiddler* 1964 helped American Jews "consolidate their Americanness" (in Wolitz's words, the "Americanization of Tevye"), *Fiddler* 2004 "helps them firm up their Jewishness."

This places a heavy burden on *Fiddler* producers in the twenty-first century, to maintain a delicate balance between nostalgia and contemporary relevance. For the Broadway production in 2004, David Leveaux hoped to re-examine some of the show's themes without changing its essence. The scenery in his production was quite different and nothing like Chagall, the character of the "fiddler" himself was more of a constant presence, sometimes interacting with the onstage orchestra, and Bock and Harnick even wrote a new Klezmer-flavored song, "Topsy-Turvy," for Yente to sing in the second act.[139] (It replaced the scene-change song, "The Rumor.") On the other hand, some of Jerome Robbins's staging, and virtually all of his choreography, remained intact. Reviews were mixed. In the wake of Thane Rosenbaum's pre-opening-night pre-review, some reviewers of the actual opening night seemed to have been too easily distracted by the matter of the show's "Jewishness." But the issue was not, as Ben Brantley wrote in the *Times* (2/27/04), whether a non-Jewish actor is capable of projecting "Jewish soul"; the issue was whether the production had "soul of any kind." Where some saw praiseworthy "control and restraint" (Desmond Ryan, *Philadelphia Inquirer*, 2/29/04), others saw a "paralyzing fog" (Ben Brantley, *New York Times* 2/27/04). Some found Molina's performance "impressive" (Terry Teachout, *Wall Street Journal*, 2/27/04) and "inspired" (Robert Feldberg, *The Record*, 2/27/04); others found him "tentative and wary" (Mark Steyn, *New Criterion*,

April 2004) or complained that he "doesn't have musical comedy in his bones" (Peter Marks, *Washington Post*, 2/27/04).

The following January, when Harvey Fierstein assumed Tevye duties, the production gained new life from his stage presence and comic gifts, and ran for another year. He even survived a few months alongside Rosie O'Donnell's undistinguished portrayal of Golde.[140] Fierstein explored the humor in the role without resorting to Mostellian shtick, and he proved that he could play a warm, affectionate husband and father with a deep emotional core. Of course this hardly resolved the ongoing debate, as it simply left critics free to argue whether Fierstein was a good Tevye because he is a good actor, or whether he was a good Tevye because he is a good Jewish actor.

John Lahr, in his commentary on the 2004 opening in the *New Yorker*, highlights yet another part of *Fiddler*'s message, its perspective on the Jewish "storytelling tradition."[141] The show itself is "eloquent witness" to that tradition, writes Lahr, and we understand that the omnipresent onstage fiddler himself represents the "invisible thread of narrative," as his playing "carries in its distinctive ambivalent refrain the culture's memory of loss and of wisdom." The message was delivered with special impact at the end of Leveaux's production, when the fiddler handed his instrument to a young boy. But this is not just a "passing on of the narrative tradition" in Jewish culture; it is in fact a "foreshadowing of the American musical itself," writes Lahr. The storytelling tradition would survive and prosper in the century to come in the hands of songwriters and dramatists whose ancestors would settle in America as if following the migration of Tevye and his family. As Mark Steyn has written, *Fiddler* is "a piece of collective autobiography, a farewell to the world those Lower East Siders left behind."[142]

It is appropriate, then, that *Fiddler on the Roof* should help mark the end of a storied period in the evolution of the Broadway musical, not only by standing as one of its most successful and powerful exemplars, but also by commenting symbolically on the history it helps to make. The paradigms of Rodgers and Hammerstein had proven their worth in the post-*Oklahoma!* years, constituting what Mark N. Grant calls (paraphrasing Lehman Engel) the "common-practice period" of the American musical between 1940 and 1965.[143] Contributions to that history in the years just before the conception of *Fiddler*—especially *West Side Story* (1957), *Gypsy* (1959), and *The Sound of Music* (1959)—had exemplified the tradition in its most refined and artistically viable state. Amid turbulent changes in American society, the years after *Fiddler*'s premiere, the nearly eight years of its initial Broadway run, would see the radical departures of *Hair* (1968) and the dramatic innovations of Stephen Sondheim (starting with *Company* in 1970). *Fiddler* demonstrates that an overture is not an essential component of the formula, that the integration of music and story can be accomplished in multiple interesting ways, and that even a show with a pogrom can draw audiences in droves, but above all it demonstrates how beautifully the formula can work in the hands of expert practitioners. *Fiddler* aims to keep alive not only the bittersweet aura of Jewish history but also the Broadway musical itself. The fiddler plays his tune, and *Fiddler* plays on.

7

HERE IN EDEN

• • •

THE MID-1960S AND *THE APPLE TREE*

After *Fiorello!* in 1959, Jerry Bock and Sheldon Harnick had established them-selves as major contributors to the Broadway canon, and the critical acclaim of *She Loves Me* in 1963 had proven their range and originality, if not commer-cial viability. In the second half of the 1960s, however, as *Fiddler on the Roof* evolved from smash hit to cultural phenomenon, their stature as musicians and dramatists rose to an exclusive, iconic level. They accepted the resulting responsibilities with grace and humility. While monitoring cast changes and maintenance of *Fiddler* on Broadway, they also kept close watch over national tours and overseas premieres and generally did what they could to keep the show's integrity intact. In the years to come they resisted offers to return to the Aleichem characters, notwithstanding rumors of a sequel tentatively titled *Tevye in America*.[1] Bock said in 2002, "You won't believe how many offers we've had to do *Son of Fiddler, Daughter of Fiddler, Fiddler IV*," but "it wasn't even a temptation."[2] They did have discussions in the early 2000s about a made-for-television version of *Fiddler on the Roof*, to be directed by Alan Ackerman and starring Victor Garber as Tevye. The project was to be financed by Disney and filmed in a Czech village, but fell apart because of security concerns and new budget-busting insurance costs in the aftermath of the tragedies of September 11, 2001. The care and feeding of *Fiddler* can be an all-encompassing endeavor: it is not unusual to find more than two hun-dred current or upcoming productions of the show, all over the world, listed on the website of its licensing organization.[3]

When the *Fiddler* explosion was just beginning to reverberate in late 1964, however, Bock and Harnick were simply looking for new ideas and projects. Their next major effort, their sixth as a team, would premiere on Broadway as *The Apple Tree* in the fall of 1966. Amidst the twists and turns of the new show's development they also found time to make smaller contributions to other new Broadway productions, to create a new television musical, and to write music for beer commercials. They were in demand, they were at the top of their form, and they relished the opportunities and hard work.

BAKER STREET

Bock and Harnick had probably known for years about the development of a musical known as *Baker Street*, based on a selection of Arthur Conan Doyle's Sherlock Holmes stories. Jerome Coopersmith, who had written for television in the 1950s, had drafted a libretto for the show and had been seeking support and collaborators since the late fifties or early sixties. Around 1962 Coopersmith did some work with composer Alan Friedman and lyricist Dennis Marks, and a premiere had been announced for February 1963, but the production schedule was delayed by disagreements over the score and by a change of director, from Michael Langham to Joshua Logan.[4] At some point Bock and Harnick had been offered the chance to write the show's score but had declined, citing conflicts with other projects.[5] Eventually Marian Grudeff and Ray Jessel were brought in to write the music, Logan bowed out, and Harold Prince was hired to direct, fresh from *She Loves Me* and just starting to assume producer's duties for *Fiddler*.[6] Prince took the job because he wanted more directorial experience, and he was able to devote all his efforts to the project in the fall of 1964, following *Fiddler*'s opening in September. All the while, however, he had persistent concerns about Grudeff and Jessel's score. As the production played its pre-Broadway tryouts in Boston and Toronto he convinced the producer to bring in Bock and Harnick for a last-minute infusion of new creative energy, and they eventually wrote four new songs for the show, all uncredited and intended to remain a secret.[7] After still more delays *Baker Street* finally opened in New York, on February 16, 1965, and ran for 313 performances.

Coopersmith's adaptation, drawn from four different Holmes stories, centers on Queen Victoria's Diamond Jubilee in 1897 and Holmes's attempts to prevent Moriarty from stealing the Crown Jewels. The librettist also created a love-interest for the main character in Irene Adler, an actress. Reactions by New York critics varied widely—John Chapman in the *Daily News* (2/17/65) called it "an absolutely captivating entertainment," Martin Gottfried in *Women's Wear Daily* (2/17/65) summed it up as a "good-looking bore"—although all of them liked a moment in the second act when the Queen's Jubilee procession was portrayed entirely by Bil Baird's puppetry. Reviewers also generally agreed that the music was the show's weakest element, and several made unflattering comparisons with music from two other shows set in London,

Lerner and Loewe's *My Fair Lady* (1956) and Lionel Bart's *Oliver!* (1960). Indeed many of the Grudeff–Jessel songs do have strong echoes of those scores. When Holmes talk-sings "It's So Simple" to display his powers of deduction, he seems to be mimicking Henry Higgins, and when Irene anticipates her night out with Holmes to help him track down Moriarty, her song "What a Night This Is Going to Be" sounds like a close relative of Eliza Doolittle's song about a night out, "I Could Have Danced All Night." Songs by the band of street urchins known as the Baker Street Irregulars ("Leave it To Us, Guv," "Roof Space") leave the impression that the boys are close friends, perhaps business associates, of Fagin and the Artful Dodger ("Consider Yourself," "Be Back Soon").

Bock and Harnick apparently made no effort to match the styles of their songs with the existing ones; the result is a bit of a hodgepodge.[8] In Boston they wrote "I'm in London Again" for Irene to sing in Act 1 when she is performing her stage show, and "I Shall Miss You" for Moriarty, who is holding Holmes captive and preparing to detonate a time bomb—part of a reworked Act 1 finale. For the lyric of "I Shall Miss You" Harnick drew inspiration from a line in an earlier version of the script; some of the lyrics of the Grudeff–Jessel song that was replaced, "A Veritable Work of Art," were then written into the dialogue.[9] In Toronto they added "Cold, Clear World," in which Holmes explains his hyper-rationality to Irene, replacing a Grudeff–Jessel song about sensory acuity, "The Five Senses." Irene responds with a Grudeff–Jessel song, "Finding Words for Spring." After Bock and Harnick returned to New York, Prince persuaded them to write a different song for Irene and they came up with "Buffalo Belle," a production number that eventually replaced "I'm in London Again" during the Broadway run.[10]

Whether or not the new material changed *Baker Street* in any substantial way—or in any positive way, for that matter—Prince was apparently satisfied, or at least mollified. Though a tiny blip on the radar screen for Bock and Harnick, the songs offer an informative glimpse at some of their first work post-*Fiddler*. The climactic final phrase of "I Shall Miss You" is one that Harnick has cited as a favorite: "When the stately Holmes of England is no more."[11] This sly reference to Noël Coward's song "The Stately Homes of England," from his musical *Operette* (1938), is delivered in plain emphatic quarter notes moving down a natural minor scale, except that the penultimate note, step two of the scale, is lowered. The result is a Phrygian half step between this note and the final tonic, a tiny remembrance of melodies with lowered second steps in the *Fiddler* score (e.g., the end of the "Fiddler" tune and melodies based on the *Ahavah rabbah* mode). What is distinctive about Bock's work in general in the songs for *Baker Street* is a pronounced affection for chromaticism, especially in "I'm in London Again," which is vocally challenging, and "I Shall Miss You," which has sinister series of semitones slithering around the steps of a minor scale. While chromatic moments are not uncommon in Bock's earlier work, from Tamiment songs to "If I Were a Rich Man" ("All day long I'd biddy, biddy bum" and so forth), his only previous exploration of this extent of chromatic saturation was his song with Larry Holofcener from at least a decade earlier, "Show Me a Better Man" (Example 2.2).

THE CANTERVILLE GHOST

For the remainder of 1965, now with musical stakes in two shows currently playing on Broadway, Bock and Harnick accepted an assortment of new assignments. Bock wrote a song and incidental music for William Goodhart's play *Generation*, which opened in October and played for 300 performances. Henry Fonda starred as a father befuddled by the values and behavior of his pregnant daughter and her beatnik husband. It was, therefore, the second time Bock contributed music to a play about impending parenthood and generational differences, after *Never Too Late* in 1962 (see chapter 4). Bock's song for *Generation*, with lyrics by the playwright, was "I Put My IBM Card in that Old Pianola," an amalgam of Al Jolson and rock and roll that the daughter and son-in-law sing to showcase his poetic gifts.[12] During this period Bock and Harnick together wrote songs for two Ballantine Beer commercials, one a "Riddle Song" in a light comic vein, the other a jazzy syncopated number with a melody obsessed with interlocking thirds and a curious atonal ending.[13] Harnick recalls receiving some sort of recognition or award for their efforts from an organization of television advertisers.

In 1966, while simultaneously moving through the final stages of development for their next major Broadway musical, Bock and Harnick also wrote songs for a made-for-television musical, *The Canterville Ghost*, based on the Oscar Wilde novella. The production debuted on ABC on November 2, 1966, a few days after *The Apple Tree* opened on Broadway. It was part of a series of original programs, collectively titled ABC Stage '67, that included dramas, documentaries, variety shows, and musicals. Memorable entries in the series included Stephen Sondheim's *Evening Primrose* (broadcast on 11/16/66), the Burt Bacharach–Hal David rock musical *On the Flip Side* (12/7/66), and dramas by Sam Peckinpah (*Noon Wine*, 11/23/66), Truman Capote (*A Christmas Memory*, 12/21/66), and Jean Cocteau (*The Human Voice*, 5/4/67).[14] *The Canterville Ghost* was directed by John Robins and starred Douglas Fairbanks,

Jr., Michael Redgrave, Natalie Schaefer (who had just completed her third and final season as Mrs. Thurston Howell III on *Gilligan's Island*), and Peter Noone, at that time riding a wave of popularity as the lead singer of Herman's Hermits.

Wilde's novella, first published in serial form in 1887, is a classic ghost story with a mischievous commentary on Americans and American values.[15] When the American Ambassador and his family arrive to occupy Canterville Castle, they are unfazed by warnings of a haunting spirit lurking within. Despite the best efforts of the ghost of Sir Simon de Canterville to frighten them into leaving, the Americans become quite content in the stately English manor. They interact with the ghost and befriend him. The two young twin boys of the family play tricks on him. This leaves Sir Simon in abject distress, and eventually the family's fifteen-year-old daughter, Virginia, learns the root of the problem: the ghost longs only to leave the spirit world and join his wife, whom he had killed in 1575, in eternal rest. Simon tells Virginia that only the prayers and tears of a young girl can help him to rest in peace, and she agrees to do her part. While her family frantically searches for her, Virginia travels with Simon into the netherworld and sheds a tear of redemption. When she returns, she tells her family that the ghost is gone, and they give the skeleton a proper burial. In an epilogue, Virginia is depicted several years hence, telling her new husband, the Duke of Cheshire, that she can never tell anyone, including him, about her experience with the ghost of Sir Simon: "He made me see what Life is, and what Death signifies, and why Love is stronger than both."[16]

Bert Shevelove, an old friend of Harnick's from their early years in New York—and the co-writer, with Larry Gelbart, of *A Funny Thing Happened on the Way to the Forum* (1962)—made the adaptation for the television musical. He stayed much closer to the original story than Edwin Blum did for the 1944 film version of *Canterville* starring Charles Laughton, and is generally more faithful than later versions as well, such as George Zateslo's adaptation for a 1986 television movie starring John Gielgud. Even so, there are two substantive differences between Shevelove's adaptation and Wilde's original, alongside other smaller variations: Shevelove makes the Duke of Cheshire more of a presence early on in the story, to develop the romance with Virginia; and his version closes with Virginia's return to the material world, omitting the funeral and flash-forward of Wilde's epilogue. Shevelove first communicated his ideas about the adaptation to Bock and Harnick in the form of a detailed outline, dated April 1966.[17]

This outline includes obvious opportunities or specific suggestions for songs at several places. The opening scene, when the Ambassador's family arrives at

Douglas Fairbanks, Jr. (Ambassador) and Michael Redgrave (Ghost) in
TheCanterville Ghost *(1966) (Photofest)*

the castle, seems to have been conceived as a musical montage, and Bock and
Harnick obliged with "Welcome to Canterville Hall." Soon after, Shevelove set
up a classic romantic scene for the young lovers, Virginia and the Duke of
Cheshire, and for this the songwriters wrote a pair of songs: in "I Worry," Virginia explains that she is filled with the anxieties and doubts of a teenager
(Example 7.1a), and in "If You Never Try," the Duke responds with a proclama-
tion of his openness and willingness to explore (Example 7.1b).[18] Later in the
outline Shevelove wrote, "Virginia and the Duke arrive home from a dance.
There is a love scene and song." Bock and Harnick complied with an up-tempo
love song for the Duke to sing to Virginia, "You're Super." For the ghost's big
musical scene the songwriters adopted Shevelove's suggestion precisely: "The
ghost is in a dreadful state. His honor and the honor of all ghosts are in the
balance. He sings an elaborate song, called 'Vengeance.'" And at the end of the
outline, where Virginia helps deliver Simon from his spiritual agony, Shevelove
suggested that Virginia sing a little verse of "cryptic prophecy"; Bock and Harnick responded with a moment of solemnity, "Peace." All these elements came
together in a full libretto, including all song lyrics, dated July 15, 1966.[19]

Shevelove's oddest idea proposed a recurring "commercial jingle" at three places in the original story where Wilde depicts the Ambassador's family as unrepentant pitchmen, like carnival barkers eager to make a fast buck selling magic potions. In Wilde's original, when the housekeeper explains that a red stain on the floor continues to return even after it has been cleaned away— Simon puts it there, to mark the spot where he killed his wife—one of the sons responds that "Pinkerton's Champion Stain Remover and Paragon Detergent will clean it up in no time" and proceeds to scrub it clean.[20] In his outline at this point Shevelove wrote that the Ambassador's wife "cleans the spot from the floor, singing a little commercial jingle in praise of the product." Later Wilde has the Ambassador advising the ghost to oil his noisy chains, using

> a small bottle of the Tammany Rising Sun Lubricator. It is said to be completely efficacious upon one application, and there are several testimonials to that effect on the wrapper from some of our most eminent native divines. I shall leave it here for you by the bedroom candles, and will be happy to supply you with more should you require it.[21]

Shevelove suggested: "He has some all-purpose oil that he has been using on his hunting rifles. That should do the trick. He gives it to the ghost and again we hear the commercial jingle, this time in praise of the all-purpose oil." And still later, when Wilde's ghost emits a peal of "demoniac laughter," the Ambassador's wife offers him "a bottle of Dr. Dobell's tincture" to help with indigestion.[22] Shevelove changed this to a headache remedy and again suggests a "commercial jingle in praise of the little pills."

Bock and Harnick accepted all three of these suggestions. At those three places in the show, the characters break into song in praise of their products, as if suddenly transformed into advertisers on late-night info-mercials. First they sing about a stain remover called "Undertow," second about a lubricant named "Rattletrap," and third about their headache remedy, "Overhead." The jingles are all based on the same melody (as Shevelove proposed) but presented in contrasting styles, making the melodic similarities easy to miss: the first is a sort of jazz waltz, with "doo be doo" fill-ins inserted between phrases of the main melody, the second is presented as a show tune, and the last is rendered in a brassy pop style. (Above the first measure of the lead sheet for the third one Bock wrote, "'Tiajuana [sic] Brass' style."[23]) To present these ideas this way certainly makes the point about the crass commercialism of the ugly Americans very strongly, but it also holds an odd presence in the flow of the drama. The commercials seem to occupy some ghostly netherworld between standard musical-comedy moments, where the characters break into song (as they do, of course, else-where in the show), and diegetic moments, where the characters recognize that they are singing. These three send-ups of American enterprise are neither, and they are both.

The other songs in the show demonstrate typical dramatic range and musical variety. The ghost's big number, "Vengeance," is a dramatic *tour de force*, in the tradition of Billy Bigelow's "Soliloquy" from *Carousel* or "Rose's Turn" from *Gypsy* or an operatic mad scene. Simon releases a fury of threats and complaints, recalling some of his more successful efforts at scaring unwelcome guests and promising to bring a whole new experience of fright to the Ambassador and his family. Harnick got ideas for the lyric from passages in Wilde's original, as when Simon revels in the memory of creating an uproar "by merely playing ninepins with his own bones upon the lawn-tennis ground."[24] In Harnick's versification this becomes:

> As the night was warm and windless all the guests were strolling 'round
> So I suddenly appeared upon the lawn tennis ground.
> With a minimum of moaning, just a few selected groans
> I played a game of nine-pins with me own bleached bones![25]

Bock's musical setting for "Vengeance" includes simple mocking melodies, moments of recitative, and a dramatic ending worthy of *verismo* opera. The song "Peace," on the other hand, is more of a hymn, using simple materials to evoke an archaic religious setting. Still more different are the songs for the young lovers. "You're Super" could almost be a current pop song—by, say, Herman's Hermits—but it is a little too square; the Duke makes us question whether one chap can be both aristocratic and groovy. And the pairing of their songs "I Worry" and "If You Never Try" uses musical contrast to help establish the contrast in their characters, something that the libretto itself does not develop much at all. Virginia's anxieties are expressed in a minor key (C), in a rhythmically restless melody (Example 7.1a). The Duke's song is in a major key (F) with frequent returns to the raised fourth step (B♮) and its upward resolution (Example 7.1b), using the resolving appoggiatura to depict security and confidence as Bock had done before, notably in half-step resolutions in the melody of "On the Side of the Angels" from *Fiorello!* (cf. Example 3.2). When the Duke's melody moves on to a B section ("A wee baby bird . . ."), he recalls and re-interprets a turning figure that is central to Virginia's tune (bracketed in Examples 7.1a and 7.1b). The motivic linkage not only helps make a musical connection between the characters; it also shows how the Duke is able to accept Virginia's worries and overcome them with hopefulness.

a. "I Worry," opening phrases (Bock Papers, box 14, folder 11)

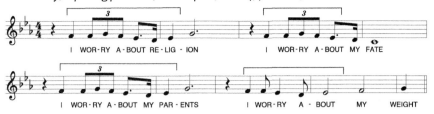

b. "If You Never Try," first A and B sections (Bock Papers, box 14, folder 10)

Example 7.1: Melodies of the young lovers in The Canterville Ghost

But was it all for naught? *The Canterville Ghost* was one of the least successful products of the Bock–Harnick partnership. Jack Gould in the *New York Times* (11/3/66) called it a "wildly incoherent mishmash." Barbara Delatiner in *Newsday* (11/3/66) summarized the show as a "graceless, unimaginative, humorless charade." Part of the problem was the singing: only Michael Redgrave, as the ghost, and Peter Noone, as the Duke, showed any musical ability at all. The singing voices of the other actors begged for anonymous overdubbing. Harnick has said that the director of the show was too "laid back" and did not devote sufficient effort to casting.[26] But this was only part of the show's misfortune; at every turn it was plagued by dubious creative decisions. Many of the songs had the potential to charm but were weighed down by presentation and context. It is difficult to judge whether the three odd "commercials" were simply ill-conceived or whether they could have worked, or at least worked better, at the hands of a more attentive, imaginative director. Harnick confessed, "Jerry Bock and I may not have taken *The Canterville Ghost* seriously enough." They wrote their songs "and then walked away from it, instead of trying, in any way we could, to make the show (not just the score) as good as possible." If they had followed through with production and refinement, as they always did with their musicals for Broadway, they could and undoubtedly would have done more to correct earlier misjudgments. *The Canterville Ghost* displays, in effect, an early stage of a creative process that was not seen through to the end.

THE APPLE TREE

Bock and Harnick were unable to devote sufficient time and energy to a television musical during this same period because they were busy preparing their next show for Broadway. It is a project they had been working on since long before *Canterville* came along, since the immediate aftermath of *Fiddler on the Roof* in late 1964, and by the spring of 1966 they were preparing to start rehearsals. Of course they were eager to build on their recent success, but with no end in sight for the *Fiddler* phenomenon, they were also in no particular hurry. Their sixth major musical, *The Apple Tree*, finally premiered at the Shubert Theater on October 18, 1966, more than two years after *Fiddler* opened around the corner at the Imperial.

The impetus for the new project once again reflected their desire to break new ground, to try something different rather than retracing old steps. In December 1964 Bock and Harnick told Lewis Funke of the *Times* that they were conceiving a set of "three individual pieces all to be performed in a single evening, all to have the same book writer, director, designer, choreographer, stars, and casts."[27] Bock later explained:

> Writers will sometimes take a wonderful tale, and because they believe they're bound to fill a certain amount of time, like two hours, they take that story and stretch it as much as possible. We thought we'd like to try to do the stories in the amount of time they should take, and if it was forty minutes for one, twenty for another, a half hour for another, so be it. We'd still fill the evening but give each story its rightful due.[28]

As it happened, Stuart Ostrow, who had produced and directed Meredith Willson's *Here's Love* in 1963, was thinking along the same lines and signed on to produce Bock and Harnick's new show during the early stages. He told the *Times*:

> Let's face it—too many musicals run out of steam by the time the second-act curtain goes up. The padding is strictly according to formula—a big

production number here, a big ballet scene there. What we will be doing will be adaptations of shorter works—stories, one-act plays. The field is vast. It has great potential. The shorter musical form permits Bock and Harnick to choose dramatic situations previously not considered practical for traditional two-act musical comedy and drama.[29]

Or as Ostrow more cynically put it in 1999, "Television had reduced the audience's attention span to half-hour programming—why not try it on stage?"[30]

Harnick remembers reading "hundreds and hundreds of stories" in search of source material for their suite of one-act musicals.[31] They considered writings of Nelson Algren, Marcel Aymé, Donald Barthelme, Giovanni Boccassio, Jorge Luis Borges, Truman Capote, Anton Chekhov, Charles Dickens, Guy de Maupassant, Nikolai Gogol, Nathaniel Hawthorne, Ernest Hemingway, Henry James, James Joyce, D. H. Lawrence, Bernard Malamud, Katherine Mansfield, Herman Melville, Frank O'Connor, Katherine Ann Porter, Edgar Allan Poe, Mark Twain, Émile Zola, and Mikhail Zoshchenko, among others.[32] They enlisted the services of a "college professor of literature" for help with sources and ideas.[33] They made three initial choices—de Maupassant's "Boule de Suif," Malamud's "Angel Levine," and Aymé's "Martin, the Novelist"—but decided that these stories lacked cohesion as an evening of theater. They started adapting Capote's "Along the Paths to Eden" but then learned that the rights had been withdrawn.[34] By June of 1965 they had settled on stories by American writers focused on male–female relationships: Bruce Jay Friedman's "Show Biz Connections," Hawthorne's "Young Goodman Brown," and Twain's "The Diary of Adam and Eve." They invited their *She Loves Me* collaborator, Joe Masteroff, to make the adaptations, but he was already committed to Kander and Ebb's next project, *Cabaret*. Instead Jerome Coopersmith, with whom they had worked briefly on *Baker Street*, took the job and began drafting a libretto. The announced title for the show was *Come Back! Go Away! I Love You.*[35]

Bock, Harnick, and Coopersmith worked for the second half of 1965 and the early months of 1966 on the Friedman and Twain treatments. They made substantial progress on the Hawthorne but struggled with the ending: "None of us were really sure what Hawthorne was saying," recalls Harnick.[36] Eventually they abandoned Hawthorne and turned their attention instead to Frank R. Stockton's "The Lady or the Tiger," for which Coopersmith drafted a general scenario. At some point, however, Bock and Harnick began to feel constrained by their relationship with their librettist. Coopersmith had written a script for the Twain story that Harnick found "very clever" and "theatrically sound," but that did not seem amenable to musical treatment. Ostrow told them, "in so short a form (shorter even than a first act of an average musical), the librettist and lyricist might be getting in each other's way."[37] Eventually Coopersmith agreed to step aside, retaining a program credit (for "additional book material") and a financial stake, and Bock and Harnick took responsibility for the libretto themselves. The book is officially credited to both of them equally, although Harnick actually did most of the writing (or rewriting Coopersmith) himself, with assistance from Bock in the form of "conferences and suggestions."[38] In the case of the Twain adaptation, Harnick made very few substantive adjustments in what Coopersmith had originally given him: he introduced "minor changes, cuts, additions, and transpositions," but "the end product was still *essentially* [Coopersmith's] libretto."[39] He created a fairly complete version of the Friedman story, and he began to flesh out Coopersmith's scenario for the Stockton into what he has described as a "little jazz opera."[40]

Bock, Harnick, and Ostrow had hoped that Jerome Robbins would direct, but in early spring 1966, Robbins was unable to commit to their lineup of Friedman–Stockton–Twain. Robbins had other commitments, plus basic questions about the conception of a single show drawn from three disparate sources.[41] Instead Ostrow made inquiries with Mike Nichols, who had already made a name for himself as the Tony-winning director of the plays *Barefoot in the Park* (1963), *Luv* (1964), and *The Odd Couple* (1965), and who would have been in the final pre-release production stages of his feature film directorial debut, *Who's Afraid of Virginia Woolf?* (1966). Nichols agreed to do it—it would be his first experience directing a musical—but only if the Friedman story, which he felt was "simply too dark," was replaced.[42] He suggested instead a musical treatment of Jules Feiffer's illustrated story "Passionella," a property he had come to know a few years earlier, when it was adapted in a show he directed in summer stock in New Jersey. In that adaptation it was called *The World of Jules Feiffer* (1962) and included music by Stephen Sondheim.[43] Bock and Harnick reluctantly agreed to the switch and went back to work, and by the summer of 1966 they had their complete show ready for rehearsals, reordered as Twain–Stockton–Feiffer.

To help with the staging of musical numbers, Ostrow brought in Herbert Ross, whose choreography had continued to gain respect since *The Body Beautiful* and who had received a Tony nomination for his work with Stephen Sondheim and Arthur Laurents on *Anyone Can Whistle* (1964). The main choreographer for the show would be Lee Theodore, who had played one of the bar girls in the original Broadway production of *Tenderloin*. Otherwise the members of the production team were new to the Bock–Harnick orbit: orchestrator Eddie Sauter, musical director and vocal arranger Elliot

Lawrence (who had won a Tony award in 1962 for his musical direction of *How to Succeed in Business Without Really Trying*), and scene and costume designer Tony Walton (who would win the first of three Tony awards a few years later, working with Stuart Ostrow again on *Pippin*).

The show was renamed *The Apple Tree*. The change in title, explained Harnick, recognized that "each story seemed to have a kind of devil figure" and "was about a male subdued by a cunning, fatally appealing female."[44] At the same time, the songwriter-librettists continued to have concerns about the thematic coherence of the stories they had selected, even as the first stage of their work was complete in early summer 1966. They recalled Jerome Robbins's parting words: "Keep this evening homogeneous. It must add up to something."[45] They asked for further delays. Ostrow told them, however, that Nichols was only available then, for rehearsals starting on July 18. The show had to go on.

The production would require only three principal characters, a leading couple and a foil who also served as a narrator and balladeer. Ostrow remembers seriously considering an African-American actor, Al Freeman, Jr., for the male lead but deciding that Broadway was not ready for a mixed-race romance. He also recalls auditioning a young Dustin Hoffman for the role but discovering that Hoffman could not sing at all. (Mike Nichols would remember him when he was casting his next project, his film *The Graduate*.) Alan Alda, who had worked on Broadway since 1959, most recently in Bill Manhoff's *The Owl and the Pussycat* (1964), won the role with a rendition of "If I Only Had a Brain."[46] Barbara Harris took the female lead. Her star had been rising since arriving on Broadway with the Second City improvisational troupe from Chicago in 1961, moving on to an acclaimed production of Brecht's *Mother Courage and Her Children* (1963) and to the part of Daisy Gamble in the Burton Lane–Alan Jay Lerner musical *On a Clear Day You Can See Forever* (1965), for which she received a Tony nomination. The third main role was played by Larry Blyden, who had worked on Broadway since 1949, often in secondary lead parts such as Sammy Fong in Rodgers and Hammerstein's *Flower Drum Song* (1958), for which he received a Tony nomination.

Part 1: "The Diary of Adam and Eve"
The Stockton and Feiffer stories have straightforward narratives that could be preserved in most details in the stage adaptations. The Twain material, on the other hand, began as two separate publications, *Extracts from Adam's Diary* (1893) and *Eve's Diary* (1905), that had to be woven together into a dramatic unity.[47] The final stage version, named "The Diary of Adam and Eve," retains the original sense of a "diary" recorded by Adam and Eve in the Garden

of Eden, interleaving elements of the two separate perspectives to tell the familiar story. It also preserves some of the homespun charm of the original, while adding a few new witticisms. The story begins when God awakens a sleeping Adam (a dramatic device not found in the original sources), who begins to name the creatures around him, as "flyers," "crawlers," "swimmers," and the like. This is an embellishment of part of Twain's *Eve* diary, where she describes her relationship with Adam: "During the last day or two I have taken all the work of naming things off his hands, and this has been a great relief to him, for he has no gift in that line, and is evidently very grateful."[48] Eve soon emerges onto the scene, although Adam has not yet named or even identified this new creature, and she remarks that she feels like an "experiment," just as in Twain's original:

> For I feel like an experiment, I feel exactly like an experiment; it would be impossible for a person to feel more like an experiment than I do, and so I am coming to feel convinced that that is what I *am*—an experiment; just an experiment, and nothing more.[49]

And so forth. The libretto develops the relationship between a moody, stand-offish Adam and a chatty, personable Eve, just as in Twain. It reinforces stereotypes of the cranky but compliant husband and his demanding but irresistible wife. The two gradually become closer and more affectionate, adopting Eve's suggestion to use the new words "us" and "we," and they begin to call each other by name. The Snake arrives to enlighten Eve about the material world, but in Twain's Eden a forbidden fruit is not the cause of original sin. Instead it is "chestnuts": Adam has invented humor, and Twain's Serpent explains to Adam that when he uttered the First Chestnut of humor, "all nature broke loose in war and death." The libretto adds an extra joke— "Why did the chicken cross the road?"—and then uses Twain's joke as Adam's second example of his new invention:

> I was thinking about [Niagara Falls]. And I thought, "How wonderful it is to see that vast body of water tumble down there." And then I thought, "Yes, but it would be a lot more wonderful to see it tumble up!"[50]

Because Adam has uttered chestnuts, he and Eve must leave the Garden, and they go on to have children and enjoy what appears to be a stable family life. An accelerated chronology ultimately takes us to Eve's death, and Adam's final speech, using the last line of Twain's Eve diary as a sentimental eulogy: "Wheresoever she was, there was Eden."[51]

The music is not continuous throughout this first act of *The Apple Tree* but has a dominant presence, providing not only character exploration and comic

Alan Alda (Adam) and Barbara Harris (Eve) in Act 1 of The Apple Tree *(1966) (Billy Rose Theater Division, The New York Public Library for the Performing Arts, Astor, Lennox, and Tilden Foundations)*

moments but also integral plot development and dramatic intensifications. Bock and Harnick originally began the show with their song "Useful," in which Adam reflects on his surroundings and his presence in the Garden, followed by "Beautiful, Beautiful World," in which Eve expresses awe at the world around her.[52] The show opened this way in the pre-Broadway tour in

Boston (starting September 10), but Barbara Harris was having difficulty with breathing and phrasing in her song.[53] By the time the show opened in New York on October 18, Adam's opening number had been dropped entirely and Eve's replaced by the new song "Here in Eden," also an exclamation of wonder over the natural surroundings, with a brief reference to a "tiny reservation" that sets the drama in motion: she lacks companionship.

The remainder of the music for the Twain adaptation stayed the same from Boston to New York (Table 7.1). Eve's second song is "Feelings," an exploration of her physical and emotional responses to Adam. Harnick's clever ending sets up the expectation of a certain rhyming word but delivers something different:

> What is the source of this congestion
> That I must learn to rise above?
> Is there a name for this condition?
> Yes, there's a name . . .
> And it is hell![54]

Bock sets the "Feelings" lyric in an unusual asymmetrical meter alternating a triple beat grouping with three duples, notated in the published vocal score as alternating measures of 3/4 and 6/4. The vocal line is mostly thirds and leaps and difficult shifts and breathing patterns—actually more challenging, it would seem, than the song that gave Barbara Harris problems, "Beautiful, Beautiful World."

Soon after "Feelings," Adam sings its counterpart, "Eve." He notices the "rubbish" filling up their hut, like "flowers and plants," and resists her efforts at physical affection, yet finds that "She's an interesting creature / This Eve." Bock makes a musical connection between this number and Eve's recent song: a prominent falling half-step motive in the introduction to "Feelings" is referenced by a conspicuous rising half-step figure in the introduction to "Eve." Motivic half steps also figure prominently in the next song, "Friends," Eve's self-examination while studying the human likeness she sees in a pool of water. The idea for this song came directly from Twain's Eve diary:

> I went away and sat on the moss-bank with my feet in the water. It is where I go when I hunger for companionship, some one to look at, some one to talk to. It is not enough—that lovely white body painted there in the pool—but it is something, and something is better than utter loneliness. It talks when I talk; it is sad when I am sad; it comforts me with its sympathy; it says, "Do not be down-hearted, you poor friendless girl; I

Eden Prelude

"Here in Eden" (Eve)

"Feelings" (Eve)

"Eve" (Adam)

"Friends" (Eve)

"The Apple Tree (Forbidden Fruit)" (Snake)

"Beautiful, Beautiful World" (Adam)

"It's a Fish" (Adam)

"Go to Sleep, Whatever You Are" (Eve)

"What Makes Me Love Him?" (Eve)

Eden Postlude

will be your friend." It *is* a good friend to me, and my only one; it is my sister.[55]

But when she finishes the song, the Snake arrives to point out that Eve has merely discovered her own reflection. He then sings his big number, "The Apple Tree (Forbidden Fruit)," and again an opening half-step motive catches our attention and reminds us of "Feelings" and "Eve." Now the half step has a sinister, luring character ("Listen . . . closely / Let me fill you in"), showing that the Snake has taken over a musical idea that once linked Adam and Eve and made it his own. In the song he lets Eve in on the secret that the apples are not forbidden but are actually sources of knowledge and wisdom, developing an idea from Twain's Adam diary: "She says the snake advises her to try the fruit of that tree, and says the result will be a great and fine and noble education."[56]

That song segues immediately into Adam's rendition of "Beautiful, Beautiful World," the number that was originally sung by Eve at the top of the show, before it was replaced by "Here in Eden." "Beautiful, Beautiful World" remained in the later spot, giving Adam the opportunity to display his newly enlightened perspective on the world around him.[57] Adam also sings the next song in the show, "It's a Fish," about a new creature that Eve has brought home, which she supplies with milk and cradles with maternal affection, following Twain's Adam diary.[58] Eve responds with her lullaby for their first child, "Go to Sleep, Whatever You Are," followed by another verse of "It's a Fish," which moves time forward to their second offspring: "I'll be damned if she didn't catch another!"[59] Finally Eve sings a touching reflection on her life with Adam, "What Makes Me Love Him?" Above a spare, music-box-like accompaniment—the published score calls it a "simple country folk style . . . à la dulcimer"—she confesses an inability to explain her affections, even while remaining sure that they are genuine. The lyric is drawn from the final pages of Twain's Eve diary, an extended reflection that starts with the same sentiments:

> The Garden is lost, but I have found *him*, and am content. He loves me as well as he can; I love him with all the strength of my passionate nature, and this, I think, is proper to my youth and sex. If I ask myself why I love him, I find I do not know, and do not really much care to know. . . .[60]

It is a phenomenon full of mystery, Eve realizes, a secret that endures and ensures the perpetuation of the species.

The first act of *The Apple Tree* is Bock's most extended exercise in musical integration. He had employed recurrent chord progressions and motivic ideas as thematic elements in his other shows, but here the saturation reaches a higher degree of musical connection and dramatic meaning. It starts with the first sounds we hear, the "Eden Prelude," actually an instrumental version of "Go to Sleep, Whatever You Are" (Example 7.2a). A descending chromatic line in an inner voice announces a recurring organic thread for the entire act, and beyond, starting from the upper note of an octave (the upper D in the bass clef of mm. 1–2), moving to a major seventh above the tonic (C♯ in mm. 3–4), minor seventh (C♮, mm. 5–6), and then the third of the subdominant (B, m. 7), concluding on ♭6 as the fifth of a dominant pivot chord (B♭, m. 8). Soon after this we hear a chromatic descent again in Eve's song "Here in Eden," in the same key and also in an inner voice, this time going a step further from step 1 down to step 5 (Example 7.2b, the chromatic descent from D down to A in the upper notes of the bass clef). A chromatic motion from 1 down to 5 also appears in the song that "Here in Eden" replaced at the beginning of the show and that became Adam's later song, "Beautiful, Beautiful World" (Example 7.2c). Now it is in the bass line (and in the key of B♭) and so invokes the tradition of the "lament" bass that Bock had used before, in the "New York Prologue" of *Wonders of Manhattan* and elsewhere (see chapter 2).[61] Later, at the end of "The Diary of Adam and Eve," the trend continues, first with the return of the inner chromatic movement of "Go To Sleep, Whatever You Are," as first heard in the Prelude, and then in the undergirding of "What Makes Me Love Him?," winding downward from a tonic E in an inner voice to steps ♮7 (D), 6 (as both C♯ and C♮) and 5 (B) in the bass line (Example 7.2d). The avoidance of root position tonic chords helps portray the uncertainty and questioning of the lyric.

Bock claims "no conscious effort to connect leitmotifs or parallel chromatics or search for commonalities in writing other than the composer's natural

a. "Eden Prelude," mm. 1–8

b. "Here in Eden," opening phrases

c. "Beautiful, Beautiful World," refrain

Example 7.2: Chromatic descents in "The Diary of Adam and Eve" (Continued)

musical instincts rather than a mindful musical plan." Whether conscious or not, the consistency of thought in the first act of *The Apple Tree* gives the score a solid, satisfying musical cohesion and dramatic unity. In one sense the recurrent lines represent the organic matter shared by the originators of human life on earth, the seeds of their blossoming growth and prosperity, in and out of the Garden. Little chromatic moments in other songs tie the thread together as

d. "What Makes Me Love Him?," first verse

Example 7.2: (Continued)

well: inner-voice chromatic ascents in "Eve" and "It's a Fish," and a chain of resolving suspensions in "Friends." But more specifically, the chromatic lines bind the characters together, connecting Eve's "Here in Eden" and "What Makes Me Love Him?" with Adam's "Beautiful, Beautiful World." The ideas coalesce in the lullaby to the product of their union, "Go To Sleep, Whatever You Are," first heard in the Prelude and then played once again as a Postlude just before the first-act curtain. It is indeed a beautiful artistic world, filled with diversity and richness and yet inherently inter-connected through basic genetic material.

Part 2: "The Lady or the Tiger?"

Although initially imagined as co-equals with "The Diary of Adam and Eve," parts two and three of *The Apple Tree* eventually became more modest creations, more like comedy sketches than one-act musical plays. In recent times, when all three parts of *The Apple Tree* are performed together, the second and third are usually played in close succession, with only a brief pause between them, as a single second act. The first act has sometimes been separated out and paired with a different work of comparable dimensions, such as Rice-Lloyd Webber's *Joseph and the Amazing Technicolor Dreamcoat*.[62] In spite of the contrasts, however, Bock and Harnick did what they could to establish linkages between the parts, musical and otherwise. Of course the same actors appear in all three vignettes, and the two main leads play roles that fulfill analogous dramatic functions from one story to the next. The actor who plays the Snake in the first act serves as a narrator for acts two and three. (Following advice from Jerome Robbins, this actor in the original production, Larry Blyden, wore a tuxedo in all three.[63]) The color brown recurs on the walls in Adam's hut, as the color of his suspenders when he makes a joke, as the color of a house in a song in part two, and as a character name at the end of part three. Musically, the acts are connected in obvious ways that theatergoers notice immediately, and in more subtle ways.

In the case of the second tale, "The Lady or the Tiger?," the adapters ultimately discovered, remembers Harnick, that the story is "essentially an intellectual joke" that does not lend itself to broad musical expression.[64] It comes across as a comic chamber opera with a smattering of dialogue. The story is set in a "faraway kingdom" ruled by King Arik, whose justice system consists of choosing between two doors. If an accused man chooses the door leading to a ferocious tiger and certain death, this is considered proof of his guilt. If he chooses the other door, leading to a beautiful woman and immediate matrimony, he is deemed innocent. The king's daughter Barbara (pronounced bar-BEAR-ah) finds herself in a dilemma when she is caught in an embrace with her beloved, the military hero Sanjar, and the King submits Sanjar to the choice of doors. Barbara finds out the secret of the doors, and she promises to tell Sanjar which to choose, but she cannot decide whether to direct him to the lady—actually her servant, Nadjira—or the tiger. The piece ends as the original story does, with Barbara in conflict and the audience left to ponder her anguished decision.

The musical contrast of this vignette with the previous one is apparent as soon as the Act 2 overture begins, with a brass fanfare and a loud, rowdy march. Bock introduces two key elements here: the raised fourth step of the fanfare (the E♮ in Example 7.3a) and the prevalence of the lowered seventh in the melodic lines (the A♭'s in Example 7.3b). These non-scale tones help portray a wild, unruly scene. They also recall the modal basis for some of *Fiddler*'s music, especially the *Mi shebberakh* mode, which features both ♯4 and ♭7 (Examples 6.7b, 6.8b). After the march the Balladeer (narrator) arrives, strums his guitar, and begins to tell the tale in "I'll Tell You a Truth," featuring a melody containing both the lowered (minor) third scale step in the upper register and the unaltered (major) third in the lower, exactly like the *Adonai malach* mode (Example 6.7c). Bock's adoption of these modes—or at least, important elements of these modes—in settings not intended to evoke Jewish musical traditions is consistent with Jack Gottlieb's examples of Jewish elements in American popular music in general.[65] The Balladeer's country-folk song soon gives way to a processional march of the King and Barbara and their subjects, "Make Way." It features a raised fourth, connecting back to the opening interval of the Overture (Example 7.3a), and then repeatedly moves back and forth between the tonic and lowered seventh ("His Royal Tallness!" and so forth), recalling the first main tune of the Overture (Example 7.3b).

These elements continue to resonate throughout the entirety of "The Lady or The Tiger?" In a demonstration of his justice system, the King sings an

a. Fanfare

b. First melody

Example 7.3: "The Lady or the Tiger?," elements of Overture

elaborated version of the opening motive, in the same key of B♭ (Example 7.4a, cf. Example 7.3a). It comes back again when Sanjar returns from battle and his loyal subjects proclaim victory (Example 7.4b). When the King uses a developed version of this motive to reprimand his daughter for keeping company with Sanjar, it takes on a sinister, menacing quality (Example 7.4c). By the end of the story, the raised fourth scale step has become a central thematic element, even when it is not part of a restatement or development of the opening motive. Barbara's dramatic aria "Tiger, Tiger," in which she lays out her options and anguish just before the climactic final scene, features a tortured arpeggio on the tonic D minor chord, coming to rest on nearly shouted ♯4's (Example 7.4d). Bock had used raised fourth scale steps many times before, but never with this frequency, and never before to such dramatic effect.

In addition to linking material, frequent underscoring, and passages of musicalized speech, the mini-drama contains nine principal numbers after the Overture (Table 7.2). The songs supporting the central part of the story either maintain an edgy, satirically barbaric tone or comically migrate to an opposite, saccharine extreme. A duet for Barbara and Sanjar, "Forbidden Love," is a Latin-tinted foxtrot, sandwiched around what could be a dance number for Fred and Ginger, "In Gaul" ("In Gaul / We'd live so simply / No more feathers and fuss / Just the children and us"). Both songs were added by Bock and Harnick after the Boston opening, replacing "One Third Princess," in which Barbara describes herself as one third princess, one third woman, one third tigress.[66] As Barbara subsequently realizes that Sanjar is destined for trial, she asks the Royal Tiger-Keeper, portrayed by the Balladeer/Narrator, to tell her which door will lead to the tiger, and he responds with "Forbidden Fruit." This becomes the moment of strongest connection with

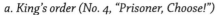

a. King's order (No. 4, "Prisoner, Choose!")

Pris - 'ner,_____ Choose! It's your chance to prove your in - no - cence or guilt! Sa lute!

b. Declaration of victory (No. 6, "Victory Is Ours, Nadjira")

Vic - to - ry is ours!_____

c. King's outrage (No. 8, "Barbara! How Could You?")

For a com - mon man _____ to make love to you _____ Is a sin a - gainst the gods!

brass

d. Barbara's anguish ("Tiger, Tiger")

Your dy - ing screams _____ Haunt - ing my dreams _____

Example 7.4: "The Lady or the Tiger?," recurrences of opening motive (cf. Example 7.3a)

Table 7.2: Songs in "The Lady or the Tiger?," part 2 of The Apple Tree

---

Overture
"I'll Tell You a Truth" (Balladeer)
"Make Way" (King Arik, Court)
"Forbidden Love/In Gaul" (Barbara, Sanjar)
"Forbidden Fruit" (Balladeer)
"I've Got What You Want" (Barbara)
"Tiger, Tiger" (Barbara)
"Make Way" (reprise) (King Arik, Court)
"Which Door?" (Company)
"I'll Tell You a Truth" (reprise) (Balladeer)

"The Diary of Adam and Eve," as the Balladeer sings about the inside informa-tion using the same music he sang earlier, as the Snake advising Eve about the fruit trees in the Garden.

After that the connections continue in more subtle ways, as Barbara, now holding Sanjar's fate in her hands, sings a seductive torch song, "I've Got What

You Want" ("I've got what you want / I've got what you need / I know how much you want it / Yeh! Yeh! Sanjar"). The entire number is oriented around a more harmonically complex version of the "lament" bass that Adam and Eve shared in the first act (Example 7.5a, cf. Example 7.2). The bass descent from step 1 down to 5 in the key of C includes only the lowered seventh step (B♭), skipping over the true leading tone, starting a trend continued by subsequent versions of this bass line for the rest of the show.[67] This is followed directly by "Tiger, Tiger," in which Barbara has her Ethel Merman moment, taking over the stage and laying out her unsavory options. A harmonically richer lament bass again emerges, when she graphically describes the kind of greeting Sanjar is likely to receive from the tiger (Example 7.5b). She swings back and forth from jealousy to guilt (cf. Example 7.4d), summed up in a brief quiet moment: "I don't want him dead / Better dead than wed." The bass line that became a symbol of male-female connection and union in the first act now haunts the decision that threatens to split them apart.

The music of the final trial scene builds to a fever pitch, starting with the arrival of the King and the reprise of the processional music from the opening. Sanjar melodramatically wonders, "Which door should I choose"; Barbara wonders which door she should tell him to choose. The King and his subjects take over the melody and wonder the same things, in a texture that becomes gradually thicker and louder with each new canonic entry. As Sanjar prepares to select a door, deciding whether to take Barbara's advice while Barbara decides exactly what advice to give, the music becomes primordially barbaric: "Yeh, yeh, manna, / Yeh, yeh callu / Yeh, yeh, manna callu / Yeh, yeh." But

a. "I've Got What You Want," opening phrase

b. "Tiger, Tiger," middle section

Example 7.5: "The Lady or the Tiger?," bass descents

Example 7.6: "The Lady or the Tiger?," ending

when the door finally opens we see only the Balladeer, strumming his guitar and comically arresting the feverish crescendo. His concluding reprise of his opening country-folk song plainly summarizes the conundrum at the heart of the story: "If you have loved, / You understand / How love and hate / Can walk hand in hand." The song's final strains, just before the curtain falls, could only conclude on the most tonally ambiguous note of the scale, the raised fourth scale step (F♯ in the key of C), one last time (Example 7.6).

Part 3: "Passionella"

The moral choices faced by characters in the third vignette, "Passionella," are less morbid but no less momentous. A narrator—the Snake/Balladeer again—tells the Cinderella story of an ordinary chimney sweep, Ella, who longs only to be a movie star. After she loses her job, her godmother appears in her television screen and transforms her into Passionella, a glamorous, curvaceous beauty and star of the silver screen. The catch is that Passionella only exists in the evening hours, "from Huntley-Brinkley to the Late Late Show." At other times of day she is Ella again. She does achieve wealth and fame, but she is not happy, and she meets her Prince Charming, Flip, a mega-hipster who convinces her that honesty and realism are the keys to happiness. She makes a movie as Ella, about a chimney sweep, and wins both the Academy Award and Flip's heart. But to Flip she is still Passionella, made up to look like a chimney sweep for the movie, and when the Late Late Show signs off during their first night together, Ella realizes that Flip is about to discover her deep dark secret. As it turns out, that is just fine with him, because at the same moment he reverts to his true self, a nerdy guy named George L. Brown. And that is a happy ending.

The final score for part three of *The Apple Tree* features a Prelude and seven main songs (Table 7.3). Ella's first number, "Oh, To Be a Movie Star," in which she reveals her deepest star-struck fantasies, begins with a four-bar introduction that includes quick chromatic slides in the F major melody, approaching step 5 (C) by half steps from above (E–E♭–D–D♭ in mm. 2 and 4 of Example 7.7). These chromatic flickers shrewdly anticipate the lament bass line supporting the main tune of the song to come, harmonized more like those in the first act than those of the second. This is the first of a series of songs for Ella/Passionella, fashioned to evoke Hollywood glamour and trace her path to fame. (The original production also included a five-minute

Table 7.3: Songs in "Passionella," part 3 of The Apple Tree

Prelude

"Oh, To Be a Movie Star" (Ella)

"Gorgeous" (Passionella)

"(Who, Who, Who, Who) Who Is She?" (Passionella, Company)

"I Know" (Passionella, Company)

"Wealth" (Passionella)

"You Are Not Real" (Flip, Company)

"George L." (Ella, George)

Example 7.7: "Oh, To Be a Movie Star," opening phrase

animated film depicting the transformation.[68]) In "Gorgeous" she exclaims amazement at her new look. She has received not only a total physical transformation but also newly developed vocal gifts, including an operatic high D at the final cadence (surpassing by a minor third the similarly flamboyant final vocal flourish of "Ice Cream" in *She Loves Me*). In "(Who, Who, Who, Who) Who Is She?" she and a group of subway riders marvel at her fame and beauty, in the style of a forties up-tempo shuffle. In "I Know" she revels in her celebrity, all too happy to agree with her fawning admirers:

> MEN: Passionella, how I love you!
>
> PASSIONELLA: I know.
>
> MEN: If you knew how I adore you!
>
> PASSIONELLA: I know.
>
> MAN 1: I can't sleep at night for thinking about you!
>
> PASSIONELLA: It's understandable.

MAN 2: I want you.

MAN 3: I want you.

MEN: I want you.

PASSIONELLA: It must be awful.

And in "Wealth" she reflects on the remarkable life she is leading, filled with limitless creature comforts and constant attention wherever she goes, but finally admits that she has still failed to find true happiness. The female lead of *The Apple Tree* had already been a dominant presence in the first and second acts, but by this point, in the wake of the "I've Got What You Want" and "Tiger, Tiger" at the end of Act 2 and this series of songs dominating Act 3, the evening is hers.

When Flip finally does get his chance, he bursts forth in a big way, with a spirited, mocking country-rock waltz, "You Are Not Real." He pulls no punches in explaining to Passionella that her stardom and riches are fictive and hollow: "How does it feel / To be the world's ideal / When you know an' I know / That you are not real." It is the strongest statement of this vignette's central theme, as Harnick has articulated: "Really what 'Passionella' is about—it's not a satire, or a burlesque, of Marilyn Monroe. It's a satire of an approach to realism that certain movies take, which goes way beyond realism and becomes something that's unreal."[69] It is also built almost entirely of a repeating lament bass line, with a routine harmonization as in Act 1, and again moving directly from tonic to the flattened seventh step (Example 7.8). Only the bridge/chorus ("Instead of a soul . . ." / "How does it feel . . ."), which moves through a complete diatonic circle of fifths, strays from the main harmonic pattern. Bock thereby links not only Flip's big number with Ella's first song (Example 7.7), but also connects this pairing with the musical pairing of Adam and Eve in Act 1 (Example 7.2). Harnick's lyric for the second verse of "You Are Not Real" likewise recalls the earlier story, when Flip sings on behalf of "the sons of Adam," explaining his views about "you daughters of Eve." Along with Barbara's big numbers in Act 2 (Example 7.5), these intra-show connections build a solid case for uniting these three stories in a single

Example 7.8: "You Are Not Real," opening phrase

evening of theater, as a dramatic and musical exploration of male–female relationships.

When the show opened in Boston Bock had brought back the central musical idea yet one more time, in Ella's concluding love ballad, "I'm Lost." This song presents the chromatic descent connecting steps 1 and 5 in an inner voice as in the opening of Act 1, not as a bass line (cf. Examples 7.2a, 7.2b). Sometime before the New York opening, however, Bock and Harnick reworked the ending and removed "I'm Lost."[70] They made the connection to Act 1 in a different way, by reprising the music of the second part of the Eden Prelude, where the melody specifically anticipates the title phrase of Eve's lullaby, "Go To Sleep, Whatever You Are." In the new ending Ella and Flip—soon to be revealed as George—sing to each other using the same melodic phrases heard in the first act, backed by essentially the same orchestration. It puts a ribbon on the whole musical package and ties it into a bow.

The Sum of Its Parts

Nevertheless, commentators have been mostly critical of the experience of The Apple Tree as a single evening of theater. Any musical threads, plus the consistent themes of male-female relationships and temptations from dev-ilish figures, have not generally been deemed sufficient to create a satisfying dramatic unity. Ethan Mordden wrote that "the show reveled in heteroge-neity."[71] The Variety reviewer ("Ares") of the original Broadway production called it "essentially a package of three skits executed in revue fashion" (9/14/66). Harnick himself tended to agree: "We came out with less than the sum of our parts, not more. . . . The pieces were not honestly tied together."[72] It cannot help that parts two and three are so different from part one, in both conception and style. Critics have generally liked "The Diary of Adam and Eve": Whitney Bolton wrote that it was "worth the admission price all by itself" (New York World Telegraph, 10/20/66); Richard P. Cooke found in it "a great deal of insight and pathos" (Wall Street Journal, 10/20/66). But they have generally not been kind to the other two: Walter Kerr described "The Lady or the Tiger" as "swiftly, and much too cursorily, outlined" (New York Times, 10/19/66); Martin Gottfried summarized "Passionella" as a "sad attempt to be both serious and funny about the Marilyn Monroe career" (Women's Wear Daily, 10/19/66). The second and third stories just betray a completely dif-ferent sensibility from the first one. They are more like sketches from a revue; they transport Bock and Harnick back to summers in the Poconos or Adiron-dacks. Reviewing the original production, Cecil Smith compared "Passionella" to an episode of the Bullwinkle cartoon's "Fractured Fairy Tales" (Los Angeles Times, 10/20/66). Forty years later, Ben Brantley was no kinder: "The second act is steeped in a makeshift glitz that brings to mind 1960s television variety revues. . . . This in turn makes you more conscious than you should be of how closely the latter part of *The Apple Tree* resembles a middling segment from an old *Carol Burnett Show*" (*New York Times*, 12/15/06).

But how much of a difference would it make if all three parts were equal, in style and substance, and were thoroughly unified, musically and dramatically? The experience of three short dramas is entirely different from that of one long one. No matter how good a short story may be, the experience of reading it can never be the same as the extended commitment of reading an equally fine novel. In the theater, audiences naturally get more from the long dramatic arc, from the development of plot and character over the course of a full evening, than they do from a series of first-rate vignettes. Surely this is why groupings of one-act musicals have been so rare in the history of Broadway. Ethan Mordden could recall only four as of 2001, two by Victor Herbert (*Dream City* [1906] and *The Magic Knight* [1906]), and two by Jerome Moross (*Ballet Ballads* [1948] and *A Day in Hollywood, A Night in the Ukraine* [1980]).[73] At one time Richard Rodgers is said to have abandoned plans to create a musical with two separate parts.[74] Cy Coleman and Dorothy Fields's *Sweet Charity* was originally conceived as one half of a musical, to be paired with a separate original piece by Elaine May, before it was expanded to its full size.[75] Producers do not want to leave their audiences hungry or feeling cheated out of a complete evening of entertainment. These considerations may also help explain why plans to make a film adaptation of *The Apple Tree* were abandoned in 1969.[76]

Without a long-range dramatic structure, audiences look for other unifying threads, and in the original Broadway production of *The Apple Tree* they found one in Barbara Harris. Critical praise for Harris's performance as Eve/Barbara/Ella/Passionella was unanimous. Walter Kerr found her "exquisite, appetizing, alarming, seductive, out of her mind, irresistible, and from now on unavoidable" (*New York Times*, 10/19/66). George Oppenheimer wrote that she was a "doll and a dream, possessed of more talent than any young or old star on our musical stage today" (*Newsday*, 10/20/66). Harris won the Best Actress Tony in 1967 against formidable competition from Lotte Lenya (*Cabaret*) and Mary Martin (*I Do! I Do!*). Otherwise the original production of *The Apple Tree* did not fare as well in the other Tony categories in which it was nominated, for music, choreography, costumes, direction, Best Actor in a Musical, and Best Musical; it was *Cabaret*'s year. The show ran for more than thirteen months, 463 performances, and closed on November 25, 1967. According to Harnick, business fell off sharply after Barbara Harris left the cast in early November.[77]

More than anything else, *The Apple Tree* is an opportunity to witness the work of a single actress who is asked to demonstrate a broad range of dramatic, comedic, and musical gifts; without such a talent, it suffers. This is one reason that productions of the complete *The Apple Tree* are relatively rare. In Harnick's words, "It is murderous to find an actress who can do all three roles."[78] A Broadway revival finally arrived in 2006, forty years after the original, because finally a performer of Kristin Chenoweth's abilities came along to pull it off. Bock said, "We haven't until Kristin had the performer who could do it."[79] She even sang her own high D at the end of "Gorgeous"; Harris's had to be dubbed in and played as a joke. Chenoweth's reviews looked a lot like Harris's: Ben Brantley called her "blindingly radiant," with the "feral comic instincts of Lucille Ball" (*New York Times*, 12/15/06); Joe Dziemianowicz wrote that she was the "ideal leading lady for a show built for a knockout comic diva" (*Daily News*, 12/15/06). Chenoweth was nominated for a Drama Desk Award but denied a Tony nomination. (The 2006 production received just one Tony nomination, for Best Musical Revival, and lost to John Doyle's revival of *Company*.) Her co-stars, Brian d'Arcy James and Marc Kudisch, were equally splendid but destined to be spectators in their own show.

The 2006 revival also afforded Bock and Harnick the opportunity to consider how their show had aged in forty years, and they located several spots for updating and refining. They made minor adjustments in the first two stories, adopting suggestions from the director, Gary Griffin. For "Passionella" they consulted with the story's original author, Jules Feiffer, who saw the incipient version of this production, in the City Center "Encores!" series in 2005, and gave them ideas for sharpening the story's satiric edge.[80] They tried different things but ultimately added just one new line for the narrator: "And then one night, Passionella met the right man. She met him at a star-studded benefit for a new disease that had recently been discovered by the pharmaceutical industry." (Harnick: "It always received a very gratifying audience response.") The revival ran on Broadway for ninety-nine performances from December 2006 up until March 2007, when the star needed to move on to other commitments in film and television.

Again, as with *Fiddler*, it is John Lahr who has insightfully summarized a show's essential lesson, in his *New Yorker* review of the revival.[81] Evocations of Eden have been rare on Broadway, writes Lahr, because the musical comedy itself already appropriated "the notion of paradise on earth: abundant, joyous, unreflective, and radically innocent—a place where the concepts of sin and curiosity had no purchase." He cites an Edenic moment in the Lane–Harburg song "The Begat" from *Finian's Rainbow* (1947), which has Adam and Eve frolicking in the Garden "as free as the summer breeze." He might have also mentioned the "Garden of Eden Ballet," Michael Kidd's showstopping reverie at the end of Act 1 of Cole Porter's *Can-Can* (1953): amidst dancing inchworms, flamingos, and sea horses, Eve (Gwen Verdon) celebrates the abundance of earthly delights, and temptations. But sometime in the 1960s, writes Lahr, the musical, like the American society it was designed to entertain, lost its innocence. Once it had been banished from its paradise, the path ahead became precarious, overgrown with harsh realities. *The Apple Tree* stands at the crux of this shift, on the one hand reaping the fruits of the Garden, on the other confronting the daunting complexities of fame and happiness. After the Fall, it searches, wanders, explores. It knows that life beyond the Garden is necessary for growth and evolution, that possibilities are abundant in the paradise of the imagination, but it is not entirely sure where it is going or how it is going to get there.

8

HAVE YOU EVER SEEN A PRETTIER
LITTLE CONGRESS?
• • •
THE LATE 1960S AND *THE ROTHSCHILDS*

During the thirteen-month run of *The Apple Tree* at the Shubert Theater in late 1966 and most of 1967, Bock and Harnick could find titles of their major musicals on two Broadway marquees, something they had last experienced when *Fiorello!* and *Tenderloin* played simultaneously for six months in 1960 and 1961. Indeed, when *Fiddler on the Roof* shifted operations from the Imperial Theater one block down to the larger Majestic in February 1967, their two shows became close neighbors on West 44th Street, separated by only one other theater, the Broadhurst, where Kander and Ebb's *Cabaret* had opened the previous November. (It moved to the larger Imperial in March.) Meanwhile, *Fiddler*'s rival for Broadway longevity, Jerry Herman's *Hello, Dolly!*, was playing across the street at the St. James. One imagines a stroll down 44th Street from Broadway to Eighth Avenue while all the shows were in performance, in a fantasy world where there is no street noise and all the doors have been left open, sampling the diverse flavors of the American musical theater at a pivotal historical juncture. As we progress down the block, Bock and Harnick in contemporary mode give way to Kander and Ebb recalling idioms of one part of European history while Bock and Harnick in historical mode explore the culture and traditions of another part, finally punctuated by Jerry Herman's tuneful spectacle. An air of innovation permeates the first part of the trip, giving way to celebrations of traditions, Broadway and other, in the latter part. We need expand the stroll only by a few blocks, and by a year or so, and we would hear something quite different coming from the stage door of *Hair*. Stretch the time warp and geography a little further and we start to hear Sondheim and *Company*.

Bock and Harnick may have been in the vortex of the music-theatrical world there on 44th Street at that memorable time, but they were not inclined to stand around and look for ways to get both marquees in the same camera shot. Ideas for new major projects were always percolating. In general, however, the late 1960s were as tempestuous for the Bock–Harnick partnership as they were for the whole of American society. The team devoted some effort to a film version of *She Loves Me* in 1967–69, until a studio executive pulled the plug (see chapter 5). They declined an offer to write the music and lyrics for a new musical called *The Happy Time*, fearing that they would be re-exploring old terrain: its "emotional quality was too close to that of *Fiddler*, although on the surface there was no resemblance at all," Harnick explained.[1] (Instead Kander and Ebb wrote the music for the show, and it became their next Broadway production after *Cabaret*.) A project Bock and Harnick did pursue, a new musical based on the life and naval exploits of Lord Nelson, resulted in a cache of new songs and ideas but fell apart over disagreements with the librettist. And they had yet another unrewarding experience with show-doctoring. When they finally did create a new Broadway musical, *The Rothschilds*, the show's development and production were plagued with difficulties of all sorts, and the experience left the partnership strained beyond repair.

MUSICAL HISTORIES

All of Bock and Harnick's main projects from this time had historical themes, recalling their first big success, *Fiorello!* The idea for a musical about Lord Nelson originated with producers Warren Tute and Richard Pilbrow, who brought Bock and Harnick together with the British playwright John Arden. The collaboration was first announced in early 1965, just after *Fiddler* opened, with the hope of a premiere in London on Trafalgar Day, October 21, 1967.[2] Arden produced a story outline in June 1966, and Bock and Harnick were able to start work in earnest later that year, after the opening of *The Apple Tree*.[3] The plot was to follow Nelson's career, leading up to his victory over the Spanish and French fleets at Trafalgar in 1805, which spoiled Napoleon's plans to invade England. Arden saw it as a

> character study of a particular kind of naval genius. Nelson is a very strange man when you juxtapose his successful naval career with his very odd and not very happy private life. And it is a play that seems to me to be raising a lot of issues that one might call serious issues, which need not necessarily be diminished by the fact that it's a musical.[4]

He emphasized that he imagined a "serious" musical, but not a "solemn one." The working title was *Trafalgar*.

Bock and Harnick did some background research and Bock made his usual tape recording of musical ideas for the score.[5] The composer sought inspiration from sheet music of songs from Nelson's era that was furnished by the producers, and he gave at least some of his original songs a scent of a sailor's hornpipe or sea chanty, with Aeolian modalities and distinctively repeated folkish motivic cells.[6] Using the material on the tapes as inspiration, Harnick produced twelve lyrics, with titles such as "The Ballad of the Battle of St. Vincent," "Glory is My Object," and "Your Anxious Wife."[7] He told Lewis Funke of the *New York Times* that he became intrigued by the subject matter, even though it might have appealed mostly to British audiences, because he was "drawn to Nelson as a human being. He was a universal man, a naval genius who was a fighter, a man of humble origins who fought the Establishment of his time—and also got seasick when he went to sea."[8]

Ultimately, however, Arden saw it differently. The playwright had no sympathy for Nelson and began to envision a smaller, less conventional treatment of the material, engaging anti-war themes and raising questions about Nelson's heroism. In early 1968, after conferring with the songwriters and hearing their ideas, he "asked for his book back," telling them, "You take your music, and I'll have my play."[9] He then reconceptualized the entire piece as *The Hero Rises Up*, a kind of ballad opera employing existing songs and improvisations.[10] Arden's reworked piece premiered in London on November 11, 1968, staged in the round and experimentally flavored with elements of different theatrical styles and audience participation.[11] Bock and Harnick also hoped to go forward with their plans and in 1968 still considered *Trafalgar* to be an ongoing project, but they never found another librettist to join them.[12] Even twenty-one years later, in a "musical synopsis" of *Trafalgar* dated September 3, 1989, Bock was still apparently planning to develop the material into something workable, but this too has failed to reach fruition.[13]

A few months after parting company with Arden, Bock and Harnick accepted a request for help with another historically based musical. *Her First Roman*, an adaptation of George Bernard Shaw's *Caesar and Cleopatra*, featured book, music, and lyrics by Ervin Drake, best known as the composer of popular songs such as "I Believe," which had been made famous by Frankie Laine (1953), and a more recent hit, Frank Sinatra's "It Was a Very Good Year" (1966). Drake had also written music and lyrics for the musical *What Makes Sammy Run?*, which played on Broadway for 540 performances in 1964 and 1965. If Drake's track record seemed promising enough, then the actors hired for the two leads also seemed to work in the show's favor. Cast in the role of Caesar was Richard Kiley, who won his first Best Actor Tony in 1959 for *Redhead* and more recently, in 1966, had won his second, for *Man of La Mancha*. The role of Cleopatra went to Leslie Uggams, a recent Broadway sensation and Best Actress Tony winner for *Hallelujah, Baby* (1967).[14]

And yet all was not well in the rehearsal studio during the summer of 1968. Three different choreographers were eventually employed.[15] The original director, Michael Benthall, clashed with the producers over staging issues, and over the degree to which Shaw's original plot and dialogue should be incorporated into the adaptation. Ultimately Benthall resigned in mid-August 1968, just at the beginning of the pre-Broadway tour in Boston, and was replaced by Derek Goldby, a recent Tony nominee for his direction of Tom Stoppard's *Rosencrantz and Guildenstern Are Dead* (1967).[16] Goldby oversaw a restructuring of the book to include more Shaw, less Drake. But Goldby also had reservations about the score and brought in Bock and Harnick to advise Drake and to write some new songs. In the end, three of Drake's songs were essentially replaced by Bock–Harnick numbers, three were removed without being replaced, and others were reworked. The changes were made in Boston in late August, and in Philadelphia in September, leading up to a New York opening on October 20, 1968. The show was mercilessly panned by the critics and closed on November 2, after seventeen performances.

Clive Barnes wrote in the *Times* (10/21/68), "it is the music and lyrics that spoil the evening," but he was in the minority; most of the blame fell on Drake's adaptation of Shaw's play. Many felt that the book relied too heavily on Shaw—that, in other words, the midstream decision to move the story closer to the original source was misguided and deleterious. Ken Mandelbaum summarizes the result as the "Cliff Notes" version of the play: "occasional passages of Shaw's dialogue, but simplified and watered down." Further, writes Mandelbaum,

> what Drake failed to realize was that Shaw was less interested in telling the story of Caesar and Cleopatra than he was in using their story to comment satirically on contemporary morality. All that was left in the musical was the plot, with Shaw's all-important philosophical musings absent.[17]

Some of Bock and Harnick's songs for *Her First Roman* also rely extensively on Shaw, especially "Caesar Is Wrong," which is directly based on a long speech from *Caesar and Cleopatra*.[18] That is not to say it lacks charm, however: the music of "Caesar Is Wrong" is a colorful *waltz macabre*, projecting the same warped sensibility as "Tiger, Tiger" from *The Apple Tree* while reviving the Dorian-flavored chord progressions of *Fiddler*'s "Sabbath Prayer." The other two Bock–Harnick contributions, "Old Gentleman" and "Ptolemy," are likewise fresh and entertaining. For that matter, the songs that Drake wrote are also consistently interesting. They can be heard in what was billed as the "cast album" for the show—because it reunited Kiley and Uggams—made on its twenty-fifth anniversary in 1993, and featuring all of Drake's original songs (some with revised lyrics), none of Bock and Harnick's.[19] The problem is that these songs just do not belong with Drake's final libretto, and one might reasonably ask whether they could work with any other adaptation of Shaw's play. As Barnes wrote in the *Times* (10/21/68), "The basic mistake is to believe that you can take a play more than sixty years old and hold up the action every so often for a feeble song or a little bit of *Aida*-like spectacle and imagine you have a musical on your hands." Perhaps Lerner and Loewe's musical adaptation of a Shaw play in *My Fair Lady* just made it look too easy.

Despite arriving on the scene in the eleventh hour, Bock and Harnick were unable to insulate themselves from the ambient tensions. Harnick had surveyed the situation in Boston and found it "hopeless," feeling uninspired to be part of an enterprise that seemed destined for failure. He felt that the director, Derek Goldby, was a source of problems, not only because Goldby had requested and encouraged the ill-advised infusion of Shaw material, but also because Harnick found Goldby to be less-than-forthright with other members of the creative team.[20] Bock, however, wanted to make it work and felt loyal to Goldby. They stayed on to try to help out, but neither could be content with the circumstances. In truth, this conflict turned up the heat on tensions that had already been simmering. Harnick told Harold Flender in 1971 that at some point prior to their involvement in *Her First Roman* he had proposed to Bock that they collaborate on an opera. When Bock resisted, a tense discussion ensued about working outside of the partnership.[21] Harnick had then made his own plans in the summer of 1968, not to write an opera but to collaborate with Burton Lane on a full-scale musical based on Herbert Tarr's best-selling novel *Heaven Help Us!* Harnick explained to Sam Zolotow in the *Times* that the arrangement had been discussed with his long-time partner: "Without relinquishing our association, which is very valuable to us, we both felt that from time to time working with other craftsmen might be a stimulating experience."[22] Just before *Her First Roman* opened in New York in October, Harnick reiterated their position: "Jerry and I have talked this over and we've agreed we should be free to work with other collaborators if such occasions occur. Certainly, we haven't split up."[23] A collaboration between Harnick and Lane never evolved beyond the planning stages—they remained close personal friends, with apartments in the same building in Manhattan and second homes in the same area of Long Island—but Harnick admits that just the discussion of working apart from Bock had been a source of disquiet and guilt for both of them.

Harnick would ultimately satisfy his desire to collaborate on an opera several times over (see chapter 9). Around the time of *Her First Roman* he began to take a small step in that direction, with his own "mini-opera" *Frustration*. The idea came to him during friendly chamber music sessions:

> At one time, I was a member of a chamber music trio that met every few weeks. I played violin, the pianist was Charles Strouse, and the clarinetist was our *Apple Tree* producer, Stuart Ostrow. There wasn't a great deal of literature for piano, violin and clarinet, and some of the pieces for that combination were simply too difficult for us to play (e.g., Bartók's *Contrasts*). Consequently, every time we met, we played the same repertoire. Our wives, who had been a good audience at first, soon tired of hearing the same pieces played over and over again. When we began to play, they would go into another room to chat.
>
> At one of our sessions, Charles Strouse told us that he had written a suite for us. It was in three short movements, each of which was dedicated to one of our wives. This brought the women back into the living room. The suite, by the way, was charming. This spurred Stuart and me to write pieces as well. Then Charles wrote a three-minute "opera" for our three wives to sing accompanied by our trio. Not to be outdone, I wrote a six-minute "opera" (although it called for only two women's voices). I was studying French at the time and I was constantly amused by the dreadful gaffes I made. This inspired me to write a text for my opera which sounded as though it had been badly translated from a French libretto by a beginning French student. To complement Charles's opera, which was called *Satisfaction*, I called mine *Frustration*.

Through a friend, Harnick was able to arrange a public premiere of *Frustration* on a program of chamber operas at the Smithsonian Museum of Natural History in Washington on June 10, 1969.[24] It is a gentle spoof of Debussy's *Pelléas et Mélisande* with fractured English ("I cannot him find, and I him love!" and so forth) and cleverly deployed Impressionist clichés, including lush chords and whole-tone and pentatonic figures—"P. D. Q. Debussy," perhaps. The work was published a few years later and has occasionally appeared on various programs of short operas since then.[25]

THE ROTHSCHILDS

All the while, Bock and Harnick were toiling on a new major musical and adding another title to their growing list of historical treatments. The producer Hillard Elkins had first approached them with the idea of making a musical about the Rothschilds family in 1963, having acquired the rights to Frederic

Morton's popular book, *The Rothschilds: A Family Portrait* (New York: Atheneum, 1962). Because they did not care for the dramatization Elkins showed them, by the British writer/playwright Wolf Mankowitz, Bock and Harnick had declined and stayed focused on their next show, then known as *Tevye*. Elkins continued to search for collaborators in the years to come, as he was producing the Strouse/Adams musical *Golden Boy* (premiered 10/20/64) and other things. When he came back to Bock and Harnick in early 1968, not long after *The Apple Tree* closed, he showed them a new version of a libretto, by a television writer and aspiring playwright, Sherman Yellen. Yellen's colorful and imaginative treatment convinced them to sign on, despite reservations about presenting a new show involving Jewish characters and themes while *Fiddler on the Roof* was still playing on Broadway. They also surely recognized potential difficulties in the creative team that was being formed: to direct, Elkins had hired the replacement director and apparent source of friction for *Her First Roman*, Derek Goldby.

Bock and Harnick wrote music for their seventh major musical, *The Rothschilds*, throughout the remainder of 1968, with diversions for *Her First Roman* and other things, and well into the next year and the next, until it finally opened in New York on October 19, 1970. The production was delayed at several points by financing and by conflicts within the creative team, some of which are documented in Christopher Davis's book about Hillard Elkins, *The Producer*.[26] Most of the problems centered on Elkins himself: his and Goldby's "temperaments and talents do not suit," writes Davis; Elkins is accused by Yellen of holding "secret meetings, cabals, alliances"; Bock and Harnick felt inadequately consulted about postponements and other things.[27] Part of the problem may have been that Elkins was also occupied during this period with production duties for *Oh! Calcutta!*, which opened on Broadway on June 17, 1969, and with the surrounding hoopla and lawsuits. But the *Rothschilds* material itself presented many challenges as well, dramatic and musical. The tensions boiled over in August 1970, during the pre-Broadway tour in Detroit, when Elkins fired Derek Goldby and replaced him with Michael Kidd. Kidd also became the show's choreographer, replacing Eliot Feld. Cast members liked Goldby and had not been consulted about the change. Harnick approved of the switch, while Bock remained loyal to Goldby, as he had been when they were working with him on *Her First Roman*.[28] In March 1971, when *The Rothschilds* was four-and-a-half months into its inaugural run, Harnick described the entire experience as "two years of great emotional turmoil and confusion and pain."[29]

Other members of the production team managed to avoid the turmoil, to some degree at least. For important musical jobs Bock and Harnick renewed their association with a pair of collaborators from *Fiddler on the Roof*: musical director and vocal arranger Milton Greene and orchestrator Don Walker. (Walker had also done orchestrations for *Baker Street*.) Scenery and costumes were designed by John Bury, who had received a Tony nomination for his design of Harold Pinter's *The Homecoming* in 1967.

The Libretto and Its Formulation

Morton's book is only a general source for the story told in *The Rothschilds*. Yellen's libretto is a free dramatization of historical events, with some scenes and dialogue that might have happened as he depicts and others that are purely invented to fulfill dramatic needs. The script is generally less grounded in historical fact than that of Bock and Harnick's previous historically based show, *Fiorello!*[30] Yellen's scope is limited to events of the first hundred pages or so of Morton's book, depicting the life of Mayer Rothschild in the Jewish ghetto of Frankfurt and his rise to financial success in the latter decades of the 1700s, ultimately passing the torch to his five sons in the early decades of the next century. (The rest of Morton's book then carries the family's history forward to the date of publication, 1962.) Yellen's most imaginative conceit, in the initial version of his libretto, the one that so enchanted Bock and Harnick, was to begin the show with an "auction," not of goods but of years, as a way of introducing the scenes and themes of the show.[31] Later in Act 1 there was a similar auction in the court of Napoleon, with "liberté, égalité, and fraternité" on the block. In Act 2 there were auctions in England and Austria, offering goods both metaphorical ("our new free enterprise society") and material (gold and peace bonds). Bock and Harnick found abundant musical possibilities in these scenes and wrote a recurring auction song and theme that would give musical support to Yellen's unifying framework.[32]

The auction metaphor, however, did not survive the pre-Broadway tour. Harnick told Frank Kelly in 1974:

> We all began to feel that the auction device was not consistent and was confusing some people—that at the very beginning the auction device was kind of poetic and that the auctioneer was auctioning off a year, but as it was used throughout the show, particularly when it got to the last time it was used, he was auctioning off bonds, and it was a realistic thing.[33]

Soon after the Detroit premiere the creative team restructured the opening and several other scenes, removing the metaphorical auctions and generally giving the show a more conventional look. They extended Mayer Rothschild's life six years beyond his actual demise, to give more stage time to an endearing character. Elkins also brought in advisers to suggest further revisions, usually over Yellen's objections. The librettist recalls input from visitors such as Mel Brooks, who proposed adding a scene of a Jewish uprising, and William Gibson, who suggested a bar mitzvah. Joseph Stein also showed up; he added a joke about a candlestick, remembers Yellen. The Boston theater critic Elliot Norton was on hand as a consultant as well, according to Christopher Davis.[34]

Although most of this counsel was rejected, the libretto was nonetheless quite different by the time *The Rothschilds* opened in New York in October 1970. The new version began with a scene in the palace of Prince William of Hesse, in 1770 Frankfurt. To contrast with the glitter and wealth of the aristocracy, this scene ends with an abrupt shift to the gates of the Frankfurt Jewish ghetto, where Mayer Rothschild is taunted and told to "do his duty" by removing his hat and bowing to a group of children, then forced to pay the gatekeeper to enter his own neighborhood.[35] In the Rothschild shop he finds his betrothed, Gutele, who worries about their future and about official quotas that will likely delay their marriage by years, but Mayer shares grand ideas for rising above their poverty and circumventing the system. He goes to the Frankfurt Fair to sell rare coins and attracts the notice of Prince William, who accepts a rare coin in exchange for an expedited marriage approval. By befriending the Prince's assistant, Budurus, Mayer gains entry to the Prince's court and, through shrewd maneuvering and business acumen, gains a position with the official bankers. Mayer and Gutele are married and bear five sons, first Amshel, then Solomon, Nathan, Jacob, and Kalman.[36] Soon the boys themselves become astute workers in the family's shop, despite persistent ethnic oppression. During a pogrom they descend with their parents into a cellar to hide, and then, in a compelling bit of stagecraft, emerge as young men sixteen years later, already successful businessmen. The Rothschilds begin their rise to power and wealth as they help the Prince arrange a loan to a Danish relative. Then, after Napoleon's army has invaded and sent the Prince into exile, the family plans to collect on the Prince's debts in Europe's financial capitals. As Act 1 ends they anticipate their dispersal across the continent: Solomon to Vienna, Amshel to Prussia, Jacob to Prague, Kalman to Hamburg, and Nathan to London.[37]

The first part of Act 2 is centered on Nathan and his accumulating influence and prosperity in London financial circles. When he negotiates a loan to help England win its war with France, his insistence that the loan be connected to equal rights for Jews earns the hand in marriage of a strong-willed woman, Hannah Cohen. The Rothschild brothers meet with Prince Metternich, leader of the Crowned Heads of Europe, who agrees to remove restrictions against Jews in exchange for the Rothschilds' financial support, but when the leaders gather at Aix-la-Chappelle, the Prince does not deliver on his promises, and the Rothschilds must find a new way to achieve their goals. After Mayer dies, his sons carry the legacy forward by devising a bold, risky plan to sell peace bonds in competition with the Prince. The plan succeeds, and the Prince is forced to yield to their demands. In the final scene the Prince visits the Rothschilds in their childhood home in the Frankfurt ghetto and agrees to arrange for the Crowned Heads to sign a Declaration of Rights for European Jews. The Rothschilds accept new aristocratic titles, Baron von Rothschild, and celebrate a victory over oppression in the name of their beloved father.

The creators of *The Rothschilds* have never backed away from their rather fanciful treatment of history. At one point they gave the show a subtitle, "A Musical Legend," as a claim of creative license.[38] The linkage of financial aspirations with victories over Jewish oppression is entirely invented: the Rothschilds were noted philanthropists, but in reality they attended the Congress at Aix-la-Chappelle to advance their power and financial fortunes, not to make deals on behalf of their former neighbors in the Frankfurt ghetto. As Harnick said of the show just before the Detroit opening, "If it were just about five guys who made a lot of money, it would be nothing. To a certain extent, power is the theme."[39] More importantly, they wanted to draw parallels between minority struggles within any culture, at any point in history. "When you get bright, aggressive young people who begin to see a way to break out of the ghetto," Harnick told Harold Flender, "and society at large decides that society will try to keep them in the ghetto, what do they do? . . . We were trying to suggest . . . don't be too angry at black militants because we went through the same thing."[40] And: "Although, specifically, it had to do with anti-Semitism, anybody who looks at the show and thinks about the show will realize it is about racial prejudice in general."[41]

Evolution of the Score

Changes in the score between Detroit and New York were considerable (Table 8.1). Of course the songwriters had to rethink the opening and other scenes that had been metaphorical auctions, often requiring new songs, but they also worked to soften the overall tone of the show, which they came to regard as unappealingly strident. Harsh edges were removed from lyrics, and some of the more acerbic songs were either reworked or removed altogether.[42] A song about Mayer's humiliation at the ghetto gate, "Jew, Do Your Duty," in which street urchins instruct him to "Bow, Jew, and lick my shoe! / Come and kiss, my beauty!," was cut because it "seemed to cast a pall over the succeeding scenes . . . from which it was difficult to recover," recalled Bock.[43] Another song that was excised, "I Will Bow," made "an ineradicable and damaging association between our leading character (a Jew) and either abject servility, or a deep involvement with money," according to Harnick.[44] The desire to de-emphasize pure financial gain also motivated the removal of the song "Mayer's Fine Coins," and its companion song, "William's Fine Troops," subsequently replaced by a new number, "He Tossed a Coin," that finds adventure and romance in Mayer's business dealings.[45] Even Nathan's courtship changed its tone: in Detroit, Hannah gave her suitor a piece of her mind with force and acidity in "You're a Fraud, Sir"; this was eventually replaced by a Broadway-style lovefest, "I'm in Love! I'm in Love!"[46] By the time the show completed its pre-Broadway tour it was more dramatically cohesive and crowd-pleasing, but it had lost its edge, seeming less inclined to confront the harsh realities of its central themes.

The songs that appeared on both the Detroit and New York programs (the **bold** titles in Table 8.1) became the backbone of the score. "Sons" portrays

Table 8.1: *Musical numbers listed on* The Rothschilds *program in Detroit, with titles that remained in the show for the New York opening in* **bold**

ACT 1

"The Royal Hessian Auction"
"Jew, Do Your Duty"
"I Will Bow"
"Mayer's Fine Coins"
"William's Fine Troops"
"Sons"
"Everything"
"My Cousin Christian"
"The French Imperial Auction"
"Rothschild and Sons"

ACT 2

"The British Free Enterprise Auction"
"They Say"
"This Amazing London Town"
"Messenger Ballet"
"They Say" (reprise)
"You're A Fraud, Sir"
"Gold Smugglers' Gavotte"
"The Grand Alliance Auction"
"Have You Ever Seen A Prettier Little Congress?"
"Never Again" [later renamed **"Stability"**]
"Bonds"

the expansion of the Rothschild family and legacy in Act 1 with a contrapuntal central section reminiscent of layered passages in "The Bum Won" from *Fiorello!*, "Good Clean Fun" from *Tenderloin*, and the *Fiddler* Prologue. As each new son is introduced and educated about the family business, he sings his own melody, and this is then combined with the melodies of his brothers as the song progresses. By the time all four sing together—the fifth son arrives as a newborn at the end of the song—we hear a four-part layering and Bock's characteristically free use of dissonance (Example 8.1). Especially in the first few bars, he allows frequent clashes of half and whole steps between the parts, savoring the sense of individuality and independence implied by simultaneous melodies that do not dovetail with each other in completely consonant ways. Another song that stayed in the show, "Everything," has the sons explaining to their mother what they want from life: "We want everything, everything, everything other men aspire to / What another's entitled to, we're entitled to too." Shortly after that they celebrate their agreement with

Example 8.1: "Sons," four-part layering

the Prince, and look ahead to a prosperous financial future, in the song "Roth-schild and Sons." Part of the strength of the first act comes from these musical portrayals of the father and his sons and their journey out of the ghetto. Eventually the creative team strengthened the theme further at the end of the act by adding a reprise of "Sons," in which, as Mayer instructs his sons to disperse across Europe, we hear each of the son's individual melodies (heard earlier as contrapuntal layers) in the underscoring.[47]

Second-act songs that stayed in the show from Detroit to New York include two depicting Nathan's activities in London: a scene-setter, "This Amazing London Town," and a demonstration of Nathan's skill and style on the floor of the stock exchange, "They Say." Then at the end of the act a trio of songs gives dramatic musical voice to the scenes with Prince Metternich. In "Have You Ever Seen a Prettier Little Congress?" the Prince opens the Congress at Aix-la-Chappelle with self-congratulatory proclamations. This is followed by "Never Again" (later expanded and renamed "Stability"), which makes clear exactly what kind of perfect world the Prince expects the Congress to create:

> Never again
> Shall servant be master
> Never shall pawns aspire to be kings
> Coddling an upstart is courting disaster;
> We've witnessed the chaos equality brings.

The chorus of attendees responds:

> Hear! Hear!
> Stability! Stability!
> The world's been made free
> For people like you
> And people like me.
> Stability! Stability!
> The upstart will pay
> Who stands in the way of
> Stability![48]

It is a notion of "stability" that the Rothschilds resolutely reject, and they finally pave the way to achieving their goals, financial and humanitarian, in the bidding war of the song "Bonds."

The remainder of the score at the New York opening was composed during the pre-Broadway tour (Table 8.2, new songs in regular type). After the creators jettisoned Yellen's auction framework, they set the scene differently in Act 1 with "Prologue: Pleasure and Privilege," sung by Prince William and the

Table 8.2: Overview of The Rothschilds *at the New York premiere, with titles that appeared on the Detroit program in* **bold**

ACT 1

    Prologue: Hesse, 1772.
        "Pleasure and Privilege" (Prince William and His Court)
1. The gate of the Frankfurt ghetto, 1772.
2. The Rothschild shop, 1772.
        "One Room" (Mayer, Gutele)
3. The Frankfurt fair, 1773.
        "He Tossed a Coin" (Mayer, Vendors)
4. The palace of Prince William, 1773.
5. The Rothschild shop, 1788.
        "Sons" (Mayer, Gutele, young sons)
6. The Rothschild shop, 1788.
7. The Rothschild shop, 1804.
        "Everything" (Gutele, grown sons)
8. The palace of Prince William, 1804.
        "Rothschild and Sons" (Mayer, grown sons)
        "Allons!" (Joseph Fouché, Grenadiers)
9. The Rothschild shop, 1804.
        "Rothschild and Sons" (reprise) (Mayer, grown sons)
        "Sons" (reprise) (Mayer, Gutele)

ACT 2

1. The London Royal Stock Exchange, 1805.
        "Give England Strength" (John Herries, Bankers, Brokers)
        "This Amazing London Town/They Say" (Nathan, Bankers, Brokers)
2. The London Royal Stock Exchange, 1806.
        "They Say" (reprise) (Bankers, Brokers)
3. Rothschild shop/Hannah Cohen's Garden, 1806–1811.
        "I'm in Love! I'm in Love!" (Nathan)
        "I'm in Love! I'm in Love!" (reprise) (Nathan, Hannah)
4. The Rothschild home, 1812.
        "In My Own Lifetime" (Mayer)
5. The ballroom at Aix-la-Chapelle, 1818.
        "Have You Ever Seen a Prettier Little Congress?" (Prince Metternich, Nobility)
        "Stability" (Prince Metternich, Nobility) [formerly **"Never Again"**]
6. The Rothschild home, 1818.
7. The ballroom at Aix-la-Chappelle/the Ghetto, 1818.
        "Bonds" (Prince Metternich, Rothschild Sons)
8. The Rothschild home, 1818.

members of his court. At the beginning of Act 2 the collaborators replaced "The British Free Enterprise Auction" with a hymn, "Give England Strength," sung by the English bankers. Act 1 also includes "One Room," for Mayer and Gutele at the beginning of their lives together, she just hoping for a simple home, he dreaming about a better life outside of the ghetto; "He Tossed a Coin," for Mayer to demonstrate his sales skills at the Frankfurt fair; and "Allons!," sung by Napoleon's Grenadiers when they arrive to seize Hesse. In Act 2, in addition to the new song after Nathan meets Hannah, "I'm in Love! I'm in Love!," and its reprise as a duet after he has finally won her affections, Bock and Harnick added what has become the show's signature song, "In My Own Lifetime." This number became possible when they extended Mayer's life deeper into the second act and wanted to feature him one last time before his passing. The elder Rothschild imagines a peaceful world free of bigotry, with elegant, flowing phrases that struggle at first to ascend beyond a flatted seventh ("In my own **life**-time") but eventually soar and triumph ("This Moses wants to see the promised land / In my own lifetime").

Dramas of Musical Style

Bock sought inspiration for the *Rothschilds* score following his usual practices. As with his absorption of songs on a Beatrice Kay album when writing music for *Tenderloin*, or Theodore Bikel albums for *Fiddler*, or more recently, sheets of English folk songs when preparing to write music for *Trafalgar*, for *The Rothschilds* he immersed himself in late Baroque, Classical and early Romantic Western European art music. He told Lewis Funke of the *Times* that he spent "hours and hours . . . refamiliarizing himself with the work of Handel, Haydn, Mozart, and Beethoven, German lieder and Viennese folk songs" in preparation for composing the *Rothschilds* score.[49] On an index of some of the early tapes he made for Harnick he described some of his original melodies as "Haydnish" or "Rachmaninoff" or "18th century / also a bit o Bach."[50] Thus the finished score is filled with stylistic evocations and concert music clichés. We hear this right away at the beginning of the Overture, in music that Bock originally wrote to introduce the metaphorical auction, featuring dotted rhythms in the manner of the French operatic overture.[51] Then in the first song, "Pleasure and Privilege," he calls upon scalar passages, motivic patterns, and classic cadential figures to evoke an eighteenth-century court. As similar materials appear again and again throughout the score, Bock joins an older tradition that had already shown how art-music models could be adapted for popular entertainment—the operetta. The bouncy rhythms and triadic gestures of "Rothschild and Sons" are reminiscent of a Gilbert and Sullivan song such as "When I Was a Lad" from *H. M. S. Pinafore*.

The patter song "I'm in Love! I'm in Love!" is closer to a Gilbert and Sullivan model such as "I Am the Very Model of a Modern Major-General" from *The Pirates of Penzance* than is the earlier jazz-inflected Bock–Harnick patter song "Tonight at Eight" from *She Loves Me*. The Act 2 opener "Give England Strength" is a direct homage to the masters of English operetta, mimicking the choral work of the likes of "He Is an Englishman" from *H. M. S. Pinafore*; Harnick's punch line at the end of the song, "May Bonaparte be blown apart," could have come directly from the pen of W. S. Gilbert. Music for the court scenes in Act 2 is more reminiscent of Viennese musical traditions. The waltz of "Stability," for example, calls to mind a Johann Strauss, Jr. classic such as *Wiener-Blut*, op. 354.

But there is also a whole other side of the musical language of *The Rothschilds*, first heard at the end of "Pleasure and Privilege" when the scene dramatically shifts to the Frankfurt ghetto. As the classically tailored melody reaches its final formulaic cadence, on the lines "A world of pleasure and privilege / Elegant, elite / A private arcadia / Where life . . . is sweet," suddenly the tonality shifts to minor and the tone becomes dark. Over open fifths in the strings and ominous clanging bells, a crier intones "Hear ye, hear ye / Jews and aliens of Frankfurt / Cease all trade and traffic and remain confined in your homes until morning." A cello solo responds with an expressive sigh on the notes of the *Ahavah rabbah* mode (Example 8.2, cf. Example 6.7a).[52] During the course of the show, elements of Jewish music become more and more part of the complete musical fabric, in tandem with the rise of the Rothschilds' wealth and power. Bock explained his basic strategy at the beginning of a detailed note to orchestrator Don Walker:

> The 1st ACT is late 18th century classic—open—so that one can see the pure and impure with equal definition—the sound should be Haydn-Mozart and a forecast of Beethoven—bare—yet not barren—Within this outline is a Semitic strain—not in terms of "Fiddler" but buried under the graces of the outline—with the potential to pour out suddenly, privately, impulsively. . . .
>
> In the second act the layers become thicker—the individual/single perverse strains are put off by the lust invitations of a romantic world—fraught with wealth, power, love (+) plus and ironically cop-out—And these 19th cent. sounds are fuller—richer—but no less haunting—except that it takes more to push through to haunt than it did before.[53]

He wrote this note before the opening in Detroit and thus went on to describe a number of songs that never made it to New York. Still, he remained faithful to his original conception as he wrote new songs on the road.

The first song where the "Semitic strain" fully emerges is "Everything," which Bock calls "the first wrench from tradition—the open, instinctive Yiddish sound turned into a militant, dedicated purpose."[54] He accomplishes this in part by re-deploying the *Ahavah rabbah* mode on D heard earlier in the cello (Example 8.3, cf. Example 8.2). (Scale-step 2, the E♭, is in the accompaniment, as the flatted fifth of the dominant A$^{7(-5)}$ chords.) As the melody repeats the title word it reiterates the minor seventh C♮ on each first syllable, finally breaking away (and briefly out of the mode) to the major seventh C♯ (spelled as D♭) on the continuation of the line ("**oth**er men aspire to").

But Jewish flavorings do not always arrive with such force and clarity: indeed, some of the sounds that Bock introduces to disrupt the purity of classical tonality are simply dissonant or chromatic, not necessarily identifiable with specific ethnic traditions. His intentions are clear in his original music for the first auction, which begins with an undisturbed classical orientation but then arrives at what he calls a "music box figure" (Example 8.4a).[55] He wrote to Walker:

> What looks like a music box figure should be treated more aggressively/impulsively, cruder, shopworn, quasi spooky. It should sound both comfortable and *un*-comfortable—maybe a bit too loud for classic propriety—maybe the voice is accompanied by too little so the voice is vertically alone and harsher/uneasy, and the continuo underneath is *not quite right*.[56]

The music box melody is frankly Lydian on F at first, featuring the raised fourth step B♮ in the third bar, and after that the tonality is colored by two notes from outside the scale (the E♭ and D♭ in the sixth and seventh bars).

Example 8.2: Cello solo at end of "Pleasure and Privilege"

Example 8.3: "Everything," first vocal phrase

a. "The Auction," "music box figure" (Bock Papers, box 7, folder 3)

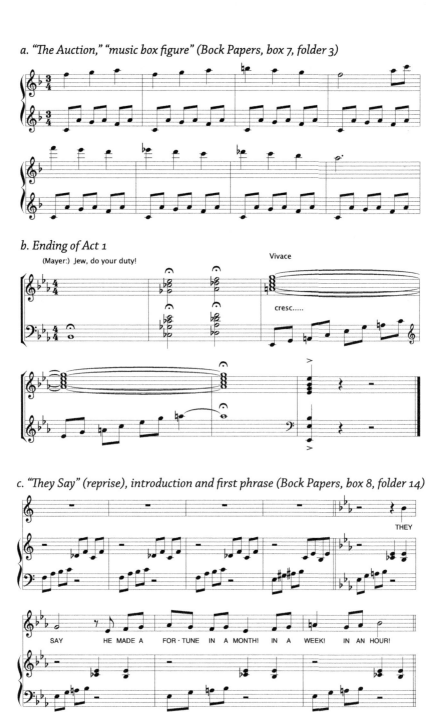

b. Ending of Act 1

(Mayer:) Jew, do your duty!

Vivace

cresc.....

c. "They Say" (reprise), introduction and first phrase (Bock Papers, box 8, folder 14)

THEY

SAY   HE MADE A   FOR - TUNE   IN   A   MONTH!   IN   A   WEEK!   IN AN HOUR!

Example 8.4: Tonality and inflections in The Rothschilds

(Continued)

d. "Have You Ever Seen a Prettier Little Congress?," first section (Bock Papers, box 7, folder 16)

Example 8.4: (Continued)

These impurities take the ear away from pure F major, as a tiny metaphor for the incursion of the Rothschild brothers into the European aristocracy.

Bock explained to Walker that he used this melodic idea later in the score "as Mayer might borrow what he's heard and learned before." This means not only that the melody itself will recur—as it did in the cut songs "Money," "Mayer's Fine Coins," and "William's Fine Troops"[57]—but also that distinctive elements of the melody will make return appearances, when the circumstances call for tonal disruptions. So at the end of Act 1, after the reprise of "Sons" and in response to Mayer's stirring directive to his sons, "Jew, do your duty," the return to the tonic E♭ major is interrupted by the projection of a four-note motive featuring a raised fourth scale step (A♮) upward through four octaves (Example 8.4b). Similarly, in "They Say" near the beginning of Act 2, when the London bankers closely follow Nathan's every movement on the floor of the stock exchange, we hear an accompaniment packed with raised fourths and lowered sixths and then a melody with stepwise movement and a prominent raised fourth just as in the music box melody (Example 8.4c).[58] And when Prince Metternich sings "Have You Ever Seen a Prettier Little Congress?" in a pivotal scene at Aix-la-Chappelle in Act 2, the tritones in the bass between the tonic E♭ and raised fourth A♮, as well as the prominence of the raised fourth and other chromatic notes in the melody itself, undercut the Prince's arrogant proclamations (Example 8.4d).[59] This is exactly what Bock was thinking of when he told his orchestrator that the "classic layers" of his score would ultimately be infused with "streaks of obliqueness, perverseness, anger—in other words, humanity."

When the competition between the Prince and the Rothschilds reaches a climax in "Bonds," these elements continue to resonate and provide a musical commentary in support of the drama. As the bidding shifts back and forth between the combatants, the music shifts back and forth between a princely waltz that grows increasingly distressed and the earthy Rothschilds music that becomes more and more assertive, its ♯4's and ♭7's finally assuming a central, secure place in the song's basic sound. Despite an unprecedented number of changes from early drafts to Broadway, and despite innumerable personal conflicts within the creative team, and potential crises during the pre-Broadway tour, Bock and Harnick had remained true to their original conception of the show's score, and they had shown once again a remarkable range and versatility.

The Show and Its Contexts

The Rothschilds ran for 505 performances, through January 2, 1972. It featured Hal Linden as Mayer, in his first major role on Broadway after more than a decade of supporting and replacement parts, plus an acclaimed run off-Broadway as Billy Crocker in Cole Porter's *Anything Goes* (1962).[60] The other meaty acting assignment in *The Rothschilds* goes to a single actor who plays four different characters, Prince William, Joseph Fouché (Napoleon's Minister of Police), John Herries (Chancellor of His Majesty's Exchequer), and Prince Metternich. This role was originated by Keene Curtis, who had appeared in Orson Welles's film *Macbeth* (1948) and had worked steadily on Broadway (although not in musicals) since 1955. Familiar names among the secondary roles included Broadway veteran Leila Martin (Gutele), Tony nominee (for *Rosencrantz and Guildenstern Are Dead*) Paul Hecht (Nathan Rothschild), and two actors who would subsequently embark on successful careers on stage and in films, Jill Clayburgh (Hannah Cohen) and Chris Sarandon (Jacob Rothschild). A fourteen-year-old Robby Benson made his Broadway debut in the role of the young Solomon Rothschild.

Hal Linden (Mayer Rothschild) with a cast member of The Rothschilds *(1970)*
(Photofest)

The Rothschilds received nine Tony nominations but won only two, for Best Actor in a Musical (Hal Linden) and Best Supporting or Featured Actor in a Musical (Keene Curtis). In most of the other nominated categories (Best Musical, Score, Lyrics, Book, Director, Scene Design) the awards went to a Broadway landmark, Stephen Sondheim's *Company*. This is no great surprise:

critical appraisals of *The Rothschilds* were decidedly mixed. Clive Barnes in the *Times* (10/20/70) stopped short of unqualified praise but admitted that the show was "interesting, in parts very witty, has a certain moral force and, best of all, it has style." Richard Watts in the *Post* (10/22/70) also had his doubts—he wrote that "the Rothschilds are too unfailingly triumphant for the best interests of dramatic suspense"—yet allowed that "the production is so visually attractive, there is enough ingenuity in the telling of its undeniably placid success story, and it is so well acted that it becomes striking, interesting, and certainly highly unusual." Critics who dissented were especially vicious. Martin Gottfried wrote in *Women's Wear Daily* (10/21/70) that in *The Rothschilds* Bock and Harnick took a "depressing step backward" to "the operetta, the patchwork musical, the shorthand story sprinkled with songs, dances, and production numbers," all in all a "vulgarization of musical theater." Brendan Gill in the *New Yorker* (10/31/70) found the show "vulgar, silly, and totally unhistorical." He wrote that the music threatened "constantly to turn into other and more familiar songs, some of them by Jerry Bock"; that the lyrics were "often so bad as to be funny"; and that the book revealed "no feeling whatever for the period with which it is concerned."

Several critics found the first act stronger than the second and questioned the purpose of the romantic storyline between Nathan and Hannah. Barnes called this romance a digression that "detracts from the steady development of the story." In any case, wrote John Chapman in the *Daily News* (10/20/70), the portrayal of the courtship was "not particularly romantic." Harnick came to agree with this assessment, accepting criticism from within the Bock family:

> We were thinking traditionally, so we thought, "We've got to have a love story in it." So Sherman Yellen, who wrote the book, with all of our agreement wrote a love story in the second act for one of the sons, Nathan Rothschild, who goes to England. In real life, he did meet Hannah, they fell in love, and they got married. It wasn't until after we had opened that Jerry Bock and I were in a taxicab with Jerry's twelve-year-old son and he [the son] said, "You guys really blew it." We said, "What do you mean?" He said, "The love story is about the father and the five sons, not about Nathan and Hannah." And he was right. We didn't blow it; the show was good. We ran about fourteen months. But it's true that the second act, instead of remaining about those five boys, got overshadowed by Nathan.[61]

After the show closed on Broadway, Harnick and Michael Kidd addressed these and other criticisms in significantly pruning the libretto for a successful tour of California, also starring Hal Linden. Then in 1990, for a production Off-Off-Broadway by the American Jewish Theater, Harnick trimmed the dialogue even more, to minimize the Nathan–Hannah romance and keep the primary focus on the brothers. This scaled-down production, economizing acting roles and reducing the size of the cast from forty to fifteen, was greeted by a generally warmer critical reception than the original and eventually moved to a larger Off-Broadway house, the Circle in the Square Downtown, where it played for 379 performances.[62]

Critics at any time, of any production, have made unavoidable comparisons between The Rothschilds and its Jewish-themed predecessor in the Bock-Harnick catalogue, which played on Broadway for six more months after The Rothschilds closed. The Rothschilds has been called "a rich man's Fiddler," "Fiddler with money," "Fiddler on the Continent," and "Violinist on a Pedestal."[63] A joke circulated about a rejected song for the show, "Now That I'm a Rich Man."[64] The Variety reviewer of the original Broadway production (Hobe, 10/21/70) suggested that the five Rothschild sons were "the obvious answer to the problem of Tevye's five marriageable daughters." In a pre-emptive defense published in the Times a few days before the New York opening, Bock and Harnick noted that they had first been approached about the Rothschilds project well before they completed Fiddler, and that "the only similarity between the two musicals is that they are about Jewish families." Harnick observed:

> Tevye's people were resigned to their poverty. The Rothschilds were determined to break out of theirs. And, although shtetl life was meager and circumscribed, there was a warmth that people do look back on with a kind of nostalgia. There never was any nostalgia for the austere, restricted life that pervaded the walled-in ghettos of Frankfurt and elsewhere.[65]

Indeed that was the essence of the challenge for the creators of The Rothschilds—to tell an endearing story in the absence of nostalgia or sentimentality for the characters and settings. They succeeded in establishing a warm sense of family in the first act, as Bock, Harnick, and Joseph Stein did for Tevye and his family, but in the second act they risked being overtaken by the Rothschild brothers' drive toward power and wealth. The addition of the moral component, the family's concern for equal rights for Jews—exaggerated though it may be—hopes to rescue the story from the clutches of materialism and greed. In Fiddler on the Roof we never lose sympathy for Tevye's beliefs in tradition, nor with his struggles against his oppressors, but in The Rothschilds our feelings about the sons can too easily shift from sympathy in the first act to ambivalence, indifference, possibly even distaste, in the second.

We ultimately realize that the Rothschilds' story is not as transferable, not as transcendent of culture and ethnicity, as are *Fiddler*'s appeals to universal values and sensibilities. As Tevye moves through his changing world, he remains one of us; the Rothschilds progress from one of us to one of them. The names say it all: we are on a first-name basis with Tevye and his family—surnames are not necessary in the *shtetl*—but for Mayer Rothschild and his progeny, the family name is a symbol of their power, their legacy, their aristocratic pretensions. Likewise for the shows themselves: Bock and Harnick's musical dramatization of some of Sholem Aleichem's stories was known as *Tevye* through several drafts of Joseph Stein's libretto in 1962–1964 (see chapter 6); with *The Rothschilds*, however, they were always on a last-name basis.

If *The Rothschilds* does veer away from a humanistic core, it becomes more vulnerable to harsh stereotyping, as Martin Gottfried bluntly implied in the opening sentence of his 1970 review: "*The Rothschilds* is a musical about Jews and money."[66] Jewish theatergoers who want to embrace the show as they did *Fiddler* can easily teeter back and forth between pride and disenchantment. In a thoughtful article in the *Village Voice* in 1970, Julius Novick wrote that after seeing *The Rothschilds* he had "never felt so clearly that a yarmulke is a badge of honor," and yet he also found that "it roused me at moments to exasperation and contempt."[67] As Alisa Solomon observed in 2006, *Fiddler* resonated with Jewish audiences by fusing values of the old and new countries; the Rothschilds family, however, "never needed to engage the promise of America and they did not leave behind a murdered world for which their grandchildren could be nostalgic."[68] On the other hand, the Nobel laureate Elie Wiesel, writing in the *Times* during the off-Broadway run in 1990, found comfort in the legend and in his own experience.[69] "The name of Rothschild made me daydream, as it did many Jewish children," Wiesel reminisced. "Envied by the high society that accepted them reluctantly, the Rothschilds were our princes and protectors, recalling the glory and pride of ancient days." The Rothschilds "do not hide their desire to make money," wrote Wiesel, but it is a "means and not an end. A means of proving to the world that Jews are as smart and as vulnerable as other people; and that they know how to deal with humiliation, of which poverty is only one painful aspect." Many who share Wiesel's sentiments and heritage might identify with Sholem Aleichem's monologue "If I Were a Rothschild," which was published in English translation in the same collection that contains the stories of Tevye and his daughters. Indeed the Yiddish version of *Fiddler on the Roof* renders the lyric of "If I Were a Rich Man" as "Ven Ich Bin A Rothschild."[70]

The reception of *The Rothschilds* by the world at large was another matter. There was still ample interest in shows upholding Broadway traditions in the early 1970s, when *The Rothschilds* played on Broadway alongside *Fiddler on the Roof*, Ethel Merman in *Hello, Dolly!*, Lauren Bacall in *Applause*, and the like. But when *The Rothschilds* opened in October 1970, *Hair*, subtitled "The American Tribal Love-Rock Musical," was halfway through its third year; Burt Bacharach's pop-oriented score for *Promises, Promises* was still playing well as it neared the end of its second year; and the musically eclectic erotic revue *Oh! Calcutta!* showed no signs of going away after its first sixteen months. The Sondheim/Prince musical *Company* had opened the previous April, challenging audiences to focus less on narrative structures, more on recurring themes and ideas. During the more than fourteen months of the run of *The Rothschilds*, Broadway offered more Sondheim, in the form of *Follies* (opened 4/4/71), and more musicals with alternative scores: Rice and Lloyd Webber's rock-based *Jesus Christ Superstar* (10/12/71); Melvin Van Peebles's *Ain't Supposed to Die a Natural Death* (10/20/71), part of what has been called a "black musical renaissance"; and *Hair*-mastermind Galt MacDermot's *Two Gentlemen of Verona* (12/1/71).[71] The new directions that Bock and Harnick had dedicated themselves to exploring for each new show had always stayed within the boundaries of the conventional book musical, their modest tinkerings in *The Apple Tree* notwithstanding. They would not be following the lead of their former collaborator Harold Prince, who was becoming Stephen Sondheim's chief ally in redefining the Broadway musical. If *Fiddler on the Roof* offered one last spectacular example of what a Rodgers and Hammerstein-style musical could be, then *The Rothschilds* was one more demonstration of how well worn the old formulas had become. In a milieu of cultural transformation and societal unrest—of protest marches and celebrations of the counterculture—a big Broadway musical about the rise to power and wealth of an eighteenth-century Jewish patriarch and his ambitious sons was easily marginalized.

The position of *The Rothschilds* within the work of Bock and Harnick is likewise tenuously wrought. Of course it has been dwarfed by *Fiddler*, but then so have all their other shows. Its music represents the team at its most mature, and yet it has failed to gain a wide following and does not seem poised for the kind of belated emergence enjoyed by *She Loves Me*. It does have its ardent admirers, but its long-term popularity still falls somewhere south of *Fiorello!* and *The Apple Tree*, north of *Tenderloin* and *The Body Beautiful*. In the end, the creators' early assessments still ring true, despite substantial later improvements. Harnick said in 1973: "We did the best we could; we came in with a show that I felt rather good about ultimately; I thought we came close."[72] For Bock in 1974, *The Rothschilds* was an "incomplete show": "there were moments that were right, and moments that were wrong, and problems that we did not solve."[73] Considering the tensions and difficulties of the show's development, it is hardly surprising that the result failed to meet standards that the team had set for themselves. Less-than-ideal working conditions easily yield counterproductive artistic compromises. Reflecting on the experience and its impact on the partnership in March 1971, when *The Rothschilds* was in its fifth month on Broadway, Harnick could only say, "I don't know what the resolution is yet."[74]

9

TOPSY-TURVY

• • •

SEPARATE PATHS SINCE THE EARLY 1970S

There were outward signs in the early 1970s that the songwriting partnership of Jerry Bock and Sheldon Harnick had survived the tensions and difficulties of their latest show. When Max Wilk interviewed them (separately) in 1971, as *The Rothschilds* and *Fiddler on the Roof* continued to play on Broadway, they spoke as members of a team. Reflecting on these conversations in his book on American popular songwriters, Wilk summarized Bock's and Harnick's attitudes toward the future: "And so, for two craftsmen, who wish to exercise their considerable talents to enrich the American theater, . . . the search for their next project goes on."[1] In 1971, 1972, and 1973 Bock and Harnick wrote satirical songs for Mayor John Lindsay to sing at the annual Inner Circle dinner for New York political reporters, upholding a tradition they began in 1966.[2] In October 1972 they sang three of their songs, one newly written, for a theatrical gala organized to raise money for the McGovern–Shriver presidential campaign.[3] And they appeared together to help celebrate special events, including the premiere of the film version of *Fiddler on the Roof* on November 3, 1971, and milestones for the first stage run of *Fiddler* on July 21, 1971 (longest-running musical) and June 17, 1972 (longest-running Broadway show), before it established the record for longevity with its final performance on July 2, 1972.[4]

But these were only public faces, masking different private realities: issues of team survival were too fresh and unsettled to share with an interviewer in 1971; at this point they could write songs for political revues with minimal effort, perhaps even minimal personal contact; it is easy to smile for photographs on a red carpet. The truth is, Bock and Harnick were drawn increasingly apart during this time. They had stopped discussing new project possibilities, stopped thinking as a team. "Jerry and I were furious with each other and really didn't speak for years," Harnick reflected in 1990. "For a while the feelings between us were very bad."[5] They have acknowledged no defining moment of separation, no tempestuous meeting or icy phone call that became a critical turning point, just a gradual parting of ways. "Jerry and I kind of drifted apart and never managed to drift back together," Harnick told an interviewer in 1985.[6] More than two decades later, Bock remembered it the same way: "It's not that we said we would never work together again. We just needed to take some time away from each other."[7]

Relations did begin to improve in 1985, when the former partners worked side-by-side once again to help fine-tune a production of *Fiorello!* at the Goodspeed Opera House. "Thank God we have ongoing business with the productions that we've written," Harnick said in 1990.[8] After that they continued to serve as creative advisors for important new productions of their shows in many venues, most notably the Broadway revivals of *Fiddler on the Roof* in 1990 and 2004, *She Loves Me* in 1993, and *The Apple Tree* in 2006. They have shared stages numerous times to accept joint honors and awards, and in 2008 Harnick was on hand to help celebrate Bock's eightieth birthday with the Encompass New Opera Theater at the National Arts Club in New York. But their reconciliation stopped short of a new major collaboration. Harnick has said that he has proposed new large projects to Bock on several occasions but failed to arouse his friend's interest.[9] Bock has seemed open to new suggestions but ultimately unwilling to retrace old steps. "I'm sorry we're not writing together," Harnick said in 2003. "This is his choice."[10] They have worked together as a songwriting team only once since the early 1970s, to write the song "Topsy-Turvy" for the 2004 *Fiddler*. "It felt like yesterday," Bock told an interviewer.[11] "Once we started, it was as if we'd never stopped writing together. We wrote it in a few days."[12]

We can never know all the forces that conspired to break up one of Broadway's most celebrated songwriting teams after fourteen years and a string of distinguished contributions to the American musical theater. Certainly, the conflicts that arose about the creative leadership of *Her First Roman* and *The Rothschilds* in the late 1960s were important factors. But as Bock explained in 2008, "The back of the camel had been weakened by other straws along the way, so that *The Rothschilds* straw broke a vulnerable back, not one broken by a sudden blow." Perhaps he was referring to conflicts that had arisen earlier in the decade, during discussions they had about writing an opera and working outside the partnership, not long before Harnick announced a collaboration with Burton Lane in 1968 (see chapter 8). In any event, by the early 1970s both were ready for new professional challenges. Bock was eager to write both words and music, having nothing left to prove as the composer half of a songwriting team. Harnick was interested in exploring other forms of musical-dramatic expression besides the Broadway musical. And it is no mere coincidence that their attitudes evolved during the time when *Fiddler on the Roof* was emerging as a certifiable phenomenon: exploration had become a luxury that they could now afford. Having reached a whole new level of personal and professional comfort, they could be more selective, more reflective. Put another way, their earlier successes may have depended on a certain hunger, born of youthful ambition and financial necessity, that had now been essentially satisfied. The tale of their partnership is a reminder that the creation and production of a work of musical theater entails an extraordinary convergence of diverse creative spirits, complex logistical forces, and deep cultural insight, and that the experience of creating any financially successful show on Broadway, let alone a *Fiddler on the Roof*, is enough to strike a chord of satisfaction in its creators that reverberates long and far.

As Bock and Harnick moved on to new projects in new arenas with new collaborators in the decades since their partnership dissolved, neither found the same success working alone or with other partners that they once enjoyed working with each other. Their personal chemistry, the compatibility of their artistic sensibilities, have proven to be rare and elusive commodities. Like other great songwriting teams, or like consortia of great scientists or athletes, their individual creative energies coalesced into some magical whole that was somehow greater than the sum of its extraordinarily talented parts. Although it is not a requirement, they happened to be good friends as well. We are left to ponder the formidable lists of distinguished works produced by songwriting partnerships with greater longevity—Rodgers and Hart, Kander and Ebb—and imagine what might have been. There is plenty left to celebrate, but it is a celebration tinged with regret. It is easy to sympathize with Harnick's own sentiments in 1999: "Every time I see one of our shows, I realize we had something special, and it saddens me."[13]

BOCK AND BOCK

Jerry Bock's interest in writing his own lyrics has been constant throughout his life. Even while writing songs with assorted friends in high school and college, with Larry Holofcener and George Weiss in the 1950s, and with Sheldon Harnick after that, he was also serving as his own lyricist for dozens of independent songs not connected to a particular show or project.[14] In the 1970s, then, as he and his long-time partner drifted apart, Bock followed a natural impulse to expand his solo efforts. As he said in 2008, "the experience and approval from peers gave me the heart to write by myself rather than with a new partner, as had been my instinct to do so since unpartnering with

Sheldon." Bock first worked on individual songs and groups of songs that told stories or explored themes. While he has kept these efforts mostly private, in recent decades he also began to develop new, more visible projects for the musical theater, including two major musicals that somehow veered away from paths to Broadway, and, in the first decade of the twenty-first century, a very successful series of musicals for young audiences.

In the Studio

Some of Bock's private songs from the 1970s are as much personal explorations as they are musical creations. In 1972 he recorded what he calls a concept album entitled *Album Leaves*, and in 1974 another, *Trading Dreams*. These are attempts at "telling a story through songs only."[15] *Album Leaves*, for example, is undisguised autobiography, a series of songs sung by Bock himself, backed by a small band, that traces the composer's life story from early childhood through young adulthood. It begins with an introductory song, "Album Leaves," that establishes both an ambience for the collection and a musical theme that recurs as connective material in several of the songs to come. On subsequent tracks we learn about his first exposure to some important life lessons ("Utopia"), friendships ("Trio [Willie, George, and Me]"), memories of his father ("Travelin' Salesman"), memories of his mother and grandmother ("Piano Man"), rites of passage ("Birthday Party"), adolescent crushes ("Proposal"), the magic of musical discovery ("Lis Nin' To Music"), the comforts of love and family ("Home Towns"), and the commitment of matrimony ("The Marriage Band"). The album closes with a final reprise of the opening song. The styles of the songs are mostly consonant with the time period being surveyed: Bock explores not only his own personal history but also the sounds and colors of his musical upbringing in the language of show tunes and classic jazz.

The songs in *Album Leaves* show that indeed Bock is a capable lyricist and is as comfortable with wordplay as he is with shaping a melodic line or inventing a soundscape. In "Proposal," for example, the protagonist finds himself helplessly smitten with two equally alluring sisters. He can think of no solution but to have them both:

> Dora, Eva,
> I believe a
> Boy can weave a dream,
> You and me, oh
> What a trio
> Coffee, sugar, cream.

In "Home Towns" he finds "home" wherever he is enveloped by love and family:

> I consider my hometown to be
> Anyplace where love lived next to me
> Lookin' at the sky,
> Stretched out flat,
> Where was that?
> That was one of my hometowns.

The most affecting song in the collection is "Piano Man," in which Bock reminisces about the baby grand in his childhood home and hours spent entertaining his mother and grandmother. Accompanied by a cascading triplet riff, sounding like figures from a Czerny etude dipped in Fats Waller, Bock paints a vivid scene of music and family:

> Her name was Grandma Rosie,
> A lady frail and small,
> Who loved to hear him play the piano
> Anytime at all.
> He pleased his mama,
> He pleased his papa,
> But my how Grandma Rosie bloomed.
>
> He'd always try to play the notes he heard inside his head,
> And Grandma would reward him while she listened in her bed,
> With teardrop medals from Rosie's petals
> For Grandson's baby grand.

Eventually the song recalls the day "a Rose began to fade" and the grandson played for her one last time "in a place where people prayed." It is through the love and support of his family, the lyric explains, that he was eventually able to become a true "Piano Man."

In *Album Leaves* Bock essentially offers an explanation for a reputation he has earned since 1970 for avoiding the spotlight of public attention. He is more comfortable, the album seems to say, expressing himself in song than in a speech or interview. If he has a story to tell, he will let his music do the talking. His other private compositions from the 1970s and '80s likewise tell colorful tales of creative exploration and expansion. Although some of the songs were reportedly written for a songwriting competition or television show, they have remained stored in Bock's proverbial trunk until recently, when he began to collect and organize them for digital preservation.[16] These songs range across the spectrum, from basic ballads ("We Are One," "Write Me a Love Song") to a bossa nova ("Like Our Love"), a gospel anthem ("Lord, Lift the Ark"), and an anti-materialistic Christmas song ("A Christmas Present").[17] In a CD compilation Bock has called *Noblesse O' Blues*, also *Bounty of Blues*, he offers eight takes on classic jazz, employing figures and feels of typical blues numbers (but not using twelve-bar blues progressions).[18] Accompanied only by himself at the piano, he sings about blues traditions ("They Don't Write Blues," to a honky-tonk beat), self-examination ("Mirror, Mirror Blues," a cabaret-style ballad), lost love ("We Spell Blue," an up-tempo belter), loneliness ("Still Blue," a tear-drenched torch song), the comfort of the blues in the face of romantic loss ("Noblesse O' Blues," a defiant up-tempo minor-key show tune), waiting for love ("Lemon and Lime Blues," a melancholy ballad), remembrance of past love ("Anniversary Blues," recalling early riff-based blues), and finally redemption ("No Blues No More," another throwback, with a strong scent of ragtime).[19] Overall the collection leaves the strong impression that a need to sing, play, and write in the style of classic jazz has finally burst forth after years of semi-dormancy, a tendency we may have already detected anyway in earlier Bock songs such as "Too Close For Comfort" (*Mr. Wonderful*, 1956), "Just My Luck" (*The Body Beautiful*, 1958), "Since I've Been To You," (recorded by Ethel Ennis in 1964), "Popsicles in Paris" (*To Broadway with Love*, 1964), and "I've Got What You Want" and "Tiger, Tiger" (*The Apple Tree*, 1966).

Yet another private compilation from the 1970s, possibly extending into the early 1980s, consists entirely of solo piano music in triple meter, a focused exploration of the waltz and its metric brethren. Bock calls it *Three/Four All*. The song titles alone capture a sense of the rich character and humor of the collection:

1. Papa Pa-Oom
2. The Dip
3. Der Rosie's Cavalier
4. Bali Low
5. You Bah B'Dah
6. Gershlude
7. One Anna Two Anna Three
8. Chaplinesque
9. Marching Disorders
10. Octave-Genarion
11. Beat's Me!
12. Triple Tongue On Wry
13. A Dozen Bakers

All work independently as piano pieces—collected together like a set of character pieces by Chopin or Schumann—but some could also be songs awaiting (or missing) a lyric. Stylistically they either rest comfortably in, or comment provocatively on, jazz and so are companions to *Noblesse O' Blues*. The title of the sixth track, "Gershlude" may offer a clue to Bock's overall inspiration for the collection, in its hint at Gershwin's Three Preludes for Piano (1926). To an even greater extent than Gershwin's preludes, Bock's collection explores boundaries of style, as in "Der Rosie's Cavalier," where he takes figures suggesting a waltz by Johann Strauss II and morphs them into swing-era syncopations. In "You Bah B'Dah," similarly, ragtime struggles to disrupt the facade of an ordinary waltz. Indeed the interaction, sometimes competition, between clichés from different stylistic traditions emerges as a theme for the entire collection. On a page kept among an assortment of papers in his archive, Bock seems to have been considering different, revelatory titles for the collection: "Welcome Intrusions" or "The Welcome Intruder (A Fable of Waltzes)."[20]

Musical Theater and Film

Bock continued with his private explorations throughout the 1970s and '80s. In 1990 he told an interviewer that he was "writing words and music for a performance piece on the theme of food." "It's not a musical, as such," explained Bock; "I'm inventing the form as I go along."[21] But during those same years he was equally focused on writing music for the public arena, potentially the Broadway stage. His first major post-Harnick theatrical project originated in the early 1970s—probably while *The Rothschilds* was still playing on Broadway—with Stuart Ostrow, the *Apple Tree* producer who had recently produced the successful musical *1776* (1969). Perhaps inspired by Anthony Schaffer's popular award-winning play *Sleuth* (which opened on November 12, 1970), Ostrow had begun to conceive a "murder-mystery-musical" he called *Caper*. To write the book he had recruited the novelist Evan Hunter (also known as the author of popular mystery novels, under the name of Ed McBain), and he had at first made an agreement with Richard Rodgers to write the music. Bock got involved, to write both music and lyrics, when Ostrow learned that Bock was open to projects without Harnick, and in light of what seemed to be a lack of enthusiasm by Rodgers. As Ostrow told the *New York Times* when the creative team was announced in May 1973, the challenge was to use music "in a way that helps to make the suspense mount." The problem, said Hunter, is that "suspense and mystery seem to disappear the minute someone opens his mouth to sing."[22] Their solution was to create a "protagonist [who] is progressively endangered when singing each new musical number and is ultimately put to death by the musical's finale." The project fizzled, however, when Hunter withdrew after "many unsuccessful book attempts," recalls Ostrow. Even so, Bock had written a number of songs for the show, and Ostrow still, in 2009, had not lost hope for bringing the concept to fruition.[23]

Bock continued to imagine projects for the big stage and at one point tried to interest Joe Masteroff in a musical adaptation of the Oscar-winning Danish film *Babettes Gæstebud* (known in America as *Babette's Feast*, 1987). Instead of a musical, however, Bock's next public project after *Caper* was the score for a film, Sidney Lumet's *A Stranger Among Us* (1992). He got involved with this effort in the early 1990s through the film's orchestrator, his old friend Jack Elliott, who had done dance arrangements for the original productions of *Fiorello!* and *Tenderloin* and had arranged incidental music for the original score of *She Loves Me*.[24] In the years since, Elliott had worked extensively in television and film. The project seemed a natural fit for Bock: the story is set in a Hasidic community in Brooklyn and features scenes of religious services, Sabbath prayers, and Jewish traditions. Naturally, many of his melodies for the film feature raised fourths and lowered sevenths, and Elliott's orchestrations echo Klezmer traditions, picking up where the *Fiddler* dance music left off. A scene showing a Sabbath meal essentially comments on the parallel scene in *Fiddler*, underscored with a melody based on the *Ahavah rabbah* mode (see Example 6.7a). One of the film's central ideas is the cultural contrast between the Hasidim and the New York around them, as seen through the eyes of a gritty (and non-Jewish) New York police detective (played by Melanie Griffith). Bock's music supports this idea just as his score for *The Rothschilds* portrays the emergence of Jewish outsiders within the European aristocracy. As the detective becomes more and more aware of Hasidic laws and traditions, and more and more immersed in the community—she lives with the Rebbe's family in order to solve a murder—clichés of Jewish music become more and more integrated into the soundtrack. At the beginning of the film there is a clear separation between the straight-ahead soft jazz style of New York at large and the Klezmer sounds of the Hasidim, but by the end, with the murder solved and the detective enlightened, the two sound worlds have merged. The underscoring of the final scene, when the detective displays her new understanding and appreciation to a Jewish colleague on the force, accomplishes this within just a few beats, moving from the main title theme in basic jazz style to a figure that mixes the lowered third and raised fourth of the *Mi shebberakh* mode (Example 6.7b) with the raised seventh of major or harmonic minor, rising upward through three octaves, nearly re-creating the ending of the first act of *The Rothschilds* (see Example 8.4b).

For the remainder of the 1990s Bock held Broadway aspirations for a major musical about the tax code. He was first approached with the idea in late 1991 or early 1992 by Jerry Sterner, playwright of the 1989 off-Broadway hit (and later a hit movie) *Other People's Money*. Sterner had already tried to develop the concept with the songwriting team of Richard Maltby Jr. and David Shire, who had recently written an off-Broadway revue, *Closer Than Ever*, but eventually decided to change collaborators and attracted Bock's interest.[25] Sterner and Bock developed book and songs throughout 1992 and 1993, brought an accomplished director, Jerry Zaks, on board, and seemed destined for a Broadway opening sometime in 1994 or 1995.[26] For one reason or another, however, the project remained in development until 1997, when Stuart Ostrow agreed to present a workshop version in Houston, Texas. Ostrow had joined the Theater faculty of the University of Houston in 1995 and had relocated and revived his Musical Theater Lab, a support program for fledgling musicals that he had started in New York in the mid-1970s.[27] Once called *Washington, D. C.*, finally *1040*, the musical premiered in workshop form in Houston on November 14, 1997. The story concerned "a middle-aged real-estate mogul and his estranged daughter who become key players in the campaign to reform the tax code. Along the way, they salvage their relationship, the mogul finds his conscience and the daughter grows up emotionally."[28]

With four scheduled performances, however, and under the aegis of something called a Musical Theater *Lab*, the idea was to shape and mold the show into something with a commercial future. This never happened, reportedly, because Sterner and Ostrow could not agree on further revisions. According to Ostrow, Sterner had already made substantial changes prior to the opening, to focus more on the father-daughter relationship, but refused to revise the script further during the four workshop performances. After that the creative team dissolved and Sterner developed his script into a non-musical play that was tepidly received at the Rich Forum of the Stamford (Connecticut) Center for the Arts in November 1998. (*Variety* [1/4/99–1/10/99]: "If Sterner believes that *1040* is less about tax reform than about a father-daughter relationship, the playwright has to build up the characters of Murray and Emily and explore their relationship more fully.") Bock's extensive score, consisting of around twenty musical numbers or scenes, languished after that.[29] This, Ostrow said in 2009, is a shame: "Jerry Bock wrote a wonderful score trying to put a pink sequined gown on a girl who hadn't bathed."

The Houston experience did have one providential byproduct, however. While on location for the *1040* premiere in 1997 Bock became acquainted with another member of the school's Theater faculty, Sidney Berger, who ran a professional summer Children's Theater Festival and was ever watchful for new material. When Berger learned of the children's songs that Bock had written decades earlier, released in 1963 as *New Songs We Sing in School* (see chapter 4), he proposed to write a libretto for a new musical molded around the existing songs. Bock agreed, and eventually wrote two new songs for the show as well, and the result, known as *The Magic Journey*, "about a guardian angel looking after several runaway children," premiered in Houston in the summer of 2000.[30] The show was a success, but it was still essentially a revue, and Bock was inspired to return to Houston the following summer and collaborate with Berger on an entirely new book musical for children, *Danny and the Dragon*, based on an original story by Berger, with music and lyrics by Bock. This also played well, and Bock and Berger continued to write children's shows together for subsequent summers, eventually creating seven new mini-musicals between 2000 and 2007:

The Magic Journey (2000)
Danny and the Dragon (2001)
Brandon Finds His Star (2002)
The Adventures of Pinocchio (2003)
The New Adventures of Pinocchio (2004)
The Land of Broken Toys (2005)
The Princess Who Could Not Be Heard (2007)[31]

Story ideas for the shows originated with Berger, who would typically send Bock a first draft of a script in December and then collaborate long distance through the winter and spring. Bock wrote both lyrics and music for all of the songs. Their last two shows addressed themes of sensitivity and disability: in *The Land of Broken Toys*, a disabled boy's toys teach him how to rise above his physical limitations; in *The Princess Who Could Not Be Heard*, a deaf princess who is rejected by her own family because of her hearing disability finds acceptance among circus performers.[32]

Their third effort, *Brandon Finds His Star* (2002), about a pair of unlikely space travelers who learn to accept themselves as they are, has found its way into the catalogue of Music Theater International (which also licenses Bock–Harnick shows) and so has the potential for wider visibility.[33] Its score holds no surprises: the music is witty and colorful and saturated with Bockisms. In "When You Find Your Star," raised fourths and flatted sevenths call to mind "This is Love" (Example 1.1c), "Ethel Baby" (*Mr. Wonderful*), "Lovely Laurie" (cut from *Tenderloin*), and the *Rothschilds* "music box" tune (Example 8.4). In "The Wizard of Ahhhs," triplet figures surrounding step 5 with $\sharp 4$ and $\flat 6$ echo the Hungarian flavorings of "A Romantic Atmosphere" and the verse of "A Trip to the Library" from *She Loves Me*. "The Blue Planetarian Blues" features a chromatic lament bass line that revives a thematic element of *The Apple Tree*, especially bluesier numbers such as "I've Got What You Want" and "Tiger, Tiger" (see Example 7.5), not to forget some of the songs in the more recent *Noblesse O' Blues* collection. The composer's familiar facility with stylistic appropriation is on display in "Spanglish," which moves back and forth between a tango and a rumba. Lyric highlights include "Sing a Song of Planets," a patter song that serves as a learning aid for the planets of the solar system, and "When You Find Your Star," a touching ballad about personal identity ("Racing through the skies / Searching for a star / Seems so very far to roam / Then you find your star and know at last / Stars are often found at home").

Bock embraced each project for the children's theater festival with full professional commitment. "Jerry treats the festival as he would a Broadway production," Berger has said.[34] But it was not an unlikely passion for a composer of Bock's experience and ability, then well into his seventies. Clearly he had found a collaborator, and a supportive professional environment, that motivated and inspired him with no less intensity than a weekly revue at Tamiment or a pre-Broadway tryout in Boston. Although the festival shut down after the 2008 season, Bock and Berger continued to discuss possible projects together, now aiming towards adult audiences in prominent venues, possibly leading to an opening on Broadway. As Stuart Ostrow said of both Bock and Harnick in 2009, "the best is yet to come."

HARNICKIANA

If the early lives and professional evolutions of Jerry Bock and Sheldon Harnick were striking in their similarities, the paths they followed since their last major collaboration in 1970 are just as striking for their contrasts. While Bock has worked quietly in his studio year after year, Harnick has pursued and embraced a visible public presence. He has become the spokesman for his former team and has welcomed opportunities to monitor and advise and promote new productions of their work across the globe. At the same time he has nurtured a robust creative drive by exploring all corners of dramatic music, from traditional musical theater to animated television shows to grand opera. He has worked not just as a lyricist, with a variety of new collaborators, but also as a translator, librettist, and composer. He has become a distinguished elder statesman of the dramatic musical arts and a prominent, distinctive voice in American culture of the last decades of the twentieth century and beyond.

Table 9.1 organizes Harnick's work since the late 1960s into five areas of activity, starting in the left column with a flurry of translations in the 1970s and '80s. The second category/column represents a wholly new passion, opera, beginning with his librettos with Jack Beeson in the 1970s and including works large and small, plus one cantata with Joe Raposo in 1980. The remaining columns in the table consist of projects that flow more directly from Harnick's earlier work in the musical theater, although his creative roles vary. For the works listed in the third column he assumed his customary role as lyricist only, but for the next group (column four) he wrote both book and lyrics, and in the final column are two musical theater projects in which he did everything himself—music, book, and lyrics. The table also includes, for the sake of completeness, his first book musical, the project he began with David Baker and Ira Wallach in 1953, earlier known as *The Fair-Haired Boy*, or *Horatio*, or *Smiling the Boy Fell Dead*, and finally called *Pluck and Luck, or the ABC's of Success*, because Harnick returned to it in 2004 (see chapter 2).[35] It straddles the third and fourth columns, reflecting his recent involvement with the book as well as the lyrics.

These are just the "major" projects—the ones that presumably commanded the greatest expenditures of time and creative energy. Harnick's more modest undertakings from recent decades are equally numerous and diverse, ranging from songs for films with Cy Coleman (*The Heartbreak Kid* [1972], *Blame It On Rio* [1984]), to music for television (*Marriage is Alive and Well* [with Fred Karlin, 1980], *The Way We Were* [with Larry Grossman, 1981]), to an "opera spuffo" with Marvin Hamlisch (*The Audition* [2006]). For Israel's Fiftieth Birthday Celebration in 1998 he wrote new ceremonial lyrics for "To Life."[36] And for Jerome Robbins's ballet "Ives, Songs" (premiered at the New York City Ballet in 1988) he translated Louis Gallet's French text of one song by Charles Ives, "Elegie."[37] Harnick has likewise been a willing participant in theatrical galas, often benefiting charitable causes, and in tribute events, both as celebrant and honoree.

Translations

In a 1986 interview with Bob Cioffi, Harnick described his interest in translations in the 1970s as an outcome of the earlier tensions with his long-time partner. He turned away from Broadway during this time, he said, as a way of managing his own "inner grief and conflicts" in the aftermath of *The Rothschilds*. Rather than seeking a new collaborator for something original, he found ways to "write with dead composers."[38] It was a trend that actually

Table 9.1 Major Works of Sheldon Harnick with New Collaborators or Alone, 1967–2009

	Translations	Opera Libretti	Musical Theater Lyrics	+Book	+Music
	Stravinsky, L'histoire… (1967)				
1970	Ravel, L'enfant… (1971)		M. Rodgers, Pinocchio (1973)		Dragons (1973–2006)
		Beeson, Captain Jinks… (1975)	Raposo, Alice (1975)		
	Lehár, Die lustige Witwe (1977)	Beeson, Dr. Heidegger's… (1978)	R. Rodgers, Rex (1976)		
	Legrand, Les parapluies… (1979)				
1980	Bizet, Carmen (1981)	Raposo, Sutter's Gold [cantata] (1980)		Raposo, A Wonderful Life (1978–2005)	
	Mozart, L'Oca del Cairo (1982)			Legrand, Christmas Carol (1979–87)	
1990	J. S. Bach, Two Cantatas (1988, 1990)	Shepard, Love in Two Countries (1991)	Lawrence, Peter Rabbit (1991)		
		Beeson, Cyrano (1994)			
		Black, Phantom Tollbooth (1995–2008)			
		Mollicone, Coyote Tales (1998)	Legrand, Aaron's Magic Village (1997)		
2000	Legrand, L'amour fantôme (2001)			Baker, Pluck and Luck, or The ABC's of Success (2004–?)	The Doctor In Spite of Himself (2003–?)

began several years earlier, in 1967, when his and Bock's previous collaborator Bil Baird (*Peter and the Wolf* [1958], *The Man in the Moon* [1963]; see chapter 4) asked Harnick to provide a new English translation of the French text by C. F. Ramuz for Stravinsky's *L'histoire du soldat*, for a performance by Baird's marionettes with the Philadelphia Chamber Orchestra. Harnick had been studying French privately and welcomed the opportunity to update and Americanize the two most common English translations of the narration, by Rosa Newmarch (1924) and by Michael Flanders and Kitty Black (1955).[39] Then in 1970 and 1971 he returned to another translation project that he had begun some years earlier, Ravel's opera *L'enfant et les sortilèges*. Harnick's translation of Colette's original French libretto was premiered at the Manhattan School of Music in April 1971 and has seen wide use since then.[40]

Harnick's gifts as a translator attracted even more attention a few years later, in 1977, for a production of Lehár's *Die lustige Witwe* [*The Merry Widow*]. The project started, explains Harnick, with a frantic phone call from Julius Rudel, at that time the music director of the New York City Opera:

> The company was doing a joint production with the San Diego Opera featuring Beverly Sills as the lead. Tito Capobianco, the director of the San Diego Opera, had commissioned an English translation. But the results were so terrible that Sills refused to do it. Julius asked me if I could come to the rescue. He said I had ten days. I told him that would be impossible since I didn't even know the opera.[41]

But Harnick took the challenge and produced translations of Viktor Léon and Leo Stein's lyrics that were acceptable to Sills by working "day and night for nine days." The following year he was able to refine his lyrics for a recording by Sills, Rudel, and company, which won the Grammy for Best Opera Recording in 1978, and the year after that Harnick translated and adapted the operetta's dialogue for publication.[42] Harnick's version remains one of several that are available and still used, including in a performance at Northwestern University in March 2009, with the translator/adapter/alumnus in attendance.

Thus began Harnick's busiest years as a translator. His next project provided English text for a staged version of Jacques Demy's 1964 film *Les parapluies de Cherbourg* [*The Umbrellas of Cherbourg*], essentially an opera with music by Michel Legrand, best known for two signature songs, "Watch What Happens" and "I Will Wait For You." Harnick and Legrand, in association with Charles Burr, made few changes in the basic structure or drama of Demy's original text, and the story plays on stage about as well as it does on film—as a sumptuous romantic tragedy, best enjoyed by those who can get lost in

Legrand's lush score and overlook quirky details of plot and characterization. (Fans of a young Catherine Deneuve can find additional reasons to like the film.) The original staged version premiered at the Public Theater/Cabaret in New York in February 1979, followed by performances in Los Angeles and San Francisco in 1980, and has since been revived in an "elevated concert version" at Sundance (Utah) in 1999 and fully staged by the Two River Theater Company (New Jersey) in 2005.[43] Harnick translated for Legrand again in 2001, this time for a stage musical, *L'amour fantôme*, with book and lyrics by Didier van Cauwelaert; an anticipated performance in London never happened.[44]

Harnick's growing reputation as an adept translator and generous collaborator led to a commission from the Houston Grand Opera for a new English translation of Bizet's *Carmen* that premiered in Houston in January 1981. Then in 1983, during the run of Peter Brook's condensed (French-language) version of that opera, *La tragedie de Carmen*, in New York, Harnick was called upon to adapt his translation as an English text for Brook's version, to be presented in half of the performances each week, in repertory with the original French for the other half. During this same time Harnick also translated Giovanni Battista Varesco's libretto for a reconstructed and little-known comic opera by Mozart, *L'Oca del Cairo* [*The Goose from Cairo*, 1783], for the Lyric Opera of Kansas City (1982). A few years later Harnick translated two of J. S. Bach's secular cantatas for staged performances by the Bach Aria Group in New York and on Long Island. (Even the *New York Times* could not resist trumpeting a new project for Bach and Harnick.[45]) The first, *Der Streit zwischen Phoebus und Pan* [*The Contest Between Phoebus and Pan*], which is probably the most opera-like of Bach's works in this genre, premiered in 1988; the second, *Der Zufriedengestellte Aeolus* [*The Appeasement of Aeolus*], in 1990.[46] Harnick has also been involved in many other smaller translation projects over the years but has generally turned his attention in other directions since 1990.

Opera Libretti

Harnick's interest in opera began in the mid-1960s, after he had seen Julia Migenes, the original Hodel in *Fiddler on the Roof*, perform in Menotti's *The Saint of Bleecker Street* with the New York City Opera.[47] But Jerry Bock had shown no interest in writing an opera, and a subsequent attempt to write an opera with another unnamed "composer friend" had run aground. So when the distinguished composer and Columbia University professor Jack Beeson, who had won wide acclaim for operas such as *The Sweet Bye and Bye* (1956) and *Lizzie Borden* (1965), proposed a collaboration with Harnick in 1972, acting on a suggestion from Beeson's former student John Kander, Harnick was both intrigued and wary.[48] He welcomed the opportunity, but he knew he would need guidance. Fortunately he soon discovered that Beeson was able to provide exactly the assistance that Harnick needed. Beeson gave him a complete account of the requirements of an opera libretto, and the collaboration thrived.[49] Their first project together was an adaptation of a 1901 play, Clyde Fitch's *Captain Jinks of the Horse Marines*, developed over a three-year period and premiered on September 20, 1975, by the Kansas City Lyric Theater.

Fitch's story is a natural for musical adaptation. A beautiful American opera singer, Aurelia Trentoni, who has made a name for herself in Europe, arrives to conquer New York, and a handsome young dandy, Captain Jinks, makes a bet with friends that he will be able to seduce her. When Jinks meets Aurelia, however, he falls in true love and regrets his callous wager. As Aurelia prepares for her American debut, performing Violetta in *La Traviata*, forces conspire against the two lovers, and Aurelia becomes distraught when she learns about Jinks's bet. Fortunately she is still able to perform beautifully, and eventually Jinks is able to convince her of his sincerity and the depth of his love. The play ends with a jubilant toast to the diva and her newly betrothed, as the crowd sings a spirited chorus of an old song, "Captain Jinks" (William Lingard and T. Maclagan, 1868).

The story was a popular target for Burlesque in the years following the original premiere, and the play was made into a movie in 1916.[50] In 1925 a musical version appeared on Broadway, with a book by Frank Mandel and Laurence Schwab, lyrics by B. G. DeSylva, and music by Lewis E. Gensler and Stephen Jones, although reviewers were unable to detect much of Fitch's original story in the show, aside from character names and general plot outlines. (Bide Dudley in the *Evening World* [9/9/25]: "A plot does intrude now and then, but quickly it is batted on the head with the mallet of Terpsichore and all is well again.") For their operatic adaptation, Harnick and Beeson closely followed Fitch's original story but gave the character of Aurelia more emotional range and greatly expanded the role of an impresario, a character based on Colonel James Mapleson, who had built the Academy of Music into a prominent opera house in New York between 1878 and 1883.[51] They also added a budding romance between Aurelia's maid and one of Jinks's friends, in addition to many other smaller changes in the original story and characters. As Beeson observed, the collaborators had to cut "some of what was comedy in 1901, and might still be in the spoken play," because these lines "make no effect when the matrix is music."[52] On the other hand, they of course added extensive lyrical passages for characters to explore inner feelings in arias, as when Aurelia sings about her childhood in Act 1, and when Mapleson muses about the life of an impresario at the beginning of Act 2.

In general they wrote a "numbers opera," divided into arias, recitatives, and ensembles like *La Traviata*, and also a "love letter to Italian opera" dedicated especially to "singers and opera buffs," wrote Beeson in his autobiography.[53] *Captain Jinks* ends with a song, not a tribute to Jinks himself but a collective hymn to the power of music ("Music can reach us as no other art / Music can soften the hardest heart," and so forth).

This message in fact resonates with one of the principles Harnick had learned about the collaborative process for an opera, after reading biographies of opera composers and correspondence between composers and librettists: "the quality of the music is what ultimately determines the life of an opera." Whereas the lyricist for a musical could play a more dominant role in the process, when writing an opera libretto, Harnick observed, "it was my obligation to accommodate my composer in every way I could."[54] He also came to feel that opera is more concerned than musical theater with grand gestures and epic themes:

> You're not as worried about details. It's the sweep of it. You're not worried about filling in the history and the events, one leading to another. They're the broad strokes, just these sweeps of color that lead to these big emotional statements. That's what opera is about.[55]

What is clear above all is that Harnick had quickly and skillfully made the transformation from musical theater lyricist to operatic librettist, thereby opening up a whole new outlet for his creative energies.

The success of their initial effort led Harnick and Beeson to seek a story source for a second collaboration right away. Beeson had already received a request from the National Arts Club in New York for a one-act chamber opera, and had hoped to find usable material in the transcript of the divorce trial between Aaron Burr and his second wife.[56] When this failed to bear fruit— Beeson had thought, erroneously as it turns out, that Mrs. Burr's attorney was Aaron Burr's rival, Alexander Hamilton, Jr.—they shifted attentions to Nathaniel Hawthorne's short story "Dr. Heidegger's Experiment" (published in *Twice-Told Tales*, 1837). This tale is perfectly proportioned for a chamber opera, with five central characters and a compact but rich plot about the desire for eternal youth. It has been a popular story source, the subject of at least five other operatic treatments, by Paul Schwartz (*The Experiment*, 1953), Sam Raphling (*Dr. Heidegger's Experiment*, 1956), Stephen Burton (*Heidegger's Experiment*, 1974), Leo Smit (*Magic Water*, 1978), and Richard Wargo (*The Crystal Mirror*, 1979).[57] The Beeson–Harnick version, titled *Dr. Heidegger's Fountain of Youth*, premiered at the National Arts Club in New York on November 17, 1978.

In Hawthorne's story, the doctor plans a special evening and invites four guests: three "white-bearded gentlemen" and a "withered gentlewoman" who has a romantic past with each of the three men. Dr. Heidegger takes a dried, withered rose from a book and demonstrates the miraculous restorative powers of a liquid that was obtained, he tells them, from the Fountain of Youth—the substance that had once eluded Ponce de Leon but that has now been found in Florida. The doctor's guests are eager to test the liquid on themselves, and they drink heartily and frequently as they feel the years fall away and gain the energy and vitality of long-forgotten youth. But their startling renewal also rekindles old romantic rivalries, and the revelry eventually degenerates into shouting and shoving, an overturned table, and a vase of magical water falling pathetically to the floor. The rose, and the guests, then return to their true ages, and the doctor thanks them for demonstrating the perils of time manipulation. The guests, however, only crave more regression, and they resolve "forthwith to make a pilgrimage to Florida, and quaff at morning, noon, and night from the Fountain of Youth."[58]

In his adaptation Harnick takes more liberties with Hawthorne's text than he did with Fitch's play for *Captain Jinks*—and more than he did with the sources for the second and third parts of *The Apple Tree* as well. Unlike the original story, the opera begins with Dr. Heidegger reading from the book before removing the dried rose; he reads a passage from Paracelsus explaining the moral lesson for the drama to come. In addition, Harnick reorders some of the early events and changes the location of the Fountain of Youth from Florida to Brazil. He also revises the guest list: instead of three men and one woman, he wrote roles for two men and two women, thus changing the personal dynamics of the quartet when they begin to argue and fight at the climax. (The two men compete over one of the women, while the other woman feels spurned and disgusted and tries vainly to attract romantic interest herself.) Above all Harnick adds depth and detail to events and characterizations, enriching the texture and color of the drama. As the characters watch their years falling away, for example, they celebrate their good fortune in an imitative quartet:

> To the unfurrowed brow
> To the unclouded eye,
> To vigor and fire
> In boundless supply,
> To beauty of form,
> Beauty of face,

And movements that flow
With careless, easy grace;

Heavenly gifts
Which only the old can treasure in truth!
To the most precious boon in life—
To youth!

Elsewhere the characters rhapsodize similarly about their restored conditions in graceful poetic lines. In the end the doctor gets the last word, telling
his friends, "if the vast and varied richness of life can no longer fill your
glasses, why then in truth, I pray you find it. I pray you may find your Fountain of Youth." As his friends embark on their journey to Brazil, Dr. Heidegger
himself turns to toast the audience, one more time: "I pray you may all find
your Fountain of Youth."

Within a year of the premiere of *Dr. Heidegger* Beeson and Harnick had
found a source for their third project together (all told, Beeson's eighth opera)
in Rostand's *Cyrano de Bergerac*. Their goal was to follow up a chamber piece
with a grand opera, and also to employ large choral forces.[59] Of course this is
a story with a rich history of translations and adaptations, from its first appearance on American soil in 1898 to the many subsequent productions on
Broadway and on film. As a source for a musical entertainment, *Cyrano* had
provided fertile material for Burlesque (in Weber and Fields's *Cyranose de
Bric-a-Brac*, 1898) and had been adapted for the musical stage when the play
was still in its infancy by Victor Herbert (1899, book by Stuart Reed, lyrics by
Harry B. Smith).[60] A musical version variously known as *Cyrano*, *Roxane*, *The
White Plume*, and *The Vagabond King*, with book and lyrics by Charles O. Locke,
music by Samuel Pokrass with late additions by Vernon Duke, abandoned
plans for New York openings during two separate pre-Broadway tours in the
1930s. More recently, Michael J. Lewis wrote the music for an adaptation on
Broadway starring Christopher Plummer (1973, book and lyrics by Anthony
Burgess), and Harnick contributed to the translations for a Dutch musical
version that came out after he and Beeson were finished with theirs (1993,
music by Ad Van Dijk, book and lyrics by Koen Van Dijk).[61] The first purely
operatic treatment of the Cyrano story was by Walter Damrosch (1913,
libretto by W. J. Henderson). Later operatic adaptations include versions in
French by Franco Alfano (1935, libretto by Henri Cain), in Polish by Romuald
Twardowski (1962), in Estonian by Eino Tamberg (1974, libretto by Jaan
Kross), and in Italian by Marco Tutino (1987, libretto by Danilo Bramati). Beeson and Harnick worked on this enormous project for virtually the entire

decade of the 1980s, at one point anticipating a premiere at the New York City Opera.[62] Instead their opera was first performed in German translation by the Theater Hagen in Hagen, Germany on September 10, 1994.[63]

Still awaiting its first American performance, the Beeson–Harnick *Cyrano* is known mainly through Beeson's commentary in his 2008 memoirs.[64] (In 1997 he reworked some of the music as a concert piece, *Interludes and Arias from Cyrano*, in hopes of attracting interest in the complete work.[65]) Beeson quotes a program note by Harnick giving details of the libretto's poetic structure (mostly eschewing the alexandrines of Rostand's original), rhyming style (selective, as in his previous two libretti), and refinements of the original text (especially his efforts to give greater substance and intelligence to the character of Roxane).[66] It was surely a disappointment to find such a lot of hard work failing to find an audience, but the partners nevertheless continued to seek new source material for their next collaboration throughout the early 1990s, until they finally concluded, around 1997, that they were unable to find a project of mutual interest and then "each went on his way."[67] Harnick's eighteen (nonexclusive) years of work with Jack Beeson became his most successful collaborative relationship after his fourteen (more-or-less exclusive) years with Jerry Bock.

These experiences also inspired Harnick to pursue operatic projects with others. In 1988 he told Derrick Henry of the *Atlanta Journal Constitution* that he was "writing librettos for two one-act operas, *The Blind Men and the Donkey*, based on a French medieval farce, with composer Jonathan Tunick, and *That Pig of a Labete*, based on a Maupassant short story, with RCA recording executive Thomas Z. Shepard."[68] Although the collaboration with Tunick never reached fruition, Harnick and Shepard eventually completed both the Maupassant project and another one-act opera based on a story by Nikolai Leskov, *A Question of Faith*, for a premiere in New York in 1991, under the collective title *Love in Two Countries*.[69] Shortly after that Harnick collaborated on an opera for children based on Norton Juster's popular book *The Phantom Tollbooth*, assisting the author with the libretto. The music was composed by Harnick's long-time friend Arnold Black, who had worked for many years as a musical consultant and composer in the advertising industry. *The Phantom Tollbooth* premiered in Wilmington, Delaware in 1995 and was subsequently revised into a format closer to that of a musical, to enhance its marketability. The new version premiered in Washington, D. C. in September 2008 and toured the United States through March 2009.

Harnick produced his most recent libretto in collaboration with Henry Mollicone, a prolific American composer especially known for his choral and dramatic works who was a protégé of Leonard Bernstein in the 1970s.[70] In the mid-1990s Harnick and Mollicone began developing ideas for two operas, one about Albert Einstein that never got off the ground, and another based on Native American legends that piqued the interest of the leadership of the Lyric Opera of Kansas City, who was looking for a new work to help celebrate the institution's fortieth year.[71] Mollicone and Harnick workshopped the first act of their new opera in Kansas City in 1996 and both acts in Utah in the summer of 1997, in preparation for its premiere in Kansas City on March 7, 1998.

Harnick arrived at the opera's theme and title, *Coyote Tales*, after combing books of Indian legends for stories that could be brought together into a single episodic music drama. The main connection between the stories is the coyote, a character common to legends of many different tribes, usually in the tradition of a "trickster," a "rebel against authority and the breaker of all taboos." The coyote and his kin, in the words of Richard Erdoes and Alfonso Ortiz, "represent the sheerly spontaneous in life, the pure creative spark that is our birthright as human beings and that defies fixed roles or behavior."[72] Harnick created five scenes by adapting coyote tales from five different tribes:

ACT 1

SCENE 1: Old Man Coyote Makes The World (Crow)

source: *American Indian Myths and Legends*, selected and edited by Richard Erdoes and Alfonso Ortiz (New York: Pantheon, 1984), 88–93.

SCENE 2: Coyote And The Great Spirit / Coyote Keeps His Name (Okanagon)[73]

source: *Pale Moon: Tales of the American Indians*, selected and edited by John Long (Merrillville, Ind.: ICS Books, 1995), 12–14.

SCENE 3: How Coyote Brought Fire To The People (Karok)

source: *Indian Legends of the Pacific Northwest*, selected and introduced by Ella E. Clark (Berkeley: University of California Press, 1953), 187–189.

SCENE 4: Coyote In Love With A Star (Klamath)

source: *Coyote Was Going There: Indian Literature of the Oregon Country*, compiled and edited by Jarold Ramsey (Seattle: University of Washington Press, 1977), 210–211.

ACT 2

SCENE 5: Coyote and Pavayoykyasi (Hopi)

source: *Hopi Coyote Tales; Istutuwutsi*, selected and introduced by Ekkehart Malotki and Michael Lomatuway'ma (Lincoln: University of Nebraska Press, 1984), 140–149.

Using the style of libretto construction that he by this time knew very well, Harnick extracted key phrases and central ideas from the sources and reimagined them as poetic sung dialogue and arias. Coyote first oversees the creation of the world from a root and a ball of mud, then becomes endowed with a special gift of resurrection. He gives the world fire, dances with a star, and, in the second act, steals the bride of a mythical figure, Pavayoykyasi. The tales are stitched together through several devices: via a narrating Storyteller; by bringing back the Skookums, the guardians of fire from scene 3; and by bringing Coyote back to life twice—after he is dropped from the sky at the end of Act 1, and after he is killed by Pavayoykyasi at the end of Act 2. At the same time, Harnick was careful not to mix elements of different tribal traditions, following advice he had received from Native American students at Haskell Indian Nations University.[74] The opera concludes with praise for Coyote, not, presumably, for his malicious theft of a beautiful maiden in Act 2, but "For giving us breath / For calling us forth to this beautiful place / For the power to hear and the power to see / For giving us life." The Storyteller finally observes, "As you behave, we shall too, Old Man Coyote / We are you."

Coyote Tales was performed again by students at the Oberlin Conservatory in 2000, with the composer conducting and the librettist in attendance.[75] Harnick and Mollicone continued to explore other projects together, at one point planning an opera based on the life and work of environmentalist Rachel Carson.[76] The funding for this project never materialized, but for Harnick it would have provided an amusing symmetry within his career, recalling the inspiration for one of his early songs, "The Sea Is All Around Us" (see chapter 2). In 2009 Harnick and Mollicone were still discussing possible new projects together, this time a "musical theater work."

Sheldon Harnick in the Musical Theater Since 1970

Harnick has consistently devoted his efforts in the decades since *The Rothschilds* not only to translations and opera libretti, but also to musical theater and songwriting projects of all sorts. He has written lyrics for puppet shows, a television program, and an animated film. He has assumed the familiar role of lyricist for a legend of the musical theater, Richard Rodgers, and for a legend of film and commercial music, Michel Legrand. He has also spearheaded adaptations of legendary sources, Dickens's *A Christmas Carol* and the Frank Capra film *It's a Wonderful Life*. Building upon his rich previous experience in the musical theater, he has found new confidence as a writer of dialogue as well, and as a composer. "I never thought of myself as having that kind of talent," he said in 2006.[77] His modesty is disarming, and it is genuine.

Harnick had explored new songwriting partnerships even before his last show with Jerry Bock premiered (see chapter 8), and he continued to do so in the early 1970s, as *The Rothschilds* and *Fiddler on the Roof* completed their Broadway runs. In 1973 he was once again affiliated with Bil Baird's troupe of marionettes, writing songs with Mary Rodgers for a production of *Pinocchio* at the Bil Baird Theater in New York. Critics were mostly enchanted with the show—Harnick's wife provided the pre-recorded singing voice for the title character—and with the book by Jerome Coopersmith, who had gone back to writing for television after his work with Bock and Harnick in the initial stages of *The Apple Tree* in the mid-1960s. By far the more attention-grabbing collaboration of this era, however, was Harnick's work with Mary Rodgers's father, who was not in good health but seemed to draw vitality from the process of creating yet another musical theater piece. Actually, Richard Rodgers had first inquired about Harnick's availability several years earlier, even before the subject of working outside the partnership had arisen with Jerry Bock. Harnick felt obligated to decline at the time, but in the post-*Rothschilds* period he felt open to a new arrangement "if the property were right."

Harnick and Richard Rodgers first agreed to collaborate with Michael Stewart in 1972, on a musical version of Joseph Kesselring's popular farce *Arsenic and Old Lace*.[78] Stewart had written a draft of a book, but the songwriters could find no room for music in it and sent Stewart back to the drawing board. After one more unsuccessful attempt Stewart withdrew. Harnick concluded that the play was not adaptable as a musical, but Rodgers insisted that they continue the search for a writer who would be willing to try. Harnick recalls Rodgers inviting, and receiving polite demurrals from, Joseph Stein and Abe Burrows, among others. Finally Rodgers found a willing collaborator in Tom Stoppard, whose *Rosencrantz and Guildenstern Are Dead* had won the Tony for Best Play in 1968. Stoppard agreed to make an effort and send a draft for feedback from Rodgers and Harnick. Harnick recalls:

> So, two weeks later [Stoppard] sent this treatment to Rodgers, and Rodgers called me and said, "You've got to come to my office and see what he did." . . . It started with the twelve corpses in the basement, getting out of their graves, and marching up a ladder into heaven. Once they got to heaven, they did an opening number of some sort. Then the rest of it was the play. And at that point Rodgers said, "Okay, I give up."

Rodgers and Harnick remained on the lookout for acceptable source material for the next two years, until Richard Adler, coauthor with Jerry Ross of music for *The Pajama Game* (1954) and *Damn Yankees* (1955), found it for them.[79] Adler explains in his autobiography that he had been considering a show based on the life of King Henry VIII for some time and was happy to cede the idea to Rodgers and Harnick while taking on producer's duties himself.[80] To write the book Adler first recruited Jerome Lawrence and Robert E. Lee, but when these authors lost interest Adler engaged Sherman Yellen, still willing to give Broadway a try despite his *Rothschilds* experience.[81] The show would also feature a well-known (and famously temperamental) actor, Nicol Williamson, starring as the King. *Rex*, as it was called, evolved throughout 1975, leading up to a pre-Broadway tour in Wilmington, Delaware, Washington, D. C., and Boston in February through April 1976, and a Broadway opening on April 25.

When Rodgers and Harnick received a workable script from Yellen, probably in early 1975, Rodgers asked Harnick to locate a song opportunity and write out a complete lyric awaiting a musical setting. This would be their first song together. Harnick has described his relief some time later when he received the master's approval for his effort; he later learned that Rodgers had been equally apprehensive about getting the melody just right.[82] As work progressed, Harnick realized that Rodgers could only write music when he was working from an existing lyric, probably because of the mild

Richard Rodgers, Nicol Williamson (Henry VIII), Penny Fuller (Anne Boleyn, Princess Elizabeth), and Sheldon Harnick preparing for Rex (1976) (Photofest)

stroke he had suffered.[83] At that point in his life Rodgers could collaborate only as he had with Oscar Hammerstein II, starting from a complete lyric, not as he had in his younger days with Lorenz Hart, either starting from a partial lyric or title, or from no lyric at all. Harnick welcomed the challenge and tried experimenting with formal structures, to avoid falling back on AABA formulas.[84] Rodgers, meanwhile, wrote some beautiful tunes but made no effort to dress the score in sixteenth-century garb. "I wrote my musical impressions of the people and the country at that time," Rodgers said. "I didn't go to period music, in the same way that I didn't go to Siam to write *The King and I*."[85] Harnick was surely struck by the difference in compositional philosophy between his current collaborator and a former partner who routinely immersed himself, and his score, in the musical style of his subject matter.

Harnick has candidly admitted that some of the lyrics in *Rex* are "less than first-rate." When his lyrics did meet his highest standards, he believes, Rodgers's music was likewise transcendent; at other times, the music was "only as good as the lyric."[86] It is not difficult to imagine which songs in *Rex* Harnick might elevate above others (see Table 9.2). At the beginning of the show, the King's latest composition, "No Song More Pleasing," sung by his minstrel, takes its place among Rodgers's classic waltzes. The song "Elizabeth," a lullaby about Henry's child with his second wife Anne, and apparently the first song Rodgers and Harnick wrote together, features a melody that is not easy to sing but is shaped with the sure hands of master craftsmen. "So Much You Loved Me," written for Anne to sing after the King has spurned her—although cut before the New York opening—is a classic Rodgers ballad.[87] Occasionally Rodgers employs not only familiar elements of his distinctive style but specific musical gestures from his legendary catalogue: "Away From You," the gorgeous moment when Henry and (in the reprise) Anne first confess their love for each other, revitalizes the 5-#4-6-5 turning figure from "Some Enchanted Evening" (*South Pacific*); "As Once I Loved You," the lament by Henry's first wife as their marriage disintegrates, follows in the footsteps of "If I Loved You" (*Carousel*). If Rodgers sometimes seems to be channeling Rodgers, however, some accused Harnick of trying to channel Hammerstein. Martin Gottfried, reviewing the opening of *Rex* in the *New York Post* (4/26/76), heard in Harnick's lyrics "a deliberate attempt to write in the Hammerstein style," with both good and bad results. Douglas Watt in the *Daily News* (4/26/76) likewise felt that Harnick was "paying obeisance to Hammerstein." Even Richard Adler wrote in his memoirs that the collaboration had had a "negative effect" on the lyricist: Harnick told him, "it's a little like collaborating with God."[88] In an interview during the Boston tryout, Harnick essen-

Table 9.2: Overview of Rex (1976)

ACT 1

1. Greenwich Palace
   "Te Deum" (Company)
2. Henry's Tent
   "No Song More Pleasing" (Smeaton)
3. Field of Cloth of Gold
   "Where Is My Son?" (Henry)
   "At the Field of Cloth of Gold" (Company)
4. French Pavilion "Basse Dance" (Company)
5. Comus' Chambers
6. Hever Castle
   "The Chase" (Will, Comus, Smeaton, Gentlemen of the Court)
7. Hampton Court Palace
   "Away from You" (Henry)
8. Chapel
   "As Once I Loved You" (Catherine)
9. The Throne Room
10. Hampton Court Corridor
11. Queen Anne's Bedroom
    "Elizabeth" (Smeaton, Lady Margaret, Lady-in-Waiting)
12. Comus' Lab
    "What Now?" (Henry)
13. The Palace
    "No Song More Pleasing" (reprise) (Jane, Henry)
    "Away From You" (reprise) (Anne)
14. The Tower of London
15. The Coronation
16. The City of London
    "Te Deum" (reprise) (Company)

ACT 2

1. Hampton Court Palace
   "Christmas at the Hampton Court" (Mary, Edward, Elizabeth)
2. The Great Hall at Hampton Court Palace
   "The Wee Golden Warrior" (Will, Edward, Elizabeth, Mary)
   "Sword Dance" and "Morris Dance" (Sword and Morris Dancers)
   "The Masque" (Ladies and Gentlemen of the Court)
3. The Throne Room
   "From Afar" (Henry)

(Continued)

4. Hampton Court Corridor
    "In Time" (Elizabeth, Will)
5. Comus' Laboratory
6. Henry's Bedroom
7. The Throne Room
    "In Time" (reprise) (Elizabeth, Edward)
    "Te Deum" (reprise) (Entire Company)

tially pled guilty to these charges. "I've begun to explore simpler lyrics," he said. "I'm consciously trying to avoid flashiness, the cleverness of the intricate rhyme. I'm trying to get more direct, more emotionally naked; to find fresh images to communicate genuine feeling."[89]

Rex was flogged by the critics and abdicated after forty-nine performances. Many blamed Yellen's book for the failure: Clive Barnes in the *Times* (4/26/76) called it "basically tedious and quite excessively vulgar on a number of planes"; Allan Wallach wrote in *Newsday* (4/26/76) that Yellen's book "covers too much ground historically and, paradoxically, doesn't tell us enough," that Yellen failed "to take a cohesive point of view toward the central character." Yellen stands behind his work but admits that his own writing style, working "against sentiment," was not a perfect complement for Rodgers's romanticism. He also regrets that Nicol Williamson was cast in the lead role—a "brilliant actor" but "an extraordinarily difficult person to work with." Adler traces the problems to his decision not to meet the asking price of a more accomplished director (Michael Bennett) and the basic distaste naturally generated by a lead character who is a homicidal, misogynistic tyrant.[90] Ken Mandelbaum asked the question that was surely on the minds of many audience members: "What made Adler, Rodgers, and Harnick think Henry VIII a good subject for a musical?"[91] The creators had tried to soften Henry's hard edges during the pre-Broadway tour and had brought in Harold Prince for directorial repairs, but by then the damage was too severe, too deep-seated. Adler wrote, "I know now, in hindsight, that Elizabeth was *the* fascinating person about whom the musical should have been written in the first place."[92]

And yet *Rex* has not faded into total oblivion. In 2000, for the "Musicals in Mufti" series of the York Theater Company in New York, Harnick and Yellen revisited the script and found abundant opportunities for revision. They made "sweeping cuts," added "transitions and connective passages," and reshaped scenes, according to Harnick.[93] "We got rid of a lot of the dross," explains Yellen, and added a series of "prologues, in a kind of Shakespearian fashion," that "pulls things together." They also restored songs that had been previously cut, not only "So Much You Loved Me" but also "Tell Me, Daisy," which Henry sings when he is trying to romance Anne early in Act 1, and "The Pears of Anjou," sung by Henry just before he dies at the end of Act 2.[94] The latter song, Geoffrey Block observes, makes for a "powerful finale" to the show, "and it poetically prepares for the future rule of his daughter Elizabeth, fruit of Henry's kingship, a true renaissance."[95] Two years after the York Company's bare-bones concert performance, the new *Rex* was fully staged at the University of Findlay in Ohio, with a "large cast, regal sets, magnificent costumes, and full orchestra." At last, Harnick feels, the show was realized as the creators had envisioned it. Perhaps King Henry VIII is not such a bad subject for a musical after all.

Harnick's other songwriting projects have been richly varied. In 1972 he made two contributions to *Free to Be . . . You and Me*, a benefit record album intended to promote individuality and self-esteem among children. His poem "Housework" is performed on the album by Carol Channing; his song with Mary Rodgers, "William's Doll," based on the children's book by Charlotte Zolotow about a boy who plays with dolls, is sung by Alan Alda and Marlo Thomas (who conceived and coordinated the project).[96] A few years later, in 1991, Harnick teamed up with one of that album's composers and co-producers, Stephen J. Lawrence, to write songs for a musical adaptation of some of Beatrix Potter's *Peter Rabbit* tales for HBO, narrated by Carol Burnett. Harnick is in top form, in a ballad such as "So Near and Yet So Far," and in the comic number "Decisions, Decisions," sung by a cat trying to decide what to have for lunch ("Am I in the mood for mice? / Or am I in the mood for fish? / Spicy mice are awfully nice / But a fresh-caught fish is / Twice as delicious"). Harnick also made plans once again to write a musical with Burton Lane, this time an adaptation of *Upstairs, Downstairs*.[97] Like his earlier publicized effort with Lane (see chapter 8), and like a later project called *As Luck Would Have It*, any tangible results of the collaboration remained confined to the songwriters' studios.

In the mid-1970s Harnick also began the first of several projects with Joe Raposo, who had written music extensively for television, especially for children's shows such as *Sesame Street* and *The Electric Company*.[98] They first wrote the theme music for Alan Alda's situation comedy *We'll Get By*, which premiered on CBS in 1975, then a group of songs for a version of *Alice in Wonderland* by Bil Baird's marionettes in 1975.[99] In 1980, on a commission from the Boston Symphony, they wrote a cantata for young audiences, *Sutter's Gold*, based on the true story of August Sutter, who discovered gold on his property in the mid-nineteenth century.[100]

Harnick also worked with Raposo on one of his most ambitious and successful musical theater projects of recent decades, an adaptation of Frank

Capra's film *It's a Wonderful Life*. The impetus for the project came from Mary Jo Slater, a casting director in New York, and Eugene V. Wolsk, an old friend and a veteran Broadway producer, in 1978.[101] Harnick was persuaded to write the book himself, and fulfilled Raposo's request to provide complete lyrics first, as he had with Richard Rodgers. With both team members occasionally taking time away from this project to work on other things, they finished a first draft in 1983 and presented a two-week workshop version in New York in the summer of 1984. Making revisions all along the way, they arranged performances at the University of Michigan in 1986, at the Wagon Wheel Playhouse in Warsaw, Indiana in the summer of 1988, and at the Laguna Beach Playhouse in California in December 1989. After Raposo died of complications from lymphoma in February of 1989 (at age 51), Harnick took sole control of the project and found himself making musical additions and changes in addition to refining the book and lyrics. The show, ultimately called *A Wonderful Life*, has played consistently across the country in the two decades since, including high-profile productions at the Arena Stage in Washington, D. C. in 1991 and a concert staging in New York in 2005. A Broadway run appears unlikely, however, because of legal disputes over copyright ownership and other technicalities. The show mostly emerges every year around Christmas time in regional theaters, in productions of various sizes, before returning to hibernation the rest of the year.

As a result, *A Wonderful Life* is potentially in annual competition with another of Harnick's large musical theater projects of the last two decades, a musical rendering of Dickens's *A Christmas Carol*. The idea for this project came in 1979 from Fred Silverman of NBC, who wanted a version of the classic story for television "that eschewed the trivial, commonplace children's entertainment aspect of the piece, and concentrated on what Dickens had actually written."[102] Michel Legrand, with whom Harnick had just worked when translating *Les parapluies de Cherbourg*, wrote the music, and Harnick again wrote both book and lyrics, around the same time that he started the book and lyrics for *A Wonderful Life*.[103] The deal with NBC fell through, but Legrand and Harnick went forward with the Dickens project anyway, completing a first draft in about two years in spite of all the difficulties of intercontinental collaboration. Refinements began after performances in Elmira, New York, in November 1981 and throughout a tour of Wilmington (Delaware), Baltimore (where the show was called "Penny By Penny," to avoid confusion with other adaptations of the same material), St. Petersburg (Florida), Miami, New Orleans, and Memphis through the early weeks of 1982, starring Richard Kiley as Scrooge. After further revisions it played in Stamford, Connecticut in December 1982 and in subsequent years at Monmouth College in New Jersey and at a regional theater in Ohio.[104] By 1987 or so Harnick and Legrand considered the show complete and made it available for general licensing. It has not always made fans of reviewers but has become one of several musical versions of the story that receive seasonal productions every year. Meanwhile, Harnick's collaboration with Legrand continued to thrive, resulting in four songs for a 1997 animated film, *Aaron's Magic Village*, based on stories for children by Isaac Bashevis Singer.

One other large musical theater project has periodically consumed Harnick's energies throughout the post-*Rothschilds* era. Its origins actually go back even further, to 1963, when Harnick saw a production of Yevgeny Schwartz's political fable *The Dragon* at the Phoenix Theater in New York.[105] Harnick told Harold Flender in 1971 that the play "cries out for music," almost as if the playwright thought of it that way when he wrote it.[106] At one point Harnick tried to interest Jerry Bock in writing music for an adaptation, later Burton Lane, Milton Schafer, and Charles Strouse. He approached Joseph Stein about working on the book. But he was unable to find collaborators who shared his passion for the project and so finally followed Stein's advice and began to do all the work himself—lyrics, book, and music.[107] In 1973 he told the *New York Times* that he had completed "the first draft of a book and twelve songs" and was anticipating a Broadway opening the following year.[108] Soon thereafter, however, his professional attention was diverted to operas with Jack Beeson, translations, and his collaboration with Richard Rodgers, and he next returned to *The Dragon* and began pursuing performance possibilities in the early 1980s. The show was selected for a series of workshop performances in May 1984 by Harold Prince's National Institute for Musical Theater, and the following November it was given its first complete staging at Northwestern University.[109] Harnick then began a long process of revision and repairs, with the help of productions at Colorado College in 1986, Mesa College (Colorado) in 1987, the Empire State Institute for the Performing Arts (Albany, New York) in 1988, the University of Arizona in 1997, and the Luna Stage Company (of Montclair, New Jersey) in 2003, among others.[110] By 2008 he felt that the show was "very good" and ready for licensing and distribution.

Schwartz's play explores the nature of tyranny and the relationship between people and their leaders.[111] A dragon controls a community and provides for its citizens so long as one young maiden is sacrificed to him every year. When a wandering knight, Lancelot, discovers this arrangement he vows to rescue the next scheduled victim, Elsa, with whom he has fallen in love. Lancelot and the Dragon duel, but both appear to die in the battle. In the next year the town Mayor takes control of the community and becomes a tyrant in his own right, claiming that he killed the Dragon and planning to marry Elsa himself. But then Lancelot returns, explaining that he had only been critically injured in the duel with the Dragon and has been nursed back to health, and seizes power, and Elsa, from the Mayor. The play ends with Lancelot blissful but uncertain of the future, promising only love and happiness for his bride and his people: "if I love you everything will be wonderful."[112]

Harnick believes that when he began his adaptation, which he renamed *Dragons*, he initially drew too heavily from the original text, using it as a "crutch." As he shaped and revised he made his version more personal and distinctive, less dependent on Schwartz's. He also benefited from advice he received from his long-time friend Michael Kidd, who read a version of the script and observed that the show's central message was that "the only solution to power is to have a benevolent dictator."[113] This inspired Harnick to rework the last part of the second act to emphasize democratic principles of government: in his new ending the townspeople show that they do not want another dragon but want to have a voice in determining their own fates. Harnick's score includes a delicate ballad in which Elsa sings mournfully about her beloved, departed Lancelot ("You Could Say I Miss Him"), a sleazy soft-shoe number for the Mayor ("I Love Power"), and a trio performed by the perishing Dragon's three heads ("Passacaglia for Three Severed Heads"). As a finale Lancelot summarizes the show's ultimate message in a sort of pop anthem, "Take Care of One Another," seemingly inspired by a sentiment from one of the townspeople, a gardener, at the end of Schwartz's play:

> Be patient with us, Sir Lancelot. I do beg you to be patient. Tend us gently. The fires you light will help us grow. Take out the weeds carefully, or you might damage the new roots. You know, when you really come to think about it, when all is said and done, people need very careful treatment.[114]

Harnick's song recognizes the various threats to the safety and sanity of humanity but ultimately finds comfort in mutual love and respect:

> Take care of one another,
> The young, the old.
> Take care of one another,
> And then behold:
> This withering Sahara,
> This heartless place,
> Will bloom before we know it

And what was bleak and alien
Will wear a human face!
Yes, this is what the world can be,
If we take care of one another.[115]

Harnick has said that this song is "deeply meaningful" to him.[116] It is easy to understand why he has remained committed to bringing this show, and this message, to the stage for so many years.

Harnick finally gained full confidence as a lyricist, writer, and composer, and in the mid-2000s began working alone—and wearing a fourth hat, that of translator—on another completely new project, an adaptation of Molière's *Le médecin malgré lui* (*The Doctor in Spite of Himself*), a play that he felt had great potential as an "intimate musical."[117] It was workshopped at Northwestern University in the summer of 2009. "I will never retire while I can still lift a pen or work a word processor," he has said.[118] At the same time he can look back on a legacy in the world of dramatic music that will endure despite changing tastes and shifting sensibilities, an extensive web of artistic and personal relationships built on hard work and selfless collaboration. When he reflected on his career and creative life in 1971, just at the end of the Bock–Harnick era, he seemed to have just the right words—a habit, certainly—to sum it all up:

> I have a kind of an image in my mind having to do with talent. . . . The brain really looks like a sandy desert and . . . constantly clouds are going over this desert. And the clouds, as in a cartoon, could be labeled music, dentistry, agriculture, whatever. And they'll drop rain on this desert and depending on what your native talent is—it's like I have this image that a cloud labeled lyrics went over my desert and dropped water on it, and immediately I responded. And things began to grow.[119]

For seven decades the lyrics cloud has lingered in Harnick's creative firmament, eventually sharing space in the sky with clouds of "music" and "opera libretti" and "translations" and "dramaturgy," and it is still raining.

This chronology includes all Broadway productions, and a few noteworthy productions off-Broadway and elsewhere, to which Jerry Bock and/or Sheldon Harnick made creative contributions. Details of opening and closing dates and number of performances are taken from the in-house records of the Billy Rose Theater Division, New York Public Library for the Performing Arts (which occasionally differ slightly from sources such as Norton and Stewart). **Bold** lettering highlights major book musicals in which at least one member of the team was substantially involved.

1952   *New Faces of 1952* (revue)
        5/16/52–3/28/53   365 performances
        Directed by John Murray Anderson
        Choreography and staging of musical numbers by Richard Barstow
        Music and lyrics by Sheldon Harnick:
            "Boston Beguine"

        Two's Company (revue)
        12/15/52–3/8/53   91 performances
        Directed by John Murray Anderson
        Dances and musical numbers staged by Jerome Robbins
        Music and lyrics by Sheldon Harnick:
            "A Man's Home"

1953   *John Murray Anderson's Almanac* (revue)
        12/10/53–6/26/54   227 performances
        Sketches directed by Cyril Ritchard
        Dances and musical numbers staged by Donald Saddler
        Music and lyrics by Sheldon Harnick:
            "Merry Little Minuet" (dropped during the run)
        Music by David Baker, lyrics by Sheldon Harnick:
            "Flowers" (added during the run)

1955   *Shoestring Revue* (revue)
        2/28/55–5/21/55   96 performances
        Directed by Christopher Hewett
        Music and lyrics by Sheldon Harnick:
            "Garbage"

Music by David Baker, lyrics by Sheldon Harnick:
"Someone Is Sending Me Flowers"
"The Sea Is All Around Us"
Music by Lloyd B. Norlin, script and lyrics by Sheldon Harnick:
"Medea in Disneyland"

Catch a Star! (revue)
9/6/55–9/24/55   23 performances
Sketches directed by Danny Simon
Dances and musical numbers staged by Lee Sherman
Music by Jerry Bock, lyrics by Larry Holofcener:
"The Story of Alice"
"Fly Little Heart"
"Bachelor Hoedown"

1956   **Mr. Wonderful**
3/22/56–2/23/57   388 performances
Directed by Jack Donohue
Book by Joseph Stein and Will Glickman
Music and lyrics by Jerry Bock, Larry Holofcener, and George Weiss

The Littlest Revue (revue)
5/22/56–6/17/56   32 performances
Directed by Paul Lammers
Music and lyrics by Sheldon Harnick:
"The Shape of Things"

Shoestring '57 (revue)
11/5/56–2/17/57   110 performances
Directed by Paul Lammers
Music by David Baker, lyrics by Sheldon Harnick:
"Best Loved Girls"

1958   **The Body Beautiful**
1/23/58–3/15/58   60 performances
Directed by George Schaefer
Book by Joseph Stein and Will Glickman
Music by Jerry Bock, lyrics by Sheldon Harnick
Other productions of note:
10/12/07–10/14/07   5 performances (York Theater Company, concert
performance)

Portofino
2/21/58–2/22/58   3 performances
Directed by Karl Genus

Book and lyrics by Richard Ney
Music by Louis Bellson and Will Irwin
Music by Will Irwin, lyrics by Sheldon Harnick:
    "Prologue"
    "Opening—Come Along"
Music by Louis Bellson and Will Irwin, lyrics by Sheldon Harnick:
    "Red Collar Job"
    "Here I Come"
Music by Louis Bellson, lyrics by Richard Ney and
Sheldon Harnick:
    "Under a Spell"

1959   ***Fiorello!***
        11/23/59–10/28/61   796 performances
        Directed by George Abbott
        Book by Jerome Weidman and George Abbott
        Music by Jerry Bock, lyrics by Sheldon Harnick
        Other productions of note:
            6/13/62–6/24/62   15 performances (City Center)
            opened 10/8/62   56 performances (London premiere)
            2/9/94–2/12/94   4 performances (the first in the City Center "Encores!"
                                 series)

1960   *Vintage '60* (revue)
        9/9/60–9/18/60   8 performances
        Directed by Jonathan Lucas
        Music by David Baker, lyrics by Sheldon Harnick:
            "Ism"
            "Forget Me"

        Tenderloin
        10/17/60–4/23/61   217 performances
        Directed by George Abbott
        Book by George Abbott and Jerome Weidman
        Music by Jerry Bock, lyrics by Sheldon Harnick
        Other productions of note:
            11/6/75–11/23/75   22 performances (Equity Library Theater)
            3/24/00–3/27/00   5 performances (City Center "Encores!" series)

1961   *Smiling the Boy Fell Dead*
        4/19/61–5/7/61   22 performances
        Directed by Theodore Mann
        Book by Ira Wallach
        Music by David Baker, lyrics by Sheldon Harnick

1962   *Never Too Late*
        11/27/62–4/24/63   107 performances
        Directed by George Abbott
        Play by Sumner Arthur Long
        Music by Jerry Bock, lyrics by Sheldon Harnick:
            "Never Too Late Cha-Cha"

1963   *The Man in the Moon*
        4/11/63–4/21/63   22 performances
        Directed by Gerald Freedman
        Book by Arthur Burns
        Music by Jerry Bock, lyrics by Sheldon Harnick

        She Loves Me
        4/23/63–1/11/64   302 performances
        Directed by Harold Prince
        Book by Joe Masteroff
        Music by Jerry Bock, lyrics by Sheldon Harnick
        Other productions of note:
            opened 4/29/64   189 performances (London premiere)
            3/29/77–4/17/77   24 performances (concert
                                              performance at Town Hall)
            6/10/93–8/1/93, 10/7/93–6/19/94   355 performances (Broadway revival)
            opened 7/12/94 (London revival)
            opened 9/19/96 (Vienna, first German-language production)

1964   **Fiddler on the Roof**
        9/22/64–7/2/72   3,242 performances
        Directed and choreographed by Jerome Robbins
        Book by Joseph Stein
        Music by Jerry Bock, lyrics by Sheldon Harnick
        Other productions of note:
            opened 2/16/67   2,030 performances (London premiere)
            6/27/74–9/1/74   67 performances (Jones Beach Theater, with Zero Mostel)
            12/28/76–5/21/77 167 performances (Broadwa y revival)
            7/9/81–8/23/81   53 performances (New York State Theater)
            11/18/90–6/16/91 241 performances (Broadway revival)
            2/26/04–1/8/06   781 performances (Broadway revival)

1965   *Baker Street*
        2/16/65–11/13/65   313 performances
        Directed by Harold Prince
        Book by Jerome Coopersmith
        Music and lyrics by Marian Grudeff and Raymond Jessel

Additional music by Jerry Bock, lyrics by Sheldon Harnick (uncredited):
"I'm in London Again"
"Buffalo Belle" (replaced "I'm in London Again" during the Broadway run)
"Cold Clear World"
"I Shall Miss You"

Generation
10/6/65–6/25/66   300 performances
Directed by Gene Saks
Play by William Goodhart
Incidental music by Jerry Bock, lyrics by William Goodhart

1966   **The Apple Tree**
10/18/66–11/25/67   463 performances
Directed by Mike Nichols
Book by Jerry Bock and Sheldon Harnick; additional material by Jerome Coopersmith
Music by Jerry Bock, lyrics by Sheldon Harnick
Other productions of note:
    10/8/99–12/19/99   85 performances (Goodspeed Opera House)
    5/12/05–5/16/05   6 performances (City Center "Encores!" series)
    12/14/06–3/11/07,   99 performances (Broadway revival)

1968   *Her First Roman*
10/20/68–11/2/68   17 performances
Directed by Derek Goldby
Book, music, and lyrics by Ervin Drake
Additional music by Jerry Bock, lyrics by Sheldon Harnick (uncredited):
    "Caesar is Wrong"
    "Old Gentleman"
    "Ptolemy"

1970   **The Rothschilds**
10/19/70–1/2/72   505 performances
Directed and choreographed by Michael Kidd
Book by Sherman Yellen
Music by Jerry Bock, lyrics by Sheldon Harnick
Other productions of note:
    2/25/90–4/8/90   56 performances (Off-Off-Broadway)
    4/27/90–3/24/91   379 performances (Off-Broadway, American Jewish Theater, newly revised by Harnick)

1976   **Rex**
4/25/76–6/5/76   49 performances

Directed by Edwin Sherin
Book by Sherman Yellen
Music by Richard Rodgers, lyrics by Sheldon Harnick
Other productions of note:

10/13/00–10/15/00	5 performances (York Theater Company, concert performance, newly revised by Harnick and Yellen)
4/11/02–4/20/02	8 performances (University of Findlay [Ohio], first staged production of new version)

APPENDIX B SELECTED MEDIA RESOURCES

This listing includes audio- and videorecordings of music (or of complete shows) by Bock and/or Harnick that were commercially released or that are available in public archives. It includes only a very small sampling of new recordings of their songs by various artists in diverse styles ("covers"). Titles of major book musicals are shown in **bold**, as in Appendix A. This listing does not include recorded interviews, which are listed together with print interviews in section 4 of the bibliography.

Admiral Broadway Revue (songs or sketches credited to Bock/Holofcener)
> "County Fair" (22 April 1949): videorecording, Paley Center for Media T:27634
> "Encore" (3 June 1949): videorecording, Paley Center for Media B:25823
> "Heartburn" (8 April 1949): videorecording, Paley Center for Media T:26282
> "The Hero . . . The Heroine . . . and the Man Who's Got the Mortgage" (6 May 1949): videorecording, Paley Center for Media B:26283
> "Ingrid the Great" (8 April 1949): videorecording, Paley Center for Media T:26282
> "Today" (15 April 1949): videorecording, Paley Center for Media T:27637

"Always the Sea" (music and lyrics by Jerry Bock)
> Acquaviva and His Orchestra [instrumental arrangement by Nick Acquaviva]
> > Original release: MGM K-12434 (45-rpm single, 1957)
> > Reissue: *A Man and His Dream*, MGM E-3696 (LP, 1958)

American Musicals: Bock & Harnick
> Original release: Time-Life Records 4TL-AM14 (3 cassette tapes, 1982)
> Selections from the original cast recordings of *Fiorello!*, *Fiddler on the Roof*, and *The Rothschilds*

The Apple Tree (Bock/Harnick)
> Original Broadway cast recording: Columbia Masterworks KOS-3020 (LP, 1966)
> > Reissue: Sony Broadway SK 48209 (CD, 1992)
> Videorecording of complete concert performance (semi-staged): Theater on Film and Tape Archive, New York Public Library for the Performing Arts; videotaped at City Center, New York, 13 May 2005
> Videorecording of complete staged performance: Theater on Film and Tape Archive, New York Public Library for the Performing Arts; videotaped at Studio 54, New York, 9 March 2007

Baker Street (Grudeff/Jessel; additional songs by Bock/Harnick uncredited)
    Original Broadway cast recording: MGM E-7000 OCS (LP, 1965)
        Reissue: Decca Broadway B0005971-02 (CD, 2006)

Barbara Cook At Carnegie Hall
    Original release: Columbia M33438 (LP, 1975)
        Reissue: Sony Classical SMK 62017 (CD, 1996)
            "Dear Friend" (Bock/Harnick, from *She Loves Me*)
            "Will He Like Me?" (Bock/Harnick, from *She Loves Me*)
            "Ice Cream" (Bock/Harnick, from *She Loves Me*)

Barbara Cook's Broadway
    Original release: DRG 91484 (CD, 2004)
            "I'll Marry the Very Next Man" (Bock/Harnick, from *Fiorello!*)
            "Tonight at Eight" (Bock/Harnick, from *She Loves Me*)
            "No More Candy" (Bock/Harnick, from *She Loves Me*)
            "A Trip to the Library" (Bock/Harnick, from *She Loves Me*)
            "He Loves Me" (Bock/Harnick, from *She Loves Me*)

Blame It On Rio [feature film soundtrack]
    Original release: Varèse Sarabande STV 81210 (LP, 1984)
            "Blame It On Rio" (Coleman/Harnick)
            "I Must Be Doing Something Right" (Coleman/Harnick)

Blowin' in the Wind (Chad Mitchell Trio)
    Original release: Kapp KS-3313 (LP, 1963)
        Reissue: Folk Era 3313 (CD, 1997)
            "The Story of Alice–Part I" (Bock/Holofcener, from *Catch a Star!*)
            "Alice Revisited" (Bock/Holofcener, from *Catch a Star!*)
            "Alice: Sequel" (Bock/Holofcener, from *Catch a Star!*)

The Body Beautiful (Bock/Harnick)
    First recording: Blue Pear 1006 (LP, 1958) [recorded live from the audience]
        Reissue: Deja Vu (CD)
    First studio recording: Original Cast Records 6231 (CD, 2008)
    Composer demos and cover recordings: Original Cast Records (CD, 2008) [limited distribution]

A Broadway Christmas
    Original release: Varèse Sarabande VSD-5517 (CD, 1994)
            "Christmas Eve" (Bock/Harnick, from *She Loves Me*)
            "Christmas Gifts" (Raposo/Harnick, from *A Wonderful Life*)

Broadway Musicals of 1960
> Original release: Bayview RNBW027 (CD, 2004)
>> "Little Old New York"/"Picture of Happiness" (Bock/Harnick, from *Tenderloin*)
>> "Ism" (Baker/Harnick, from *Vintage '60*)

Broadway Swings Again (Jonah Jones Quartet)
> Original release: Capitol T-1641 (LP, 1961)
>> "'Til Tomorrow" (Bock/Harnick, from *Fiorello!*)
>> "Good Clean Fun" (Bock/Harnick, from *Tenderloin*)

Broadway's Lost Treasures
> Original release: Acorn Media AMP-6714/6706 (VHS/DVD, 2003)
>> "If I Were a Rich Man" (Bock/Harnick, from *Fiddler on the Roof*; performed by Zero Mostel at the Tony Awards ceremony, 28 March 1971)
>> "Oh, To Be a Movie Star" and "Gorgeous" (Bock/Harnick, from *The Apple Tree*; performed by Barbara Harris, with the assistance of Larry Blyden, at the Tony Awards ceremony, 26 March 1967)

Broadway's Lost Treasures II
> Original release: Acorn Media AMP-7311/7303 (vhs/dvd, 2004)
>> "The Name's La Guardia" (Bock/Harnick, from *Fiorello!*; performed by Tom Bosley and other cast members from the original Broadway production at the Tony Awards ceremony, 24 April 1960)

Cabaret Noël: A Broadway Cares Christmas
> Original release: Lockett-Palmer LPR-932512 (2-CD set, 1993)
>> "One Family" (Legrand/Harnick, from *A Christmas Carol*)

The Canterville Ghost (Bock/Harnick) [also see *Prime-Time Musicals* below]
> Original cast recording: Blue Pear 1019 (LP, 1966) [with music from three other television musicals]
> Videorecording of the complete television broadcast: Paley Center for Media T77:0161

Captain Jinks of the Horse Marines (Beeson/Harnick)
> Original recording: RCA Red Seal ARL2-1727 (LP, 1976)

Colgate Comedy Hour (song credited to Bock/Holofcener)
>> "Milly the Filly" (12 November 1950): videorecording, Paley Center for Media T:02077

Coyote Tales (Mollicone/Harnick)
> Original cast recording: Newport Classic NPD 85629 (2-CD set, 1998)

Dance to the Music from Tenderloin (Nelson Riddle and His Orchestra)
Original release: Capitol T-1536 (LP, 1961)
Instrumental versions of ten songs from the show

Doing Something Right: Randy Graff Sings Cy Coleman
Original release: Varèse Sarabande VSD-5652 (CD, 1996)
"I Must Be Doing Something Right" (Coleman/Harnick, from *Blame It On Rio*)

Dr. Heidegger's Fountain of Youth (Beeson/Harnick)
Original recording: Composers Recordings CRI SD 406 (LP, 1979)

18 Interesting Songs from Unfortunate Shows
Original release: Take Home Tunes 777 (LP, 1978)
"All of These and More" (Bock/Harnick, from *The Body Beautiful*)
"Summer Is" (Bock/Harnick, from *The Body Beautiful*)
"Ism" (Baker/Harnick, from *Vintage '60*)

Ethel Smith on Broadway
Original release: Decca DL-8993 (LP, 1959?)
"Gentleman Jimmy" (Bock/Harnick, from *Fiorello!*)
"'Til Tomorrow" (Bock/Harnick, from *Fiorello!*)

An Evening with Sheldon Harnick
Original recording: Laureate Records LL-603 (LP, 1977)
Reissue: DRG Records 021471517422 (CD, 1993)
Selected songs from Bock/Harnick shows and from Harnick's work before and after his collaboration with Bock

Fiddler on the Roof (Bock/Harnick)
Original Broadway cast recording: RCA Victor LOC-1093 (LP, 1964)
Reissue: RCA Red Seal RCD1-7060 (CD, 1986)
Original Israeli cast recording [in Hebrew]: Columbia OL-6490 (LP, 1966)
Original Israeli cast recording [in Yiddish]: Columbia OL-6650 (LP, 1967)
Original London cast recording: Columbia Masterworks SX-30742 (LP, 1967)
Reissue: Columbia Broadway Masterworks SK-89546 (CD, 2001)
Original motion picture soundtrack: UAS 10900 United Artists Records (2LP, 1971)
Reissue: EMI 72435-35266-2-7 (CD, 2001)
Videorecording of complete performance: Theater on Film and Tape Archive, New York Public Library for the Performing Arts; videotaped at Winter Garden Theater, New York, 23 March 1977

Motion picture on home video: MGM/UA Home Video M304857 (VHS, 1994)

    Reissue: MGM Home Entertainment 100256 (DVD, 2001); MGM Home Entertainment 106328 (2-disc collectors' edition DVD, 2007)

Broadway revival cast recording: PS Classics PS-420 (CD, 2004)

Videorecording of complete performance: Theater on Film and Tape Archive, New York Public Library for the Performing Arts; videotaped at Minskoff Theater, New York, 7 January 2006

Fiddler on the Roof (Cannonball Adderley Sextet)

    Original release: Capitol ST-2216 (LP, 1965)

        Reissue: Capitol 42309 (CD, 1991)

            Instrumental versions of eight songs from the show

Fiorello (Oscar Peterson Trio)

    Original release: Verve 8366-A (LP, 1960)

        Reissue: Verve 5216772 (CD, 1994)

            Instrumental versions of nine songs from the show

Fiorello! (Bock/Harnick)

    Original Broadway cast recording: Capitol WAO-1321 (LP, 1959)

        Reissue: CDP 7 92052 2 Capitol (CD, 1989)

Ford-i-fy Your Future (Bock/Harnick)

    Original cast recording: Ford Motor Company (single-sided LP, 1959, not commercially released)

        Reissue: *Hey Mister! Thinking Tractor? The Music from Ford Tractor, 1959, 1960, 1964*, Forworkma Productions (CD, 2005)

Free to Be . . . You and Me

    Original release: Bell 1110 (LP, 1972)

        Reissue: Arista ARCD-8325 (CD, 1983)

          "Housework" (Harnick)

          "William's Doll" (Mary Rodgers/Harnick)

La Gingold

    Original release: Dolphin 7 (LP, 1955)

        Reissue: DRG Archive MRS-902 (LP, 1983)

        Reissue: *John Murray Anderson's Almanac and Other Broadway-London Revues*, DRG Theater 19009 (CD, 1999)

          "Flowers" (Baker/Harnick, from *John Murray Anderson's Almanac*)

The Heartbreak Kid

    Original release: Columbia S-32155 (LP, 1973)

        "Theme from The Heartbreak Kid" (Coleman/Harnick)

Herschel Bernardi Sings Fiddler on the Roof
  Original release: CBS Masterworks OS 3010 (LP, 1966)
    Reissue: Collectables COL 7502 (CD, 2002)
      Ten songs from the show, including one that was cut during development, "When Messiah Comes"

Jan Peerce Sings Songs from Fiddler on the Roof and Ten Classics of Jewish Folk Song
  Original release: Vanguard VRS-9258 (LP, 1967)
    Reissue: Vanguard 79258-2 (CD, 1994)
      Four songs from the show, sung in Yiddish, alongside ten Jewish folk songs

Jerome Robbins' Broadway
  Original release: RCA Victor 60150-2-RC (CD, 1989)
    "Tradition" (Bock/Harnick, from *Fiddler on the Roof*)
    "The Dream" (Bock/Harnick, from *Fiddler on the Roof*)
    "Sunrise, Sunset" (Bock/Harnick, from *Fiddler on the Roof*)
    "Wedding Dance—Finale" (Bock/Harnick, from *Fiddler on the Roof*)

"Joni" (music and lyrics by Jerry Bock)
  Acquaviva and His Orchestra [instrumental arrangement by Nick Acquaviva]
    Original release: MGM K-12536 (45-rpm single, 1957)
      Reissue: *A Man and His Dream*, MGM E-3696 (LP, 1958)

Knitting on the Roof
  Original release: Knitting Factory KFW-260 (CD, 1999)
    Thirteen songs from *Fiddler on the Roof* performed by a variety of artists

The Littlest Revue
  Original recording: Painted Smiles Records PS-1361 (LP, 197-)
    "Ballad of The Shape of Things" (music and lyrics by Sheldon Harnick)

Lost in Boston
  Original release: Varèse Sarabande VSD-5475 (CD, 1994)
    "Where Do I Go From Here?" (Bock/Harnick, written for *Fiorello!*)
    "Dear, Sweet Sewing Machine" (Bock/Harnick, written for *Fiddler on the Roof*)

Lost in Boston II
  Original release: Varèse Sarabande VSD-5485 (CD, 1994)
    "When Messiah Comes" (Bock/Harnick, written for *Fiddler on the Roof*)
    "I'm Lost" (Bock/Harnick, written for *The Apple Tree*)
    "Just a Map" (Bock/Harnick, written for *The Rothschilds*)

Lost in Boston III
Original release: Varèse Sarabande VSD-5563 (CD, 1995)
"Tell Me I Look Nice" (Bock/Harnick, written for *She Loves Me*)

The Madwoman of Central Park West [Phyllis Newman's one-woman show]
Original cast recording: DRG Records CDSL-5212 (CD, 1990)
"What Makes Me Love Him?" (Bock/Harnick, from *The Apple Tree*)

Man in the Moon (Bock/Harnick)
Original Broadway cast recording: Golden Records LP-104 (LP, 1963)

"Metamorphosis" (music and lyrics by Sheldon Harnick)
The Journeymen
Original release: *Coming Attraction—Live!*, Capitol T-1770 (LP, 1962)
Reissue: Collector's Choice CCHM-416 (CD, 2004)

Mr. Wonderful (Bock/Holofcener/Weiss)
Original Broadway cast recording: Decca DL-9032 (LP, 1956)
Reissue: MCAD-10303 MCA Classics (CD, 1991)

"Never" (music and lyrics by George Weiss and Jerry Bock)
Sarah Vaughan
Original release: Mercury 70727 (45-rpm single, 1955)
Reissue: *The Complete Sarah Vaughan on Mercury*, Mercury 826 320-2 (6-CD set, 1986)

"Never Mind" (music and lyrics by George Weiss and Jerry Bock)
Steve Lawrence
Original release: Coral 61708 (45-rpm single, 1956)
Reissue: *Long Before I Knew You*, Jasmine JASCD 449 (CD, 2007)
Peggy Lee
Original release: Decca 30494 (45-rpm single, 1958)
Reissue: *The Best of Peggy Lee*, MCA/Decca 4024/4025 (LP, 1960)

New Faces of 1952
Original cast recording: RCA Victor LOC-1008 (LP, 1952?)
"Boston Beguine" (music and lyrics by Sheldon Harnick)

New Songs We Sing in School (music and lyrics by Jerry Bock)
Original recording: Golden Records LP-97 (LP, 1963)
Reissued as *Songs About Animals*, Golden Records LP-162 (LP, 1965)

On and Off Broadway (Evalyn Tyner, piano)
Original release: Capitol ST-1431 (LP, 1960)

"On the Side of the Angels" (Bock/Harnick, from *Fiorello!*)
"The Very Next Man" (Bock/Harnick, from *Fiorello!*)
"When Did I Fall In Love?" (Bock/Harnick, from *Fiorello!*)
"'Til Tomorrow" (Bock/Harnick, from *Fiorello!*)

"One Moment More" (music and lyrics by Jerry Bock)
Acquaviva and His Orchestra [instrumental arrangement by Nick Acquaviva]
Original release: MGM K-12434 (45-rpm single, 1957)
Reissue: *A Man and His Dream*, MGM E-3696 (LP, 1958)

The Phantom Tollbooth (Black/Harnick)
Original recording: Kennedy Center/Music Theater International (CD, 2007)

Prime-Time Musicals
Original release: Varèse Sarabande VSD-5858 (CD, 1997)
"I Worry" (Bock/Harnick, from *The Canterville Ghost*)
"If You Never Try" (Bock/Harnick, from *The Canterville Ghost*)

Regards to the Lindsay Years (Bock/Harnick)
Original cast recording: Mayerling Productions DRC 121473 (LP, 1973) [limited distribution]

Rex (Rodgers/Harnick)
Original Broadway cast recording: RCA Red Seal ABL1-1683 (LP, 1976)
Reissue: RCA Victor 09026-68933-2 (CD, 1997)

The Rothschilds (Bock/Harnick)
Original Broadway cast recording: Columbia S-30337 (LP, 1970)
Reissue: Sony Classical SK-30337 (CD, 1992)

She Loves Me (Bock/Harnick)
Original Broadway cast recording: MGM E4118 OC-2 (2LP, 1963)
Reissue: Polydor 831-968-2 (CD, 1987)
London production cast recording: HMV CSD-1546 (LP, 1964)
Reissue: EMI/West End Angel 8-28595-2 (CD, 1994)
Broadway revival cast recording: Varèse Sarabande VSD-5464 (CD, 1993)
Videorecording of complete performance: Theater on Film and Tape Archive, New York Public Library for the Performing Arts; videotaped at Criterion Center Stage Right, New York, 23 June 1993
London revival cast recording: First Night Records OCR CD6052 (CD, 1994)
Vienna cast recording [in German]: Capriccio 10821 (CD, 1997)

Shoestring Revue
Original cast recording: Painted Smiles Records PS-1360 (LP, 1974)

Reissue: Painted Smiles PSCD-129 (CD, 1991)
   "Someone Is Sending Me Flowers" (Baker/Harnick)
   "Garbage" (music and lyrics by Sheldon Harnick)
   "Medea in Disneyland" (Norlin/Harnick)
   "The Sea Is All Around Us" (Baker/Harnick)

Show Stopper (Herschel Bernardi)
  Original release: Columbia C 30004 (LP, 1970)
   Reissue: Collectables COL 7502 (CD, 2002)
    "Little Tin Box" (Bock/Harnick, from *Fiorello!*)
    "Sunrise, Sunset" (Bock/Harnick, from *Fiddler on the Roof*)
    "In My Own Lifetime" (Bock/Harnick, from *The Rothschilds*) [CD bonus track,
     released as a single in 1970]

"Since I've Been to You" (music and lyrics by Jerry Bock)
  Ethel Ennis
   Original release: *Once Again*, RCA Victor LSP 2862 (LP, 1964)
    Reissue: RCA 74663 (CD, 2004)

"Since My Canary Died" (Bock/Harnick)
  The Brothers Four
   Original release: *Cross-Country Concert*, Columbia CS 8746 (LP, 1963)
    Reissue: Collector's Choice (CD, 1999)
  The Smothers Brothers
   Original release: *Tour de Farce: American History and Other Unrelated Subjects*,
   Mercury MG-20948 (LP, 1964)

Smiling the Boy Fell Dead (Baker/Harnick)
  Original cast recording: Sunbeam Records LB-549 [not commercially released]

Songs I Taught My Mother (Charlotte Rae)
  Original release: Vanguard VRS 9004 (LP, 1955)
   Reissue: PS Classics PS-644 (CD, 2006)
    "Gabor the Merrier" (Harnick/Rae)
    "Merry Little Minuet" (music and lyrics by Sheldon Harnick)
    "Backer's Audition" (Harnick/Rae)
    "Gus the Gopher" (Harnick/Orzey)

The Tale of Peter Rabbit (Lawrence/Harnick)
  Original recording: Home Box Office (videocassette, 1991)

Tenderloin (Bock/Harnick)
  Original Broadway cast recording: Capitol SWAO-1492 (LP, 1960)

Reissue: Broadway Angel ZDM 7243-5-65022-2-2 (CD, 1993)
New York revival cast recording: DRG Theater 94770 (CD, 2000)
Videorecording of complete concert performance: Theater on Film and Tape Archive, New York Public Library for the Performing Arts; videotaped at City Center, New York, 24 March 2000

Tenderloin Dixieland (Phil Napoleon and His Memphis Five)
Original release: Capitol T-1535 (LP, 1960)
Instrumental versions of twelve songs from the show

"This Might Be Love" (music and lyrics by Jerry Bock)
Acquaviva and His Orchestra [instrumental arrangement by Nick Acquaviva]
Original release: MGM K-12536 (45-rpm single, 1957)
Reissue: *A Man and His Dream*, MGM E-3696 (LP, 1958)

To Broadway With Love
Original cast recording: Columbia OS-2630 (LP, 1964)
Reissue: DRG 19122 (CD, 2009)
"To Broadway With Love" (Bock/Harnick)
"Beautiful Lady" (Bock/Harnick)
"Mata Hari Mine" (Bock/Harnick)
"Remember Radio" (Bock/Harnick)
"Popsicles in Paris" (Bock/Harnick)

Two's Company
Original cast recording: RCA Victor LOC-1009 (LP, 1953)
Reissue: Sepia 1047 (CD, 2005)
"A Man's Home" (music and lyrics by Sheldon Harnick)

The Umbrellas of Cherbourg (Legrand/Harnick)
Videorecording of complete performance: Theater on Film and Tape Archive, New York Public Library for the Performing Arts; videotaped at the New York Shakespeare Festival Public Theater's Martinson Hall, New York, 4 March 1979

Unsung Musicals III
Original release: Varèse Sarabande VSD-5769 (CD, 1997)
"Penny By Penny" (Legrand/Harnick, from *A Christmas Carol*)
"A Wonderful Life" (Raposo/Harnick, from *A Wonderful Life*)
"In a State" (Raposo/Harnick, from *A Wonderful Life*)

A Visit with Sheldon Harnick
Original release: DRG Records 17008 (VHS, 1981)

Selected songs from Bock/Harnick shows and from Harnick's work before and
   after his collaboration with Bock

Your Show of Shows (song credited to Bock/Holofcener)
   "Clarence the Fireman" (22 April 1950): videorecording, Paley Center for Media
      T:31453

NOTES

CHAPTER 1: SUAVE YOUNG MEN

1. Millstein, *"Fiorello! and Harnick"*; Prideaux, *American Musicals*, 4; Kasha and Hirschhorn, *Notes on Broadway*, 153. Other useful biographical sources include Bryer and Davison, *Art of the American Musical*, 73–94; Downer, *The American Theater*, 151–167; Hawkshaw, "Words Into Song"; Hischak, *Word Crazy*, 137–144; Kelly, "Musical Plays of Bock and Harnick"; Wilk, *They're Playing Our Song* [1991], 185–194; "Sheldon Harnick: Biography" <http://www.mtishows.com/bio.asp?bID=3471>; Cioffi, "The Men Who Write the Shows"; and many of the interviews and communications listed in section 4 of the bibliography.

2. Millstein, *"Fiorello! and Harnick."*

3. Kasha and Hirschhorn, *Notes on Broadway*, 153. Hawkshaw, "Words Into Song."

4. For example, an announcement in the *Chicago Tribune* of 24 March 1949 (during Harnick's sophomore year in high school) called attention to a performance of the "Aeolian Trio," comprised of Sheldon Harnick, Margery Moulton, and Eugene Moulton, at Easter services of the Irving Park Baptist Church.

5. "Current Music News," *Chicago Tribune*, 23 June 1940.

6. Harnick, interviewed by Theodore S. Chapin, October 2001.

7. "Dramatics Hold Important Role In Youths' Lives," *Chicago Tribune*, 1 March 1942.

8. On her album *Songs I Taught My Mother* (1955), which consists of highlights of her cabaret performances during the early years of her career (for album details see Appendix B). Harnick and Rae met in college (further details below).

9. Bryer and Davison, *Art of the American Musical*, 75. See also Downer, *The American Theater*, 153.

10. Harnick, interviewed by Theodore S. Chapin, October 2001. *Carmen Jones* toured California and elsewhere after it closed on Broadway in February 1945.

11. Harnick, interviewed by Andrew Patner, March 2008.

12. Robert Simonson, "Northwestern University's Famed Waa-Mu Show to Celebrate 75 Years April 28," *Playbill*, 21 March 2006.

13. Lester, "Charlotte Rae Has Her Say."

14. "N. U. Will Open Its 19th Waa-Mu Revue on May 1," *Chicago Tribune*, 23 April 1950.

15. The event of February 14, 1971 was recorded and released on LP in 1977 as *An Evening with Sheldon Harnick* (see Appendix B).

16. Hawkshaw, "Words Into Song."

17. Downer, *The American Theater*, 153. *Finian's Rainbow* opened on Broadway in January 1947. The original cast album was released in 1948 (Columbia OL-4062).

18. Millstein, *"Fiorello! and Harnick."*

19. Biographical sources for Bock include Downer, *The American Theater*, 151-167; Ewen, *Composers for the American Musical Theater*, 230–243; Kasha and Hirschhorn,

Notes on Broadway, 25–35; Kelly, "Musical Plays of Bock and Harnick"; Prideaux, *American Musicals*; Suskin, *Show Tunes*, 252–262; Wilk, *They're Playing Our Song* [1991], 185–194; "Jerry Bock: Biography" <http://www.mtishows.com/bio.asp?bID=3354>; and many of the interviews and communications listed in section 4 of the bibliography.

20. Bock Papers, box 35, folder 23.

21. Bock Papers, box 35, folder 26.

22. Bock Papers, box 6, folders 39 and 40, and box 26, folders 21 and 22.

23. The song scores are in box 6, folder 40; the overture melodies are in box 6, folder 39. The program (box 26, folder 22) lists "Herbert Aptowitz" as the orchestra leader and first violinist.

24. Example 1.1a adds chord symbols from one score (Bock Papers, box 6, folder 39) to a melody and lyric from another (box 6, folder 40).

25. Example 1.1b combines a melody (box 6, folder 39) with lyrics that were written out on a separate page (box 26, folder 21); neither source for this song includes chord symbols.

26. Bock Papers, box 6, folder 40.

27. Personal communication, 30 October 2008. Earlier accounts of this story (occasionally differing in minor details) can be found in Ewen, *Composers for the American Theater*, 232; Kasha and Hirschhorn, *Notes on Broadway*, 26; Wilk, *They're Playing Our Song* [1991], 187; and Bock, interviewed by Harold Flender, 11 February 1971.

28. See Suskin, *Show Tunes*, 255. The same contest inspired Bock's contemporary Stephen Sondheim to write *Phinney's Rainbow* around the same time.

29. "Tops Among Teens," *Chicago Tribune*, 20 June 1948.

30. Bock Papers, box 19, folders 11 and 12.

31. The surviving score for "Babe's What They Call Me" (Bock Papers, box 19, folder 11) is just a melody without lyrics or chord symbols. The lyrics added in Example 1.2a are taken from a surviving page of the script (Bock Papers, box 19, folder 12). The "Great Wisconsin" score (Bock Papers, box 19, folder 11; cf. Example 1.2b) also has no lyric, and a piece of surviving sheet music in the same folder is missing its first page. A surviving script page (Bock Papers, box 19, folder 12) includes only lyrics for a reprise of this song ("Well, that's the finish, folks, / Hope it beats any other year, / And till another year, / There's your Haresfoot!").

CHAPTER 2: WONDERS OF MANHATTAN

1. Harnick, interviewed by Harold Flender, 22 February 1971. During the course of the interview, the interviewer mentions that he saw *New Faces of 1952* with Bock.

2. Ballard, *How I Lost 10 Pounds*, 229.

3. Bryer and Davison, *Art of the American Musical*, 78.

4. Stewart, *Broadway Musicals*, 417.

5. Henry Hewes, "New Stars Icumen In," *Saturday Review*, 9 June 1956, p. 27. Hart's lyric begins:

I married many men, a ton of them,

And yet I was untrue to none of them,
Because I bumped off every one of them,
To keep my love alive.

. . . and includes verses such as:

Sir Peter had an incongruity,
Collecting girls with promiscuity,
Now I'm collecting his annuity,
To keep my love alive.

. . . and . . .

Sir Curtis made me cook each dish he ate,
And everything his heart could wish he ate,
Until I fiddled with the fish he ate,
To keep my love alive.

6. The brilliance of Rae's rendition is evident on a recording of *The Littlest Revue* that was released in the 1970s (see Appendix B). In 2007 she performed it at an appearance at a Barnes and Noble in Manhattan, with Harnick in the audience, that was memorialized on YouTube.

7. Sillman, *Here Lies Leonard Sillman*, 353. According to Sillman, *Three Wishes* co-writer/director Abe Burrows heard Rae perform at a backers' audition for *New Faces* and lured her away the next day.

8. Kasha and Hirschhorn, *Notes on Broadway*, 156; Bryer and Davison, *Art of the American Musical*, 78–79.

9. The film is available on DVD as *New Faces* (Critics' Choice CCD 1028, 2004).

10. Stewart, *Broadway Musicals*, 416.

11. Frank Kelly ("Musical Plays of Bock and Harnick," 32) notes that "The Boston Beguine" was also honored with a parody in *Dames at Sea* (1968), an off-Broadway send-up of 1930s movie musicals.

12. The program for *Talent '52* is in the files of the Billy Rose Theater Division of the New York Public Library for the Performing Arts. Harnick's scene, for which he wrote words and music, was staged by Fred Hebert and performed by Mary Harmon with the Boulevardiers (Douglas Luther and Pat Welch).

13. Anderson, *Out Without My Rubbers*, 236.

14. Stewart, *Broadway Musicals*, 310.

15. Jenness and Velsey (*Classic American Popular Song*, 164) make a similar observation. In fact, "Merry Little Minuet" has sometimes been mistaken for a Tom Lehrer song (Harnick, interviewed by John von Soosten and Howard Sherman, November 2006).

16. Brooks Atkinson, "Theater: Dallas Report," *New York Times*, 27 May 1954.

17. For information on Green Mansions see Melville, "Hidden History"; Ray, "Summer Stock"; Kaye, "Doris Humphrey at Green Mansions"; Boroff, "Dancers in the Adirondacks"; Clurman, *The Fervent Years*, 125–128; Smith, *Real Life Drama*, 139–145; Burnett, *One More Time*, 280–281; Strouse, *Put On a Happy Face*, 47–50. The history of Green Mansions remains sketchy because "all the guest registers, menus, photos, sheet music, [and] furnishings" were "either lost in a

fire, sold at tag sales, or sent to the dump" in the early 1970s (Melville, "Hidden History").

18. Downer, *The American Theater*, 155.

19. Harnick, interviewed by John von Soosten and Howard Sherman, November 2006.

20. A full staging was projected for 2009 by the Playwrights Theater, in partnership with the Morris Museum/Bickford Theater, but fell victim to financing difficulties.

21. Richards, "Anything for a Song."

22. Richards, "Anything for a Song."

23. He makes this remark when introducing his performance of "Garbage" during *An Evening with Sheldon Harnick* (see Appendix B).

24. These are the lyrics sung by Bea Arthur on the original soundtrack of *Shoestring Revue*. Harnick sings a different second quatrain in his performance on *An Evening with Sheldon Harnick* ("I offered you a life of love / You merely mocked it / I offered you a heart of gold / You went and hocked it").

25. From Ben Bagley's liner notes to the CD reissue of the original soundtrack (see Appendix B).

26. Gingold sang the song on her album *La Gingold* (see Appendix B).

27. On the soundtrack album, "The Sea Is All Around Us" is sung by Bill McCutcheon.

28. Harnick, interviewed by Harold Flender, 1 March 1971; Sheldon Harnick: Biography <http://www.mtishows.com/bio.asp?bID=3471>; Harnick, interviewed by Bernard Rosenberg and Ernest Harburg, 18 February 1983; Harnick, interviewed by Terry Gross, 1988.

29. <http://www.aislesay.com/FTR-LAVIN.html>

30. Alvin Klein, "After Thirty Years, the Hits Linger On," *New York Times*, 17 October 1982.

31. Bock remembers a salary of twenty-five dollars a week each (Prideaux, *American Musicals*, 4).

32. The show's history is chronicled in Sennett, *Your Show of Shows*.

33. Bock, interviewed by Martha S. LoMonaco, 13 May 1986.

34. The scripts are archived in the Kallen Papers, boxes 6, 9, and 10, and in the Liebman Papers, boxes 3–12. Almost all of the scripts from every season of the two shows are extant in one archive or the other (or both).

35. The Center's database indicates that the entire show of 25 March 1949 is available (cat. no. B:27639), but in fact the videorecording begins several minutes into the show, after the performance of "Jim Green."

36. Bock Papers, box 14, folder 18.

37. Neither Bock nor Holofcener recalls writing this song.

38. Bock, interviewed by Martha S. LoMonaco, 13 May 1986.

39. Prideaux, *American Musicals*, 4.

40. This show is preserved in the collection of the Paley Center. Bock's score for the song is in box 16, folder 42 of the Bock Papers.

41. The history of Tamiment is thoroughly documented in LoMonaco, *Every Week, a Broadway Revue*.

42. Bock, interviewed by Martha S. LoMonaco, 13 May 1986.

43. Bock Papers, box 32, folder 13. The archive includes only the program, not scores for the songs themselves.

44. Programs for these productions are preserved in the Tamiment Playhouse Records, box 1, folders 12, 13, and 15; and in the Bock Papers, box 33, folders 27 and 28.

45. Bock described his Tamiment experience in detail in his interview with Martha S. LoMonaco, 13 May 1986.

46. About half of the scores are extant, in the Bock Papers, boxes 13, folder 11, through 14, folder 9 (designated "Tamiment Playhouse Productions"), and scattered throughout the collections of songs in boxes 15, 16, and 17 (designated as individual songs by Bock alone and by Bock and Holofcener).

47. Example 2.1a transcribes the surviving score exactly as Bock wrote it (Bock Papers, box 13, folder 11). The lyrics are not extant, but the combined melodies both appear to be vocal lines (and Bock wrote "VOC" above the first measure).

48. Example 2.1b transcribes the opening bars of the lead sheet in the Bock Papers, box 13, folder 19. It shows that the song was conceived at Tamiment as a duet between characters named Betsy and Jeff. The folder also contains a handwritten piano-vocal score of the song without the character designations, as if he had been preparing a sheet-music publication.

49. The most successful such venture began at Tamiment in the summer of 1958 as *Princess and the Pea*, eventually opening on Broadway as *Once Upon a Mattress* in May of 1959 (LoMonaco, *Every Week, a Broadway Revue*, 156–160). Other large Tamiment projects never made it out of the Poconos.

50. Lead sheets for miscellaneous songs written between 1951 and 1976 may be found in boxes 15, 16, and 17 of the Bock Papers.

51. Bock Papers, box 16, folder 26.

52. Bock Papers, Box 13, folders 6 and 7.

53. See Ellen Rosand, "The Descending Tetrachord: An Emblem of Lament," *The Musical Quarterly* 65/3 (July 1979): 346–359. The music for *Wonders of Manhattan* is in box 13, folders 8–10 of the Bock Papers.

54. "Of Local Origin," *New York Times*, 22 March 1956.

55. The Chad Mitchell Trio recorded an excellent version of "The Story of Alice" in 1963 (see Appendix B). The score for this song is not in the Bock Papers.

56. In the printed program the title is spelled "Merry Lil' Minuet." Harnick's song is absent from a program for a later performance of the same show in Los Angeles, and from a program for a performance of the show in Chicago in June 1956. These documents are in the program files of the Billy Rose Theater Division of the New York Public Library for the Performing Arts.

57. Taylor, *Jule*, 189; Haygood, *In Black and White*, 212.

58. Taylor, *Jule*, 189.

59. George David Weiss: Biography <http://www.songwritershalloffame.org/index.php/exhibits/bio/C24>.

60. Taylor, *Jule*, 189.

61. Haygood, *In Black and White*, 214.

62. Ewen, *Composers for the American Musical Theater*, 235.

63. Biographical information from personal communications and from <www. holofcener.com>.

64. Bock Papers, box 26, folder 18.

65. *Sammy Davis, Jr. Reader*, 179–180.

66. Davis, *Sammy*, 227–228.

67. Haygood, *In Black and White*, 222, 239.

68. Prideaux, *American Musicals*, 4.

69. Taylor, *Jule*, 189. The long version is in the Bock Papers, box 6, folder 29.

70. Kelly makes a similar observation in "Musical Plays of Bock and Harnick," 30.

71. A playbill from a performance sometime after the premiere in New York shows that "Miami" had been removed (Bock Papers, box 26, folder 18).

72. Kasha and Hirschhorn, *Notes on Broadway*, 28.

73. An announcement of this partnership appeared in the *New York Times* on 16 December 1955, when most of the *Mr. Wonderful* score would have been complete. *Do Re Mi*, book by Garson Kanin, lyrics by Betty Comden and Adolph Green, and music by Jule Styne, premiered on Broadway in December 1960 and ran for 400 performances.

74. The score for "Never" is in the Bock Papers, box 17, folder 22; a separate lyric sheet is in box 35, folder 20. The score for "Never Mind" is in box 17, folder 23. Peggy Lee also released a single of "Never Mind" in 1958 (see Appendix B).

75. The songs Bock wrote alone are filed in boxes 15, 16, and 17 of the Bock Papers (separate lyric sheets in box 34, folders 13 through 94).

76. Scores for three of these are extant: "Always the Sea" (Bock Papers, box 15, folder 3); "One Moment More" (box 15, folder 31; lyric sheet in box 34, folder 59); and "This Might Be Love" (box 15, folder 40). For recording information see Appendix B.

77. Hischak, *Word Crazy*, 137.

78. Hischak, *Word Crazy*, 138. See also Engel, *Their Words are Music*, 152.

79. Engel, *Their Words Are Music*, 153–154.

80. Engel, *Their Words Are Music*, 153.

81. Hischak, *Word Crazy*, 143.

82. Hischak, *Word Crazy*, 144.

83. Harnick, interviewed by Theodore S. Chapin, October 2001.

84. Harnick, interviewed by Harold Flender, 22 February 1971.

85. Bock, interviewed by Harold Flender, 4 February 1971; Bock, interviewed by Nancy Sureck, 12 November 2002.

86. As discussed in Berry, "Gambling with Chromaticism."

87. The significance of this tritone in *West Side Story*, in songs such as "Something's Coming" and "Maria," has been explored by Block, *Enchanted Evenings*, 245–273; Swain, *Broadway Musical*, 221–264; and Knapp, *Formation*, 204–215. Swain (225) writes that the tritone is a "favorite interval of Bernstein in his whole corpus."

88. Geoffrey Block discusses the latter, and surveys other contrapuntal examples from Loesser, Gershwin, and others, in *Enchanted Evenings*, 205–209. William Marvin ("Simulating Counterpoint") characterizes the typical use of this technique in a Broadway

musical as a "quodlibet" and also cites examples from Irving Berlin's "Play a Simple Melody" (*Watch Your Step*, 1914) to Stephen Schwartz's "Loathing" (*Wicked*, 2003).

89. Engel, *American Musical Theater*, 123.

90. Jones, *Our Musicals, Ourselves*, 198.

91. Engel, *American Musical Theater*, 123–131. See also Swain, *Broadway Musical*, 265–270; and Grant, *Rise and Fall*, 101. In 2002 Bock specifically recalled seeing *Where's Charley?* during its original Broadway run (Bock, interviewed by Nancy Sureck, 12 November 2002).

CHAPTER 3: POLITICS AND POKER

1. Harnick, interviewed by Harold Flender, 1 March 1971.

2. Bryer and Davison, *Art of the American Musical*, 80.

3. Harnick, interviewed by Martin Charnin, 2008. Bryer and Davison, *Art of the American Musical*, 80.

4. Harnick, interviewed by Harold Flender, 1 March 1971. This could have happened just after the Dallas premiere of that show in the spring of 1954 or after it was presented at Green Mansions in the summer of 1955 (see chapter 2).

5. Harnick, interviewed by Harold Flender, 1 March 1971; Cioffi, "The Men Who Write the Shows," II:52.

6. Harnick, interviewed by Martin Charnin, 2008. Kelly has a different account, with Harnick signed first and Bock brought in on the recommendation of Stein ("Musical Plays of Bock and Harnick," 37).

7. Ewen, *Composers for the American Musical Theater*, 235–236.

8. Cioffi, "The Men Who Write the Shows," II:52.

9. Downer, *The American Theater*, 162. Similar explanations of their creative process are found in: Bock, interviewed by Nancy Sureck, 12 November 2002; Harnick, interviewed by Nancy Sureck, 16 January 2003.

10. Downer, *The American Theater*, 162; Harnick, interviewed by Nancy Sureck, 16 January 2003; Kasha and Hirschhorn, *Notes on Broadway*, 28.

11. Kasha and Hirschhorn, *Notes on Broadway*, 28.

12. This script is not in the Bock Papers but in the regular collection of the Billy Rose Theater Division of the New York Public Library for the Performing Arts. Bock did keep an early outline of the show dated October 1, 1956 that included song suggestions, but this predated his partnership with Harnick by at least three months (Bock Papers, box 19, folder 40).

13. The original demo recordings of many of these songs were released in 2008 with the soundtrack recording of the York Theater Company (see Appendix B).

14. Stone, "Landmark Symposium," 13–14.

15. Sketches for "Somebody Beautiful" are in the Bock Papers, box 3, folder 4 and box 19, folder 34; and in the Harnick Papers (New York), box 6, folder 112.

16. Bock Papers, box 19, folder 41.

17. Bock Papers, box 19, folder 41.

18. *The Body Beautiful*, 65.

19. A sketch for "A Word of Wisdom," or possibly a transcription of a melody from Bock's tape, is in the Harnick Papers (New York), box 6, folder 112.

20. Stephen Sondheim paid tribute to Harnick's rhyme here in a song that was cut from *Follies*. See Sondheim, "Theater Lyrics," 80.

21. Filichia, "Stein's Way." Stein's quip understates the show's longevity: actually, it did run for seven weeks and two days.

22. Kelly, "Musical Plays of Bock and Harnick," 42; emphasis original.

23. *Plain and Fancy* was adapted from a play known as *Betsy* by Marion Weaver, although the debt is uncredited. See Murray Schumach, "The Amish and Music," *New York Times*, 23 January 1955.

24. Kelly, "Musical Plays of Bock and Harnick," 62. See also Kasha and Hirschhorn, *Notes on Broadway*, 28.

25. Harnick, interviewed by Harold Flender, 1 March 1971.

26. Harnick, interviewed by Bernard Rosenberg and Ernest Harburg, 18 February 1983.

27. Filichia, "Stein's Way."

28. Ewen, *Composers for the American Musical Theater*, 236.

29. Hawkshaw, "Words Into Song."

30. Alvin Klein, "After 30 Years, the Hits Linger On," *New York Times*, 17 October 1982.

31. Bock Papers, box 16, folders 7, 8, 15.

32. Bock Papers, box 16, folder 11.

33. Bock Papers, box 6, folders 1–6 (scores); box 26, folders 1–6 (lyric sheets). The music is available on compact disc (see Appendix B).

34. Kasha and Hirschhorn, *Notes on Broadway*, 158–159; Ilson, *Harold Prince*, 47; Harnick, interviewed by Richard Christiansen, 29 April 2006; Harnick, interviewed by P. J. Powers, [April] 2008.

35. According to Frank Kelly, Arnold Schulman was also approached about writing the book at some point (Kelly, "Musical Plays of Bock and Harnick," 65).

36. Ilson, *Harold Prince*, 48.

37. Harnick, interviewed by Harold Flender, 1 March 1971. Harnick made a similar comment in the 2008 interview with Martin Charnin.

38. Kasha and Hirschhorn, *Notes on Broadway*, 157; Harnick, interviewed by Martin Charnin, 208.

39. Sondheim and Styne collaborated on *Gypsy* starting in the fall of 1958; the show opened in May 1959 (Taylor, *Jule*, 201; Secrest, *Stephen Sondheim*, 135).

40. Kasha and Hirschhorn, *Notes on Broadway*, 157. The fictitious date of the song is erroneously given as "1927" in this source. Other sources for Harnick's account give the date accurately as 1917 (e.g., Ilson, *Harold Prince*, 49; Harnick, interviewed by Richard Christiansen, 29 April 2006).

41. Louis Calta, "Broadway to Get 2-Play Program," *New York Times*, 20 March 1959. Prince's recollection of these events differs (*Contradictions*, 51–52). He remembers approaching Bock and Harnick as a team from the beginning. He says that they were asked to write three songs on spec, not as an audition but to prove themselves to the "the La Guardia people," who might have preferred that the music be written by Richard Rodgers or Irving Berlin. He writes that Bock and Harnick were not even told "the idea of the show" but were just asked to write music for two scenes. He says nothing about a waltz reminiscent of 1917 Irving Berlin.

42. Prince, *Contradictions*, 52; Ilson, *Harold Prince*, 47.

43. Bock Papers, box 25, folder 11.

44. Fiorello La Guardia, *The Making of an Insurgent, an Autobiography: 1882–1919*, introduction by M. R. Werner (Philadelphia: J. B. Lippincott, 1948). Ernest Cuneo, *Life with Fiorello: A Memoir* (New York: Macmillan, 1955). See Weidman, "Joining the Team," 11; and Lewis Nichols, "Musical Biography," *New York Times*, 22 November 1959.

45. Weidman, "Joining the Team," 11. See also Weidman, *Praying for Rain*, 396–398.

46. Prince, *Contradictions*, 50–53; Harnick, interviewed by Richard Christiansen, 29 April 2006; Harnick, interviewed by P. J. Powers, [April] 2008. Marie La Guardia died in 1984 at the age of 89.

47. Frank Kelly makes valuable observations about the characters, story structure, and source material in "Musical Plays of Bock and Harnick," 76–79.

48. La Guardia, *Making of an Insurgent*, 33.

49. Cuneo, *Life With Fiorello*, 82.

50. Cuneo, *Life With Fiorello*, 153–177.

51. Cuneo, *Life With Fiorello*, 163; *Fiorello!*, Act 2, scene 4.

52. Harnick, interviewed by Richard Christiansen, 29 April 2006.

53. Scott McMillin has an informative discussion of diegetic conventions in *The Musical as Drama*, 102–125.

54. This is Harnick's introduction to "'Til Tomorrow" in *An Evening with Sheldon Harnick* (see Appendix B).

55. Harnick, interviewed by Richard Christiansen, 29 April 2006.

56. Harnick, interviewed by Nancy Sureck, 16 January 2003. See also Kelly, "Musical Plays of Bock and Harnick," 70.

57. Kelly, "Musical Plays of Bock and Harnick," 69.

58. In his memoir *Praying for Rain* (412–414), Jerome Weidman recalls just the opposite shift for "Marie's Law," from an earlier to a later scene in the first act. Evidence from the New Haven, Philadelphia, and New York playbills indicates otherwise.

59. Prince, *Contradictions*, 57.

60. Cioffi, "The Men Who Write the Shows," II:53.

61. The recordings by Robert Goulet, Peggy Lee, and the Four Freshmen were released in the late 1950s and early 1960s. Liz Callaway's rendition appears on the first *Lost in Boston* CD (see Appendix B). The score for the song is included in the *Sheldon Harnick Songbook* (Warner Brothers, 1996).

62. Cuneo, *Life With Fiorello*, 17. The expression itself probably dates back to a speech by Benjamin Disraeli in the early 1860s: "What is the question now placed before society with a glib assurance the most astounding? The question is this—Is man an ape or an angel? My lord, I am on the side of the angels." *The Oxford Dictionary of Scientific Quotations*, ed. W. F. Bynum and Roy Porter (Oxford University Press, 2006).

63. Harnick, "Which Comes First, Words or Music?," 10–11.

64. Harnick, interviewed by Richard Christiansen, 29 April 2006.

65. Kasha and Hirschhorn, *Notes on Broadway*, 158–159; Cioffi, "The Men Who Write the Shows," II:54.

66. La Guardia, *Making of an Insurgent*, 104.

67. Mordden, *Coming Up Roses*, 235.

68. Kenneth Tynan, "On the Side of the Angels," *New Yorker*, 5 December 1959.

69. In the splendid recording of this song by Audra McDonald, the final orchestral flourish brings back the earlier clusters very precisely (*How Glory Goes*, Nonesuch).

70. Prince, *Contradictions*, 58.

71. Cuneo, *Life With Fiorello*, 183. (*Safire's Political Dictionary*, 396.) Weidman, *Praying for Rain*, 418–419. Harnick also recalls coming across the phrase during some of his background research (Harnick, interviewed by Richard Christiansen, 29 April 2006).

72. Harnick, interviewed by Richard Christiansen, 29 April 2006. Weidman tells essentially the same story, differing in minor details (*Praying for Rain*, 418–420).

73. Harnick demonstrated the connection in his first appearance in the "Lyrics and Lyricists" series at the 92nd Street Y, released on LP as *An Evening with Sheldon Harnick* (see Appendix B).

74. Grant, *Rise and Fall*, 32.

75. *Tenderloin* reissue liner notes, p. 14 (see Appendix B).

76. Mayfair 9655S. Kay also released *Naughty Nineties* on 78-rpm in the 1940s.

77. "You Tell Me Your Dream and I'll Tell You Mine" was written by Chas. N. Daniels (music) and Seymour Rice and Albert H. Brown (words) and copyrighted in 1899. Only the chorus is performed on the Beatrice Kay album: at first she alternates phrases with a vocal group, "The Eligibles," and then they all sing together at the end. Example 3.5 matches the key of this recording; most of the melody is sung an octave lower.

78. Harnick, interviewed by Harold Flender, 1 March 1971; Kasha and Hirschhorn, *Notes on Broadway*, 159; Bryer and Davison, *Art of the American Musical*, 83.

79. Kasha and Hirschhorn, *Notes on Broadway*, 28.

80. Prince, *Contradictions*, 54.

81. Arthur Gelb, "Rooney May Play La Guardia Role," *New York Times*, 20 April 1959.

82. A sample of Bosley's characterization is available on the video compilation *Broadway's Lost Treasures II* (VHS/DVD, Acorn Media, 2004), in a performance of "The Name's La Guardia" along with other original cast members at the 1960 Tony Awards ceremony.

83. Mordden, *Coming Up Roses*, 234; emphasis original.

84. Kelly, "Musical Plays of Bock and Harnick," 80.

85. The various ideas and revisions are mentioned in Cioffi, "The Men Who Write the Shows," II:54; Bock, interviewed by Nancy Sureck, 12 November 2002; Harnick, interviewed by P. J. Powers, [April] 2008; and personal communication, 8 June 2009.

86. Prince, *Contradictions*, 59–62. The hiatus, however, was in June 1960, almost seventeen months before the show actually closed. The show moved to the larger Broadway Theater in May 1961.

87. Hohenberg, *The Pulitzer Prizes*, 206.

88. Fischer, *Complete Historical Handbook of the Pulitzer Prize System*, 248.

89. Hohenberg, *The Pulitzer Prizes*, 264; Adler, *Mirror on the Stage*, 90–92; Bates, *The Pulitzer Prize*, 127. The awards to *Oklahoma!* and *South Pacific* were also the result

of advisory boards acting against the recommendations of juries (Hohenberg, *The Pulitzer Prizes*, 206, 211).

90. Hohenberg, *The Pulitzer Prizes*, 264.

91. Konas, "From Gershwin to Sondheim," 126.

92. Bordman, *American Musical Comedy*, 174.

93. Kenneth Tynan, "On the Side of the Angels," *New Yorker*, 5 December 1959.

94. Harnick, interviewed by P. J. Powers, [April] 2008.

95. Harnick, interviewed by P. J. Powers, [April] 2008.

96. The company posted the display graphics on its website (http://www.timelinetheatre.com/fiorello2/Fiorello2_LobbyDisplay.pdf).

97. Stewart, *Broadway Musicals*, 193.

98. Carol Lawson, "Little Flower to be Replanted on Broadway," *New York Times*, 30 March 1984. Stephen Holden, "*Fiorello!* at Goodspeed Opera," *New York Times*, 30 July 1985. Thomas O'Connor, "Lyricist Optimistic on Musicals," *Orange County Register*, 10 December 1989.

CHAPTER 4: LITTLE OLD NEW YORK

1. Prince, *Contradictions*, 67; Ilson, *Harold Prince*, 55.

2. Prince, *Contradictions*, 67.

3. Kasha and Hirschhorn, *Notes on Broadway*, 29.

4. Weidman, "Joining the Team," 12.

5. Smith, *Musical Comedy in America*, 242.

6. Werner, *It Happened in New York*, 36–116.

7. Werner, *It Happened in New York*, 70. In the musical the geography of the district is expanded to "Fourteenth to Forty-Second Street, from Fourth Avenue to the Hudson" (*Tenderloin*, 4–5).

8. Lewis Funke, "News and Gossip Gathered on the Rialto," *New York Times*, 6 December 1959.

9. Kelly, "Musical Plays of Bock and Harnick," 103.

10. Lewis Funke, "News and Gossip Gathered on the Rialto," *New York Times*, 6 December 1959.

11. An early version of the first act, annotated with Bock's handwritten ideas for songs, is in the Bock Papers, box 32, folder 40. The complete early version is in the collection of the Billy Rose Theater Division, New York Public Library for the Performing Arts.

12. Bryer and Davison, *Art of the American Musical*, 83. See also Kasha and Hirschhorn, *Notes on Broadway*, 159; Wilk, *They're Playing Our Song* [1991], 190; Harnick, interviewed by Bernard Rosenberg and Ernest Harburg, 18 February 1983; Cioffi, "The Men Who Write the Shows," II:55.

13. Kelly, "Musical Plays of Bock and Harnick," 110; Altman, *Making of a Musical*, 27. The Goldmans went on to write successfully for Broadway and Hollywood. James wrote the books for *Family Affair* (1962) and *Follies* (1971) and the Oscar-winning screenplay for *The Lion in Winter* (1968); William wrote Oscar-winning screenplays for *Butch Cassidy and the Sundance Kid* (1969), *All the President's Men* (1976), and many other distinguished films.

14. Altman, *Making of a Musical*, 26-27.

15. Kelly, "Musical Plays of Bock and Harnick," 112.

16. Kelly, "Musical Plays of Bock and Harnick," 114.

17. Cioffi, "The Men Who Write the Shows," II:54; Harnick, interviewed by Andrew Patner, March 2008.

18. *Tenderloin*, vocal selections (New York Times Music, 1960).

19. Adams, *Tenderloin*, 39–40.

20. Adams, *Tenderloin*, 40. The song's actual chorus is:

> There's a name that's never spoken
> There's a mother's heart half broken
> Just another face that's missing from the old home, that is all.
> There's a memory still living
> There's a father, unforgiving,
> There's a picture that is turned toward the wall.

21. The key structure of "My Miss Mary" features subdominant relations in the original cast recording but not in the recording from 2000 (see Appendix B).

22. For "Artificial Flowers" and "My Miss Mary," this is true only in the original cast album, not in the 2000 release. Bobby Darin's version of "Artificial Flowers" (No. 20 on the pop charts in 1960) uses the whole-step shift as in the original.

23. Bryer and Davison, *Art of the American Musical*, 82.

24. Prince, *Contradictions*, 68.

25. Prince, *Contradictions*, 67.

26. Prince, *Contradictions*, 68–69.

27. Mandelbaum, *Not Since Carrie*, 269.

28. Kelly, "Musical Plays of Bock and Harnick," 118.

29. Liner notes to the 2000 revival cast album.

30. Mandelbaum, *Not Since Carrie*, 267.

31. Kelly, "Musical Plays of Bock and Harnick," 111.

32. Bryer and Davison, *Art of the American Musical*, 83. See also Kasha and Hirschhorn, *Notes on Broadway*, 159; and Wilk, *They're Playing Our Song* [1991], 190.

33. Recordings of "Ism" are included in the collections *18 Interesting Songs From Unfortunate Musicals* and *Broadway Musicals of 1960* (see Appendix B); a score for the song is included in the *Sheldon Harnick Songbook* (pp. 114–117). "Forget Me" has been forgotten.

34. Howard Taubman, "Theater: *Vintage '60*, Bubbly and Flat," *New York Times*, 13 September 1960.

35. A videorecording of the program survives in the collection of the Paley Center. Bock's score is in the Bock Papers, box 17, folder 15.

36. Sam Zolotow, "Musical Planned by Arthur Penn," *New York Times*, 24 January 1962.

37. The album's origins are described this way in Everett Evans, "UH Children's Show Scores a Top Talent," *Houston Chronicle*, 16 July 2000; and Dylan Otto Krider, "Not By the Book," *Houston Press*, 27 July 2000. In a 1971 interview Bock said that the songs were commissioned by CBS (Bock, interviewed by Harold Flender, 11 February

1971). The album was released in 1963, then again in 1965 under the new title *Songs About Animals*.

38. "Better is Love": box 15, folder 3. "Said My Heart": box 15, folder 34. "The Lonely Stage": box 16, folder 13. "The Right Word": box 16, folder 17.

39. Box 16, folder 18.

40. *Coming Attraction—Live!* (see Appendix B).

41. Bock Papers, box 15, folder 35.

42. The score is in the Bock Papers, box 6, folders 41 and 42. Lyric sheets are in box 26, folders 23 and 24.

43. Paul Gardner, "New Bil and Cora Baird Puppet Show," *New York Times*, 12 April 1963.

44. Scores and lyric sheets for some of the songs are preserved in the Bock Papers, box 26, folders 11 and 12, and in the Harnick Papers (Wisconsin), box 1, folder 5. A copy of the script is filed in the Harnick Papers (Wisconsin), box 1, folders 1–4.

45. The event was released on record as *An Evening with Sheldon Harnick* (see Appendix B). "Worlds Apart" is sung by Harnick's wife, Margery Gray.

46. Michael Grossberg, "*Fiddler on the Roof* Lyricist Reflects on Love, Work of Past, Present," *Columbus Dispatch*, 7 March 1977.

47. Bock Papers, box 3, folder 4; box 19, folder 34. The songwriters' demo recording of this song is included on the *Body Beautiful* bonus disc (see Appendix B).

48. This is the lyric as presented on *An Evening with Sheldon Harnick*. It is slightly different in the score in the Bock Papers, box 26, folder 11.

CHAPTER 5: TO BROADWAY WITH LOVE

1. Bock, interviewed by Max Wilk, 29 August 1971.

2. Bock's surviving correspondence for this project begins with a letter dated 23 September 1961 (Bock Papers, box 29, folder 10).

3. Harnick's transcription of some of the themes from this tape is in box 6, folder 137 of the Harnick Papers (New York).

4. Prince, *Contradictions*, 98. See also Altman, *Making of a Musical*, 21–22

5. Cioffi, "The Men Who Write the Shows," II:57. At that time Robbins would have been in preparation or rehearsal for his first non-musical directing venture, Arthur Kopit's *Oh Dad, Poor Dad, Mamma's Hung You in the Closet and I'm Feelin' So Sad*, which opened at the Phoenix Theater (off-Broadway) on February 26, 1962. Lawrence, *Dance with Demons*, 300–306.

6. Sam Zolotow, "Audrey Christie Gets Stage Role, *New York Times*, 8 June 1956. Its apparent American premiere occurred in 2004 at the University of Illinois at Urbana-Champaign (http://www.pamphletpress.org/index.cfm?sec=7&story_id=4). John Simon gives the original title as *Kispatika* (*New York*, 7/12/93). Nora and Delia Ephron's screenplay for the film *You've Got Mail* (1998) is also loosely based on this play.

7. Heylbut, "You're the Top, Cole Porter!," 57.

8. Sam Zolotow, "László Comedy Heads for Stage," *New York Times*, 25 January 1962.

9. Kelly has Prince joining the production team in July 1962 ("Musical Plays of Bock and Harnick," 158). The *Times* first announced Prince's involvement in October (Sam Zolotow, "Comedienne Sets Directing Debut," *New York Times*, 3 October 1962).

10. Kelly, "Musical Plays of Bock and Harnick," 159.

11. The inspiration for *Silk Stockings*, *Ninotchka* (1939)—another Lubitsch film—was an original story by Melchior Lengyel; the original source for the film *Destry Rides Again* (1939) is Max Brand's novel of the same name; and *Lili* (1953), the film that inspired *Carnival!*, is based on a published story by Paul Gallico. See Mast, *Can't Help Singin',* 296.

12. Bock, Harnick, and Masteroff, interviewed by Peter Filichia, 28 April 1994.

13. Abbott was said to be "weighing" the invitation in September (Sam Zolotow, "Guthrie to Help Theater on Coast," *New York Times*, 7 September 1962), and in October his participation was described as "likely" (Sam Zolotow, "Comedienne Sets Directing Debut," *New York Times*, 3 October 1962).

14. Ilson, *Harold Prince*, 84.

15. Ilson, *Harold Prince*, 69–73, 82.

16. Prince, *Contradictions*, 99; Ilson, *Harold Prince*, 84.

17. Ilson, *Harold Prince*, 84.

18. Frank Kelly presents a valuable comparison of sources in "Musical Plays of Bock and Harnick," 153-158.

19. A new version of *Parfumerie* copyrighted in 2007 includes a number of changes in László's original script, most significantly an ending that is very much like Raphaelson's. E. P. Dowdall, a nephew of László, made the adaptation. The American premiere of this version (under the title *The Perfume Shop*) took place in December 2009, by the Asolo Repertory Theater in Sarasota, Florida.

20. In Raphaelson's screenplay the female lead is named Klara, the older clerk is Pirovitch, and the delivery boy is Pepi. Other names in Masteroff's script are the same as Raphaelson (Ilona) or similar (Maraczek/Matuschek). The name for the male lead is different in all three versions (Bela Horvath in László, Alfred Kralik in Raphaelson, Georg Nowack in Masteroff).

21. Downer, *The American Theater*, 161. See also Kasha and Hirschhorn, *Notes on Broadway*, 160; Bryer and Davison, *Art of the American Musical*, 84; Harnick, "Which Comes First, Words or Music?," 11–12.

22. Masteroff's first draft of Act 1 and one scene from Act 2 are kept in the Bock Papers, box 30, folder 27. An earlier rough outline of the story, dated January 24, 1962, is in box 30, folder 22.

23. Cioffi, "The Men Who Write the Shows," II:57.

24. This refrain appears on pages 12, 14, 19, and 37 of the first act in Masteroff's first draft (Bock Papers, box 30, folder 27).

25. In Act 1, pages 5 (twice), 6, and 8; in Act 2, page 40; and in Act 3, pages 13, 14 (twice), and 15.

26. Bock, Harnick, and Masteroff, interviewed by Peter Filichia, 28 April 1994.

27. From scene 2 of Masteroff's original Act 1, pages 1–18 (Bock Papers, box 30, folder 27); emphases original.

28. *She Loves Me*, 33.

29. From Masteroff's original Act 1, pages 1–42 (Bock Papers, box 30, folder 27); emphasis original. Frank Kelly traces this monologue to a passage from the first act of *Parfumerie* ("Musical Plays of Bock and Harnick," 184).

30. *She Loves Me*, 47.

31. Bock, Harnick, and Masteroff, interviewed by Peter Filichia, 28 April 1994.

32. Bock, Harnick, and Cook, interviewed by Craig Zadan, December 1979.

33. Kasha and Hirschhorn, *Notes on Broadway*, 160.

34. Bock, Harnick, and Cook, interviewed by Craig Zadan, December 1979.

35. Mordden, *Open a New Window*, 66.

36. Simon, "Loving *She Loves Me*," 58. The label has been incorrectly attributed to William A. Henry III in *Time* (6/21/93), who actually called it a "perfect revival."

37. Bock Papers, box 9, folder 21.

38. Gottlieb, *Funny, It Doesn't Sound Jewish*, 88.

39. See Bellman, "Toward a Lexicon for the *Style hongrois*"; and Bellman, *The* Style Hongrois *in the Music of Western Europe*. Bellman does not discuss chromatic turns extensively, but many of his examples contain them.

40. Ewen, *Composers for the American Musical Theater*, 230.

41. Kasha and Hirschhorn, *Notes on Broadway*, 31.

42. Bellman, *The* Style Hongrois *in the Music of Western Europe*, 121.

43. Bellman, *The* Style Hongrois *in the Music of Western Europe*, 121; Pethö, "Style Hongrois," 206.

44. *She Loves Me*, 13. For the Broadway revival in 1993 the program did specify that the story was set in Budapest in 1934.

45. Bock, Harnick, and Cook, interviewed by Craig Zadan, December 1979.

46. Bock Papers, box 30, folder 28.

47. Bock, Harnick, and Masteroff, interviewed by Peter Filichia, 28 April 1994.

48. Bock, Harnick, and Masteroff, interviewed by Peter Filichia, 28 April 1994.

49. "The Touch of Magic" score is in the Bock Papers, box 10, folder 13; the lyric sheet is box 30, folder 12. The monologue is on page 91 of the published libretto.

50. Bock, Harnick, and Masteroff, interviewed by Peter Filichia, 28 April 1994. See also Cioffi, "The Men Who Write the Shows," II:57.

51. "Hello Love": Bock Papers, box 9, folder 10 (score), and box 29, folder 21 (lyric sheet). "Christmas Eve": box 9, folder 3 (score), and box 29, folder 17 (lyrics).

52. Bock, Harnick, and Masteroff, interviewed by Peter Filichia, 28 April 1994. In 2000 Sondheim included "Tell Me I Look Nice" in his list of "Songs I Wish I'd Written (At Least in Part)" (Frank Rich, "Conversations With Sondheim," *New York Times Magazine*, 12 March 2000, 40). The score for "Tell Me I Look Nice" is in the Bock Papers, box 10, folder 9 (score), and box 30, folder 9 (lyrics).

53. Bock Papers, box 10, folder 1.

54. Bock Papers, box 9, folder 18 (score), and box 30, folder 1 (lyrics).

55. Bock, Harnick, and Masteroff, interviewed by Peter Filichia, 28 April 1994.

56. Kasha and Hirschhorn, *Notes on Broadway*, 160–162; Cioffi, "The Men Who Write the Shows," II:58.

57. Kerr was not amused by the story or by the "sort of musical number that goes out of its way to peddle plot information." He was no stranger to the lonely dissent,

having previously expressed firm reservations about critically acclaimed classics such as *The Most Happy Fella* (1956) and *West Side Story* (1957).

58. Prince, *Contradictions*, 99–100.

59. "She Loves Me! She Loves Me!," *New York Post*, 11 June 1993.

60. Edward Sothern Hipp, "She Loves Me," *Newark Evening News*, 19 January 1964.

61. Prince, *Contradictions*, 101–102.

62. Bock, Harnick, and Masteroff, interviewed by Peter Filichia, 28 April 1994.

63. Prince, *Contradictions*, 102.

64. Prince, *Contradictions*, 100.

65. Bock, Harnick, and Masteroff, interviewed by Peter Filichia, 28 April 1994.

66. Bock, Harnick, and Masteroff, interviewed by Peter Filichia, 28 April 1994.

67. Avery Corman, "Curtain Call for the 'Ice Cream' Team," *New York Times*, 3 October 1993.

68. Avery Corman, "Curtain Call for the 'Ice Cream' Team," *New York Times*, 3 October 1993.

69. Matt Wolf, "Bugged by the Beatles No Longer," *New York Times*, 4 July 1994.

70. A. H. Weiler, "Movies—From Joyce to Zola," *New York Times*, 1 October 1967.

71. Bock Papers, box 32, folder 4.

72. Bock Papers, box 30, folder 30.

73. Bock Papers, box 30, folder 32. Masteroff, interviewed by Philip Lambert, 11 June 2009. Bock and Harnick also do not recall who wrote the version with the new songs.

74. The Edwards script is in the Bock Papers, box 31, folder 1.

75. Details were announced in *Variety* on August 6, 1969.

76. Bock, Harnick, and Masteroff, interviewed by Peter Filichia, 28 April 1994. See also Cioffi, "The Men Who Write the Shows," II:59.

77. *Variety*, 22 October 1969.

78. Bock, Harnick, and Masteroff, interviewed by Peter Filichia, 28 April 1994.

79. Harnick, interviewed by Robert Armin, 16 December 2002.

80. Bock, Harnick, and Masteroff, interviewed by Peter Filichia, 28 April 1994. The verse was included in the published vocal selections from the score (Times Square Music, 1963). On Bock's original tape of song ideas this verse and chorus were consecutive but separate numbers (Harnick Papers [New York], box 6, folder 137).

81. Prince, *Contradictions*, 99.

82. Bock, Harnick, and Masteroff, interviewed by Peter Filichia, 28 April 1994.

83. Scores for the songs are in the Bock Papers, box 12, folders 17–24; lyric sheets are in box 33, folder 5. Some of the same materials are also preserved in the Harnick Papers (Wisconsin), box 3, folders 1–4. An original cast album of the show includes recordings of all but two of the Bock–Harnick songs (see Appendix B).

84. Kelly, "Musical Plays of Bock and Harnick," 211.

85. Thomas Thompson, "A Century of Show Biz with Wall-to-Wall Girls," *Life*, 22 May 1964.

86. Bock Papers, box 12, folder 22.

87. The show opened in previews when the World's Fair began on April 22. Martin Tolchin, "Troubles Plague Two Pavilion Shows," *New York Times*, 28 April 1964.

88. Samuel, *The End of the Innocence*, 47.

CHAPTER 6: TRADITION

1. "Williams, Miller Works are Best of This Century," *Washington Times*, 25 December 1999. *Fiddler* was preceded on the list by (in ranking order) *Oklahoma!*, *West Side Story*, *Guys and Dolls/Show Boat* (tie), *A Chorus Line*, *Cabaret*, *My Fair Lady*, and *Porgy and Bess*.

2. Altman, *Making of a Musical*, 22; *Variety*, 7/29/64.

3. Stone, "Landmark Symposium," 21.

4. Bock Papers, box 23, folder 11.

5. Stone, "Landmark Symposium," 11.

6. Prince, *Contradictions*, 98; Altman, *Making of a Musical*, 21–22. Bock and Harnick have recalled later discussions in which Jerome Robbins was proposed as director, but have not independently confirmed Prince's recollection about this meeting in early 1962 (see Stone, "Landmark Symposium," 15–17).

7. Wolitz, "Americanization of Tevye," 520. See also Weitzner, *Sholem Aleichem in the Theater*, 100–102.

8. Sam Zolotow, "Aleichem Stories Inspire a Musical," *New York Times*, 20 August 1962.

9. Stewart, *Broadway Musicals*, 186.

10. Stewart, *Broadway Musicals*, 186. More recently, an adaptation by Grigory Gorin has been extremely popular for more than two decades in Kiev, Ukraine, featuring Bohdan Stupka as Tevye ("*Tevye* Still Hot in Ukraine," *Ukrainian Weekly*, 4 December 2005).

11. These are the titles as given in the 1949 English translation by Frances Butwin from which the *Fiddler* team worked (Aleichem, *Tevye's Daughters*, 20–37, 53–68, 93–108, 257–272). The language in this translation is "overly sentimentalized and folksy," writes Seth L. Wolitz ("Americanization of Tevye," 523), and was superseded by a more scholarly version by Hillel Halkin in 1987 (titled *Tevye the Dairyman and the Railroad Stories*). A third English translation, by Aliza Shevrin, appeared in 2009, published by Penguin Classics to celebrate the sesquicentennial of Aleichem's birth (*Tevye the Dairyman and Motl the Cantor's Son*).

12. Stone, "Landmark Symposium," 12.

13. Aleichem, *Tevye's Daughters*, 271.

14. Frank Kelly suggests that Stein may have gotten ideas for Yente from the character of Yenta the Poultrywoman in Aleichem's story "The Little Pot" (Kelly, "Musical Plays of Bock and Harnick," 218). "The Little Pot" appears in *Tevye's Daughters*, 180–191.

15. Zborowski and Herzog, *Life Is With People*. Harnick mentioned this source, for example, in a television program broadcast shortly after the show premiered, on 18 October 1964.

16. See Altman, *Making of a Musical*, 40; Wolitz, "Americanization of Tevye," 526–527; Swain, *Broadway Musical*, 279–281; Knapp, *Formation*, 217–218.

17. *Fiddler on the Roof*, 2.

18. Bock's copies of these early scripts are archived in the Bock Papers, box 21, folders 1, 4, 5, and 6. Stein's copies are in the Stein Papers, box 26, folders 2–7, and box 27, folder 1–3.

19. Stone, "Landmark Symposium," 19.

20. *Fiddler on the Roof*, 48.

21. Aleichem, *The Old Country*, 21–41; Aleichem, *Tevye's Daughters*, 1–15.

22. Aleichem, *Tevye's Daughters*, 58.

23. Bock Papers, Box 21, folder 1, page 1-3-20; Stein Papers, box 26, folder 2.

24. Perl, *Tevya and His Daughters*, 31. Hodel's suitor is named Feferal in Aleichem and Perl.

25. Bock Papers, Box 21, folder 4, pages 1-10-68 and 1-10-69; Stein Papers, box 26, folder 6. This is undoubtedly the version they showed to Harold Prince in early 1962, when he urged them to pursue the project only if Jerome Robbins could direct.

26. *Fiddler on the Roof*, 61.

27. Wolitz, "Americanization of Tevye," 524, 527, 530.

28. Jowitt, *Jerome Robbins*, 351; Sam Zolotow, "Robbins to Direct 'Tevye,' a Musical," *New York Times*, 29 August 1963.

29. Stone, "Landmark Symposium," 17.

30. Whitfield, "Fiddling with Sholem Aleichem," 7.

31. Prince, *Contradictions*, 104–105; Altman, *Making of a Musical*, 22; Stone, "Landmark Symposium," 16–18. The *New York Times* announced Coe's departure on July 3, 1964 (Sam Zolotow, "Stage's 'Hamlet' Becomes a Film").

32. Jowitt, *Jerome Robbins*, 353.

33. Altman, *Making of a Musical*, 42.

34. Stone, "Landmark Symposium," 17. Robbins refers to a popular radio and television serial, *The Rise of the Goldbergs*, later just *The Goldbergs*, about the lives and travails of a Jewish family living in a New York tenement. The show was broadcast in various forms from the late 1920s to the mid-1950s.

35. The version of the script in box 21, folder 1 of the Bock Papers begins with the encounter between Tevye and Perchik. The version in box 21, folder 4 opens with the daughters and their Sabbath preparations.

36. This is explained by the creators in Stone, "Landmark Symposium," 19.

37. Zborowski and Herzog, *Life Is With People*, 292.

38. Zborowski and Herzog, *Life Is With People*, 130, 291.

39. Zborowski and Herzog, *Life Is With People*, 88, 349 (sons); 347 (daughters); 271 (matchmaker); 211 (beggar); 168 (rabbi).

40. Knapp, *Formation*, 221.

41. The two younger daughters also appear in some of the original stories (*Tevye's Daughters*, 145-161 ["Shprintze"]; 203–224 ["Tevye Goes to Palestine"]; 257-272 ["Get Thee Out"]).

42. See Stone, "Landmark Symposium," 13, and Bock Papers, box 23, folder 11.

43. Stone, "Landmark Symposium," 13.

44. Bock's reference to Igor Moiseyev, the great Russian dancer-choreographer, triggers a number of musical comparisons and associations in the next section of this chapter.

45. Bock Papers, box 21, folder 4. Stein Papers, box 26, folder 6.

46. Stone, "Landmark Symposium," 13.

47. Bock: "'We Haven't Missed a Sabbath Yet' [alternatively titled 'We've Never Missed a Sabbath Yet'] was our first shot at the opening number. Little did we realize

that inherent in it (3rd section), we had dropped a seed that would eventually blossom into 'Tradition'" (liner notes to Columbia Broadway Masterworks SK-89546, p. 11).

48. Stone, "Landmark Symposium," 14.

49. That was his recollection when he introduced the song during his first appearance in the "Lyrics and Lyricists" series at the 92nd Street Y in New York on 14 February 1971. The performance was released on LP as *An Evening With Sheldon Harnick* (see Appendix B).

50. See Stone, "Landmark Symposium," 24; Altman, *Making of a Musical*, 54; and Cioffi, "The Men Who Write the Shows," II:60.

51. Cioffi, "The Men Who Write the Shows," II:59.

52. "Messiah" appears on *Lost in Boston II*, "Sewing Machine" on *Lost in Boston I*. Harnick's appearances in the "Lyrics and Lyricists" series are preserved in *An Evening With Sheldon Harnick* and *A Visit With Sheldon Harnick*. For details, see Appendix B.

53. Cioffi, "The Men Who Write the Shows," II:59.

54. See Stone, "Landmark Symposium," 20; and Altman, *Making of a Musical*, 36.

55. As explained in Altman, *Making of a Musical*, 51–52. "Now I Have Everything" was revised slightly when they made the switch (Cioffi, "The Men Who Write the Shows," II:59).

56. Stone, "Landmark Symposium," 20. See also Cioffi, "The Men Who Write the Shows," II:60.

57. "American Musical Theater: Jerry Bock and Sheldon Harnick Discuss *Fiddler on the Roof*" (television broadcast, WCBS-TV, 18 October 1964).

58. This is the melodic pattern that Leonard Bernstein used to demonstrate the "infinite variety of music" in a 1959 lecture-demonstration (Bernstein, *Infinite Variety*, 34–46).

59. The actual interval of a melody played on a shofar, the ram's horn used as a call for gathering and repentance in Jewish services, varies with different instruments but ranges from a fourth to a sixth (Jeremy Montagu, "Shofar," *Grove Music Online*).

60. Joseph Swain, on the other hand, finds in the monologues a "gross awkwardness in the handling of recitative texture." He is disenchanted because the counterclockwise fifths progression "in classical tradition is associated with declining, not rising musical tension," and he detects no sense of transformation when "the music that vainly expresses [Tevye's] outrage must also express his tenderness" (Swain, *Broadway Musical*, 286).

61. Laufe, *Broadway's Greatest Musicals*, 337.

62. Knapp, *Formation*, 223.

63. Swain, *Broadway Musical*, 268.

64. Bock and Harnick, interviewed by Terry Gross, 21 June 2004 (here quoting Harnick). See also Altman, *Making of a Musical*, 118.

65. Jones, *Our Musicals, Ourselves*, 211. See also Raphael, "From Marjorie to Tevya," 70.

66. Hamm, *Irving Berlin's Early Songs*, I:xxxiv.

67. See Hamm, *Irving Berlin: Songs from the Melting Pot*, 40–46.

68. Jeffrey Magee discusses the tonal structure of these songs in Magee, "Irving Berlin's 'Blue Skies,'" 547–548. See also Slobin, *Tenement Songs*, 182.

69. Gottlieb, *Funny, It Doesn't Sound Jewish*, 107. His survey of Yingish songs appears on pages 101–116.

70. Killick, "Music as Ethnic Marker," 189, 190.

71. Idelsohn, "Features of Jewish Sacred Folk Song," 22; Idelsohn, "Musical Characteristics of East-European Jewish Folk-Song," 636.

72. As noted by Swain, *Broadway Musical*, 272.

73. See Swain, *Broadway Musical*, 276.

74. See Beregovski, "Jewish Folk Songs," 294–296; Idelsohn, *Jewish Music in Its Historical Development*, 72–89; Sapoznik, *Compleat Klezmer*, 20–22.

75. See Beregovski, "Altered Dorian Scale"; Beregovski, "Jewish Folk Songs"; Idelsohn, "Features of Jewish Sacred Folk Song"; Idelsohn, *Jewish Music in Its Historical Development*; Idelsohn, "Musical Characteristics of East-European Jewish Folk-Song"; Sapoznik, *Compleat Klezmer*; Slobin, "Evolution of a Musical Symbol"; Slobin, *Tenement Songs*; Werner, "Jewish Music." Manuel, "Modal Harmony," notes interesting similarities between these modes and scales from other regions.

76. See Beregovski, "Altered Dorian Scale"; Idelsohn, "Features of Jewish Sacred Folk Song," 23; Idelsohn, "Musical Characteristics of East-European Jewish Folk-Song," 635–636; Sapoznik, *Compleat Klezmer*, 21–22.

77. Werner, "Jewish Music"; Killick, "Music as Ethnic Marker," 190.

78. Altman, *Making of a Musical*, 100. For more information about Hasidic music of this type see Koskoff, "Contemporary Nigun Composition," and Schleifer, "Jewish Liturgical Music." Frank Kelly ("Musical Plays of Bock and Harnick," 245) discusses the connection between this song and Aleichem's "The Bubble Bursts" (*Tevye's Daughters*, 3, 9–10).

79. Bock and Harnick, interviewed by Terry Gross, 21 June 2004.

80. Altman, *Making of a Musical*, 35. See also Kasha and Hirschhorn, *Notes on Broadway*, 31.

81. Bock, interviewed by Harold Flender, 11 February 1971.

82. Bock and Harnick, interviewed by Terry Gross, 21 June 2004.

83. Gottlieb, *Funny, It Doesn't Sound Jewish*, 49.

84. Gottlieb, *Funny, It Doesn't Sound Jewish*, 65, 69.

85. Mostel, *170 Years of Show Business*, 165.

86. Margo Lemberger, "A Musical Milkman's Multi-Culti Appeal: 'Sunrise, Sunset' Glows in El Paso as 'Fiddler' Heads Back to Broadway" (*Forward*, 5 January 2001).

87. Bock, interviewed by Harold Flender, 11 February 1971.

88. Columbia Broadway Masterworks SK-89546 (CD, 2001), track 16.

89. Bikel's performance earned him a Tony nomination in 1960. Harnick and Bikel are distant cousins (Harnick, interviewed by Harold Flender, 22 February 1971).

90. Mlotek, *Mir Trogn a Gezang*, 211.

91. Knapp, *Formation*, 223–224.

92. Columbia Broadway Masterworks SK-89546 (CD, 2001), tracks 14–17.

93. Altman, *Making of a Musical*, 71, 120; Stone, "Landmark Symposium," 18; Prince, *Contradictions*, 105; Harnick, interviewed by Harold Flender, 1 March 1971; Cioffi, "The Men Who Write the Shows," II:60; Mostel, *170 Years of Show Business*, 165.

94. Sainer, *Zero Dances*, 162–164; Jowitt, *Jerome Robbins*, 354. The program aired on December 14, 1959.

95. Altman, *Making of a Musical*, 71–85.

96. Kelly, "Musical Plays of Bock and Harnick," 233.

97. Mostel, *170 Years of Show Business*, 167.

98. Stone, "Landmark Symposium," 22 (quoting Stein). Altman, *Making of a Musical*, 9.

99. See Stone, "Landmark Symposium," 22–23.

100. Stone, "Landmark Symposium," 23.

101. These final modifications are explained in Altman, *Making of a Musical*, 54, 65–66; and Stone, "Landmark Symposium," 14.

102. Bock, interviewed by Harold Flender, 11 February 1971.

103. Stone, "Landmark Symposium," 21.

104. Altman, *Making of a Musical*, 118. Emphasis original.

105. See Stone, "Landmark Symposium," 21; Altman, *Making of a Musical*, 116–118; Brown, *Zero Mostel*, 230–231; Sainer, *Zero Dances*, 162–164; Bryer and Davison, *Art of the American Musical*, 91–92.

106. Harnick, interviewed by Harold Flender, 1 March 1971.

107. Stewart, *Broadway Musicals*, 187.

108. Altman, *Making of a Musical*, 120; Brown, *Zero Mostel*, 222.

109. Harnick, in a panel discussion marking the publication of Jim Brochu's play about Zero Mostel, *Zero Hour*, held at a Barnes and Noble in Manhattan on 9 December 2009.

110. Altman, *Making of a Musical*, 119. See also Prince, *Contradictions*, 106.

111. See Altman, *Making of a Musical*, 62, 120; Stone, "Landmark Symposium," 26; Brown, *Zero Mostel*, 243–244.

112. Stone, "Landmark Symposium," 27.

113. A videorecording of a performance from this run is preserved in the Theater on Film and Tape Archive at the New York Public Library of the Performing Arts. Mostel's rendering of "If I Were a Rich Man," from the 1971 Tony Awards ceremony, can be seen on the video compilation *Broadway's Lost Treasures* (VHS/DVD, Acorn Media, 2003).

114. Bikel's account of this experience appears in his autobiography *Theo*, 321–354.

115. Altman, *Making of a Musical*, 161.

116. Cioffi, "The Men Who Write the Shows," II:61; Brett M. Rhyne, "'Fiddler on the Roof' Lyricist Featured in New Musical," *Jewish Journal*, 28 February 2003.

117. The production of this musical, by mostly African-American and Hispanic students in a school with a mostly Jewish teaching staff, produced controversy and conflict during a period of great turmoil in the city and in the school system. The eventual result was a triumph of political maneuvering and community-building, and a singular theatrical accomplishment.

118. Altman, *Making of a Musical*, 183. Norman Jewison, interviewed by Scott Simon, 13 October 2001.

119. Brett M. Rhyne, "'Fiddler on the Roof' Lyricist Featured in New Musical," *Jewish Journal*, 28 February 2003. Stone, "Landmark Symposium," 27.

120. In the audio commentary for the Collector's Edition of the DVD (2007).

121. Altman, *Making of a Musical*, 184.

122. Paul Michael Glaser's recording of "Any Day Now," accompanied by John Williams's orchestration, is included on disc 2 of the Collector's Edition of the DVD (2007), along with Harnick's explanation of the song's origins.

123. Altman, *Making of a Musical*, 201.

124. Pauline Kael, "A Bagel with a Bite Out of It," *New Yorker*, 13 November 1971. Emphasis original.

125. Robert Brustein, "Fiddling While Talent Burns," *New Republic*, 17 October 1964, 31–32.

126. Irving Howe, "Tevye on Broadway," *Commentary* 38/5 (Nov. 1964): 73–75.

127. See, for example, Ozick, "Sholem Aleichem's Revolution," and Wisse, *Modern Jewish Canon*.

128. Thane Rosenbaum, "A Legacy Cut Loose," *Los Angeles Times*, 15 February 2004.

129. "*Shtetl* Shock: L. A. Times Hits 'Roof'; Actress Hits the Road," *New York Post*, 18 February 2004.

130. Ben Brantley, "A Cozy Little McShtetl," *New York Times*, 27 February 2004.

131. Whitfield, "Fiddling with Sholem Aleichem," 120.

132. Ami Eden, "Fiddling With Tradition: Does Musical Misstep?," *Forward*, 12 March 2004.

133. In 2009 Theodore Bikel was doing something close to what Stein suggests in his one-man show *Sholem Aleichem: Laughter Through Tears*.

134. Bock Papers, box 20, folder 11. At the top of the page Bock indicated that the letter was "written, but not mailed (unfortunately!) to NY Post critic."

135. John Heilpern, "New-Ish But Still Jew-Ish: Fiddler Breaks Tradition," *New York Observer*, 7 March 2004.

136. Charles Isherwood, "Fiddled Fiddler," *The Times (London)*, 8 March 2004. Isherwood could have also pointed out that the role of Captain Von Trapp in *The Sound of Music*, the military officer whose services are so coveted by the Nazis, was originated on Broadway by an actor-singer closely identified with Jewish culture, Theodore Bikel. Bikel had also played a World-War-II-era officer on a German U-boat (in the 1957 film *The Enemy Below*) and a southern sheriff (in the 1958 film *The Defiant Ones*, for which he received an Oscar nomination).

137. Alisa Solomon, "Fiddling with Fiddler: Can the Broadway Revival of Everyone's Favorite Jewish Musical Ignore Today's Radically Different Cultural Context?," *Village Voice*, 21–27 January 2004.

138. Alisa Solomon, Part I: "How *Fiddler* Became Folklore," *Forward*, 1 September 2006; Part II: "Tevye, Today and Beyond," *Forward*, 8 September 2006.

139. Bock Papers, box 4, folder 14 (score); box 20, folder 48 (lyrics).

140. Ben Brantley in the *Times* (10/14/05): "Her accent trots the globe, through countries real and imagined. It is variously Irish, Yiddish, Long Island-ish and, for big dramatic moments, crisp and round in the style of introduction-to-theater students."

141. John Lahr, "*Fiddler on the Roof* and *Bridge and Tunnel*," *New Yorker*, 8 March 2004.

142. Steyn, *Broadway Babies Say Goodnight*, 85.

143. Grant, *Rise and Fall*, 80; Engel, *Words with Music*, 59.

CHAPTER 7: HERE IN EDEN

1. Wolitz, "Americanization of Tevye," 522–523.
2. Bock, interviewed by Nancy Sureck, 12 November 2002.
3. http://www.mtishows.com/show_detail.asp?showid=000036
4. Louis Calta, "Show on Holmes Due Here Feb. 2," *New York Times*, 5 May 1962. Stewart, *Broadway Musicals*, 44.
5. Cioffi, "The Men Who Write the Shows," III:58; Harnick, interview with Nancy Sureck, 16 January 2003.
6. Prince, *Contradictions*, 113–116; Ilson, *Harold Prince*, 109–118.
7. Bock and Harnick's contributions were acknowledged in *Variety* (2/24/65). See also Gates, "Broadway's Prince Charming," 108.
8. The show was revived in 2001 by the York Theater Company in New York, featuring a revised libretto and the score as it stood before Bock and Harnick got involved (Stewart, *Broadway Musicals*, 45).
9. The earlier version of the libretto is in the Bock Papers, box 19, folder 9 (dated November 1964).
10. The original cast recording of the show includes "I'm in London Again," while the published libretto has only the lyrics for "Buffalo Belle."
11. Harnick, interviewed by Robert Armin, 16 December 2002.
12. Bock Papers, box 6, folder 7.
13. Bock Papers, box 16, folders 5 and 6; box 35, folder 1.
14. See <http://www.tv.com/abc-stage-67/show/13585/episode_guide.html>. Each show in the series is available for viewing at the Paley Center for Media in New York.
15. Raby, *Oscar Wilde*, 51.
16. Wilde, *Canterville Ghost*, 43.
17. Bock Papers, box 34, folder 5.
18. New recordings of these two songs were included in a compilation album, *Prime-Time Musicals* (see Appendix B).
19. Bock Papers, box 34, folder 4.
20. Wilde, *Canterville Ghost*, 8.
21. Wilde, *Canterville Ghost*, 11–12.
22. Wilde, *Canterville Ghost*, 15–16.
23. Bock Papers, box 14, folder 13.
24. Wilde, *Canterville Ghost*, 13.
25. Bock Papers, box 14, folder 14.
26. Harnick, interviewed by Robert Armin, 16 December 2002.
27. Lewis Funke, "*Fiddler*'s Men at Work," *New York Times*, 13 December 1964.
28. Kasha and Hirschhorn, *Notes on Broadway*, 32.
29. Lewis Funke, "*Fiddler*'s Men at Work," *New York Times*, 13 December 1964.
30. Ostrow, *A Producer's Broadway Journey*, 87.
31. Kasha and Hirschhorn, *Notes on Broadway*, 164.
32. Lewis Funke, "The Rialto: Guild Gets Going," *New York Times*, 27 June 1965; Kelly, "Musical Plays of Bock and Harnick," 284; Ostrow, *Present at the Creation*, 35; Bock Papers, Box 19, folder 2.

33. Lewis Funke, "The Rialto: Guild Gets Going," *New York Times*, 27 June 1965.

34. Cioffi, "The Men Who Write the Shows," III:59.

35. Lewis Funke, "The Rialto: Guild Gets Going," *New York Times*, 27 June 1965.

36. The extant sketches and drafts for the Hawthorne treatment are in the Harnick Papers (Wisconsin), box 7, folder 7, and in the Bock Papers, box 1, folder 33, and box 18, folders 29 and 35.

37. Harnick, "Which Comes First, Words or Music?," 13; Harnick, interviewed by John von Soosten and Howard Sherman, November 2006.

38. Kelly, "Musical Plays of Bock and Harnick," 289. See also Harnick, interviewed by Nancy Sureck, 16 January 2003.

39. Harnick, "Which Comes First, Words or Music?," 13; emphasis original.

40. Harnick, interviewed by John von Soosten and Howard Sherman, November 2006.

41. Kelly, "Musical Plays of Bock and Harnick," 285; Thomas O'Connor, "Lyricist Optimistic on Musicals," *Orange County Register*, 10 December 1989.

42. Ostrow, *Present at the Creation*, 36. Bock and Harnick made a demo tape of their adaptation of Friedman's "Show Biz Connections," thinking that they might try to pair it with a companion piece at some point, but "never really made the effort." The piece is not represented at all in any of the archives; Harnick believes that the music was never notated.

43. Kelly, "Musical Plays of Bock and Harnick," 286; Stewart, *Broadway Musicals*, 35.

44. Kasha and Hirschhorn, *Notes on Broadway*, 165.

45. Kasha and Hirschhorn, *Notes on Broadway*, 164.

46. Ostrow, *Present at the Creation*, 37–38.

47. Twain, *The Diaries of Adam and Eve*, Afterword: 2, 6. *Adam* was first published in a souvenir booklet of the 1893 Buffalo Pan-American Exposition, then as a separate book in 1904. *Eve* first appeared in *Harper's Monthly* in 1905 and as a book in 1906.

48. Twain, *The Diaries of Adam and Eve*, Eve: 29.

49. Twain, *The Diaries of Adam and Eve*, Eve: 5.

50. *The Apple Tree*, 33. This comes from Twain, *The Diaries of Adam and Eve*, Adam: 53.

51. Twain, *The Diaries of Adam and Eve*, Eve: 109.

52. "Useful" is in the Bock Papers, box 1, folder 11.

53. Kelly, "Musical Plays of Bock and Harnick," 289.

54. *The Apple Tree*, 14.

55. Twain, *The Diaries of Adam and Eve*, Eve: 43, 45. Harnick's original lyric for the song was "Let's Pretend," apparently for Eve to sing in an attempt to bring Adam closer (Harnick Papers [New York], box 6, folder 137).

56. Twain, *The Diaries of Adam and Eve*, Adam: 41.

57. In earlier versions of the show, "Beautiful, Beautiful World" was used at this point as an abbreviated reprise, and it is this version that was included in the published libretto (p. 32). However, the complete song was included in the published vocal score and was performed in the original cast recording, in the 2005 Encores! production of the show, and in the Broadway revival in 2006.

58. Twain, *The Diaries of Adam and Eve*, Adam: 55, 57, 63, 65.

59. *The Apple Tree*, 39.

60. Twain, *The Diaries of Adam and Eve*, Eve: 95. Ideas for the lyric appear throughout pages 95–105 of Twain's Eve diary.

61. Other instances of the these types of chromatic descents in Bock's music include the endings of "Jacques D'Iraque" and "Too Close for Comfort" from *Mr. Wonderful*, the inner voice that later becomes one part in a contrapuntal duet in "A Relatively Simple Affair" from *The Body Beautiful*, the ending of "Gentleman Jimmy" from *Fiorello!*, and the "letter" portion of "Ice Cream" from *She Loves Me*.

62. Alvin Klein, "Critics Notebook: On Musicals," *New York Times*, 17 October 1999.

63. Ostrow, *A Producer's Broadway Journey*, 89. Marc Kudisch did not follow this tradition in the 2006 Broadway revival.

64. Kelly, "Musical Plays of Bock and Harnick," 289.

65. Gottlieb, *Funny, It Doesn't Sound Jewish*. Gottlieb's best-known example of an American popular song using the *Adonai malach* mode is probably Harry Warren and Mack Gordon's "At Last" (p. 130).

66. Bock Papers, box 1, folder 19, and box 18, folder 23; Harnick Papers (New York), box 6, folder 137.

67. Later in the song ("So I will give it to you / And when I give it to you . . .") the lament bass line includes both the true leading tone and the flatted seventh and is harmonized differently.

68. Ostrow, *Present at the Creation*, 40. The film was made by Richard Williams, who later directed the animation for the film *Who Framed Roger Rabbit?* (1988).

69. Harnick, interviewed by John von Soosten and Howard Sherman, November 2006.

70. "I'm Lost" was originally written for the treatment of the Capote story, "Among the Paths to Eden" (Cioffi, "The Men Who Write the Shows," III:60). It is included in the published vocal selections from the show (New York Times Music Corp., 1966) and was recorded on the *Lost in Boston II* CD (see Appendix B).

71. Mordden, *Open a New Window*, 234.

72. Kasha and Hirschhorn, *Notes on Broadway*, 165.

73. Mordden, *Open a New Window*, 234.

74. Stuart W. Little, *New York Herald Tribune*, 18 June 1965.

75. Sam Zolotow, "Musical to Rely on Fellini Movie," *New York Times*, 8 July 1965.

76. A letter from screenwriter Terry Shenk, dated April 16, 1969, and a detailed outline of a possible film adaptation of *The Apple Tree* are filed in the Bock Papers, box 19, folder 4.

77. Kasha and Hirschhorn, *Notes on Broadway*, 165. Harris's brilliance can be witnessed on the video compilation *Broadway's Lost Treasures* (VHS/DVD, Acorn Media, 2003), in a fully costumed and staged performance of "Oh, To Be a Movie Star" and "Gorgeous" from the 1967 Tony Awards ceremony.

78. Alvin Klein, "Critics Notebook: On Musicals," *New York Times*, 17 October 1999.

79. Jesse Green, "She Sings! She Acts! She Prays!," *New York Times*, 3 December 2006.

80. Harnick, interviewed by John von Soosten and Howard Sherman, November 2006.

81. John Lahr, "Lost in Paradise," *New Yorker*, 25 December 2006.

1. Sheldon Harnick, "Another Jewish Show?," in the *Rothschilds* souvenir program.

2. *The Observer*, 14 February 1965; Sam Zolotow, "Musical To Treat Nelson's Career," *New York Times*, 21 February 1966.

3. Arden's outline is in the Bock Papers, box 33, folder 12.

4. Ira Peck, "Art, Politics, and John Arden," *New York Times*, 10 April 1966.

5. An index of the recording is in the Bock Papers, box 13, folder 4.

6. The surviving scores are in the Bock Papers, box 13, folders 1–3. Sketches are in box 13, folder 5. A cover letter for a delivery of sheet music from the producers is in the Bock Papers, box 33, folder 9.

7. Bock Papers, box 33, folder 10.

8. Lewin Funke, "The Rialto: Robbins's Lab," *New York Times*, 16 October 1966.

9. *Times of London*, 11 February 1968.

10. Page, *John Arden*, 100; Schiele, *Off-Centre Stages*, 143

11. *New York Times*, 9 November 1968.

12. *New York Times*, 10 March 1968, 13 August 1968.

13. Bock Papers, box 33, folder 9.

14. The award was shared with Patricia Routledge (*Darling of the Day*).

15. Stewart, *Broadway Musicals*, 271.

16. Sam Zolotow, "Circle in the Square Delays Uptown Debut," *New York Times*, 15 August 1968.

17. Mandelbaum, *Not Since Carrie*, 209.

18. Bock Papers, box 6, folder 8.

19. Lockett-Palmer 931306. A live recording of the original show, from a pre-Broadway performance in Boston, was released in 1968 by the Society for the Preservation of Musicals (CO-7751). The published song collection from the show (Warner Brothers Publications, 1994) also includes songs that were cut in tryouts and none by Bock and Harnick.

20. Harnick, interviewed by Harold Flender, 1 March 1971.

21. Harnick, interviewed by Harold Flender, 1 March 1971.

22. Sam Zolotow, "*Heaven Help Us* Chooses Team to Turn Novel Into Musical," *New York Times*, 13 August 1968. Tarr was to make the adaptation.

23. Lewis Funke, "News of the Rialto: Tynan's Elegant Erotica," *New York Times*, 20 October 1968.

24. Paul Hume, "Mini Is What They Are," *Washington Post*, 11 June 1969. The two singers for the premiere, Lois Darling and Adriana Hardy, were accompanied by pianist William Huckaby, clarinetist Don Deroche, and violinist Henry Rubin. The other works on the program were Donizetti's *Rita* and William Goldstein's *The Peddler*.

25. Merion Music, 1973. *Frustration* was performed in New York in 1979 (Encompass Opera), 1981 (Bel Canto Opera), and 1991 (American Chamber Opera Company). The 1979 program also included Strouse's *Satisfaction*.

26. Christopher Davis, *The Producer* (New York: Harper & Row, 1972).

27. Davis, *The Producer*, 161, 164, 165.

28. Davis, *The Producer*, 272–274; Harnick, interview with Harold Flender, 1 March 1971.

29. Harnick, interviewed by Harold Flender, 1 March 1971.

30. *Tenderloin* also has a basis in history, but events and figures are already fictionalized in the original source, Adams's novel.

31. Bock Papers, box 27, folder 29.

32. Bock Papers, box 7, folders 1, 3, 12; box 26, folders 26, 30, 32.

33. Kelly, "Musical Plays of Bock and Harnick," 352.

34. Davis, *The Producer*, 271.

35. As described in Morton, *The Rothschilds*, 16.

36. The actual birth order (and name spelling) of Mayer's sons was: Amschel, Salomon, Nathan, Kalmann, Jacob. Mayer and Gutele Rothschild also had five daughters who are not included in Yellen's narrative (Morton, *The Rothschilds*, 29–30).

37. Details differ of the actual dispersal of the Rothschild sons throughout Europe (Morton, *The Rothschilds*, 36–93).

38. Mel Gussow, "Three Costly Musicals Get Set for Season," *New York Times*, 11 August 1970.

39. Mel Gussow, "Three Costly Musicals Get Set for Season," *New York Times*, 11 August 1970.

40. Harnick, interviewed by Harold Flender, 4 March 1971.

41. Cioffi, "The Men Who Write the Shows," III:61.

42. Davis, *The Producer*, 294; Kelly, "Musical Plays of Bock and Harnick," 360–362.

43. Kelly, "Musical Plays of Bock and Harnick," 353. See Bock Papers, box 7, folder 25; Morton, *The Rothschilds*, 16.

44. Kelly, "Musical Plays of Bock and Harnick," 358. Bock Papers, box 7, folder 24.

45. Bock Papers, box 8, folders 2, 20.

46. Bock Papers, box 8, folder 22.

47. In a pre-Detroit version of the libretto, dated July 1970 (Bock Papers, box 27, folder 27), the finale of Act 1 is the song "Just a Map," a tender ballad in which Gutele expresses melancholy apprehension about the departure of her sons. The vocal score for this song is in the Bock Papers, box 8, folder 1; lyrics are in box 27, folder 4. "Just a Map" has been recorded and released on the second *Lost in Boston* CD (see Appendix B); a complete vocal score appears in *The Sheldon Harnick Songbook* (Warner Brothers, 1996).

48. Bock Papers, box 8, folder 7; box 27, folder 13.

49. Lewis Funke, "*Rothschilds* Held No Kin to *Fiddler*," *New York Times*, 15 October 1970.

50. Bock Papers, box 8, folder 25.

51. Bock Papers, box 7, folder 3.

52. The cello solo shown in Example 8.2 can be heard on the original cast recording (see Appendix B), although it may have been excluded from the score in the original stage production.

53. Bock Papers, box 27, folder 25. Although Bock has always worked closely with his orchestrators, this is a rare instance of extant written instructions (probably because any other such notes remained in the possession of their recipients).

54. Bock Papers, box 27, folder 25.

55. Bock Papers, box 7, folder 3.

56. Bock Papers, box 27, folder 25. Emphases original.

57. Bock Papers, box 8, folders 2, 3, 20.

58. Bock Papers, box 8, folder 14.

59. Bock Papers, box 7, folder 16.

60. In November 1967 Linden replaced Larry Blyden as the Snake/Balladeer/narrator for the final three weeks of the Broadway run of *The Apple Tree*.

61. Bryer and Davison, *Art of the American Musical*, 92.

62. The director of this production was Lonny Price, who had played one of the young sons in the 1972 California tour.

63. Alan Bunce, *Christian Science Monitor*, 26 October 1970; quoted in Solomon, "Family Fortune"; quoted in Degan, "Musical Theater Since World War II," 438; Clive Barnes, *New York Times*, 2 March 1990.

64. Stone, "Landmark Symposium," 14.

65. Lewis Funke, "*Rothschilds* Held No Kin to *Fiddler*," *New York Times*, 15 October 1970.

66. Martin Gottfried, "The Theater," *Women's Wear Daily*, 21 October 1970.

67. Julius Novick, "Rich Jews," *Village Voice*, 5 November 1970.

68. Solomon, "Family Fortune."

69. Elie Wiesel, "Treasured Family Is the Secret Wealth of *The Rothschilds*," *New York Times*, 23 September 1990.

70. The original story is in *Tevye's Daughters*, 16–19. The Yiddish version of *Fiddler* played for a few weeks in Tel Aviv in 1967, after the Hebrew version had played and toured for more than eighteen months (Altman, *Making of a Musical*, 122–133); cast albums were recorded in both Hebrew and Yiddish (see Appendix B). Jan Peerce's album of Jewish folk songs and songs from *Fiddler* also includes "Ven Ich Bin A Rothschild."

71. Warfield, "From *Hair* to *Rent*"; Wollman, *The Theater Will Rock*, 73–119.

72. Kelly, "Musical Plays of Bock and Harnick," 412. Harnick made the remark in a "discussion at Hofstra University" on 28 October 1973.

73. Kelly, "Musical Plays of Bock and Harnick," 412. Bock made the remark in an interview with Kelly on 23 May 1974.

74. Harnick, interviewed by Harold Flender, 1 March 1971.

CHAPTER 9: TOPSY-TURVY

1. Wilk interviewed Bock on August 29, 1971, Harnick on November 6, 1971. Recordings of both interviews are in the collection of the Rodgers and Hammerstein Archive of Recorded Sound, New York Public Library for the Performing Arts. Wilk's comment quoted here appeared in the 1991 expanded edition of his book, which was based on the 1971 interviews and apparently written shortly thereafter (*They're Playing Our Song* [1991], 192). The original 1973 edition of his book does not include a chapter on Bock and Harnick.

2. According to articles in the *New York Times* and documents in their personal archives, Bock and Harnick provided material for Inner Circle shows in 1966, 1969, 1970, 1971, 1972, and 1973. Scores and sketches of most of these efforts are preserved in the Harnick Papers (New York). Also in 1973, on December 14, some of their material was featured in a farewell fete for Mayor Lindsay at the New York State Theater, which was recorded for limited release as *Regards to the Lindsay Years* (see Appendix B). Bock and Harnick's earliest involvement with the music of mayoral politics—not

including *Fiorello!*—was a song "The A. D. Men and the Lindsay Volunteers," written for John Lindsay's Inaugural Ball in 1965 (Harnick Papers [New York], box 3, folder 75 and box 6, folder 117). Harnick discussed these experiences in his interview with Harold Flender on 4 March 1971.

3. Bock Papers, box 33, folders 22–24; Harnick Papers [New York], box 3, folder 84, and box 6, folder 121. The new song, called "He Didn't," listed the many things President Nixon had not done (such as invading Sweden), because, as the last line says, "we'd rather not talk about the things he did!" Bock and Harnick also performed "On the Side of the Angels," with lyrics revised for the political moment (and with vocal contributions from Margery Harnick), and "A Little Tin Box."

4. A photograph published in the *Daily News* on June 18, 1972 shows Bock and Harnick on stage at the Broadway Theater performing material that was "cut from the show" as part of the festivities celebrating their new record (for longest-running Broadway show).

5. Everett Evans, "*Fiddler*'s Enduring Appeal Surprises Creators," *Houston Chronicle*, 26 August 1990; Stephen Holden, "A Hit Songwriter Is About to Become a Cabaret Performer," *New York Times*, 10 April 1990. On the other hand, Bock has said that "There's never been any anger" (*Houston Chronicle*, 16 June 2007).

6. Kasha and Hirschhorn, *Notes on Broadway*, 166.

7. Everett Evans, "Prize-Winning Composer Caters to Young Audience," *Houston Chronicle*, 16 June 2007.

8. Stephen Holden, "A Hit Songwriter Is About to Become a Cabaret Performer," *New York Times*, 10 April 1990. See also Everett Evans, "*Fiddler*'s Enduring Appeal Surprises Creators," *Houston Chronicle*, 26 August 1990.

9. Kasha and Hirschhorn, *Notes on Broadway*, 166; Cioffi, "The Men Who Write the Shows," I:46, III:62; Gerald Nachman, "Sheldon Harnick Tries an Even More *Wonderful Life*," *San Francisco Chronicle*, 20 May 1990.

10. Harnick, interviewed by Nancy Sureck, 16 January 2003.

11. Matthew Gurewitsch, "Tradition? The Delicate Task of Retuning *Fiddler*," *New York Times*, 26 February 2004.

12. Everett Evans, "Prize-Winning Composer Caters to Young Audience," *Houston Chronicle*, 16 June 2007. Bock made a similar comment during his and Harnick's interview with Terry Gross, 21 June 2004.

13. Don Shirley, "S. T. A. G. E. Varies Its Yearly Ritual," *Los Angeles Times*, 21 February 1999.

14. Scores for many of these songs are archived in box 15 of the Bock Papers.

15. Most of these songs are not represented in the Bock Papers at the New York Public Library for the Performing Arts (and may not have been notated), although a CD of *Album Leaves* was generously provided by Bock as source material for the final chapter of this book.

16. Bock told Nancy Sureck in 2002 that he wrote ten songs for a songwriting competition "probably" in the 1970s (Bock, interviewed by Nancy Sureck, 12 November 2002). The finding aid for the Bock archive at the New York Public Library for the Performing Arts indicates that "a dozen of the songs by Bock were written between 1974–1976 with the idea of using them in TV variety shows."

17. Bock Papers, box 15, folders 11, 22, 23, 46, and 54. Some of the songs in the group may have been part of *Trading Dreams*.

18. Bock generously made this CD available for the research that led to this book.

19. The Bock Papers include scores for different (and differently titled) versions of "Still Blue" ("How Are You?," box 15, folder 17) and "Lemon and Lime Blues" ("Waitin' for Love," box 15, folder 45).

20. Bock Papers, box 16, folder 3. The connection of this page to the triple-meter collection now known as *Three/Four All* is hypothetical, not specifically made by any of Bock's notations or other explanatory markings.

21. Everett Evans, "*Fiddler's* Enduring Appeal Surprises Creators," *Houston Chronicle*, 26 August 1990.

22. Lewis Funke, "Ed McBain Will Pull a 'Caper' To Bock's Music," *New York Times*, 6 May 1973. Rupert Holmes showed that it could be done in his book for Kander and Ebb's murder-mystery musical *Curtains* (2007).

23. As of 2009 Bock had not donated materials for *Caper* to his archive at the New York Public Library for the Performing Arts.

24. Bock, interviewed by Nancy Sureck, 12 November 2002.

25. Kevin Kelly, "Playwright Jerry Sterner Takes On a Taxing Subject," *Boston Globe*, 17 May 1991 (announcing the collaboration with Maltby and Shire); Kevin Kelly, "When It Comes to *Other People's Money*, The Play's The Thing," *Boston Globe*, 8 November 1991 (indicating that Sterner was looking for a new composer and lyricist); David Nicolette, "Play is a Sweet Deal for Businessman-Turned-Writer," *Grand Rapids Press*, 5 April 1992 (announcing Bock's involvement).

26. Alex Witchel, "Zaks is Booked," *New York Times*, 24 April 1992; Sterner, interviewed by Elaine Terris, 5 May 1992; Bruce Weber, "On Stage, and Off," *New York Times*, 21 May 1993; Ira J. Bilowit, "Broadway at Mid-Season: Classics, Revivals, and Adaptations Dominate," *Back Stage*, 6 January 1995.

27. Ostrow, *Present at the Creation*, 124–132. The Musical Theater Lab operated in New York churches in 1974 and 1975, and at the Terrace Theater of the Kennedy Center in Washington, D. C. from 1976 to 1981. It had a brief stay at Harvard in 1983–84 but had been dormant until Ostrow moved to Houston in 1995.

28. Everett Evans, "*1040* Tuning Into Tax Reform," *Houston Chronicle*, 9 November 1997.

29. As of 2009 Bock had not donated materials for *1040* to his archive at the New York Public Library for the Performing Arts. Sketchy information about the music appeared in Everett Evans, "*1040* Tuning Into Tax Reform," *Houston Chronicle*, 9 November 1997.

30. Everett Evans, "UH Children's Show Scores a Top Talent," *Houston Chronicle*, 16 July 2000. The new songs were "Because" and "We Are One."

31. The information comes from an interview with Sidney Berger on 12 March 2009. Bock and Berger did not collaborate in 2006.

32. Some information about these shows has been accessible on the web in university press releases: <http://www.uh.edu/news-events/archive/nr/2005/06june/061505ctf_jbock.html>; <http://www.uh.edu/news-events/archive/nr/2007/05may/051707childrenstheafest_jbock.html>.

33. http://www.mtishows.com/show_detail.asp?showid=000244. As of 2009 none of these shows was represented in the Bock Papers at the New York Public Library for the Performing Arts.

34. http://www.uh.edu/news-events/archive/nr/2005/06june/061505ctf_jbock. html

35. Harnick's mini-opera *Frustration* (1969) arguably belongs on a chart of his major works since 1967 but does not fit neatly into any of the categories (see chapter 8).

36. Harnick Papers (New York), box 3, folder 73.

37. Harnick Papers (New York), box 6, folder 116.

38. Cioffi, "The Men Who Write the Shows," I:45.

39. Henry, "Language No Barrier"; Hawkshaw, "Words into Song."

40. Robert Sherman, "Students Produce a Spirited Ravel," *New York Times*, 20 April 1971. See Henry, "Language No Barrier," and Harnick, interviewed by Harold Flender, 4 March 1971.

41. Henry, "Language No Barrier."

42. Angel S-37500 (LP, 1978). The score and book were published by Theodore Presser.

43. "The 'Umbrellas' of Sundance," *Deseret News*, 11 July 1999. Naomi Seigel, "Doomed, But Beautiful," *New York Times*, 2 October 2005.

44. The story source for this show may be Jean-Michel Olivier's novel of the same name (Lausanne: *Age d'homme*, 1999), although the script given to Harnick did not indicate as much. This show should not be confused with Legrand and van Cauwelaert's *Amour*, an *opera bouffe* based on a story by Marcel Aymé that was a success in Paris in 1997 (under the title of the original story, "Le passe-muraille") and had a brief run on Broadway in 2002 (in an English adaptation by Jeremy Sams).

45. Barbara Delatiner, "Harnick's New Partner: Bach," *New York Times*, 19 June 1988.

46. These are cantatas BWV 201 (1729, text by Picander after Ovid) and 205 (1725, text by Picander after Virgil), respectively.

47. Sheldon Harnick, "How Do You Write a Libretto?," liner notes for the premiere recording of Jack Beeson/Sheldon Harnick, *Captain Jinks of the Horse Marines* (see Appendix B). The essay is reprinted in Beeson, *How Operas Are Created*, 392–394. *The Saint of Bleecker Street* premiered at the New York City Opera on March 18, 1965 and remained in the company's repertory the following fall.

48. Beeson, *How Operas Are Created*, 392.

49. Harnick, "How Do You Write a Libretto?"

50. Playbills from some of these shows are in the collection of the New York Public Library for the Performing Arts.

51. Cone, *First Rival of the Metropolitan Opera*; Stockdale, *Emperors of Song*, 17–90. In the original play the character of Mapleson is briefly mentioned (Fitch, *Captain Jinks*, 28).

52. Jack Beeson, " . . . And What, If Not Who, is *Captain Jinks of the Horse Marines*?," liner notes for the premiere recording of Jack Beeson/Sheldon Harnick, *Captain Jinks of the Horse Marines* (see Appendix B). The essay is reprinted in Beeson, *How Operas Are Created*, 395–397.

53. Beeson, *How Operas Are Created*, 395, 397.

54. Harnick, "How Do You Write a Libretto?"

55. Hawkshaw, "Words Into Song."

56. Beeson, *How Operas Are Created*, 412–413.

57. The Schwartz version was completed in 1953 but first performed at Baldwin-Wallace College in Ohio on January 27, 1956 (Ross Parmenter, "World of Music: Casals Says No," *New York Times*, 29 January 1956). The Raphling premiered at the Greenwich House in New York on February 18, 1956 (*Central Opera Service Bulletin*, December 1967). Burton's version was composed in 1974 but premiered in Virginia in 1988 (Joseph McLellan, "Sprightly 'Heidegger's Experiment,'" *Washington Post*, 14 July 1988). The most accomplished composer of the group, Leo Smit, wrote his version in California in 1978; it received its premiere performance in Buffalo (Herman Trotter, "The Keys to the Past: Remembering Leo Smit," *Buffalo News*, 9 April 2000; New York Public Library for the Performing Arts, Leo Smit Papers, box 14, folders 4, 5, and 6). Wargo wrote his version when he was a senior at the Eastman School of Music in 1979; it was premiered there the same year (*Central Opera Service Bulletin*, Summer 1979).

58. Hawthorne, "Dr. Heidegger's Experiment," 158–167.

59. Beeson, *How Operas Are Created*, 438–440.

60. Bordman, *American Musical Theater*, 186, 191. See also Fields, *From the Bowery to Broadway*, 147.

61. Bordman, *American Musical Theater*, 737, 797.

62. Beeson, *How Operas Are Created*, 447–448.

63. Beeson, *How Operas Are Created*, 448–453. Beeson kept a detailed journal of his work on *Cyrano* with the hope that it would one day be published.

64. Beeson, *How Operas Are Created*, 438–454. Further information is available in tapes of eighteen hours of interviews with Susan Hawkshaw for the Yale University Oral History of American Music project.

65. Beeson, *How Operas Are Created*, 488.

66. Beeson, *How Operas Are Created*, 440–441.

67. Beeson, *How Operas Are Created*, 487.

68. Henry, "Language No Barrier."

69. Mel Gussow, "Theater in Review," *New York Times*, 10 April 1991. Both works are available in the Presser Rental Library (http://www.presser.com/marketing/catalogs/webOpera.pdf).

70. Bill Forman, "Mollicone for the Masses," *metroactive*, 22–28 March 2006 (http://www.metroactive.com/metro/03.22.06/mollicone-0612.html).

71. William S. Goodfellow, "Utahans, Creators Will Get First Look at *Coyote Tales*," *Deseret News*, 3 August 1997.

72. *American Indian Myths and Legends*, 335.

73. The title of scene 2 is given differently in the published score and on Mollicone's website (http://www.henrymollicone.com/coyote.html). In the original source (*Pale Moon . . .*) the title is "Coyote Keeps His Name."

74. Hawkshaw, "Words into Song."

75. Donald Rosenberg, "Tales of Wily Coyote Give Depth to Lyrical Opera's Ohio Premiere," *Cleveland Plain Dealer*, 17 November 2000.

76. Misty Edgecomb, "Natural Notes: Composer Joins College of the Atlantic Effort to Create Operatic Salute to Environmentalist Rachel Carson," *Bangor Daily News*, 5 October 2001.

77. Terry Morris, "The Musical Man: Lyricist to Present Evening of Songs, Stories at Gala," *Dayton Daily News*, 28 April 2006.

78. Louis Calta, "*Selling of President* Set for Broadway," *New York Times*, 7 February 1972.

79. "Rodgers, Harnick Team Up For *Rex*," *New York Times*, 17 April 1974.

80. Adler, *You Gotta Have Heart*, 266. According to James Leve, however, Fred Ebb was given the opportunity to write lyrics for this project; he declined because he felt "intimidated by the prospect of working directly with Rodgers" and "did not care for the premise" (Leve, *Kander and Ebb*, 103, 326).

81. "Musicals are very taxing, tiring, and unrewarding for the book writer, who is always in a no-win position," said Yellen in 1976. "Most people, even critics, are a little humble in the face of the score. I mean, they don't presume to be able to write, or re-write, the music. But when it comes to the book, everybody, even stage managers, think they know how to fix it." Stasio, "*Rex*: The Making of a Musical," 11.

82. Beeson, *How Operas Are Created*, 402.

83. Kasha and Hirschhorn, *Notes on Broadway*, 166; Stasio, "*Rex*: The Making of a Musical," 103; Cioffi, "The Men Who Write the Shows," III:62.

84. Kasha and Hirschhorn, *Notes on Broadway*, 166.

85. Stasio, "*Rex*: The Making of a Musical," 10.

86. Robert Armin, interview with Sheldon Harnick, 16 December 2002.

87. "So Much You Loved Me" does appear on the cast recording (see Appendix B). See also Block, *Richard Rodgers*, 240.

88. Adler, *You Gotta Have Heart*, 269.

89. Stasio, "*Rex*: The Making of a Musical," 10.

90. Adler, *You Gotta Have Heart*, 267, 269.

91. Mandelbaum, *Not Since Carrie*, 100.

92. Adler, *You Gotta Have Heart*, 269. Emphasis original.

93. Harnick, introduction to the published vocal selections (Hal Leonard, 2005).

94. Revised versions of scripts are in the Harnick Papers (New York), box 4, folders 87–90.

95. Block, *Richard Rodgers*, 239.

96. The album also inspired a book and television special, which was released on video in 1974 (http://www.freetobefoundation.org/history.htm).

97. Mel Gussow, "For Bloomgarden, It's a Good Season," *New York Times*, 1 November 1974.

98. Harnick and Raposo first met in 1965 in Boston, where Raposo was conducting the orchestra for a production of *She Loves Me*. Judith Weinraub, "With a Song in His Heart; Sheldon Harnick Composing *Wonderful* Music," *Washington Post*, 17 November 1991.

99. Cioffi, "The Men Who Write the Shows," I:46.

100. Cioffi, "The Men Who Write the Shows," I:47.

101. Cioffi, "The Men Who Write the Shows," I:46.

102. Leah D. Frank, "Harnick's *Christmas Carol* Is Not Just for Kids," *Stamford Advocate*, 10 December 1982.

103. Cioffi, "The Men Who Write the Shows," I:46.

104. Cioffi, "The Men Who Write the Shows," III:64.

105. Howard Taubman, "Theater: Bold Fairy Tale," *New York Times*, 10 April 1963.

106. Harnick, interviewed by Harold Flender, 4 March 1971.

107. Harnick, interviewed by Max Wilk, 6 November 1971; Cioffi, "The Men Who Write the Shows," III:62; Peter Filichia, "Long Struggle with *Dragons*," *Newark Star-Ledger*, 7 November 2003; Harnick, interviewed by Philip Lambert, 28 July 2008.

108. Louis Calta, "News of the Stage," *New York Times*, 11 November 1973.

109. Donal Henahan, "Will the Broadway Musical Enliven American Opera?," *New York Times*, 22 April 1984. Sid Smith, "Sheldon Harnick's Roundabout Road to Broadway," *Chicago Tribune*, 8 November 1984.

110. See Cioffi, "The Men Who Write the Shows," I:46, III:64; Maggie Ziomek, "ESIPA Picks Two Plays for Reading," *Albany Times Union*, 9 June 1988; Thom Walker, "UA's *Dragons* Offers Delightful Musical Satire," *Arizona Daily Star*, 21 February 1997; Jim Beckerman, "Lyricist's Labor of Love Gets Staging in Montclair," *The Record*, 16 November 2003.

111. Schwartz, *The Dragon*, Introduction by Harold Shukman, 139. The play was withdrawn by Soviet officials after single performances in Leningrad and Moscow in 1944. When it was revived in 1962, shortly after Schwartz's death, it suffered a similar fate, although it was popular in Poland in 1961. See also: "Writer Irwin Shaw is Returning to the Theater After a Decade," *New York Times*, 19 March 1963.

112. Schwartz, *The Dragon*, 218.

113. Peter Filichia, "Long Struggle with *Dragons*," *Newark Star-Ledger*, 7 November 2003.

114. Schwartz, *The Dragon*, 218.

115. *Sheldon Harnick Songbook*, 110–113.

116. Harnick, interviewed by Robert Armin, 16 December 2002.

117. His first public comments about this project came in his interview with Nancy Sureck on 16 January 2003.

118. Catherine Foster, "*Fiddler* Lyricist Has Kind Words for Revue at Stoneham Theater," *Boston Globe*, 7 March 2003.

119. Harnick, interviewed by Harold Flender, 4 March 1971.

SELECTED BIBLIOGRAPHY

* * *

1. ARCHIVES

Jerry Bock Papers, 1945–2004. JPB 02-10. Music Division, New York Public Library for the Performing Arts.

Sheldon Harnick Papers. JPB 04-11. Music Division, New York Public Library for the Performing Arts.

Sheldon Harnick Papers, 1937–1968. Wisconsin Historical Society Archives.

Lucille Kallen Papers, 1938–1999. *T-Mss 2000-026. Billy Rose Theater Division, New York Public Library for the Performing Arts.

Richard Kiley Papers, 1939–1999. *T-Mss 2005-014. Billy Rose Theater Division, New York Public Library for the Performing Arts.

Max Liebman Papers, 1903–1981. *T-Mss 1981-006. Billy Rose Theater Division, New York Public Library for the Performing Arts.

Zero and Kate Mostel Papers, 1915–1977. *T-Mss 1993-007. Billy Rose Theater Division, New York Public Library for the Performing Arts.

Joseph Stein Papers, 1942–1969. Wisconsin Historical Society Archives.

Michael Stewart Papers, 1948–1987. *T-Mss 1990-018. Billy Rose Theater Division, New York Public Library for the Performing Arts.

Tamiment Playhouse Records, 1927–1987. Tamiment Library/Robert F. Wagner Labor Archives, Elmer Holmes Bobst Library, New York University.

2. PUBLISHED SCORES

The Apple Tree. Music by Jerry Bock, lyrics by Sheldon Harnick. Vocal selections: New York Times Music Corp., 1966. Vocal score: Appletree Music, 1968.

Baker Street. Music and lyrics by Marian Grudeff and Raymond Jessel. [Additional songs by Bock and Harnick, uncredited.] Vocal selections: Marks Music, 1964.

The Body Beautiful. Music by Jerry Bock, lyrics by Sheldon Harnick. Vocal selections: Valando Music, 1962.

Captain Jinks of the Horse Marines. Music by Jack Beeson, libretto by Sheldon Harnick. Vocal score: Boosey & Hawkes, 1983.

Coyote Tales. Music by Henry Mollicone, libretto by Sheldon Harnick. Vocal score: ECS Publishing, 1999.

Dr. Heidegger's Fountain of Youth. Music by Jack Beeson, libretto by Sheldon Harnick. Vocal score: Boosey & Hawkes, 1978.

Fiddler on the Roof. Music by Jerry Bock, lyrics by Sheldon Harnick. Vocal selections: Times Square Music, 1964. Vocal score: Sunbeam Music, 1965.

Fiorello! Music by Jerry Bock, lyrics by Sheldon Harnick. Vocal selections: Times Square Music, 1959. Vocal score: Tams-Witmark, 1959.

Frustration. A mini-opera in one act for two female voices, violin, B-flat clarinet, and piano. Music and libretto by Sheldon Harnick. Bryn Mawr, Penn.: Merion/Presser, 1973.

The Merry Widow. Music by Franz Lehár, original lyrics by Victor Leon and Leo Stein; English lyrics by Sheldon Harnick. Vocal score: Chappell, 1977.

Mr. Wonderful. Music and lyrics by Jerry Bock, Larry Holofcener, and George Weiss. Vocal selections: Warner Brothers, 1989.

Rex. Music by Richard Rodgers, lyrics by Sheldon Harnick. Vocal selections: Hal Leonard, 2005.

The Rothschilds. Music by Jerry Bock, lyrics by Sheldon Harnick. Vocal selections: New York Times Music, 1970.

She Loves Me. Music by Jerry Bock, lyrics by Sheldon Harnick. Vocal selections: Times Square Music, 1963; Broadway Revival Edition: Warner Brothers, 1994. Vocal score: Tams-Witmark, 1963.

The Sheldon Harnick Songbook. Vocal score: Warner Brothers, 1996.

Tenderloin. Music by Jerry Bock, lyrics by Sheldon Harnick. Vocal selections: New York Times Music, 1960.

3. PUBLISHED LIBRETTI

The Apple Tree. Book by Sheldon Harnick and Jerry Bock, based on stories by Mark Twain, Frank R. Stockton, and Jules Feiffer. Additional book material by Jerome Coopersmith. Lyrics by Sheldon Harnick. New York: Random House, 1967.

Baker Street. Book by Jerome Coopersmith, based on the stories of Sir Arthur Conan Doyle. Music and lyrics by Marian Grudeff and Raymond Jessel; additional lyrics [uncredited] by Sheldon Harnick. Garden City, N.Y.: Doubleday, 1966.

The Body Beautiful. Book by Joseph Stein and Will Glickman. Lyrics by Sheldon Harnick. New York: Samuel French, 1957.

Captain Jinks of the Horse Marines. Libretto by Sheldon Harnick, based on the play by Clyde Fitch. New York: Boosey and Hawkes, 1976.

Fiddler on the Roof. Book by Joseph Stein, based on Sholem Aleichem's stories. Lyrics by Sheldon Harnick. New York: Crown, 1964.

Fiorello! Book by Jerome Weidman and George Abbott. Lyrics by Sheldon Harnick. New York: Popular Library, 1960.

Mr. Wonderful. Book by Joseph Stein and Will Glickman. Music and lyrics by Jerry Bock, Larry Holofcener, and George Weiss. New York: Hart Stenographic Bureau, 1956.

She Loves Me. Book by Joe Masteroff, based on a play by Miklós László. Lyrics by Sheldon Harnick. New York: Dodd, Mead, 1963.

Tenderloin. Book by Jerome Weidman and George Abbott, based on the novel by Samuel Hopkins Adams. Lyrics by Sheldon Harnick. New York: Random House, 1961.

4. INTERVIEWS AND COMMUNICATIONS

Sidney Berger:
  Interviewed by Philip Lambert, 12 March 2009.
  Personal communication, 9 April 2009.
Jerry Bock:
  Interviewed by Harold Flender, 4 February, 11 February 1971. American Jewish Committee Oral History Collection, New York Public Library.

Interviewed by Max Wilk, 29 August 1971. Rodgers and Hammerstein Archive of Recorded Sound, New York Public Library for the Performing Arts.

Interviewed by Martha S. LoMonaco, 13 May 1986. Tamiment Playhouse Records, Tamiment Library/Robert F. Wagner Labor Archives, Elmer Holmes Bobst Library, New York University.

Interviewed by Nancy Sureck, 12 November 2002. Music Division Oral History Project, New York Public Library for the Performing Arts.

Personal communications, 30 October, 24 November 2008; 9 February, 10 February, 2 April, 6 April, 3 December 2009.

Jerry Bock and Sheldon Harnick:

Discussing *Fiddler on the Roof*, 18 October 1964. Television broadcast, WCBS-TV ("American Musical Theater"). Paley Center for Media T:64032.

In conversation, 12 May 1975. Theater on Film and Tape Archive, New York Public Library for the Performing Arts.

Interviewed by Liane Hansen, 7 May 2000. Radio broadcast, National Public Radio ("Weekend Edition Sunday"). <http://www.npr.org/ramfiles/wesun/20000507. wesun.15.rmm>

Interviewed by Terry Gross, 21 June 2004. Radio broadcast, National Public Radio ("Fresh Air"). <http://www.npr.org/templates/story/story.php?storyId=1966952>

Jerry Bock, Barbara Cook, and Sheldon Harnick:

Interviewed by Craig Zadan, December 1979. Television broadcast, Public Broadcasting Service (accompanying the broadcast of the BBC production of *She Loves Me* on "Great Performances").

Jerry Bock, Joe Masteroff, and Sheldon Harnick:

Interviewed by Peter Filichia, 28 April 1994. Theater on Film and Tape Archive, New York Public Library for the Performing Arts.

Sheldon Harnick:

Interviewed by Harold Flender, 22 February, 1 March, 4 March, 1971. American Jewish Committee Oral History Collection, New York Public Library.

Interviewed by Max Wilk, 6 November 1971. Rodgers and Hammerstein Archive of Recorded Sound, New York Public Library for the Performing Arts.

Interviewed by Bernard Rosenberg and Ernest Harburg, 18 February 1983. E. Y. Harburg Papers, Billy Rose Theater Division, New York Public Library for the Performing Arts.

Interviewed by Terry Gross, 1988. Radio broadcast, National Public Radio ("Fresh Air"). Re-aired on 26 December 2003. <http://www.npr.org/templates/story/story. php?storyId=1570466>

Interviewed by Susan Haskins and Michael Riedel, 19 July 1993. "Inside Broadway: Sheldon Harnick." Theater on Film and Tape Archive, New York Public Library for the Performing Arts.

Interviewed by Michael Riedel and Susan Haskins, 29 October 1997. "Theater Talk: Lyricists Susan Birkenhead, Sheldon Harnick, Deborah Grace Winer." Theater on Film and Tape Archive, New York Public Library for the Performing Arts.

Interviewed by Michael Kantor, 5 August 1998. Raw footage for Kantor's film *Broadway: The American Musical*. Theater on Film and Tape Archive, New York Public Library for the Performing Arts.

Interviewed by Theodore S. Chapin, October 2001. American Theater Wing, "Career Guides: The Lyricist." <http://americanTheaterwing.org/careerguides/detail/the_lyricist>

Interviewed by Robert Armin, 16 December 2002. <www.robertarmin.com/Harnick.htm>

Interviewed by Nancy Sureck, 16 January 2003. Music Division Oral History Project, New York Public Library for the Performing Arts.

Interviewed by Matt Windman, 26 July 2004. <www.theaterscene.net>

Interviewed by Richard Christiansen, 29 April 2006. <http://www.timelineTheater.com>

Interviewed by Leonard Lopate, 4 April 2006. "Sheldon Harnick and the American Songbook." Radio broadcast, WNYC. <http://www.wnyc.org/shows/lopate/episodes/2006/04/04/segments/58748>

Interviewed by John von Soosten and Howard Sherman, November 2006. "Downstage Center." Radio broadcast, XM Satellite Radio. < http://americanTheaterwing.org/media/downstage/mp3/Episode126.mp3>

Interviewed by Andrew Patner, March 2008. Radio broadcast, WFMT. <http://www.wfmt.com/main.taf?p=1,1,41,25,2>

Interviewed by P. J. Powers, [April] 2008. < http://www.vimeo.com/913984>

Interviewed by Martin Charnin, [2008]. Included on the *Body Beautiful* bonus disc.

Interviewed by Philip Lambert, 28 July 2008.

Personal communications, 1 March, 8 June, 9 December 2009.

Lawrence Holofcener:

Personal communications, 12 February, 13 February, 3 August, 21 November, 23 November 2008.

Norman Jewison:

Interviewed by Scott Simon, 13 October 2001. Radio broadcast, National Public Radio ("Weekend Edition").

Joe Masteroff:

Interviewed by Philip Lambert, 11 June 2009.

Henry Mollicone:

Personal communication, 16 March 2009.

Stuart Ostrow:

Personal communication, 22 March 2009.

Joseph Stein:

Interviewed by Philip Lambert, 30 November 2009.

Jerry Sterner:

Interviewed by Elaine Terris, 5 May 1992. American Jewish Committee Oral History Collection, New York Public Library.

Sherman Yellen:

Interviewed by Philip Lambert, 4 June 2009.

5. GENERAL

Abbott, George. *Mister Abbott*. New York: Random House, 1963.

Adams, Samuel Hopkins. *Tenderloin*. New York: Random House, 1959.

Adler, Richard. *You Gotta Have Heart: An Autobiography*. New York: Donald I. Fine, 1990.

Adler, Thomas P. *Mirror on the Stage: The Pulitzer Plays as an Approach to American Drama*. West Lafayette, Indiana: Purdue University Press, 1987.

Aleichem, Sholem. *Tevye the Dairyman and Motl the Cantor's Son*. Translated by Aliza Shevrin; introduction by Dan Miron. New York: Penguin, 2009.

Aleichem, Sholem. *Tevye the Dairyman and the Railroad Stories*. Translated from the Yiddish and with an introduction by Hillel Halkin. New York: Schocken Books, 1987.

Aleichem, Sholem. *Tevye's Daughters: Collected Stories of Sholem Aleichem*. Translated by Frances Butwin. New York: Crown, 1949.

Aleichem, Sholem. *Wandering Star*. Translated by Frances Butwin. New York: Crown, 1952.

Altman, Richard, with Mervyn Kaufman. *The Making of a Musical:* Fiddler on the Roof. New York: Crown, 1971.

American Indian Myths and Legends. Selected and edited by Richard Erdoes and Alfonso Ortiz. New York: Pantheon, 1984.

Anderson, Hugh Abercrombie. *Out Without My Rubbers: The Memoirs of John Murray Anderson*. As told to and written by Hugh Abercrombie Anderson. New York: Library Publishers, 1954.

Atkey, Mel. *Broadway North: The Dream of a Canadian Musical Theater*. Toronto: Natural Heritage Books, 2006.

Atkinson, Brooks. *Broadway*. Revised edition. New York: Macmillan, 1974.

Avenary, Hanoch. "The Concept of Mode in European Synagogue Chant: An Analysis of the Adoshem Malak Shtejger." *Journal of Synagogue Music* 7/1 (November 1976): 47–57.

Ballard, Kaye. *How I Lost 10 Pounds in Fifty-Three Years: A Memoir*. New York: Back Stage Books, 2006.

Banfield, Stephen. *Sondheim's Broadway Musicals*. Ann Arbor: University of Michigan Press, 1993.

Bates, J. Douglas. *The Pulitzer Prize: The Inside Story of America's Most Prestigious Award*. New York: Birch Lane, 1991.

Beeson, Jack. *How Operas Are Created by Composers and Lyricists: The Life of Jack Beeson, American Opera Composer*. Lewiston, N. Y.: Edwin Mellen, 2008.

Bego, Mark. *Bette Midler: Still Divine*. Introduction by Rita Coolidge. New York: Cooper Square Press, 2002.

Bellman, Jonathan. "The Hungarian Gypsies and the Poetics of Exclusion." In *The Exotic in Western Music*, edited by Jonathan Bellman (Boston: Northeastern University Press, 1998), 74–103.

Bellman, Jonathan. *The* Style Hongrois *in the Music of Western Europe*. Boston: Northeastern University Press, 1993.

Bellman, Jonathan. "Toward a Lexicon for the *Style hongrois*." *Journal of Musicology* 9/2 (Spring 1991): 214–237.

Beregovski, Moshe. "The Altered Dorian Scale in Jewish Folk Music (1946)." In *Old Jewish Folk Music: The Collections and Writings of Moshe Beregovski*, edited and translated by Mark Slobin (Philadelphia: University of Pennsylvania Press, 1982), 549–567.

Beregovski, Moshe. "Jewish Folk Songs (1962)." Ibid., 285–510.

Bernstein, Leonard. *The Infinite Variety of Music*. New York: Simon and Schuster, 1966.

Berry, David Carson. "Gambling With Chromaticism? Extra-Diatonic Melodic Expression in the Songs of Irving Berlin." *Theory and Practice* 26 (2001): 21–85.

Bial, Henry. *Acting Jewish: Negotiating Ethnicity on the American Stage and Screen* Ann Arbor: University of Michigan Press, 2005.

Bial, Henry Carl. "Acting Jewish on the American Stage and Screen, 1947–1998." Ph.D. dissertation, New York University, 2001.

Bialosky, Marshall. Review of Beeson/Harnick, *Captain Jinks of the Horse Marines. Notes* 42/1 (September 1985): 167–169.

Bikel, Theodore. *Theo: An Autobiography.* Madison: University of Wisconsin Press, 1994. Re-publication, with a new postscript, 2004.

Block, Geoffrey. "Bock, Jerry." *Grove Music Online.*

Block, Geoffrey. "The Broadway Canon from *Show Boat* to *West Side Story* and the European Operatic Ideal." *Journal of Musicology* 11/4 (Fall 1993): 524–544.

Block, Geoffrey. *Enchanted Evenings: The Broadway Musical from* Show Boat *to Sondheim and Lloyd Webber.* 2d ed., expanded. New York: Oxford University Press, 2009.

Block, Geoffrey. *Richard Rodgers.* New Haven: Yale University Press, 2003.

Bock, Jerry: Biography. <http://www.MTIshows.com/bio.asp?bID=3354>

Bock, Jerry: Song Catalog. <http://www.songwritershalloffame.org/songs/C327>

Bock, Jerry, and Sheldon Harnick. <http://encyclopedia.jrank.org/articles/pages/1167/Bock-Jerry-actually-Jerrold-Lewis-and-Sheldon-Mayer-Harnick.html>

Bordman, Gerald. *American Musical Comedy from Adonis to Dreamgirls.* New York: Oxford University Press, 1982.

Bordman, Gerald. *American Musical Theater: A Chronicle.* 3rd ed. New York: Oxford University Press, 2001.

Bordman, Gerald. *American Operetta: From H. M. S. Pinafore to Sweeney Todd.* New York: Oxford University Press, 1981.

Boroff, David. "Dancers in the Adirondacks." *Dance Magazine* 32/8 (August 1958): 42–44, 72–73.

Brahms, Caryl, and Sherrin, Ned. *Song by Song: The Lives and Work of 14 Great Lyric Writers.* Bolton: Ross Anderson, 1984.

Brewster, Janice L. "Spotlight on George David Weiss." *Music Educators Journal* 78/6 (February 1992): 50–52.

Brown, Jared. *Zero Mostel: A Biography.* New York: Atheneum, 1989.

Brustein, Robert. "Fiddling While Talent Burns." *New Republic*, 17 October 1964, 31–32.

Bryer, Jackson R., and Richard A. Davison, Eds. *The Art of the American Musical: Conversations with the Creators.* New Brunswick, N. J.: Rutgers University Press, 2005.

Buchler, Michael. "Modulation as a Dramatic Agent in Frank Loesser's Broadway Songs." *Music Theory Spectrum* 30/1 (Spring 2008): 35–60.

Bukoff, Ronald Nick. "A Trip to the Library, or, The Curse of 'Marian the Librarian': Images of Libraries and Librarians on the Musical Stage." *Studies in Popular Culture* 22/1 (October 1999): 27–41.

Burnett, Carol. *One More Time: A Memoir.* New York: Random House, 1986.

Cioffi, Bob. "The Men Who Write the Shows—Sheldon Harnick." *Show Music* 5/2 (November 1986): 45–57 [part I]; 5/3 (April 1987): 49–61 [part II]; 5/4 (Fall 1987): 58–65 [part III].

Clurman, Harold. *The Fervent Years: The Story of the Group Theater and the Thirties*. New York: Knopf, 1945.

Cohen, Sarah Blacher, Ed. *From Hester Street to Hollywood: The Jewish-American Stage and Screen*. Bloomington: University of Indiana Press, 1983.

Cone, John Frederick. *First Rival of the Metropolitan Opera*. New York: Columbia University Press, 1983.

Conrad, Christine. *Jerome Robbins: That Broadway Man, that Ballet Man*. London: Booth-Clibborn Edition, 2000.

Contino, Rosalie H. "Costume Designer Patricia Zipprodt: Her Contribution to the American Theater." Ph.D. dissertation, New York University, 1997.

Coyote Was Going There: Indian Literature of the Oregon Country. Compiled and edited by Jarold Ramsey. Seattle: University of Washington Press, 1977.

Crittenden, Camille. "Whose Patriotism? Austro-Hungarian Relations and 'Der Zigeuner-baron.'" *The Musical Quarterly* 82/2 (Summer 1998): 251–278.

Cuneo, Ernest. *Life with Fiorello: A Memoir*. New York: Macmillan, 1955.

Davis, Christopher. *The Producer*. New York: Harper & Row, 1972.

Davis, Jr., Sammy. *Sammy: An Autobiography; With Material Newly Revised from Yes I Can and Why Me*. With Jane and Burt Boyar. New York: Farrar, Straus, and Giroux, 2000.

Degan, John. "Musical Theater Since World War II." In *The Cambridge History of the American Theater, Vol. 3: Post-World War II to the 1990s*, edited by Don B. Wilmeth and Christopher Bigsby (Cambridge: Cambridge University Press, 2000), 419–465.

Delorenzo, Joseph P. "The Chorus in American Musical Theater: Emphasis on Choral Performance." Ph.D. dissertation, New York University, 1985.

Downer, Alan S, Ed. *The American Theater*. Washington, D. C.: Voice of America, U. S. Information Agency, 1967.

Draughon, Francesca, and Knapp, Raymond. "Gustav Mahler and the Crisis of Jewish Identity." *Echo* 3/2 (2001).

Engel, Lehman. *The American Musical Theater*, Rev. ed., New York: Macmillan, 1975. Original ed., New York: Collier, 1967.

Engel, Lehman. *Their Words Are Music: The Great Theater Lyricists and Their Lyrics*. New York: Crown, 1975.

Engel, Lehman. *Words with Music*. New York: Macmillan, 1972.

Eskin, Blake. "*Fiddler* Crabs." <nextbook.org, 5 March 2004>

Everett, William A., and Laird, Paul R., Eds. *The Cambridge Companion to the Musical*. Cambridge: Cambridge University Press, 2002.

Ewen, David. *Composers for the American Musical Theater*. New York: Dodd, Mead, 1968.

Ewen, David. *New Complete Book of the American Musical Theater*. New York: Holt, Rinehart, and Winston, 1970.

Eyman, Scott. *Ernest Lubitsch: Laughter in Paradise*. New York: Simon & Schuster, 1993.

Feiffer, Jules. *Passionella and Other Stories*. Seattle, Wash.: Fantagraphics, 2006.

Fields, Armond, and Fields, L. Marc. *From the Bowery to Broadway: Lew Fields and the Roots of American Popular Theater*. New York: Oxford University Press, 1993.

Filichia, Peter. "Stein's Way: The York Theater Company Devotes Its Fall Musicals in Mufti Series to Legendary Book Writer Joseph Stein." <http://img.theatermania.com/off-broadway/news/09-2007/steins-way_11534.html>

Fischer, Heinz-D., and Fischer, Erika J. *Complete Historical Handbook of the Pulitzer Prize System 1917–2000*. Munich: Saur, 2003.

Fishgall, Gary. *Gonna Do Great Things: The Life of Sammy Davis, Jr.* New York: Scribner, 2003.

Fitch, Clyde. *Captain Jinks of the Horse Marines*. New York: Doubleday, Page, 1902.

Frankel, Aaron. *Writing the Broadway Musical*. New York: Drama Book Specialists, 1977.

Franklin, Ruth. "Shtetl Shtick." *New York Times*, 29 February 2004.

Fraser, Barbara Means. "A Structural Analysis of the American Musical Theater Between 1955 and 1965: A Cultural Perspective." Ph.D. dissertation, University of Oregon, 1982.

Freed, Isadore. *Harmonizing the Jewish Modes*. New York: The Sacred Music Press, 1958.

Frieden, Ken. *A Century in the Life of Sholem Aleichem's Tevye*. Syracuse, N. Y.: Syracuse University Press, 1997.

Fuld, James J. *The Book of World-Famous Music: Classical, Popular, and Folk*. 5th ed., rev. New York: Dover, 2000. Original ed., New York: Crown, 1966.

Furia, Philip. *The Poets of Tin Pan Alley: A History of America's Great Lyricists*. New York: Oxford University Press, 1990.

Gates, Gary Paul. "Broadway's Prince Charming." *Holiday* (April 1966): 99–104, 107–108, 110.

Gilman, Sander L. "There Ain't No There There: Reimagining Eastern European Jewish Culture in the 21st Century." *Shofar: An Interdisciplinary Journal of Jewish Studies* 25/1 (2006): 1–4.

Godine, Amy. "The Red Woods." *Adirondack Life* 34/5 (July/August 2003): 48–56, 85–93.

Goldberg, Isaac. *George Gershwin: A Study in American Music*. New ed. Supplemented by Edith Garson. With foreword and discography by Alan Dashiell. New York: Frederick Ungar, 1958.

Goldberg, Marie W. "The Real Tevya of Old Russia." *New York Times*, 15 September 1957.

Goldman, Eric A. *Visions, Images, and Dreams: Yiddish Film Past and Present*. Ann Arbor, Mich.: UMI Research Press, 1983.

Gottlieb, Jack. *Funny, It Doesn't Sound Jewish: How Yiddish Songs and Synagogue Melodies Influenced Tin Pan Alley, Broadway, and Hollywood*. Albany, N. Y.: State University of New York in Association with the Library of Congress, 2004.

Gottlieb, Jack. "The Music of Leonard Bernstein: A Study of Melodic Manipulations." D.M.A. dissertation, University of Illinois, 1964.

Grant, Mark N. *The Rise and Fall of the Broadway Musical*. Boston: Northeastern University Press, 2004.

Green, Stanley. *The World of Musical Comedy*. 4th ed., rev. San Diego, Calif.: A. S. Barnes, 1980.

Gurewitsch, Mathew. "Tradition? The Delicate Task of Retuning *Fiddler*." *New York Times*, 26 February 2004.

Hamm, Charles. *Irving Berlin: Songs from the Melting Pot; the Formative Years, 1907–1914*. New York: Oxford University Press, 1997.

Hamm, Charles, Ed. *Irving Berlin's Early Songs*. Music of the U.S.A. II, 3 vols. Ann Arbor, Mich.: A-R Editions, 1994.

Harnick, Sheldon: Biography. <http://www.mtishows.com/bio.asp?bID=3471>

Harnick, Sheldon. "In His Own Words: Writing Lyrics." *Northwestern Magazine*, Summer 2004. <www.northwestern.edu/magazine/northwestern/summer2004/features/harnick/index.htm>

Harnick, Sheldon: Song Catalog. <http://www.songwritershalloffame.org/songs/C328>

Harnick, Sheldon. "Which Comes First, Words or Music?," *Dramatists Guild Quarterly* 4/1 (Spring 1967): 9–14. Excerpted as introduction to *The Apple Tree*, in *The Best Plays of 1966–67*, edited by Otis L. Guernsey Jr. (New York: Dodd, Mead, 1967), 214–216. Reprinted with minor revisions as "What Comes First in a Musical? The Libretto," in *Playwrights, Lyricists, Composers on Theater*, edited by Otis L. Guernsey Jr. (New York: Dodd, Mead, 1974), 38–44.

Hawkshaw, Susan. "Words Into Song." *Northwestern Magazine*, Summer 2004. <http://www.northwestern.edu/magazine/northwestern/summer2004/features/harnick/index.htm>

Hawthorne, Nathaniel. "Dr. Heidegger's Experiment." In *Young Goodman Brown and Other Tales* (New York: Oxford University Press, 1987), 158–167.

Haygood, Wil. *In Black and White: The Life of Sammy Davis, Jr.* New York: Knopf, 2003.

Heller, Charles. *What to Listen for in Jewish Music.* Toronto: Ecanthus Press, 2006.

Henry, Derrick. "Language No Barrier As Broadway's Harnick Takes Librettist's Role." *Atlanta Journal and Constitution*, 10 July 1988.

Heylbut, Rose. "You're the Top, Cole Porter!" *Etude* 74/7 (September 1956): 23, 56–57.

Hillman, Jessica. "Goyim on the Roof: Embodying Authenticity in Leveaux's *Fiddler on the Roof*." *Studies in Musical Theater* 1/1 (2007): 25–39.

Hillman-McCord, Jessica. "From the Shtetl to 42nd Street: Nostalgia and Postmemory in Jewish American Musicals, 1961–Today." Ph.D. dissertation, University of Colorado at Boulder, 2007.

Hirsch, Foster. *Harold Prince and the American Musical Theater.* Rev. ed., New York: Applause, 2005. Original ed., Cambridge: Cambridge University Press, 1989.

Hischak, Thomas S. *Word Crazy: Broadway Lyricists from Cohan to Sondheim.* New York: Praeger, 1991.

Hofler, Robert. "*Fiddler* Director, Scribe Get Physical Over Column." <variety.com, 2 March 2004>

Hohenberg, John. *The Pulitzer Prizes.* New York: Columbia University Press, 1974.

Hopi Coyote Tales: Istutuwutsi. Selected and introduced by Ekkehart Malotki and Michael Lomatuway'ma. Lincoln: University of Nebraska Press, 1984.

Howe, Irving. "Tevye on Broadway." *Commentary* 38 (November 1964): 73–75.

Idelsohn, A. Z. "The Features of the Jewish Sacred Folk Song in Eastern Europe." *Acta Musicologica* 4/1 (Jan.–March 1932): 17–23.

Idelsohn, A. Z. *Jewish Music in Its Historical Development.* New York: Henry Holt, 1929. Reprint, with a new introduction by Arbie Orenstein, New York: Dover, 1992.

Idelsohn, A. Z. "Musical Characteristics of East-European Jewish Folk-Song." *The Musical Quarterly* 18/4 (Oct. 1932): 634–645.

Ilson, Carol. *Harold Prince: From* Pajama Game *to* Phantom of the Opera. Foreword by Sheldon Harnick. Ann Arbor: U. M. I. Research Press, 1989.

Indian Legends of the Pacific Northwest. Selected and introduced by Ella E. Clark. Berkeley: University of California Press, 1953.

Isherwood, Charles. "Fiddled Fiddler." *The Times*, 8 March 2004.

Jenness, David, and Velsey, Don. *Classic American Popular Song: The Second Half-Century, 1950–2000.* New York: Routledge, 2006.

Johns, Duke. "Connections: An Interview with Jack Beeson." *Music Educators Journal* 66/2 (October 1979): 44–49.

Jones, John Bush. *Our Musicals, Ourselves: A Social History of the American Musical Theater*. Foreword by Sheldon Harnick. Waltham, Mass.: Brandeis University Press, 2003.

Jowitt, Deborah. *Jerome Robbins: His Life, His Theater, His Dance*. New York: Simon and Schuster, 2004.

Juster, Norton. *The Phantom Tollbooth*. New York: Epstein & Carroll, 1961.

Kael, Pauline. "A Bagel with a Bite Out of It." *New Yorker*, 13 November 1971, 133–139. Reprinted in *Deeper into Movies* (New York: Atlantic Monthly Press, 1973), 327–333.

Kasha, Al, and Joel Hirschhorn. *Notes on Broadway: Conversations with the Great Songwriters*. Chicago: Contemporary Books, 1985.

Kaye, Meli Davis. "Doris Humphrey at Green Mansions, 1947." *Dance Chronicle* 18/3 (1995): 405–418.

Kelly, Francis P. "The Musical Plays of Jerry Bock and Sheldon Harnick." Ph.D. dissertation, University of Kansas, 1978.

Killick, Andrew P. "Music as Ethnic Marker in Film: The 'Jewish' Case." In *Soundtrack Available: Essays on Film and Popular Music*, edited by Pamela Robertson Wojcik and Arthur Knight (Durham, N. C.: Duke University Press, 2001), 185–201.

Kirshenblatt-Gimblett, Barbara. "Imagining Europe: The Popular Arts of American Jewish Ethnography." In *Divergent Jewish Cultures: Israel and America*, edited by Deborah Dash Moore and S. Ilan Troen (New Haven: Yale University Press, 2001), 155–191.

Kislan, Richard. *The Musical: A Look at the American Musical Theater*. Rev. ed., New York: Applause, 1995. Original ed., Englewood Cliffs, N. J.: Prentice-Hall, 1980.

Klein, Alvin. "After 30 Years, the Hits Linger On." *New York Times*, 17 October 1982.

Knapp, Raymond. *The American Musical and the Formation of National Identity*. Princeton: Princeton University Press, 2005.

Knapp, Raymond. *The American Musical and the Performance of Personal Identity*. Princeton: Princeton University Press, 2006.

Kodaly, Zoltan. *Folk Music of Hungary*. Enlarged edition revised by Lajos Vargyas. Translation by Ronald Tempest and Cynthia Jolly, revised by Laurence Picken. New York: Praeger, 1971.

Konas, Gary Paul. "From Gershwin to Sondheim: The Pulitzer Prize-Winning Musicals." Ph.D. dissertation, University of California at Davis, 1993.

Koskoff, Ellen. "Contemporary Nigun Composition in an American Hasidic Community." *Selected Reports in Ethnomusicology* 3/1 (1978): 153–174.

La Guardia, Fiorello. *The Making of an Insurgent, an Autobiography: 1882–1919*. Introduction by M. R. Werner. Philadelphia: J. B. Lippincott, 1948. Reprint, Westport, Conn.: Greenwood Press, 1985.

László, Miklós. *Parfumerie*. Copyright by the author, 1936. Adaptation by E. P. Dowdall, 2007.

Laufe, Abe. *Broadway's Greatest Musicals*. Rev. ed. New York: Funk & Wagnall's, 1977. Original ed., 1969.

Laurents, Arthur. *Original Story By: A Memoir of Broadway and Hollywood*. New York: Knopf, 2000.

Lawrence, Greg. *Dance with Demons: The Life of Jerome Robbins*. New York: G. P. Putnam's Sons, 2001.

Lawson-Peebles, Robert, Ed. *Approaches to the American Musical*. Exeter, Devon: University of Exeter Press, 1996.

Lemberger, Margo. "A Musical Milkman's Multi-Culti Appeal: 'Sunrise, Sunset' Glows in El Paso as 'Fiddler' Heads Back to Broadway." *Forward*, 5 January 2001.

Lester, Rob. "Charlotte Rae Has Her Say." <http://www.talkinbroadway.com/rialto/past/2006/12_8_06.html>

Leve, James. *Kander and Ebb*. New Haven: Yale University Press, 2009.

Levine, Joseph A. *Synagogue Song in America*. Crown Point, Ind.: White Cliffs Media Company, 1989.

LoMonaco, Martha Schmoyer. *Every Week, a Broadway Revue: The Tamiment Playhouse, 1921–1960*. Westport, Conn.: Greenwood Press, 1992.

Loney, Glenn, Ed. *Musical Theater in America: Papers and Panels of the Conference on the Musical Theater in America*. Westport, Conn.: Greenwood, 1984.

Long, Robert Emmet. *Broadway, the Golden Years: Jerome Robbins and the Great Choreographer-Directors*. New York: Continuum, 2001.

Magee, Jeffrey. "Irving Berlin's 'Blue Skies': Ethnic Affiliations and Musical Transformations." *The Musical Quarterly* 84/4 (Winter 2000): 537–580.

Mandelbaum, Ken. *Not Since Carrie: Forty Years of Broadway Musical Flops*. New York: St. Martin's, 1991.

Manuel, Peter. "Modal Harmony in Andalusian, Eastern European, and Turkish Syncretic Musics." *Yearbook for Traditional Music* 21 (1989): 70–94.

Marvin, William. "Simulating Counterpoint in Broadway Musicals: The Quodlibet as Compositional Procedure." Paper delivered at the Annual Meeting of the Society for Music Theory, Columbus, Ohio, 31 October 2002.

Mast, Gerald. *Can't Help Singin': The American Musical on Stage and Screen*. Woodstock, N. Y.: Overlook Press, 1987.

Mates, Julian. *America's Musical Stage: Two Hundred Years of Musical Theater*. Westport, Conn.: Greenwood, 1985.

McClary, Susan. *Feminine Endings: Music, Gender, and Sexuality*. Minneapolis: University of Minnesota Press, 1991.

McMillin, Scott. *The Musical as Drama: A Study of the Principles and Conventions Behind Musical Shows from Kern to Sondheim*. Princeton: Princeton University Press, 2006.

Mehler, Charles Eliot. "*Fiddler on the Roof*: Considerations in a New Age." *Studies in Musical Theater* 2/1 (June 2008): 51–60.

Melville, Barbara A. "Hidden History: Salvaging Stories of Lost Communities." *Skidmore Scope* (Spring 2000). <www.skidmore.edu/scope/spring2000/feature/history.html>

Merwin, Ted. "Jew-Face: Non-Jews Playing Jews on the American Stage." <http://spinner.cofc.edu/~jwst/pages/Merwin,%20Ted%20-%20Jew-face%20+.pdf>

Miletich, Leo N. *Broadway's Prize-Winning Musicals: An Annotated Guide for Libraries and Audio Collectors*. New York: Haworth, 1993.

Millstein, Gilbert. "*Fiorello!* and Harnick." *New York Times Magazine*, 27 December 1959.

Mlotek, Eleanor G. *Mir Trogn a Gezang! Favorite Yiddish Songs of Our Generation*. New York: Workmen's Circle, 1982.

Mlotek, Eleanor G., and Mlotek, Joseph. *Pearls of Yiddish Song: Favorite Folk, Art, and Theater Songs*. New York: Workmen's Circle, 1988.

Mlotek, Eleanor G., and Mlotek, Joseph. *Songs of Generations: New Pearls of Yiddish Song*. New York: Workmen's Circle, 1998.

Mordden, Ethan. *Coming Up Roses: The Broadway Musical in the 1950s*. New York: Oxford University Press, 1998.

Mordden, Ethan. *One More Kiss: The Broadway Musical in the 1970s*. New York: Palgrave Macmillan, 2004.

Mordden, Ethan. *Open a New Window: The Broadway Musical in the 1960s*. New York: Palgrave, 2001.

Morton, Frederic. *The Rothschilds: A Family Portrait*. New York: Atheneum, 1962.

Most, Andrea. *Making Americans: Jews and the Broadway Musical*. Cambridge: Harvard University Press, 2004.

Mostel, Kate, and Madeline Gilford, with Jack Gilford and Zero Mostel. *170 Years of Show Business*. New York: Random House, 1978.

"New Faces Stop Their Own Show: Interviews and Drawings by Doug Anderson." *Theater Arts* 36 (August 1952): 18–21.

Norton, Richard C. *A Chronology of American Musical Theater*. 3 vols. New York: Oxford University Press, 2002.

Ostrow, Stuart. *Present at the Creation, Leaping in the Dark, and Going Against the Grain: 1776, Pippin, M. Butterfly, La Bête, and Other Broadway Adventures*. New York: Applause Theater and Cinema Books, 2006.

Ostrow, Stuart. *A Producer's Broadway Journey*. Westport, Conn.: Praeger, 1999.

Ozick, Cynthia. "Sholem Aleichem's Revolution" (1988). In *Metaphor and Memory: Essays* (New York: Knopf, 1989): 172–198.

Page, Malcolm. *John Arden*. Boston: G. K. Hall, 1984.

Pale Moon: Tales of the American Indians. Selected and edited by John Long. Merrillville, Ind.: ICS Books, 1995.

Parish, James Robert, and Michael R, Pitts. *The Great Hollywood Musical Pictures*. Metuchen, N. J.: Scarecrow, 1992.

Paul, William. *Ernest Lubitsch's American Comedy*. New York: Columbia University Press, 1983.

Perl, Arnold. *Tevya and His Daughters*. New York: Dramatists Play Service, 1958.

Perl, Arnold. *The World of Sholem Aleichem*. New York: Dramatists Play Service, 1953.

Pethö, Csilla. "'Style Hongrois': Hungarian Elements in the Works of Haydn, Beethoven, Weber, and Schubert." *Studia Musicologica Academiae Scientiarum Hungaricae* 41/1–3 (2000): 199–284.

Piro, Richard. *Black Fiddler*. New York: William Morrow, 1971.

Prideaux, Tom. *American Musicals: Bock & Harnick*. Liner notes to Time-Life Records 4TL-AM14 (3 cassette tapes, 1982).

Prince, Harold. *Contradictions: Notes on Twenty-Six Years in the Theater*. New York: Dodd, Mead, 1974.

Raby, Peter. *Oscar Wilde*. Cambridge: Cambridge University Press, 1988.

Raphael, M. L. "From Marjorie to Tevya: The Image of the Jews in American Popular Literature, Theater, and Comedy, 1955–1965." *American Jewish History* 74/1 (Sept. 1984): 66–72.

Ray, Andy. "Summer Stock." *Adirondack Journal*, 12 August 1988. <http://andyray.net/page8academicpapers/page18unpublished.html>

Rhyne, Brett M. "'Fiddler on the Roof' Lyricist Featured in New Musical." *Jewish Journal*, 28 February 2003.

Richards, David. "Anything for a Song: Ben Bagley, the Archeologist of Broadway." *Washington Post*, 1 January 1982.

Riedel, Michael [uncredited]. "Shtetl Shock: L.A. Times Hits *Roof*; Actress Hits the Road." *New York Post*, 18 February 2004.

Robinson, Paul A. *Opera and Ideas: From Mozart to Strauss*. New York: Harper & Row, 1985.

Rosenbaum, Thane. "A Legacy Cut Loose." *Los Angeles Times*, 15 February 2004.

Rosenberg, Bernard, and Ernest Harburg. *The Broadway Musical: Collaboration in Commerce and Art*. New York: New York University Press, 1993.

Roskies, David G. *The Jewish Search for a Usable Past*. Bloomington: Indiana University Press, 1999.

Rudisill, Amanda Sue. "The Contributions of Eva Le Gallienne, Margaret Webster, Margo Jones, and Joan Littlewood to the Establishment of Repertory Theater in the United States and Great Britain." Ph.D. dissertation, Northwestern University, 1972.

Safire, William. *Safire's Political Dictionary*. New York: Oxford University Press, 2008.

Sainer, Arthur. *Zero Dances: A Biography of Zero Mostel*. New York: Limelight, 1998.

The Sammy Davis, Jr. Reader. Edited and with an introduction by Gerald Early. New York: Farrar, Straus, and Giroux, 2001.

Samuel, Lawrence R. *The End of the Innocence: The 1964–1965 New York World's Fair*. Syracuse, N. Y.: Syracuse University Press, 2007.

Samuel, Maurice. *The World of Sholem Aleichem*. New York: Knopf, 1943.

Sanders, Ronald. "The Rothschilds on Broadway: Jews, History, and Musical Comedy." *Midstream: A Monthly Jewish Review* (December 1970): 23–31.

Sapoznik, Henry. *The Compleat Klezmer*. Transcriptions and technical introduction by Pete Sokolow. Cedarhurst, N. Y.: Tara Publications, 1987.

Sárosi, Bálint. *Gypsy Music*. Translated by Fred Macnicol. Budapest: Corvina Press, 1978.

Schiele, Jinnie. *Off-Centre Stages: Fringe Theater at the Open Space and the Round House, 1968–1983*. Hertfordshire: University of Hertfordshire Press, 2005.

Schleifer, Eliyahu. "Jewish Liturgical Music from the Bible to Hassidims." In *Sacred Sound and Social Change: Liturgical Music in Jewish and Christian Experience*, edited by Lawrence A. Hoffman and Janet R. Walton (Notre Dame, Ind.: University of Notre Dame Press, 1992): 13–58.

Schwartz, Yevgeny. *The Dragon*. In *Three Soviet Plays*, translated by Max Hayward and Harold Shukman, with an introduction by Harold Shukman (New York: Penguin Books, 1966), 135–218.

Scott, Derek B. "Orientalism and Musical Style." *The Musical Quarterly* 82/2 (Summer 1998): 309–335.

Secrest, Meryle. *Stephen Sondheim: A Life*. New York: Knopf, 1998.

Sennett, Ted. *Your Show of Shows*. New York: McMillan, 1977.

Sheed, Wilfred. *The House that George Built: With a Little Help from Irving, Cole, and a Crew of About Fifty*. New York: Random House, 2007.

Sheehy, Helen. *Margo: The Life and Theater of Margo Jones*. Dallas: Southern Methodist University Press, 1989.

The Shop Around the Corner. Feature film produced and directed by Ernst Lubitsch, 1940. Screenplay by Samson Raphaelson.

Siegel, Barbara, and Scott Siegel. "Playing Favorites." <www.theatermania.com/content/news.cfm/story/8061>

Sillman, Leonard. *Here Lies Leonard Sillman: Straightened Out At Last*. New York: Citadel, 1959.

Simon, John. "Loving *She Loves Me*." *New York* 26/27 (12 July 1993): 58, 61. Reprinted in *John Simon on Theater* (New York: Applause, 2005): 566–569.

Simon, John. "Theater Chronicle." *The Hudson Review* 23/4 (Winter, 1970–1971): 721–732.

Simon, Neil. *Rewrites: A Memoir*. New York: Simon and Schuster, 1996.

Singer, Isaac Bashevis. "Sholem Aleichem: Spokesman for a People." *New York Times*, 20 September 1964.

Slobin, Mark. "The Evolution of a Musical Symbol of Yiddish Culture." In *Studies in Jewish Folklore: Proceedings of a Regional Conference of the Association for Jewish Studies*, Spertus College of Judaica, Chicago, May 1–3, 1977 (Cambridge, Mass.: Association for Jewish Studies, 1980), 313–330.

Slobin, Mark. *Tenement Songs: The Popular Music of the Jewish Immigrants*. Urbana: University of Illinois Press, 1982.

Smith, Cecil Michener. *Musical Comedy in America: From* The Black Crook *to* South Pacific. New York: Theater Arts Books, 1950. 2nd ed., updated by Glenn Litton ("From *The King and I* to *Sweeney Todd*"), 1981.

Smith, Wendy. *Real Life Drama: The Group Theater and America, 1931–1940*. New York: Random House, 1990.

Solomon, Alisa. "Family Fortune." <nextbook.org, 27 December 2006>

Solomon, Alisa. "Fiddling with Fiddler: Can the Broadway Revival of Everyone's Favorite Jewish Musical Ignore Today's Radically Different Cultural Context?" *Village Voice*, 21–27 January 2004.

Solomon, Alisa. "How *Fiddler* Became Folklore." Part I, *Forward*, 1 September 2006. "Tevye, Today and Beyond." Part II, *Forward*, 8 September 2006.

Solomon, David Lyle. "A Stage for a Bima: American Jewish Theater and the Politics of Representation." Ph.D. dissertation, University of Maryland at College Park, 2004.

Sondheim, Stephen. "Theater Lyrics." In *Playwrights, Lyricists, Composers on Theater*, edited by Otis L. Guernsey Jr. (New York: Dodd, Mead, 1974), 61–97.

Stasio, Marilyn. "*Rex*: The Making of a Musical." *Cue* 45/16 (April 24–30, 1976): 10–11.

Stewart, John. *Broadway Musicals, 1943–2004*. Foreword by Hal Prince. Jefferson, N.C.: McFarland, 2006.

Steyn, Mark. *Broadway Babies Say Goodnight: Musicals Then and Now*. London: Faber & Faber, 1997.

Steyn, Mark. "Fiddling with *Fiddler*." *New Criterion* 22/8 (April 2004): 58–63.

Stockdale, Freddie. *Emperors of Song: Three Great Impresarios*. London: J. Murray, 1998.

Stockton, Frank R. *The Lady or the Tiger and Other Stories*. New York: Garrett Press, 1969.

Stone, Peter, moderator. "Landmark Symposium: *Fiddler on the Roof*." *Dramatists Guild Quarterly* 20/1 (1983): 10–29. Reprinted in *Broadway Song and Story: Playwrights/Lyricists/Composers Discuss Their Hits*, edited by Otis L. Guernsey, introduction by Terrence McNally (New York: Dodd, Mead, 1985), 115–134.

Strouse, Charles. *Put On a Happy Face: A Broadway Memoir*. New York: Union Square Books, 2008.

Study Guide to *Fiddler on the Roof*. <http://www.patelconservatory.org/onschooltime/0809studyguides/fiddler.pdf>

Suskin, Steven. "On the Record: Bock and Harnick's *The Body Beautiful* and Hugh Martin's *Hans Brinker*." <playbill.com, 27 October 2008>

Suskin, Steven. *Show Tunes: The Songs, Shows, and Careers of Broadway's Major Composers*. 3rd ed., rev. Foreword by Michael Feinstein. New York: Oxford University Press, 2000.

Swain, Joseph P. *The Broadway Musical: A Critical and Musical Survey*. 2nd ed. Latham, Maryland: Scarecrow, 2002. Original ed., New York: Oxford University Press, 1990.

Tavris, Carol. "A Sketch of Stanley Milgram: A Man of 1,000 Ideas." *Psychology Today* 8 (1974): 74–75.

Taylor, Theodore. *Jule: The Story of Composer Jule Styne*. New York: Random House, 1979.

Tevye. Feature film produced by Harry Ziskin, directed by Maurice Schwartz. Screenplay by Maurice Schwartz. Teaneck, N. J.: Ergo Media, 1990.

"Theater Music: Seven Views (George Abbott, Jerry Bock, Micki Grant, E. Y. Harburg, Richard Rodgers, Harvey Schmidt, Jule Styne)." In *Playwrights, Lyricists, Composers on Theater*, edited by Otis L. Guernsey Jr. (New York: Dodd, Mead, 1974), 135–144.

Twain, Mark. *The Diaries of Adam and Eve*. Foreword by Shelley Fisher Fishkin. Introduction by Ursula K. LeGuin. Afterword by Laura E. Skandera-Trombley. New York: Oxford University Press, 1996.

Viljoen, Nicol. "The Raised Fourth Degree of the Scale in Chopin's Mazurkas." *Acta Academica* 32/2 (2000): 67–85.

Vinaver, Chemjo, compiler/editor. *Anthology of Jewish Music*. New York: Edward B. Marks, 1955.

Wallach, Ira. *Hopalong-Freud and Other Modern Literary Characters*. New York: Henry Schuman, 1951.

Walsh, David, and Pratt, Len. *Musical Theater and American Culture*. Westport, Conn.: Praeger, 2003.

Ward, Jonathan. "Recruit, Train and Motivate: The History of the Industrial Musical." <www.furious.com/PERFECT/industrialmusicals.html>

Warfield, Scott. "From *Hair* to *Rent*: Is 'Rock' a Four-Letter Word on Broadway?" In *The Cambridge Companion to the Musical*, edited by William A. Everett and Paul R. Laird (Cambridge: Cambridge University Press, 2002), 231–245.

Weidman, Jerome. "Joining the Team." *Theater Arts* 43 (Dec. 1959): 10–12.

Weidman, Jerome. *Praying for Rain*. New York: Harper & Row, 1986.

Weitzner, Jacob. *Sholem Aleichem in the Theater*. Madison, N. J.: Fairleigh Dickinson University Press, 1994.

Werner, Eric, et al. "Jewish Music." *Grove Music Online*.

Werner, M. R. *It Happened in New York*. New York: Coward-McCann, 1957.

Whitfield, Stephen J. "Fiddling with Sholem Aleichem: A History of *Fiddler on the Roof*." In *Key Texts in American Jewish Culture*, edited by Jack Kugelmaus (New Brunswick, N. J.: Rutgers University Press, 2003), 105–125.

Wilde, Oscar. *The Canterville Ghost: A Hylo-Idealistic Romance*. London: Electric Book Company, 2001.

Wilk, Max. *They're Playing Our Song: From Jerome Kern to Stephen Sondheim—The Stories Behind the Words and Music of Two Generations*. Original ed., New York: Atheneum,

1973. Rev. ed. (*They're Playing Our Song*), New York: Zoetrope, 1986. Expanded ed. (*They're Playing Our Song: The Truth Behind the Words and Music of Three Generations*), Mount Kisco, N.Y.: Moyer Bell, 1991. Reprint of expanded ed. (*They're Playing Our Song: Conversations with America's Classic Songwriters*), New York: Da Capo, 1997. Rev. and updated ed. (*They're Playing Our Song: Conversations with America's Classic Songwriters*), Westport, Conn.: Easton Studio Press, 2008.

Wisse, Ruth R. *The Modern Jewish Canon*. New York: The Free Press, 2000.

Wolitz, Seth L. "The Americanization of Tevye, or Boarding the Jewish 'Mayflower.'" *American Quarterly* 40/4 (Dec. 1988): 514–536.

Wollman, Elizabeth L. *The Theater Will Rock: A History of the Rock Musical, from* Hair *to* Hedwig. Ann Arbor: University of Michigan Press, 2006.

Zborowski, Mark, and Elizabeth Herzog. *Life Is With People: The Jewish Little-Town of Eastern Europe*. Foreword by Margaret Mead. New York: International Universities Press, 1952. Reprinted in softcover as *Life Is With People: The Culture of the Shtetl* (New York: Schocken Books, 1952).

Zoglin, Richard. "Getting Beyond Zero." *Time*, 8 March 2004, 76.

INDEX

• • •

Page numbers of musical or photographic illustrations are highlighted in **bold**.

Printed in Great Britain
by Amazon

19297595R00222